SCIENCE AND TECHNOLOGY EDUCATION

INTERNATIONAL ENCYCLOPAEDIA OF
SCIENCE AND TECHNOLOGY EDUCATION - 1

SCIENCE AND TECHNOLOGY EDUCATION

By

Dr. Digumarti Bhaskara Rao
M.Sc., M.A., M.A., M.Ed., Ph.D.
Reader & Research Director
R.V.R. College of Education
Srinivasa Nagar Colony
Guntur–522 006
(India)

DISCOVERY PUBLISHING HOUSE PVT. LTD.
NEW DELHI-110 002

Published by:
Namit Wasan

DISCOVERY PUBLISHING HOUSE PVT. LTD.
4383/4B, Ansari Road, Darya Ganj
New Delhi-110 002 (India)
Phone : +91-11-23279245; 23253475; 43596065
E-mail : discoverybooksindia@gmail.com
discoverypublishinghouse@gmail.com
namitwasan9@gmail.com
web : www.discoverypublishinggroup.com

***Edition:* 2020**

ISBN: 978-81-7141-548-9 (Set)

ISBN: 978-81-7141-568-7

Science and Technology Education

Printed at:
Infinity Imaging Systems
Delhi

Preface

Science and Technology have occupied almost all spheres of human life. The wonderful achievements of science and technology have glorified the modern world and transformed the modern civilization into a scientific and technological civilization. Considering the importance of science and technology, they have been incorporated in every stage of education.

This International Encyclopaedia of Science and Technology Education is developed covering a wide range of aspects related to science and technology education for the benefit of all those who are associated with science and technology education. This Encyclopaedia is consisting of eleven volumes, namely:

1. Science and Technology Education,
2. Science Education in Developing Countries,
3. Organisational Structure of Science,
4. Science Education in Asia and the Pacific,
5. Science and Technology Education for All,
6. Values, Ethics, Talent and Girls in Science and Technology Education,
7. Popularisation of Science and Technology Education,
8. Science, Power and Society
9. Information Technology,
10. Teacher Training in Science and Technology Education and
11. Science, Technology and Society—A Curriculum Framework.

I convey my cordial thanks to UNESCO-PROAP, Bangkok, Thailand; UNESCO-ROSTE, Venice, Italy; UNESCO Paris, France; IIEP, Paris, France; Commonwealth Secretariat, London, UK; UNCTAD, Geneva, Switzerland, Queen's University, Kingston, Canada; and Alberta Education, Edmonton, Canada for their kind co-operation in preparing this Encyclopaedia.

DR. DIGUMARTI BHASKARA RAO
Secretary
Academy of Communication Culture Education
Science and Service
GUNTUR (A.P.)

Contents

1

Science

Science has helped the man to acquire supremacy over nature. It has greatly affected the way the people view themselves and the world around them. The wonderful achievements of science have glorified the modern world and illuminated the human creative potential.

In ancient times, most of the people believed that natural events and everything that happens to them are because of the actions of God and Spirits. But the ancient Greeks were among the first to use systematic observation and reasoning to analyse natural happenings. As scientific thinking gradually developed, nature has seen less and less as the product of mysterious spiritual forces. Moreover, people began to feel that nature could be understood and even controlled through science.

Science, in literal sense, means 'the pursuit of knowledge'. The word 'Science' comes from the Latin word 'Scientia' which means 'Knowledge'. The term science in the sense of knowledge was used for long to include the entire subject matter of study. Though it is correct, it does not imply that, all knowledge is science. This is very clear by the fact that all the branches of social sciences and humanities are universally excluded from the purview of sciences. The reason offered for this is that the conclusions in social sciences and humanities are beyond verification and quantification. The post-war efforts by various people to elevate the status of humanities and social sciences to science, proved to be a futile effort. Again the reason was the inability to measure, quantify and verify the human mind and behaviour. Thus, the facility to measure, quantify and verify the object in question is the part of Science, its conclusions are universal. The body of knowledge is factual and verifiable, and the results are data-based.

Science is usually defined as a systematized knowledge. It is not a casual heap of disconnected scraps, but the bonds of union and the principles of arrangement is knowledge and it is mainly practical and social.

The knowledge is ordered, but it is not ordered from the stand point of and for the sake of knowledge. Not, thus, the presence of systematization characterizes science, but the presence of a peculiar principle and method of systematized from the stand point of and for the sake of knowledge as distinct from the stand point of practice and social intercourse. Specifically, this means that the subject matter of knowledge is selected, formulated and arranged. With special reference to the exhibition of relations of intellectual dependence which its various parts sustain one another.

Many efforts, hence, were made to arrive at a precise meaning and definition of the word science by avoiding the loopholes. Let us see some of the important definitions to understand the science.

The Columbia Encyclopaedia defined science as ". . . . accumulated and systematized learning, in general usage, restricted to natural phenomenon. The progress of science is marked not only by an accumulation of facts, but by the emergence of scientific method of the scientific attitude."

According to Frederic Fitzpatrick, "Science is cumulative and endless series of empirical observations which result in the formation of concepts and theories, with both concepts and theories being subject to modification in the light of further empirical observation. Science is both a body of knowledge and a process of acquiring it."

Albert Einstein felt that "Science searches for relations, which are thought to exist independently of the searching individual." Whitehead defines science as "an attempt to systematize our knowledge of the circumstances in which recognitions occur." Ames, M. V. says that "Science is more than a compilation of facts. It is a method of thinking and working, a way of solving problems." Conant defines that "Science is an interconnected series of concepts and theories. Science is a body of knowledge and the process of acquiring and refining knowledge."

Paul Hurd opined that "Facts themselves do not make a science. Science is not simply an abstraction from empirical data, but an intellectual occasion often suggested by data. It is the discerning of order among the data that makes the science. Science is an intellectual activity which arises from personal experience and takes place in the minds of men. It is simply a way of using human intelligence to achieve a better understanding of nature and nature's laws."

B. F. Skinner defined science as "First of all, science is a set of attitudes. It is a deposition to deal with facts rather than with what some one has said about them." Green, A. W. says that "Science is a way of investigation". In the words of Poincare, "Science is built of facts as a house is built of stones, but an accumulation of facts is no more a science than a heap of stones." According to Weinbeg and Shabat, "Science is a certain way of looking at the world".

Since life in the present world invariably warrants, to variable degrees, knowledge of scientific facts and laws, science has now become everyday science for everybody. Teaching of everyday science for everybody has become an unavoidable part of general education. Science takes its place side by side with other subjects as an essential element of one's education. It affords a knowledge of certain facts and laws and an insight into methods and dates peculiar to the domain of science.

The teaching of science like any other subject as school stage can be justified for various reasons. The very nature of the subject justifies its inclusion in the school curriculum. Science prepares pupils to think and sharpen their intellect making them more careful and systematic in reasoning. It provides unique training in truth, inculcates a spirit of inquiry, develops the capacity to know the unknown and gives strength to face failures.

The report of the Education Commission (1964-66) laid much emphasis on science-based education. In its own words, "There is one thing about which we feel with no doubt of hesitation, that is, science-based education in coherence with Indian culture and values can alone provide the foundation as an instrument for the nation's progress, security and welfare."

In its recommendations on "Education and Productivity", the Commission further mentions that "Science Education should become an integral part of school education, and ultimately some study of science should become a part of all courses in humanities and social sciences."

Science education in daily life, specially at the school stage, is necessary for several reasons. Firstly, the rapid growth of science and technology is influencing almost all walks of life. In fact, this rapid growth is resulting in the production of altogether new materials, new uses of old materials as well as providing the society with powerful tools capable of bringing about changes in the environment. Secondly, significant portions of the students terminate their studies after primary education and therefore there is an imperative need to provide them education, informally or non-formally, on continuing basis about the ongoing developments in the area of science and technology having direct relevance to life. Thirdly, in view of the nature of science, the scientific laws and principles being generalisation of common experiences, the need for relating science with the life of community becomes quite obvious. A comparison between the processes of science and those used in agriculture, health and hygiene revealing the similarity between them also endorses the same view. Lastly, only the important objectives of education will bring about desired behavioural change. If science is taught in isolation, as a body of facts and principles alone, it can hardly meet the above objectives. It is therefore, all the more, necessary to make deliberate efforts to associate science education with life.

2

On What It Means to Understand Science

ANTONIO BETTENCOURT
Michigan State University, USA

Introduction

> Science is no longer the quintessence of knowledge and of what is worth knowing, but a way. It is a way of penetrating into unexplored and unmastered realms.[1]

The importance of a sound scientific education for the young generations is recognized by science educators of both technologically advanced societies and developing ones. The recognition of this importance is not, however, consistent with what we know about classroom practices in the natural sciences. These sciences are taught divorced from the lives of students, the problems of the surrounding community, the global implications they may have, etc.

The presentation of the natural sciences is, in general, textbook bound, aimed at the memorization of vocabulary and the algorithmic resolution of quantitative problems. The student side of the picture is constituted by young persons that can, at best, parrot definitions, solve numerical problems, but have little understanding of ideas, very little notion of the applications of these sciences and even less critical awareness of their role in causing and/or solving societal problems. (Driver et al. 1985; Osborne & Freyberg 1985; Gallagher 1989, 1990)

We all know that the problems of science education are complex, recurrent, and difficult to solve. They have pedagogical, social, historical, and political dimensions not always clear cut and easily addressable. This should caution us about putting too much hope on solving those problems by a pedagogical path. On the other hand, pedagogical dimensions are usually within reach of science educators and may serve as an entry point into the path that may lead if not to solution at least to alleviation.

One of the solutions that has been advocated for the problems of science education is teaching for understanding. Teachers and students should engage in a set of practices whose aim and result is the understanding of the natural sciences. The purpose of this paper is to illuminate some possible ways of conceiving what it means to understand the natural sciences.

Understanding the Natural Sciences

> Understanding is an adventure and, like any other adventure, is dangerous.[2]

The aim of science education is conceived, in this paper, as the construction of "understanding of the natural sciences." The statement immediately raises two questions: What are viable meanings for the expression "understanding of the natural sciences"? How can we pursue it?

In general we can say that we understand something when we know what that something means. The connection of understanding and meaning is now almost traditional in the philosophy of the human sciences since the analysis of Dilthey (1990, p. 102) at the turn of the century. A viable theory of understanding is then connected with a theory of meaning. Understanding the natural sciences is therefore understanding their meaning. What could be a viable meaning for the expression "the meaning of the natural sciences"?

Alan Bishop (1985, p. 26) speaking about mathematical meaning says that making mathematical meaning for an expression, idea, concept is connecting that idea, concept etc., to other ideas in mathematics, to other ideas in fields of knowledge other than mathematics and to everyday uses of those ideas. We can use this definition as a strafing point if we think of ideas in the natural sciences instead of mathematical ideas. The definition above has important advantages but still considers meaning from the point of view of ideas, concepts, etc. what we can call, for lack of a better term, the contents of the mind. Undeniably the natural sciences are ideas, concepts, theories, explanations, facts, etc. They are also practices, social relations, modes of discourse, and historical ways of evolving characteristic of specific communities of thought and action. Whenever we are reducing the natural sciences to ideas, concepts, etc. that are one of their products we are forgetting two things. One is that the constitution and maintenance of the scientific communities are not only producers but also products of the natural sciences. The other is that the ideas, concepts, that are produced by the natural sciences when divorced from the practices and communities wherefrom they were produced and that are part of their meaning makes them unintelligible. Understanding the natural sciences in understanding them as a form of life with all that is part of that form of life.

Forms of life are embodie in complexes of practices, actions, and beliefs. Understanding the natural sciences is engaging in the practices that will render the form of life that the natural sciences are, intelligible. Intelligible means here no more and no less that possible of being understood and talked about in some meaningful ways. Intelligible does not mean here transparent or fully describable. The totality of any form of life will always escape us in some way.

The practices of understanding the natural sciences are certainly related to the practices of making those sciences. They are not necessarily the same nor simple transpositions into school or other contexts.

A. Understanding as Use

According to Wittgenstein's *Philosophical Investigations* the meaning of a word is its use in the language.

> For a large class of cases—though not for all—in which we employ the word "meaning" it can be defined thus: The meaning of a word is its use in the language.[3]

We can extend this notion by saying that understanding an idea, a concept, an expression, means then, using it appropriately in the language (be it spoken or written). Any language evolves within a community of users. Appropriate and inappropriate uses have always to be referred to the proper community and the proper context. Wittgenstein seemed to hint at this when he wrote that "to imagine a language is to imagine a form of life". (1958, # 19, p. 8) In the case of the natural sciences, students and teachers understand a concept, idea or what not, when they are able to use it correctly in the discourse. Correctly here means no more and no less than acceptable to the members of the community.

The process of coming to understand is not linearly sequential but more of a circular nature. We understand a concept or idea insofar as we use it appropriately in the language. We come to understand it correctly as we use it appropriately in the language. Using, being corrected, correcting others, and being able to anticipate the correction of others are not only criteria for understanding but also the very process by which understanding as use is constructed. Wittgenstein, in the *Philosophical Investigations,* puts it very clear when he says:

> Let the use of words teach you their meaning. (Similarly one can often say in mathematics: let the *proof* teach you *what* was being proved.[4]

Putting it more clearly, we do not understand and then use but we understand as we use and we use as we come to understand. The process of constructing understanding is thus, not only circular but also endless.

The use of words expressions and concepts does not make sense unless it is bound to a community of discourse. There is no way of correctly using the words, concepts or whatever in an appropriate way unless we understand the form of life they embody and from which they spring. The reciprocal is true, we cannot understand a form of life if we do not understand the language that expresses it. One again we are immersed in the productive circularity that is part of the meaning of understanding. Any of us that has attempted to learn a different language also knows that the task is endless. It is instructive to compare this circularity of understanding with the circularity of scientific observation in physics.

> Let us examine not how observation, facts and data are built up into general systems of physical explanation, but how these

systems are built into our observations, and our appreciation of facts.[5]

B. Understanding as Representation

Another way to conceive understanding of the natural sciences is connected with the idea of representation. The meaning of something is a representation of that something. The term "representation" is here used in two different but closely interrelated meanings. Re-presentation means that in representing something we make that something present again. It may be present as mental content (e.g. image, concept, etc.) or it may be re-presented in the sense of "displayed in front of us". The second meaning is close to the sense of representation in a work of art (e.g. a painting or a play).

None of these meanings implies here the sense of an iconic copy. Neither our mental representations nor the "displays" of the works of art are copies of independently existing originals. Both ways of using the term "representation" refer to the constructive processes by which we try to penetrate, appropriate and display the meaning of the represented item. (von Glasersfeld 1983, 1986) This meaning is not a disembodied quality but always a meaning to us. A copy may be an altogether bad representation making opaque the sense of the represented thing. If Picasso had "copied faithfully" (assuming that would be possible) the massacre of Guernica he would certainly not have achieved the force and depth of meanings represented in his "Guernica."

We understand something insofar as we are able to produce or interpret an adequate representation of it. Once we have discarded the notion of representations as "iconic pictures" of something external both producing and interpreting are constructive processes of the thinking subject. (von Glasersfeld 1983, 1986)

Another characteristic of this notion of understanding is that the idea of a completely right or completely wrong representation ceases to make sense. No representation is ever totally adequate because it has always limitations. On the other hand any representation has always something to tell us about the represented thing. In the limits of any representation we confront once again the impossibility of as complete grasp of a form of life. Whenever we are representing something we are also concealing some parts or aspects of that something.

The limitations and the adequacies of any representation are never known in advance, only when the representation is used (e.g. to communicate). In constructing and using representations we come to understand and as we come to understand we construct more meaningful representations. Meaningfulness is here conceived referred to the contexts and purposes of construction and use of the representation. As soon as it is used in other contexts and for other purposes anything can happen, namely problems.

The problems we encounter with our representations are not to be avoided or repressed, they should be used as the occasions to look critically at the representation. These problems may point to weak points of an otherwise useful and elegant representation. Rutherford's model of the atom was a quite elegant way of subsuming a whole array of data from physics and chemistry. It could not justify both why atoms were stable and why their spectra were discontinuous. Bohr's model did away with the first difficulty be erecting it into a postulate and explained the second for hydrogen not only with elegance but also quantitative exactness. It too failed when trying to explain more complex atoms. Problems with a representation may also arise from difficulties inherent to the complexity or elusiveness of the represented item. The representations of human cognition may be a good example. Another source of problems may come from ideas implicitly embedded in the representation but not explicitly dealt with. The representation of the cell functions with "factory models" may conceal the fairly complex interrelations and mutual influences of each organelle on all the others because it privileges hierarchical relations.

Finally, since no representation is totally adequate in principle, understanding is also connected with multiplicity of representations. To understand ideas, concepts or practices of the natural sciences in a rich way we must deal with multiple representations of them. To represent understanding of the natural sciences only by knowledge of ideas, concepts, etc. is an altogether inadequate representation because it privileges products and forgets the processes of production not to mention that both products and processes are carried in specific social networks.

Natural sciences are full of representations. As a matter of fact, the natural sciences work almost exclusively with models and models of models. Some models, like the model of the atom are mechanical models of mathematical models or mathematical models built from mechanical models that subsume a great deal of empirical facts. There are models in the natural sciences that represent the not only scientific content but social and political ideas current at the time of their origin. One has only to think about the model of the cell where ideas about division of labour and management are embedded. The idea of competition as a way to success and social progress current in England through the Industrial Revolution is embodied in the concepts of natural selection and the whole framework of the theory of evolution. (Bernal 1953/1970, p. 165) Interestingly enough the project of building a theory of evolution based on the concept of cooperation attempted by Kropotkine (1925) never called much attention.

Understanding scientific ideas is being able to produce different representations of them, interpret various forms of their representation and also point the limitations of each. Understanding these ideas is also knowing and analyzing the representation that have been used for them and the contexts of practice and discourse where they arose.

C. Understanding as Application

We can also conceive understanding as application. This conception comes from the hermeneutic tradition. Hans-Georg Gadamer, one of the foremost contemporary scholars in hermeneutic philosophy, in his major work, *Truth and Method* (1975), explicitly states that:

> "understanding always involves something like the application of the text to be understood to the present situation of the interpreter."[6]

Understanding the natural sciences is applying them in some way to our present situation.

The idea of application we are trying to explicate here is fundamentally different from "application" in the sense commonly used in science education. The common usage originates in technological conceptions of science use and was given the status of a pedagogical instrument in Bloom's Taxonomy (Bloom 1956). Application was conceived there as the use of a general law or statement to explain or solve a concrete case. This notion was elevated to a philosophical rule of method in the deductive-nomological models of scientific explanation usually associated with logical empiricism. (Hempel 1965a, 1965b)

Once again we do not understand something in a general way and then apply it to something particular. We understand both the general and the particular in the very process of applying them to our present situation. Gadamer (1975) is very clear about this when he says:

> The interpreter dealing with a traditional text seeks to apply it to himself. But this does not mean that the text is given for him as something universal, that he understands it as such and only afterwards uses it for particular applications. Rather, the interpreter seeks no more than to understand this universal thing, the text; i.e. to understand what this piece of tradition says, what constitutes the meaning and importance of the text. In order to understand that, he must not seek to disregard himself and his particular hermeneutical situation. He must relate the text to this situation, if he wants to understand at all.[7]

In the act of understanding both what we want to understand and what we apply it to, change their meaning. Application is conceived not as a deductive process (as Bloom conceives it) but as a dialogue mediated through the interpreter (i.e. the person who wants to understand).

Understanding a scientific idea, concept, formula, problem, etc. is then applying it to the relevant situation. Finding (or making) the relevant situation is already part of the application because the situations where something applies or does not are part of its meaning.

Laboratory work can be thought of as providing many occasions where application in the sense above may happen. We must remind ourselves that, conceived in this way, laboratory is not just illustration or demonstration of a concept, but rather an occasion to refine our understanding of the concept and reconceiving the practical problem at hand. Moreover, most scientific concepts have laboratory operations as part of their meaning. On the other hand the laboratory itself, the instruments contained therein, and the practices scientist engage in there are "materialized theories" to borrow an apt metaphor of Bachelard (1934/1949, p. 12). The theoretical leadenness of the laboratory is vividly portrayed by Pierre Duhem when he writes:

> Enter a laboratory; approach the table crowded with an assortment of apparatus, an electric cell, silk-covered copper wire, small cups of mercury, spools, a mirror mounted on an iron bar; the experimenter is inserting into small openings the metal ends of ebony-headed pins; the iron oscillates, and the mirror attached to it throws a luminous band upon a celluloid scale; the forward-backward motion of this spot enables the physicist to observe the minute oscillations of the iron bar. But ask him what he is doing. Will he answer: 'I am studying the oscillations of an iron bar which carries a mirror'? No, he will say that he is measuring the electric resistance of the spools. If you are astonished, if you ask him what his words mean, what relation they have with the phenomena he has been observing and which you have noted at the same time as he, he will answer that your question requires a long explanation and that you should take a course in electricity.[8]

Summarizing we can say that understanding what something means is a never ending process of using that something in discourse, constructing representations of it and making it relevant to our present situation. In this process, the thing to be understood, the situation in which the understanding is taking place, and the interpreter, change. Another characteristic of understanding is that it happens in a social historical matrix. We understand with the tools of our culture (e.g. langugage), with our previous experience (mainly our prejudices) and within the interpretive norms of specific communities.

Understanding as Process and Practice

> For a scientific mind, all knowing is an answer to a question. If there was no question, there cannot be scientific knowledge. Nothing is self-evident. Nothing is given. Everything is constructed.[9]

Conceiving understanding of the natural sciences as the use of specific modes of discourse, the production and interpretation of representations, and application in the hermeneutic sense raises two sets of questions. The first has to do with completeness. Are these aspects all there is to understand about understanding? Certainly not, understanding is too rich to be reduced to three aspects. We only touched these because they seemed important and worth exploring. The second set has to do with the practices and processes by which we may come to understand some domain of experience, namely the natural sciences.

A. The Central Role of the "Question"

Exploring the process of understanding we can say that it starts with "a question". We understand something insofar as we know the question that something is an answer to.

> We can say, with Collingwood [1939/1982, p. 29-43], that we understand only when we understand the question to which something is an answer, and it is true that what is understood in this way does not remain detached in its meaning from our own meaning. Rather, the reconstruction of the question, from which the meaning of a text is to be understood as an answer, passes into our own questioning. For the text must be understood as an answer to a real question.[10]

Understanding starts with a question, not any question but a real question. A question that because it is real does not remain detached from us. A real question supposes that a real person (i.e. questioner) is asking about some domain of experience (i.e. an object). Said in another way a real question expresses a desire to know. This desire is what moves the questioner to pursue the question until an adequate answer has been found (i.e. made). Desiring to know opens ourselves to experiencing what is new as new and the already known as renewed under different aspects.

A real question seems to exclude immediately both the rhetorical and the pedagogical question. (Gadamer 1975, p. 327) They do not express a genuine desire to know. There is an inherent paradox in this exclusion. Rhetorical and pedagogical questions comprise most of the questions asked in school situations. The implication seems to be that genuine understanding is excluded from schools and classrooms . . . unless we try to remake our ways of questioning, thus reopening the possibility of understanding in those contexts. This is not an easy task, and surely it is a dangerous one.

B. Prejudices as Conditions of Understanding

Wherefrom do these genuine questions spring? The answer that hermeneutics gives has the sound of a provocation. They spring from our prejudices. This is surely an answer to approved thought. Prejudices, in the original sense of pre-judgments (i.e. judgements made before all the evidence is available) are the conditions of our understanding of the world. In trying to understand science we bring to it the prejudices handed down to us by our personal history, the tradition of our communities, and history of science itself. Prejudices, in this sense, are not impediments. They are the only points from where to start our questioning. (Gadamer 1975, pp. 239-245)

Student prejudices in the form of cultural or individual conceptions are the very condition of their understanding. The students' knowledge of their world claims a wisdom and a rationality that our reverence for science has difficulty in accepting. Instead of engaging with students in the questioning of our prejudices, and the prejudices of science we try to erase the students knowledge. With the best of intentions we strip ourselves from the possibility of understanding science and in the process transform it into a sort of alien dogma.

Questions, if they are genuine cannot be asked from a detached stance. The disembodied observer that asks the questions of science is a fantasy of the worst kind because it obscures the human side of science. Scientists, like everyone else, ask their questions in the context of their research traditions and within communities of practice and discourse. Even revolutions in science exhibit many continuities with their ancestors. Our questions if they are going to be ways of understanding have to be asked from the hic et nunc of our interpretive situation.

C. Historicality of Understanding

Questions and prejudices help us see understanding as an inherently historical process. We can understand the natural sciences insofar as we are part of the same historical continuity. Our own culture and our own personal history are in some ways continuous with these sciences. Understanding the natural sciences is not only an attempt at understanding a domain of experience but also an attempt at understanding ourselves (both at personal and cultural levels). (Gadamer 1975, p. 340)

Inherent continuities must not make us forget the inherent discontinuities. The otherness that asserts itself in the natural sciences is a constant invitation to our efforts of understanding and a constant warning against hasty interpretation. We understand the natural sciences insofar as, from our prejudices, our history, our culture, we relentlessly pursue their subject matter, what they are about. The subject matter is understandable only because we question these forms of life. At the same time the meaning that our understanding achieves, emerges because we question the natural sciences with our prejudices (i.e. expectations that some meaning will emerge). Understanding the natural sciences is a constant movement between what we expect and what emerges from our questioning. (Gadamer 1975, p. 236)

D. Penelope in the Science Classroom

We all know the history of Penelope, wife of Ulysses, who in order to delay her answer to marriage proposals wove a cloth during the day and unwove it during the night. Understanding the natural sciences can be conceived in these terms.

Questioning the natural sciences makes us unweave their fabric, understand not only the superficial pattern (i.e. the finished knowledge) but also the underlying frame of threads (i.e. interconnections between the ideas) and the ways in which these were woven in the first place (i.e. history and sociology of science).

The unweaving makes us also become aware of our own frames of questioning (i.e our prejudices) and also question them from the point of view of science.

Hopefully we will achieve a new tapestry that will integrate our own views with those of the natural sciences without subordination but in the eye-to-eye of genuine dialogue.

Acknowledgements

The author wishes to acknowledge the contributions of Joel B. Garb and the many discussions they had about institutions. He also recognizes his indebtedness to Perry Lanier's insistence on multiplicity of representations. He takes, however, full responsibility for all the errors and misunderstandings.

NOTES

1. Gadamer 1976/1981b, pp. 69-70.
2. Gadamer 1978/1981, pp. 109-110.
3. 1985, #43, p. 20.
4. 1958, p. 220, emphasis in the original
5. Hanson 1958, p. 3
6. Gadamer 1975, p. 274.
7. Gadamer 1975, p. 289.
8. Duhem 1914/1954, p. 218.
9. Bachelard 1960, p. 14, my translation
10. Gadamer 1975, p. 337.

REFERENCES

Bachelard, Gaston: 1949. *Le Nouvel Esprit Scientifique,* Presses Universitaires de France, Paris. (Originally published in 1934)

Bachelard Gaston: 1960. *La Formation De l'Esprit Scientifique: Contribution A Une Psychanalyse De La Connaissance Objective,* Lib. Philosophique J. Vrin, Paris.

Bernal, J. D.: 1970. *Science And Industry In The Nineteenth Century,* Indiana University Press, Bloomington. (First published in 1953)

Bishop, Alan: 1985. The Social Construction of Meaning: A Significant Development for Mathematics Education?, *For the Learning of Mathematics,* 5, 24-28.

Bloom, Benjamin. S. (Ed.): 1956. *Taxonomy Of Educational Objectives: The Classification Of Educational Goals By A Committee Of College And University Examiners,* Longmans, New York.

Collingwood, R. G.: 1982. *An Autobiography,* Clarendon Press, Oxford. (Originally published in 1939)

Dilthey, Wilhelm: 1990. The Rise Of Hermeneutics, In G. L. Ormiston & A. D. Schrift (Eds.), *The Hermeneutic Tradition: From Ast To Ricoeur* (pp. 101-114), State University of New York Press, Albany.

Driver, R., Guesne, E. & Tiberghien, A. (Eds.): 1985. *Children's Ideas In Science,* Open University Press, Milton Keynes.

Duhem, Pierre: 1914. *La Theorie Physique: Son Object—Sa Structure,* M. Riviere, Paris.

Gadamer, Hans-Georg: 1975. *Truth And Method,* Translation edited by G. Barden and J. Cumming, Crossroad, New York.

Gadamer, Hans-Georg: 1981a. Hermeneutics As Practical Philosophy *Reason In The Age Of Science* (pp. 88-112), Translated by F. G. Lawrence, MIT Press, Cambridge, MA. (German original published in 1976)

Gadamer, Hans-Georg: 1981b. What Is Practice? The Conditions Of Social Reason, *Reason In The Age Of Science* (pp. 69-87), Translated by F. G. Lawrence, MIT Press, Cambridge, MA. (German original published in 1976)

Gallagher, James J.: 1989. Research On Secondary School Science Teachers' Practices, Knowledge And Beliefs: A Basis For Restructuring, M. L. Matyas, K. G. Dobbin & B. J. Fraser (Eds.), *Looking Into Windows: Qualitative Research In Science Education* (pp. 43-57), American Association for the Advancement of Science, Washington, DC.

Gallagher, James J.: 1990. *Como O Conhecimento Novo, Adquirido Pela Pesquisa Em Ensino E Aprendizagem, Pode Ajudar A Melhorar O Ensino De Ciencias,* CAPES—Ministerio da Educacao e Cultura, Brasilia.

Hanson, Norwood R.: 1958. *Patterns Of Discovery: An Inquiry Into The Conceptual Foundations Of Science,* Cambridge University Press, New York.

Hempel, Carl G.: 1965a. The Function Of General Laws in History, *Aspects Of Scientific Explanation And Other Essays In The Philosophy Of Science,* Free Press, New York.

Hempel, Carl G.: 1965b. Studies In The Logic Of Explanation, *Aspects Of Scientific Explanation And Other Essays In The Philosophy Of Science,* Free Press, New York.

Kropotkine, P. A.: 1925. *Mutual Aid: A Factor In Evolution,* Knopf, New York.

Osborne, R. & Freyberg, P. (Eds.): 1985. *Learning In Science: The Implications Of Children's Science,* Heinemann, London.

von Glasersfeld, Ernst: 1983. On The Concept Of Interpretation, *Poetics,* 12, 207-218.

von Glasersfeld, Ernst: 1987. Preliminaries To A Theory Of Representation, C. Janvier (Ed.), *Problems Of Representation In The Teaching And Learning Of Mathematics* (pp.), L. Erlbaum Associates, Hillsdale, NJ.

Wittgenstein, Ludwig: 1958. *Philosophical Investigations,* Translated by G. E. M. Anscombe, Macmillan, New York.

3

What is Science?

SANDRA K. ABELL
Purdue University, USA

&

DEBORAH C. SMITH
University of Delaware, USA

Introduction

The ultimate goal of science education is scientific literacy for all students. Scientific literacy involves understanding not only scientific knowledge, but also understanding the nature of science—"knowledge of both why science believes what it does and how science has come to think that way" (Duschl, 1988, p. 57). Science for All Americans (Rutherford & Ahlgren, 1990) presents a set of recommendations for what knowledge of the way science works is required for scientific literacy, organized under three categories: the scientific world view (e.g., scientific ideas are subject to change), scientific inquiry (e.g., science explains and predicts; science demands evidence), and the scientific enterprise (e.g., science is a complex social activity).

If students are to become scientifically literate, in part through understanding the nature of science, it stands to reason that their teachers must understand how science works so that they can model appropriate behaviours and attitudes. Unfortunately, many science teachers misunderstand and misrepresent the nature of science (Benson, 1989; Hodson, 1988).

In disciplines such as history and mathematics, teachers' views of the discipline itself influence how they teach (Schmidt & Kennedy, 1990; Sch ram et al., 1988; Wilson & Wineberg, 1988). In science, teachers' views of the nature of the discipline can influence their students' conceptions of science (Wolfe, 1989; Zeidler & Lederman, 1987), and can serve to limit the kinds of science that children do in classrooms (Smith & Neale, 1989; Tobin & Fraser, 1988).

What views about the nature of science do teachers construct? We can begin to build a picture of their views by examining them in the context of the preservice science methods course. We are especially interested in the views held by preservice elementary teachers, since they are the ones who will soon offer young children their first school experiences with science.

Past studies have typically examined secondary science teacher viees of the nature of science (Akindehin, 1988; Billeh & Hasan, 1975; Collins, 1989; Koulaidis & Ogborn, 1989; Lederman, 1986; Lederman & Zeidler, 1987; Wavering, 1990). Furthermore many of these studies assessed teacher beliefs and knowledge through the use of a multiple choice instrument.

In contrast, Bloom (1989) examined preservice elementary teachers' conceptions of the nature of science by asking them to complete a questionnaire consisting of both short answer questions and a rating scale. Bloom categorized his students' answers to: "How would you define science?" into four groups. They were science as: (1) a study of the world; (2) a set of processes; (3) a body of knowledge; and (4) a search for new developments. In the present study we elaborate upon Bloom's work by analyzing preservice elementary teachers' definitions of science and comparing them to the characterization of science provided by *Science for All Americans.*

Procedures

Students at our respective institutions are typically juniors or seniors when they enter the elementary science methods course. Prior to this they have taken between 3 and 5 required science content courses. They are predominantly female, white, and average 21 years of age. Over several semesters each of us has administered a questionnaire to these students on the first day of the elementary science methods course. The questionnaire solicits their ideas about the nature of science and their notions about teaching elementary school science. For the purpose of this paper we will focus our analysis on 140 students' definitions of science written in response to one of the following question variations: "What do you mean by the term science? Define the discipline in your own words." or "What do you think science is about?"

To analyze these data, we have employed the technique of analytic induction (Goetz & LeCompte, 1984) in which continued readings of the student responses revealed common patterns. To organize these patterns, we independently read and categorized a subsample of responses. Arriving at similar groupings, we jointly constructed category definitions and used our categories to derive generalizations about the data. Finally we validated our generalizations by going back to the data to find confirming and discrepant cases (Erickson, 1986).

Findings

A. Single Category Responses

Among our students' responses to the question of what is science, we discerned distinctive patterns, falling into five categories. Almost 58 per cent of responses fall neatly into one of these five categories. Another 40 per cent of responses represent amalgams of two or three categories. Only 2.1 per cent of single category responses do not fit into any of the categories (see Figure 3.1). We will first define these categories and illustrate them with example responses. We will follow this with a discussion of combination answers and our assertions from the data.

The five categories we induced from our data and the frequency of responses in these categories differ somewhat from Bloom's (1989) findings. The first and most frequent category we call DISCOVERY, a category which is embedded in Bloom's "body of knowledge" and "process" categories. DISCOVERY responses define science mainly as a process of finding out what exists in the world. The terms "discovery" and "exploration" are often present.

Figure 3.1: Definitions of Science by Response Category

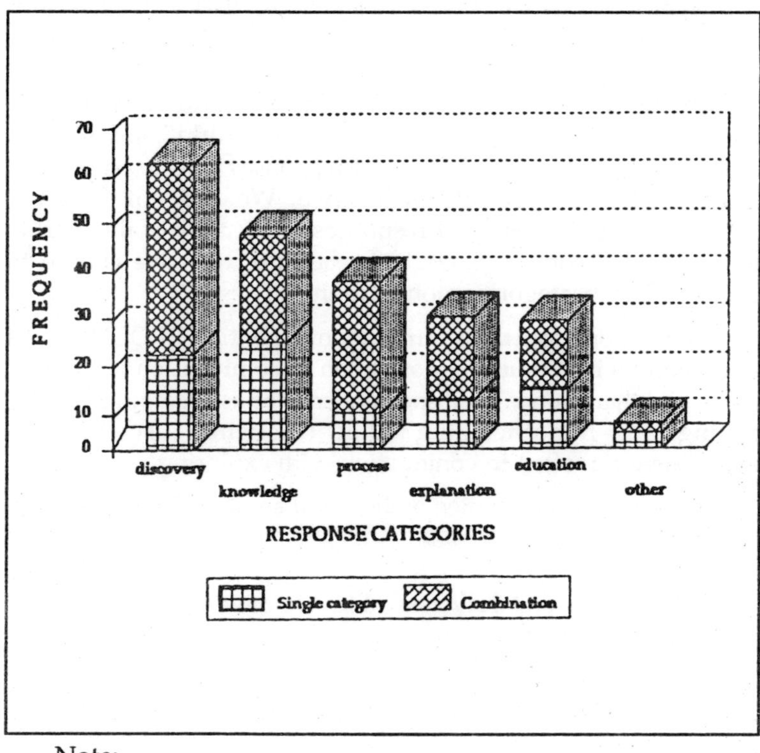

Note:

* N = 140

* Total are > 140 because some responses are recorded in more than one category

> Science to me is a term that means discovery and exploration. Whether that be the discovery through a process or unguided exploration, it means "finding out." The discipline of sciences is the guidelines and foundation for discovery and exploration.

Just over 44 per cent of our students mention discovery in their definitions of science, either solely or in combination with other categories of response (see Figure 3.1). The second most frequent response category (34.3 per cent) we call KNOWLEDGE. Respondents in this group define science as a product, as a set of ideas to be studied.

> Science involves many aspects. It is the world and the plants, animals, things and people in the world. It deals with space—the planets, stars, galaxies, and everything that goes on in space. Science covers the past, present, and future.

In this category we have combined features of two of Bloom's groupings, namely "a study of the world" and a "body of knowledge," since both types of responses tend to emphasize the knowledge products of science. We did not find the overwhelming frequency of responses of "a study of the world" type as did Bloom. This could be because we have chosen to classify his subcategories along different lines.

Almost one-fourth of our students mention PROCESSES of science in their definition, more often in combination with other categories than alone. They speak of science as observing, testing, asking, and hypothesizing. They frequently use the term experimenting, often in conjnuction with exploring.

> Science is the exploration of the world around us. It is observing, hypothesizing, discussing, and experimenting with nature and life.

This category closely resembles Bloom's in definition and frequency of response.

Twenty per cent of our students indicate that science is about explanations—focusing on the how's and why's of the world. We call this the EXPLANATION group.

> Science is the investigation and study of how the world works. It deals with the questions of why things are the way they are, what they are, and how they fit into the overall spectrum of life.

Bloom appears to lump these responses into his "study of the world" category. Because of the importance of explanation in the philosophy of science, we prefer this category to stand alone. Although we feel that EXPLANATION is a unique category, in some responses we found it difficult to distinguish EXPLANATION answers from DISCOVERY answers. As we will show below, many of the responses that discuss explanation indicate students think that the explanations exist in the world, and it is the scientist's job to discover them.

Finally we have created one category that does not appear in Bloom's classification scheme. Among our students, 19.3 per cent answer the question of what is science by defining, instead, science EDUCATION. Half of those responses mention only science education, while the other half combine EDUCATION ideas with ideas from the other categories. The responses in this category are written from the perspective of teachers teaching and learners learning science, not from that of scientists doing science.

> I think science gets children interested in the world around them. It helps them understand some of the "why" and "how" questions they may have. Science is a great "thought-provoking" subject.

Because these students are writing about science within the context of an education course, the tendency to confuse science and science education is not at all surprising. What is curious is that Bloom does not mention responses of this sort.

Combination Responses

Forty per cent of our students' definitions of science discuss more than one facet of the discipline. Their answers combine two, and sometimes three, of the single response categories. An examination of these combinations will help us to better understand these students' ideas.

Three combinations comprise over one half of all combination responses. First, 25 per cent of the combination answers discuss both DISCOVERY and PROCESS aspects of science. There seems to be a natural link between exploring the world and using specific processes to do so.

> Science is discovering and understanding. These are done through manipulating science equipment and things in the real world. Science involves hypothesizing, testing, and checking.

Sixteen per cent of the combination answers define science both in terms of DISCOVERY and KNOWLEDGE. That is, they define science as the search for knowledge and the knowledge itself.

> To me, science is about discovery. Scientists for years have made remarkable discoveries and still yearn for more . . . Science is about chemistry, environment, animals, medicine, and a variety of other things.

Finally 12.5 per cent combine DISCOVERY and EXPLANATION in their definitions of science. To them the natural world offers the explanations, and scientists are merely the conduit through which nature's explanations pass.

> Science-discovery of principles and theories. Science is based on discovery of the world (using world as a general term to include earth, animals, atmosphere, etc.) around us. An explanation of how things work and why some things occur.

Among the rest of the combination answers, only two do not involve either the KNOWLEDGE or DISCOVERY categories. The rest contain one of these two categories in various combinations with the other three. Thus our students tend to be focused on the knowledge and discovery aspects of the nature of science. Figure 3.1 illustrates the frequency of each category among the combination responses.

Assertions

Assertion #1: Our elementary science methods students have a view of the nature of science dominated by a realist perspective. In realism, the natural order is a presupposition of investigation, and objects of scientific inquiry act independently of scientists (Bynum et al., 1981). Our students often define science as a process of exploration in which data is gathered to discover the truths about the world.

> . . . [Science is] the search for the whole truth about everything . . . . They all look for answers to the big truths.

> I think science is the study of how things work in the world around us . . .The biologist studies how living organisms function whereas the physicist studies how things move and forces that act upon matter.

> Science is studying and exploring the causes and effects of certain phenomena. For example why there are 3 states of matter. It is finding out the reasons for these things.

In each of these examples, students appear to view science as a way to discover what really exists.

Their views of the processes of science belie a similar perspective. Students who discuss PROCESSES, often do so with a positivist theme: that "universal natural laws or principles may be induced with certainty from an empirical/experimental foundation" (Bentley & Garrison, 1991).

> I think that science is looking at an object or an event and finding out how it works, or why it occurs. It is asking why, giving an answer, then checking to see if your answer was correct.

> I think science is investigating the things around you, making predictions about them, and then seeing what actual [sic] happens after observing.

> When I think of scientists at work I imagine them conducting tests and experiments to prove or disprove certain assumptions or theories.

The frequency of responses in the DISCOVERY category supports the assertion that our students are realists and inductivists. Furthermore, many of the EXPLANATION responses also imply a science free from human imagination or invention, concentrating instead in understanding the "whys" and "hows" that exist in the natural world. For this reason, the EXPLANATION and DISCOVERY categories see a fair amount of overlap.

> Science is the discovery of nature. Through science nature unfolds and we are able to understand the hows and whys.

> It is the discovering of things around us. It is trying to understand or conceptualize why things work the way they do.

> Science is finding the answers to how, what, and why things occur or work. It deals with discovery of all of our surroundings . . .

> Science is the explanation of facts of why things happen . . .

> [Science is about] discovering things, or making educated guesses about the hows and whys of the world.

A few students (2 per cent) do mention that science might involve a creative dimension:

> . . . [Science is about] trying to solve problems and come up with new ideas and inventions, cures, etc.

> Science . . . requires imagination and patience.

But there are few of these statements, and they are not well elaborated. We find that our students have a limited understanding of the role of the scientist in creating explanations about the world.

Assertion #2: Our elementary science methods students often fail to see science as a unique discipline involving a specific kind of knowledge about the world. Within their amorphous views of science, the discipline takes on an almost heroic stature. Science, according to these students, is the way we make sense of the world.

> Science it about everything . . .
>
> . . . [Science is about] anything you want it to be about.
>
> . . . Science is all around us. It is about experimentation. I never realized before how much science is everywhere.
>
> Science is about investigating different things and questioning everything.
>
> . . . Science includes every subject and uses subjects to create new things.
>
> Science to me is about all different things in the world. . .
>
> I think science is about everything and everyone. . .

Charron (1991) provides evidence that students, K-12, as well as adults in the school and community, hold similar views of Science as vast and impressive. A few of our students use words like "difficult," "complicated," and "hard" in their descriptions. These students seem so overwhelmed by the notion of science that they cannot begin to make sense of its nature.

Our students' confusion about science as a discipline is also exemplified by their failure to distinguish science and science EDUCATION. Some of their responses were difficult to categorize. What at first appeared to be a discussion of science turned into a statement about education when we found a belief about students or teaching embedded in the discussion.

> Science is discovering new concepts and ideas through actual experiences. Students try out their hypothesis by doing experiments and investigations . . .
>
> Science is a way of experimenting to learn new ideas. Science is also learning about concepts used in everyday life. Science needs to be something that all can do in order to learn concepts and to discover new concepts.
>
> Science is the natural study of real life and the unknown world around us. It is full of experimenting, discovering, and learning

> more about what is around you, which makes you more knowledgeable and more willing to learn.
>
> Science is about experimenting. It is working hands-on with a subject and discovering the essence of the subject. It is being able to see how and why something works, and not just read about it.

Assertion #3: Although many of our elementary science methods students refer to how and why questions in science, they lack an understanding of the nature of knowledge claims in science. Few even use the term theory, and no one discusses theories in science—how they are developed, how they come to be accepted, or how they serve to organize knowledge and guide investigation. Within the PROCESSES group a few mention predicting as a scientific process, yet no one discusses the predictive power of theories. Bloom's students, as well, were confused about theory, even when asked directly about it.

Other aspects of science knowledge claims are missing from our students' definitions. Only one response mentions evidence and the role it plays in constructing knowledge. Not one student discusses logic (deductive or inductive) or invention in their responses. Instead they see knowledge claims as springing directly from observations and, in turn, observations directly proving the knowledge claims.

> Science is the discovery of unknown material/knowledge it is the realization of ideas by experimentation.
>
> . . . Experiments prove hypotheses.

Assertion #4: Our elementary science methods students fail to realize the social aspects of science. No one mentions the scientific community or the role it plays in communication or debate about competing theories. They exhibit no notion of human faults and failing involved in science—no mention of biases, emotions, beliefs, or ethical dilemmas. Science, to these students, is devoid of the human element. One student even states that science is outside of the social world:

> I think it is a search for explanations of why and why not in the realm outside of society.

There is a small group (3.6 per cent) that states the purpose of science is a societal one—that is, to benefit humankind.

Science is about making life good for everyone (plants, animals, people).

> I think science is about bettering society—finding cures, making life more controllable, creating a safer environment . . .

> I think science is about life, from its most simplest form to its most complex. It is about creating and building in order to better our world in which we live . . .

> [Science is about] the earth and the rest of the universe. How to use resources to make life better.

Yet even these students omit what scientists actually do to reach these goals. Overall, their responses portray science as an individualistic pursuit, and scientists as amplifiers through which the voice of nature directly flows.

Scientific Literacy?

When we examine our preservice elementary teachers' notions about science, we find them to be narrowly focused on science as "the discovery of knowledge." To assess, in part, their scientific literacy, we can consider their responses in light of the Science for All Americans (SFAA) criteria for understanding the nature of science. This document poses three categories of understanding, with specific principles under each. We will examine to what degree our students understand these principles. In the category "the scientific world view," SFAA posits that students should understand four main ideas:

- the world is understandable
- scientific ideas are subject to change
- scientific knowledge is durable
- science cannot provide complete answers to all questions

Our students rarely mention these ideas directly in their responses, but in an indirect manner they are sometimes present. The DISCOVERY group, for example, believes that the world is understandable when they say:

> Science is the discovery and study of the processes of how the world works.

Attainment of such an understanding of the world is not questioned. Only one student discusses the idea of change in science:

> Science is ever-changing.

Two others mention the durability of scientific knowledge:

> . . . Science is not just a one time thing. Science seems to be very continuous.

> . . . Science builds upon previous discoveries.

Evidence concerning students' lack of understanding of the fourth principle, the limitations of scientific knowledge, comes from those responses that portray science as everything. Those students do not seem to understand that science deals with certain kinds of questions only. A few students even indicate that science can provide the "whole truth" about all things. The second SFAA category, "scientific inquiry," identifies five characteristics of the processes of science:

- science demands evidence
- science is a blend of logic and imagination
- science explains and predicts
- scientists try to identify and avoid bias
- science is not authoritarian

Our elementary methods students do not mention evidence, logic, or imagination for the most part. A small group writes about explanation, but usually as a product, not as an activity in itself. When a prediction is mentioned it is without relation to theory. No one discusses issues of bias or authority. Overall they do not see the human role in inventing explanations or using logic in science.

In the final SFAA category, "the scientific enterprise," four principles are presented:

- sciences a complex social activity
- science is organized into content disciplines and is conducted in various institutions
- there are generally accepted ethical principles in the conduct of science

- scientists participate in public affairs both as specialists and as citizens

Our students, as stated earlier, place little emphasis on the social aspects of science. For example, no one discusses the scientific community and its role in communicating findings or debating the validity of new knowledge claims. Furthermore they do not mention ethics as a factor in the scientific enterprise. Many, however, do appear to understand that science is organized into different subdisciplines, as evidenced by some of the KNOWLEDGE responses.

> Science is studying the things around us—I believe it involves the environment, nature, some physics, the weather, space and our bodies.

> There are a number of different forms of science. These forms can be divided up into two different types: life science and number science. A few life sciences are biology and ecology, and several mathematical sciences are physics and chemistry . . .

Overall our students do not have a feel for how science is done, how scientists work together, or how the scientific world view is unique. According to SFAA, these students could not be considered scientifically literate. Yet they are to be teachers of science in our elementary schools.

Conclusions and Implications

What significance does knowing about our students' views of the nature of science have for us as teacher educators? We know from other studies that science teachers' views of science can affect how science is taught (e.g. Brickhouse, 1990). But among preservice teachers, what are the implications of their limited views of science?

We believe that our students' views about the nature of science are closely tied to their beliefs about teaching and learning. In our elementary methods courses we try to portray a conceptual change orientation toward science teaching (Anderson & Smith, 1987; Driver & Oldham, 1986) based on a constructivist philosophy of learning (von Glasersfeld, 1987). We are interested in the views about science teaching and learning that students bring with them to our science methods courses, and how these views change or are reconstructed over time.

What becomes clear is that although many students tout a hands-on approach to science teaching, their teaching orientations are typically discovery, didactic, or activity-driven (see Anderson & Smith, 1987). They believe that knowledge exists in the world or in the teacher, and that students must receive or discover it.

Songer and Linn (1991) believe that children's views of the nature of science influence their beliefs about themselves as learners of science. In a similar fashion, our students' views about science and about science learning overlap. Our students see science as a process of discovering what is out there, not as a human process of inventing explanations that work. Likewise they see learning as a process of acquiring knowledge through discovery. They fail to see the importance of the learner's physical, cognitive, and social activity in making sense of the world.

How can we help our students revise their beliefs about teaching and learning? Discussions about the nature of science could be a natural starting point. Unfortunately we know that the nature of science is merely touched upon in most elementary science methods textbooks (Abell, 1989), and often is portrayed in a positivistic light. Teacher educators need to develop a set of resources, including readings and activities (see Loving, 1991) concerning the nature of science that are appropriate for preservice elementary teachers and that will spark discussion about the scientific enterprise.

However, our students' naive realist views of science have been constructed over years of formal science instruction and may be difficult to influence. Seventh graders' views of science are strikingly similar to our college students' ideas: that scientists learn by observing the world, and that knowledge comes from directly observable facts (Carey et al., 1989). The images of science our methods students have experienced beyond seventh grade seem to have done little to change their views. According to Grosslight et al. (1991), if we want students to develop a richer understanding of the nature of science they will need experiences using scientific models to solve problems, examining alternative models and wrestling with the modification of models in light of new evidence. Thus students woud "learn that a model can be used as a tool of inquiry and that it is not simply a package of facts about the world that needs to be memorized"(p. 820).

Our students have been participants in an apprenticeship of observation (Lortie, 1975) throughout their schooling. They have formed realist and positivist ideas about science based on the science teaching they have witnessed and the science lessons they have experienced. They have likewise formed ideas about teaching and learning very different from the conceptual change orientation we espouse. We need to portray richer images of science to these preservice teachers in their science content courses. In science methods courses we must ask students to think about learners with different explanations about the world, and how to deal with these differences. Our methods students also need experiences inventing their own explanations and dealing with anomalous data and alternative explanations. The challenge for science teacher educators is great. We must help future science teachers see science teaching through new lenses; they must understand how children learn science and how scientists construct scientific knowledge in order to promote the scientific literacy of their students.

REFERENCES

"Abell, S. K.: 1989, 'The Nature of Science as Portrayed to Preservice Elementary Teachers via Methods Textbooks," In D. E. Herget (Ed.), *The History and Philosophy of Science in Science Teaching. Proceedings of the First International Conference,* Florida State University, Tallahassee, 1-14.

Akindehin, F.: 1988, "Effect of an Instructional Package on Preservice Science Teachers' Understanding of the Nature of Science and Acquisition of Science-related Attitudes," Science Education 72, 73-82.

Anderson, C. W., & Smith, E. L.: 1987, "Teaching Science," In V. Richardson-Koehler (Ed.), *Educators' Handbook: A Research Perspective,* Longman, New York, 84-111.

Benson, G. D.: 1989, "The Misrepresentation of Science by Philosophers and Teachers of Science," *Synthese* 80, 107-119.

Bentley, M. L., & Garrison, J. W.: 1991, "The Role of Philosophy of Science in Science Teacher Education," Journal of Science Teacher Education 2, 67-71.

Billeh, V. Y., & Hasan, O.E.: 1975, "Factors Affecting Teachers' Gain in Understanding the Nature of Science," Journal of Research in Science Teaching 12, 209-219.

Bloom, J. W.: 1989, "Preservice Elementary Teachers' Conceptions of Science: Science, Theories and Evolution," International Journal of Science Education 11, 401-415.

Brickhouse, N. W.: 1990, "Teachers' Beliefs about the Nature of Science and Their Relationship to Classroom Practice," Journal of Teacher Education 41, 53-62.

Bynum, W. F., Browne, E. J., & Porter, R. (Eds.): 1981, *Dictionary of the History of Science*, Princeton University Press, Princeton, NJ.

Carey, S., Evans, R., Honda, M., Jay, E., & Unger, C.: 1989, "An Experiment is When You Try It and See If It Works: 'A Study of Grade 7 Students' Understanding of the Construction of Scientific Knowledge," *International Journal of Science Education* 11, 514-529.

Charron, E. H.: 1991, "Classroom and Community Influences on Youths' Perceptions of Science in a Rural Country School System," *Journal of Research in Science Teaching* 28, 671-687.

Collins, A.: 1989, "Assessing Biology Teachers: Understanding the Nature of Science and its Influence on the Practice of Teaching," In D. E. Herget (Ed.), *The History and Philosophy of Science in Science Teaching. Proceedings of the First International Conference*, Florida State University, Tallahassee, 61-70.

Driver, R., & Oldham, V.: 1986, "A Constructivist Approach to Curriculum Development in Science," *Studies in Science Education* 13, 105-122.

Duschl, R. A.: 1988, "Abandoning the Scientistic Legacy of Science Education," *Science Education* 72, 51-62.

Erickson, F.: 1986, "Qualitative Methods in Research on Teaching," In M. Wittrock (Ed.), *Handbook of Research on Teaching* (Vol. 3), Macmillan, New York, 119-161.

Goetz, J.P., & LeCompte, M.D.: 1984, *Ethnography and Qualitative Design in Educational Research*, Academic Press, Inc., New York.

Grosslight, L., Unger, C., Jay, E., & Smith, C.L.: 1991, "Understanding Models and their Use in Science: Conceptions of Middle and High School Students and Experts," *Journal of Research in Science Teaching* 28, 799-822.

Hodson, D.: 1988, "Toward a Philosophically More Valid Science Curriculum," *Science Education* 72, 19-40.

Koulaidis, V., & Ogborn, J.: 1989, "Philosophy of Science: An Empirical Study of Teachers' Views," International Journal of Science Education 11, 173-184.

Lederman, N. G.: 1986, "Students' and Teachers' Understanding of the Nature of Science: A Reassessment," *School Science and Mathematics* 86, 91-99.

Lederman, N.G., & Zeidler, D.L.: 1987, "Science Teachers' Conceptions of the Nature of Science: Do they Really Influence Teaching Behaviour?" *Science Education* 71, 721-734.

Lortie, D. C.: 1975, *Schoolteacher: A Sociological Study,* University of Chicago Press, Chicago.

Loving, C. C.: 1991, "The Scientific Theory Profile: A Philosophy of Science Model for Science Teachers," *Journal of Research in Science Teaching* 28, 823-838.

Rutherford, F.J., & Ahlgren, A.: 1990, *Science for All Americans,* Oxford University Press, New York.

Schmidt, W., & Kennedy, M.: 1990, Teachers' and Teacher Candidates' Beliefs about Subject Matter and about Teaching Responsibilities. Research Report 90-4. Michigan State University, The National Center for Research on Teacher Education, East Lansing.

Schram, P., Wilcox, S., Lanier, P., & Lappan, G.: 1988, Changing Mathematical Conceptions of Preservice Teachers: A Content and Pedagogical Intervention. Research Report 88-4. Michigan State University, The National Center for Research on Teacher Education, East Lansing.

Songer, N. B. & Linn, M.C.: 1991, "How do Students' Views of Science Influence Knowledge Integration?" *Journal of Research in Science Teaching* 28, 761-784.

Smith, D., & Neale, D.: 1989, "The Construction of Subject-Matter Knowledge in Primary Science Teaching," In J. Brophy (Ed.), *Advances in Research on Teaching* (Vol. 2), JAI Press, 187-243.

Tobin, K., & Fraser, B.: 1988, April, "Impediments to the Teaching and Learning of Highlevel Science Outcomes," A paper presented at the Annual Meeting of the American Educational Research Association, New Orleans, LA.

von Glasersfeld, E.: 1987, "An Introduction to Radical Constructivism," In P. Watzawick (Ed.), *The Invented Reality,* Norton, New York, 17-40.

Wavering, M.: 1990, April, "What do prospective Science Teachers Understand about the Nature of Science?" Paper presented at the

Annual Meeting of the National Association for Research in Science Teaching, Atlanta, GA.

Wilson, S., & Wineberg, S.: 1988, "Peering at History from Different Lenses: The Role of Disciplinary Perspectives in the Teaching of American History," Teachers College Record 89, 525-539.

Wolfe, L.F.: 1989, "Analyzing Science Lessons: A Case Study with Gifted Children," Science Education 73, 87-100.

Zeidler, D.L., & Lederman, N.G.: 1987, April, "The Effect of Teachers' Language on Students' Conceptions of the Nature of Science," A paper presented at the National Association for Research in Science Teaching Annual Meeting, Washington, DC. (ERIC Document Reproduction Service No. ED 286, 734).

4

Objectives of Science Education

The science curriculum will be designed according to the objectives of the course. Many commissions and individuals have proposed different objectives for science teaching.

Education Commission (1964-66) stated that Science education must become an integral part of school education; and ultimately some study of science should become a part of all courses in the humanities and social sciences. The quality of science teaching is to be developed considerably so as to achieve its proper objectives and purposes, viz., to understand basic principles; to develop problem-solving. Analytical skills and ability; to apply them to the problems of material environments and social living besides promoting the spirit of enquiry and experimentation. Science strengthens commitments of man to free enquiry and search for truth as its highest duty and obligation. By its emphasis on reason and free enquiry, it even helps to lesson ideological tensions.

Although science is largely occupied with the understanding of Nature of present, its development is tending more and more to help man to understand himself and his place in the world in such developments. The commission observes that the pursuit of mere material affluence and power would be subordinated to that of higher values and the fulfilment of the needs of individual. This concept of mingling of science and spirituality is of special significance of Indian Education.

It is commonly felt that a child's education cannot be complete unless he has some knowledge of science irrespective of the field of study he wishes to pursue in latter life. Today the great advances in science rendered it absolutely necessary that a fundamental knowledge of science should be the 'sine qua non' of any person who was educated and who wished to lead a life which combined in itself something of scientific aspects of existence.

Objectives in any areas of curriculum should be regarded as the directions of growth and not as the ultimate ends to be completely reached. In this respect, science is not different from other branches. It is important that objectives should be selected towards which the growth and development of the individual may be directed from a very practical point of view. Objectives need to be selected and stated in such a way that progress towards their attainment may be appraised (Heiss, Obourn and Hoffman, 1950).

A judicious formulation and selection of worthwhile objectives for any school subject goes a long way in enriching and shaping both the teaching and testing in that subject and such objectives should be evolved in relation to the needs of the individual in his society. The three main sources for the formulation of the objectives are—

(1) the needs and capabilities of the pupil,

(2) the specific demands of his social environment, and

(3) the nature of the subject matter.

Science teachers have long recognized the need for sound objectives in curriculum planning. In an examination of over 3,000 statements written from 1901 to 1950 by secondary school teachers, Paul Hurd (1954) noted that the objectives of science teaching were the teacher's first consideration in planning curriculum. Objective strongly influence the organization of the curriculum and at the same time they provide the guidelines on the selection of teaching techniques.

National society for the study of Education in its Yearbook (1947) published the objectives under these categories, viz.

(1) functional information of habits,

(2) functional concepts,

(3) functional understanding of principles,

(4) instrumental skills,

(5) problem solving skills,

(6) attitudes,

(7) appreciations, and

(8) interests.

Bloom. *et. al.* (1959) classified the educational objectives under three domains, viz., the cognitive, the effective, and the psychomotor. The cognitive domain includes those objectives which deal with the recall or recognition of knowledge and the development of intellectual abilities and skills. The affective domain includes objectives which describe changes in interests, attitudes, values, and the development of appreciations and adequate adjustment. The work done in that period on manipulative or motor-skill was very less which includes motor activities.

Rai (1975) in his report on school Science Teaching stated that the main objectives for teaching of science should be—

1. To arouse the curiosity of the student about the world we live in and to encourage him to understand the various natural phenomena.
2. To train to acquire that habit of making observation in a planned way.
3. To develop in him science attitude.
4. To give him an idea how a scientist works.

The aims and objectives of teaching general science according to All India Seminar on Teaching of Science (1963) should be—

1. To familiarize the pupil with the world in which he lives and make him understand the impact of science on society so as to enable him to adjust himself to his environment.

2. To acquaint him with the scientific method and enable him to develop scientific attitude.
3. To give the pupil a historical perspective, so that he may understand the evolution of scientific development.

The Directorate of Extension programmes for Secondary education, Government of India, in its brochure on 'Evaluation in General Science' sets some of the objectives of teaching general science in secondary schools as—

1. The pupils studying general science should acquire knowledge of the fundamentals of science useful to all in everyday life.
2. They should develop the ability to apply the knowledge in every day life.
3. They should acquire experimental skills such as:
   (a) handing apparatus and instruments;
   (b) arranging apparatus for an experiment; and
   (c) preserving apparatus, chemicals, specimens, models, etc.
4. They should acquire constructional skills such as:
   (a) improvising simple instruments and appliances, and
   (b) repairing certain instruments and appliances of everyday life.
5. They should develop drawing skills such as:
   (a) drawing and sketching certain objects, instrument sand arrangements; and
   (b) photography in certain objects and specimens.
6. They should be able to locate reliable and recent information from appropriate sources.
7. They should be able to interpret scientific data given in various forms such as tabular, graphical, scientific, etc.
8. They should develop the power of minute observation of their surroundings.

9. They should develop the power of oral expression in science to discuss, argue, describe and raise questions using scientific terminology.
10. They should develop the scientific method in thinking and action.
11. They should adopt the scientific attitude in making statements, accepting information and forming beliefs.
12. They should develop interest in scientific reading and hobbies.
13. They should be able to appreciate the impact of science on life, bath personal and social, the struggle through which science has advanced, and the inspiring works of the scientists.

The following similar set of objectives was formulated by the principals of Delhi Higher Secondary Schools in the third summer camp organized by the extension department of the Central Institute of Education, Delhi.

1. To develop in the student a scientific attitude.
2. To develop in the student critical thinking.
3. To enable the student to acquire the fundamentals of scientific method.
4. To develop in the student skill in laboratory techniques.
5. To enable the student to be creative.
6. To develop in the student the ability to apply scientific knowledge and principles to problems of everyday life and new situations.
7. To enable the student to comprehend scientific terms, concepts, symbols, various tables and their uses.
8. To enable the student to construct and interpret graphs, diagrams and models.
9. To enable the student to collect and interpret data for the solution of problems.
10. To enable the student to be familiar with the natural resources of his environment and their uses.

11. To enable the student to be familiar with the trends in modern science.
12. To enable the student to appreciate the beauty and order in nature.

Approach paper on science and mathematics in General Education (1985) developed by NCERT thought of the possibility of fulfilling the following objectives for secondary level for enabling the students—

1. To study a few aspects of physical and life sciences in detail with a special emphasis on those areas of concern like food, shelter, health, energy, nutrition, and major components of environment;
2. To appreciate the need of quantification in the scientific students;
3. To develop in science and ability to put the interest into action;
4. To manipulate tools, equipment in a proper manner;
5. To identify the factors operating in the environment; and
6. To collect data, classify and draw reasonable inferences.

These objectives of secondary stage are to be fulfilled along with the objectives of primary and middle stages which include collection of information; classification of objects, events, etc.; identification of cause and effect relationship; development of scientific attitudes; acquainting with natural phenomena; giving emphasis to the relevance of science to daily life, etc.

Bhaskara Rao (1989) stated that a teacher must formulate some definite objectives and specifications . . . in order to achieve desirable behavioural changes among pupils. He emphasized on objectives such as knowledge, understanding, application, skill, interest, scientific attitudes, and appreciation.

The objectives of science explained by various individuals, commissions and conferences are concerned to biology also. Certain specific objectives are also developed only for biology. Let us observe then now.

First Asian Regional conference on school Biology (1966) held at Manila recommended the following aims and objectives of school biology teaching in Asia.

1. To develop and instil in student the scientific attitude of inquiry and experimentation.
2. To provide sufficient understanding of the concepts of biology to enable students to become worthy citizens of the world.
3. To provide the opportunities for a practical understanding of the method of biologists which give them confidence to attempt the solution of problems which they have to face in their individual and social lives.
4. To give the student the incentive to pursue the study at higher level of biology and related fields.
5. To encourage respect and feeling for living things.

And the latest national Policy on education—1986 states that 'Science Education will be strengthened so as to develop in the child well defined abilities and values such as the spirit of inquiry, creativity, objectivity, the courage to question, and on aesthetic sensibility.

All the above aims and objectives of science stress, directly or indirectly, the importance of scientific attitude, scientific aptitude, skills, abilities and interest. And also we can sense that a pupils of biology should be in a position to utilize his classroom learning in daily life through proper achievement and application.

REFERENCES

Bhaskara Rao, Digumarti and Digumarti Pushpa Latha (1995). Achievement in Science. New Delhi: Discovery Publishing House.

Bhaskara Rao, D. (1995) Jeevasashtra Bodhana (Teaching of Biology). Guntur: Creative Press.

5

Instructional Objectives of Science Education

Objectives decide the teaching learning processes in a curriculum and they determine the place of a subject in the curriculum in shaping the content.

The objectives of teaching science should be formulated on a solid philosophical, psychological, sociological and scientific footing. The utility, appropriateness, practicability, and timeliness of the objectives should be considered. The main sources for the formulation of objectives are—the needs and capabilities of the learner, the needs of the society, the nature of the subject matter, the feasibility constraints, and the nature of the educational system.

The objectives thus formulated should be specific, useful, unambiguous, feasible and in accordance with the aims of education.

The objectives have been mainly divided into 3 domains, viz., Cognitive, Affective, and Psychomotor, by Bloom and his associates. Here, the objectives and specifications developed by National Council of Educational Research and Training, India are given for Biology, Physics and Chemistry.

Instructional Objectives of Biology

1. Knowledge

The pupil acquires KNOWLEDGE of biological terms, facts, concepts, principles and processes.

Expected Learning Outcomes

The pupil

1. *recalls* biological facts, concepts, principles etc.
2. *recognizes* biological apparatus, specimen facts, concepts, principles, etc.

2. Understanding

The pupil develops UNDERSTANDING of biological terms, concepts, principles and processes.

Expected Learning Outcomes

The pupil

(1) *translates* biological terms, symbols, formulae, data etc. from one form to the other.

(2) *cites illustrations* of biological principles, concepts, phenomena etc.

(3) *identifies* relationship between various concepts, processes etc.

(4) *detects* errors in biological experiments, processes etc.

(5) *compares* biological terms, concepts, principles etc.

(6) *classifies* specimen, facts, concepts etc.

(7) *interprets* biological concepts, data, graphs.

(8) *explains* biological concepts, principles, processes and phenomena.

3. Application

The pupil APPLIES knowledge and understanding of Biology in unfamiliar situations.

Expected Learning Outcomes

The pupil

(1) *analyses* the given data or observed biological facts and phenomena to identify different components and their relationships.

(2) *formulates* hypotheses on the basis of given data or observed facts and phenomena.

(3) *suggests* appropriate and alternative experimental procedures, for a given purpose.

(4) *gives* reason for certain causes and effects in biological phenomena.

(5) *draws* conclusions, generalisations and inferences from the gives data.

(6) *predicts* biological phenomena from the observed facts or given data.

(7) *judges* the relevance, adequacy and consistency of biological concepts and principles in the given data, experimental procedures and other biological phenomena.

4. Skill

The pupil develops SKILL in

A. drawing diagrams, charts, graphs, sketches etc.

B. manipulating apparatus and instruments.

C. collecting, mounting and preserving specimens.

D. observing biological specimens, phenomena structures, etc.

E. reporting biological information, evidence and results, using scientific terminology.

Expected Learning Outcomes

A. Drawing skills

The pupil

(1) *draws* diagrams, charts etc. of observed or given specimens, material, apparatus and instruments *faithfully*.

(2) *completes* the incomplete diagrams correctly.

(3) *recognizes* the various structures in the sketches and diagrams concerned with various functions.

(4) *labels* sketches and diagrams methodically and correctly.

(5) *draws* sketches and diagrams neatly at a *reasonable* speed.

B. *Manipulative skills*

(6) *arranges* the apparatus systematically.

(7) *handles* the apparatus and instruments carefully

(8) *reads* the instruments and apparatus with precision.

(9) *maintains* the apparatus and instruments in order.

(10) *improvises* apparatus and models, using locally available materials.

C. *Collecting, Mounting and Preserving Skills*

(11) *locates* the right habitual for a particular specimen.

(12) *gathers* the required specimen during the appropriate seasons.

(13) *handles* efficiently the appropriate equipment and instruments for collection of specimens.

(14) *uses* the appropriate material economically to mount the specimens.

(15) *selects* the right preservatives for different specimens.

D. *Observing Skills*

The pupil

(16) *notices* the relevant details in the given specimens and biological phenomena carefully.

(17) *reads* the apparatus and instruments correctly.

(18) *discriminates* between closely related structures, parts and specimens accurately.

(19) *locates* the desired parts in a dissection or specimen exactly.

(20) *detects* errors in experimental set-up and procedures.

E. *Reporting Skills*

The pupil

(21) *selects* the appropriate biological terminology in describing specimens and biological phenomena.

(22) *uses* the appropriate terms in proper sequence and right context.

(23) *puts* the ideas in clear, precise and unambiguous terms.

(24) *records* the evidence or data from various sources faithfully.

(25) *tabulates* the data or evidence in appropriate form.

(26) *presents* the biological information on a logical order.

(27) *summarizes* the data and evidences in accordance with the desired pattern.

5. Appreciation

The pupil APPRECIATES the biological phenomena in nature and the role of Biology in human welfare.

Expected Learning Outcomes

The pupil:

(1) *recognizes* the unity of life in diversity of form.

(2) *signifies* the inter-relationship among various types of organisms.

(3) *develops* insight into the means and methods of biology used for exploiting nature for human welfare.

(4) *understands* the role of tools and techniques of biology in the development of life sciences.

(5) *realises* the struggle for existence among living organisms and the role of adaptation for adjustment.

(6) *gets thrilled* at the beauty of nature and is convinced of the role of biology in developing aesthetic sense in human beings.

(7) *feels* the importance of biology as inquiry in exploring the secrets of nature.

(8) *visualizes* the impact of biology on Social behaviours.

6. Interest

The pupil develops INTEREST in the living world.

Expected Learning Outcomes

The pupil

(1) *enjoys* collecting, mounting, preserving and displaying biological specimens.

(2) *participates voluntarily* in biological club activities.

(3) *frequently* writes biological articles in school and other magazines.

(4) *visit of his own* the botanical gardens, zoos and museums and other places of biological interest.

(5) *undertakes* hobbies such as improvising biological models, gardening, and field-study in *his spare time.*

(6) *reads* regularly the books and journals on the life and works of biologist *with pleasure.*

7. Scientific Attitude

The pupil develops SCIENTIFIC ATTITUDE towards biological phenomena.

Expected Learning Outcomes

The pupil

(1) *becomes inquisitive* about the biological phenomena.

(2) *is open minded* in accepting others' view points.

(3) *believes* in cause and effect relationship.

(4) *does not accept* things without proof of justification.

(5) *suspends judgements* in the absence of adequate evidence.

(6) *shows* perserverence in undertaking biological activities.

(7) *manifests* intellectual honesty in reporting results of experiments.

Instructional Objectives in Chemistry

1. Knowledge

The pupil acquires KNOWLEDGE of terms, concepts, processes, techniques and principles relating to chemistry.

Expected Learning Outcomes

The pupil

(1) recalls the terms, facts, concepts, processes, principles etc.

(2) recognizes the terms, facts, concepts principles and processes.

2. *Understanding*

The pupil develops UNDERSTANDING of terms, concepts, facts, theories, principles and techniques of chemistry.

Expected Learning Outcomes

The pupil

1. translates symbolic statements into verbal statements and vice versa.
2. illustrates terms, concepts and principles by citing examples.
3. identifies relationships, between various concepts, reactions, chemicals, terms, etc.
4. compares between related terms, concepts, reactions, and other chemical phenomena.
5. uses appropriate units to express various quantities.
6. classifies substances, facts, concepts, reactions, phenomena etc.
7. locates an error in a known experimental set up, statements and apparatus, and rectifies it.
8. performs simple, chemical calculations by substituting the formulae.
9. extrapolates from known information.
10. explains chemical reaction, concepts, phenomena.

3. *Application*

The pupils APPLIES knowledge of concepts and principles to new or unfamiliar situations pertaining to chemistry.

Expected Learning Outcomes

The pupil

1. analyses situation related to chemical data, phenomena etc.
2. formulates hypothesis on the basis of given or observed findings, facts, process data etc.
3. suggests procedure to test hypothesis using the underlying concepts, principles, laws etc.
4. establishes relationships, between causes and effects in the chemistry involved in the situations.
5. draws inference using concepts, principles, processes etc. in newer situation.
6. suggests new methods or alternative apparatus, chemical and procedures to test a hypothesis or to verify the inferences.
7. gives reasons for happenings, reactions etc. in unfamiliar cases.
8. predicts chemical changes on the basis of known facts and principles.
9. judges relevance, adequacy, consistency, fallacy etc. in the given data, observations, changes etc.

4. *Skills*

The pupil develop SKILLS required in chemistry such as manipulating skills, observational skills related to practical work.

A. Manipulative Skills

The pupil

1. arranges the apparatus systematically.
2. handles the apparatus and chemicals properly.
3. reads the instrument with correct procedure.
4. revises appropriate apparatus.
5. keeps the apparatus and chemicals in order.

6. improvises apparatus and uses alternatives efficiently.
7. prepares a sequential plan for observation.

B. Observational Skills

8. reads the instruments with precision and in sequential manner.
9. notices the relevant changes in chemical reactions using senses.
10. detects errors in experimental set ups and procedures.
11. discriminates between the closely related substances, reactions, phenomena etc.

C. Reporting Skills

12. arrives at concordant value, calculates and obtains correct results in the volumetric analysis.
13. infers correct results (e.g. group tests in qualitative analysis on the basis of observations).
14. uses proper formulae to communicate.
15. reports the results in a systematic manner.

5. Appreciation

The pupil APPRECIATES achievements in chemistry and its role in nature and society.

Expected Learning Outcomes

The pupil

1. shows thrill and excitement at the discoveries in chemistry and chemical processes occurring in nature.
2. enjoys collection and exhibiting pictures of chemists' chemical activities and cuttings about developments in chemistry.
3. realises the role of various types of reactions introducing spectacular and colourful experiments such as colour changes, crystal development, chemical garden etc.

4. feels thrilled in clearing his own experimental achievements as well as those of others.
5. gets satisfaction in reading about the achievement and sacrifices of great chemists.

6. *Interest*

The pupil develops INTEREST in chemical pursuits.

Expected Learning Outcomes

The pupil

1. collects specimens of material such as minerals voluntarily.
2. reads with satisfaction extra literature from books and journals on allied topics in chemistry.
3. performs extra experiments in his spare time.
4. engages in chemical hobbies and science clubs activities.
5. visits places of chemical interest such as factories. Science clubs, museums, exhibitions and allied institutions to get additional information in chemistry.
6. takes part in debates, lectures, paper reading etc. on his own.
7. enjoys preparing models and charts and collects informations, from books and journals.
8. improvises apparatus for his experiments without any ones guidance.

7. *Scientific Attitude*

The pupil develops scientific ATTITUDES toward chemical phenomena.

Expected Learning Outcomes.

The pupil

1. does not accept or reject anything without valid reasons.
2. has a keen desire to know how and why of anything that happens.
3. is prepared to face hazards in his investigations.

4. admits his mistakes unhesitatingly.
5. suspends judgement till it is repeatedly confirmed.
6. is unbiased in his approach to problems.
7. does not ignore any detail even if it is of not direct relevance to the work in hand.
8. shows intellectual honesty in reporting data, procedure and results.

Instructional Objectives in Physics

1. *Knowledge*

The pupil acquires KNOWLEDGE of terms, facts, concepts, definitions, fundamental laws, principles and processes in the field of Physics.

Expected Learning Outcomes

The pupil

1. recalls, terms, facts, concepts principles and processes related to Physics.
2. recognizes various terms, facts, concepts and principles of Physics.

2. *Understanding*

The pupil develops UNDERSTANDING of terms, facts, concepts fundamental laws, principles and processes in the field of Physics.

Expected Learning Outcomes

The pupil

1. translates verbal statements into symbolic equation and vice versa.
2. gives illustrations of principles of physics.
3. sees relationship between cause and effects of physical phenomena.
4. compares the various methods, concepts, principles etc.
5. detects errors in given statements, circuit, arrangements etc. and rectifies the same.

6. classifies as per criteria, the objects, facts, concepts etc.
7. gives explanation of physical phenomena, principles, concepts, etc.
8. reads and interprets graphs representing physical quantities and relationships.
9. solves numerical problems involving physical quantities principles, concepts, etc.
10. recognizes the significance and limitations of physical principles.

3. *Application*

The pupil APPLIES his knowledge and understanding of Physics to unfamiliar situations.

Expected Learning Outcomes

The pupil

1. analyses the unfamiliar situations, statements, observations, evidences etc.
2. formulates hypotheses based on data, observation etc.
3. devises new experiments for verification of the hypotheses and for known laws and principles etc.
4. establishes relationship between cause and effect, the known and unknown.
5. selects the principles relevant to a phenomenon.
6. gives reasons to explain unfamiliar physical phenomena.
7. draws inferences and conclusions from the given data or observed phenomena.
8. makes predictions on the basis of data, evidence etc.
9. judges the relevance, adequacy and consistency in statements, data, evidences, etc.

4. *Skills*

The pupil develops

A. Observing skills
B. Manipulating skills

C. Drawing skills

D. Reporting skills

A. Observing Skills

The pupil

1. reads instruments, measures physical quantities, accurately.
2. takes observations in a systematic and sequential manner.
3. takes the number of observations necessary.
4. reads graphs accurately.

B. Manipulating Skills

The pupil

5. selects appropriate apparatus, tools etc.
6. checks the tools, apparatus, equipment regarding its working.
7. knows the limitation of the apparatus etc.
8. sets the apparatus in a proper way.
9. performs the experiment with reasonable speed, accuracy, neatness.
10. makes correct substitution in formula (if any).
11. calculates the result accurately.
12. interprets data and draws conclusion.

C. Drawing Skills

13. draws neat, proportionate and correct diagrams.
14. labels the diagram correctly.
15. shows direction of force, say of current.
16. traces the circuit diagram correctly.
17. draws graph, selecting proper scale.

D. Reporting Skills

18. presents the observations in an appropriate manner/ sequence.

19. presents the calculations/results in proper sequence/ manner/units.
20. calculates (and compares) the per centage error etc. using appropriate symbols and formulae.
21. explains orally the procedures, precautions and limitations of the equipments, apparatus and experiments.

5. Appreciation

The pupil APPRECIATES the contribution of Physics to human happiness.

Expected Learning Outcomes

The pupil

1. follows and adjusts to the impact of Physics on society and individual.
2. derives pleasure in understanding the scientific advances in inter-planetary travels, radio astronomy, electronics etc.
3. feels that more inventions and discoveries are possible.
4. shows respect and admiration for great scientists.
5. manifests a spirit of scientific enquiry.

6. Interest

The pupil develops INTEREST in the world of Physical science.

Expected Learning Outcomes

The pupil

1. puts questions in scientific discussions frequently.
2. reads scientific literature and biographies of prominent scientists with satisfaction.
3. takes up scientific hobbies in his spare time.
4. takes part in science talks and debates willingly.
5. visits places of scientific interest on his own.
6. organises and actively participates in science club activities.

7. contributes articles on topics of scientific interest frequently.
8. enjoys observing natural and man-made surroundings.

7. Scientific Attitude

The pupil develops scientific ATTITUDE through the study of physical science.

Expected Learning Outcomes

The pupil

1. respects the teacher of physics.
2. records and interprets his observations honestly.
3. bases his judgements on verified facts and not on opinion.
4. willing to consider new ideas and discoveries.
5. is prepared to reconsider his own judgement.
6. develops independent thinking.
7. pursues his activities with precision and consistency undaunted by failures.
8. shows spirit of team work, self-help and self-reliance.
9. realises the danger in the misuse of scientific knowledge.

6

School Science Education: Remediation or Reconstruction?

E. W. JENKINS
The University of Leeds, U.K.

Introduction

Concern to incorporate some understanding of the nature of science within school curricula is a feature of science education in a number of countries. Examples include *Project 2061* in the U.S.A., the PLON materials in the Netherlands and the science component of the national curriculum in England and Wales, although significant changes to the last of these serve to emphasize the vulnerability of historical and philosophical interests to other curriculum pressures (Sorsby 1991, p. 2). Matthews has identified these curriculum initiatives as one element of a rapprochement between history, philosophy and science teaching, commenting that the 'advocates of increasing the profile of HPS in science teaching and in teacher training are in part arguing for a . . . science education that teaches (science) in its social, historical, philosophical, ethical and technological contexts' (Matthews 1990, p. 26). Attempts at such rapproche-ment are not new (Jenkins 1990) and the reasons for their contemporary re-emergence deserve more attention than they have received, not least as a means of exposing the different primary motives of, on the one hand, science educators and, on the other, those whose principal professional and scholarly interests lie in the history, philosophy or sociology of science.

In this paper, it is suggested that, as far as the community of science educators is concerned, any willingnss to enter into a rapprochement with scholars in the history, philosophy and sociology of science derives at least as much from a concern about the perceived state of health of the scientific enterprise as from a ready acceptance of the educational benefits of historical, philosophical or sociological insights into the nature of the scientific disciplines. This concern may be manifest in a variety of ways, e.g. public or professional debate about declining student enrolment or gender imbalance in science courses, the instrumental claims that relate science education to economic prosperity, the long-standing challenge to science educators that science offers a training but not an education, and the controversies generated by a wide range of science-based environmental, medical or industrial issues. Not surprisingly, therefore, different rationales are invoked to justify the incorporation of HPS within school science education. A brief view of some of these rationales, together with the tensions they generate in the rapprochement to which Matthews has referred, forms the substance of the first section of this paper.

Locating the distribution of HPS to science education among concerns that have to do with wider questions about science and science education in society has a number of consequences, of which two are considered in this paper. First, it suggests that some of the obstacles to curriculum reform not only lie outside the education system but are beyond the immediate control of teachers working within it. Second, it raises an important question about the contribution that studies in the history, philosophy and sociology of science might make to science curriculum development. This paper concludes with the claim that historical, philosophical and sociological insights into science should not be seen as a means of rescuing science curricula in difficulty. Rather, they should be regarded as an important element in the contemporary struggle to define a school science education 'for all' intended to empower young people as citizens in ways that traditional school science curricula are widely seen having failed to do (Yager 1983).

Some Curriculum Rationales for HPS

The history of school science education in the United Kingdom suggests at least three broad answers to the question

'Why the history of science?' First, the history of science has been seen as offering a 'humanizing' element in an otherwise dehumanizing school scientific education, a claim advanced with particular vigour in the years immediately following the first world war. A second rationale was much in evidence in the 1950s, when the case for historical and philosophical studies of science was pressed in the context of premature specialisation in science at school and the wider debate about the 'two cultures' (Snow 1959). Such studies, it was claimed, could constitute the common ground between the arts and science specialists. The third, and perhaps the most enduring, rationale has been that of providing students with a richer insight into the nature of science than that commonly provided or encouraged by conventional science teaching, a concern that transcends national boundaries and extends beyond students of school age (Matthews 1990). Conant's *Harvard Case Histories in Experimental Science,* first published in 1948, is a celebrated example of this concern into curriculum practice (Conant 1948).

More recently, the Harvard *Project Physics* course, first published in 1970 and subsequently translated into several languages, had, as one of its goals, helping 'students to see physics as the wonderfully many-sided human activity that it really is' (Brush 1989, p. 56). Likewise, the first statutory version of the national curriculum in England and Wales referred to students developing 'their knowledge and understanding of the ways in which scientific ideas change through time and how the nature of these ideas and the uses to which they are put are affected by the social, moral, spiritual and cultural contexts in which they are developed' (DES and Welsh Office 1989, p. 36).

The common and noteworthy feature of all these attempts to accommodate an HPS dimension within science curricula is that historical and philosophical insights into the nature of science have been cast in roles that are all essentially supportive of predetermined, and commonly pre-professional, goals of science education itself. Some attempts might be categorised as remedial, others as 'humanistic garnishing' but all might be seen as called in aid of science curricula in difficulty. The concern to 'humanize' science education in the immediate aftermath of the two world wars in which science played such a devastating role requires perhaps little comment. In contrast, one of the major goals of *Project Physics* was to attract more students to the study of introductory physics, itself a comment on the presumed inadequacy of existing curriculum offerings in this subject. Most recently, several initiatives e.g. the inclusion of historical perspectives in *Science for All Americans* in the U.S.A., have been justified by the rhetoric of scientific literacy, itself a problematic, if not meaningless term, and one too easily equated with the 'public understanding of science' i.e. understanding science on the scientists' terms (Layton, Davey and Jenkins 1986, Jenkins 1989). There are, of course, good arguments in favour of the 'public understanding of science ' (Royal Society, 1985). Asimov, for example, has claimed that 'without an informed public, scientists will not only be no longer supported financially, they will be actively persecuted' (Asimov 1984). Persecuted or not, it seems likely that some degree of public understanding of science underpins the political support required both for the successful prosecution of science in a modern, industrialized democracy and for the ability of the scientific community to counter opposition, e.g. from religious fundamentalists or animal rights groups. Ultimately, however, a willingness to entertain historical, philosophical or sociological insights within science curricula has stemmed from a sense, not always articulated, that science education can be amended in the cause of remedying some of the perceived problems of science itself, e.g. a shortage of qualified scientific personnel or diminishing public support for the scientific endeavour. When these problems disappear, diminish or are replaced by new or more pressing issues, the case for HPS in science education may be seen as correspondingly weakened, undermined or irrelevant. The case for HPS in science education, therefore, is historically contingent and historical, philosophical and sociological insights into the scientific enterprise have occasionally been burdened with educational responsibilities that they cannot hope to meet.

To the extent that HPS has been used to support science curriculum objectives established without reference to the history, philosophy or sociology of science, such use has something in common with the development of science, technology and society (STS) courses that have been such a distinctive feature of science education in the 1980s. Both types of initiative are commonly thought to enrich, humanize or contextualise science education without seriously challenging its traditional purposes and both require pedagogical strategies likely to be unfamiliar to many science teachers although a claim that STS amounts to a redefinition of school science education should not be ignored (Alberta Ministry of Education).

Some Obstacles to Curriculum Reform

However, well-founded, the claim that students should learn something of the 'nature of science' as an integral part of their science education presents formidable problems. Among these, attention has been drawn frequently to the difficulties facing science teachers who are required to articulate more clearly than hitherto their own understanding of the nature of science and to adopt new pedagogies in order to achieve learning outcomes that are different in form and content from those normally associated with 'learning science'. There is evidence that teachers are not only aware of these problems but also recognise them as a source of anxiety. For example, a recent study of teachers' views of science and their implications for science education in England and Wales, has concluded that 'teachers were unclear about "scientific method', despite its importance in the national curriculum then being introduced into maintained schools (Lakin and Wellington 1991, p.16). Although some valuable insights into teachers' views about the philosophy of science are available (Abell 1989, Rowell and Cawthron 1982, Koulaidis and Ogborn 1989), the only common features may be 'a lack of reflection about the nature of science and a feeling of security tinged with elitism', this last being a reference to the belief that science offers a paradigm for other disciplines to follow (Lakin and Wellington 1991, p. 16). The conventional responses to difficulties of this kind are curriculum development, inservice education and, as a longer term contribution to resolution of the difficulties, the incorporation of HPS within programmes of initial training for the teaching profession. However, those seeking to incorporate the nature of science within school science curricula may find the climate less hospitable than that confronting the curriculum reforms of a generation or so ago. It is not simply that many teachers find an exploration of the nature of science at odds with what has been referred to as their 'standard view of science education' i.e. a 'straightforward commonsense view, which claims no specific links with any particular philosophical view of science method' (Millar 1989, p. 40). There may also be opposition from some scholars, from students and from parents. Delamont, referring to scholarship in the so-called 'new history and sociology of science', has acknowledged that some of this work makes 'many sociologists of science uneasy, disturbs many scientists, and distresses educated lay people' and she reminds us that NHSS scholars have been blamed for undermining establishment faith in, and, in consequence, funding for, science (Delamont 1990, p. 157). Her caution that students might react strongly against the incorporation of NHSS ideas into their science education is reinforced by Lakin and Wellington's timely reminder that students have certain expectations of science lessons.

> They don't expect reading and discussion or drama and role play—they do expect Bunsen burners and practical work. They don't want to find out that science is not a set of facts, that theories change, and that science does not have all the answers—they want the security of a collection of truths which are indisputable.[1]

These expectations are not simply an aspect of the hidden curriculum of science education or an insight into Kuhn's 'route to normal science' (Kuhn 1962). They are fostered by the unproblematic presentation of science in the media, burnished by members of the scientific community, and form part of the wider attempt to insulate science from influences that are keen to threaten its 'neutrality' and independence (A.S.E. 1982, Joseph 1983). This insulation of science from matters of political, social or religious controversy is long standing (Mason 1953) and, arguably, is an essential condition for the success of science in understanding and controlling natural phenomena (Collingridge and Reeve 1986, Kuhn 1962). It is thus hardly surprising if students' expectations of their science lessons are shared by many of their teachers.

> 'Many science teachers believe that science is a set of facts and is divorced from morality'[2]

The incorporation of a more generous and scholarly understanding of the nature of science within science curricula also raises problems for an aspect of the teacher's work that seems likely to increase, rather than decrease in public importance. This is the assessment of progress in students' understanding. Consider the following comment from a teacher about the now abandoned Attainment Target 17 (The nature of science) in the first Statutory version of the science component of the national curriculum in England and Wales.

> AT17 will not be taught until it is assessed. How do you assess something that doesn't have a set of right answers? (*idem*).

Although the nature of this question is not such that it would command much sympathy from teachers of some other subjects in the school curriculum, notably English or history, it is an important question for science teachers. It needs to be answered not so much as an aid to developing appropriate assessment instruments, although these are likely to be important, but to bring into focus the knowledge and understanding that advocates of HPS are seeking to incorporate within school science education.

To assist in this task, there are some curriculum exemplars and a substantial and supportive literature (e.g. Herget 1989, Matthews 1990, 1991, Shortland and Warwick 1989) although it should be noted that much of this literature is historical, rather than philosophical or sociological in character and not always readily accessible to teachers.

Substantial problems, however, remain. Feyerabend's *Against Method* (1975), revelations such as those in *The Double Helix* (Watson, 1968) and the writings of sociologists *cum* anthropologists of science such as Latour and Woolgar (1979) offer a formidable challenge to traditional school science education. This challenge, serious enough at the epistemological level, also threatens conventional beliefs about the conduct of science and about the values and behaviour of those engaged professionally in it. It is, however, a far from straightforward task to respond to these challenges in ways that will satisfy both those whose scholarship makes possible the challenge and those who commonly perceive their task as advancing science by teaching it. The differences between these communities are substantial, not least in terms of the degree of commitment to the scientific endeavour. A historian, philosopher or sociologist of science has no reason to be a partisan of science, a position that, in the case of history, has generated such distinctions as science history, written by scientists, and history of science, written by historians (Debus 1971). In contrast, partisanship is of the essence in science education, although this, of course, should not be of an uncritical kind.

There is too, the difficult problem of the status of historical, philosophical or sociological knowledge, not least relative to that generated by the 'hard' sciences. Scholarship in the former three disciplines embraces a freedom to argue that the construction of scientific facts and ideas owes much to philosophical preconceptions, social influences and a range of rhetorical strategies. In contrast, scientific research and, at least up to now, science education, would seem to depend on an implicit assumption that consensible and, to this degree, objective, facts can be discovered, rather than invented. In addition, consensibility is hardly the trademark of historians, philosophers or sociologists. Historians display a range of approaches to making sense of the past and attempt to categorize each other's historiographical position using terms such as whiggist, contextualist and post-modernist. These historiographical differences are important, not least in the extent to which they accommodate different commitments to notions such as 'objectivity' and the role of the present in constructing the past. Not surprisingly, the disputes are sometimes bitter (LaCapra 1989, Jelavich 1989). Likewise, within the sociology of science, distinctions are drawn between 'strong' and 'weak' sociological explanations and between a Kuhnian, NHSS approach on the one hand, and that of the Metron/Columbia school on the other. As for the philosophy of science, it is perhaps sufficient to note that the past half-century or so has seen a remarkable transformation of its relationships with the history of science. Hitherto largely independent of, even incompatible with, historical approaches to understanding the nature of science, the philosophy of science, like much else, has been historicized but here too, as might be expected, there is vigorous debate (Nickles 1991, Nersessian 1991).

What is beyond doubt, however, is that 'the sort of ideology of science which, explicitly or implicitly, provided coherence and security for generations of science teachers is now an antique, (Ravetz 1990a, p. 20). By what, therefore, is it to be replaced?

Towards a Reconstructed Science Curriculum

To begin to answer this question, it is necessary to recognise that, seminal though they have been, the insights provided by historians, philosophers and sociologists into the nature of science constitute only one among several contemporary challenges to the ideology of science referred to above and to the science education which helps to sustain it. Studies of cognition in practice (Lave 1988), of everyday understanding (Semin and Gergin 1990), and of the ways in which scientific knowledge is used in lay contexts (Layton, Davey and Jenkins 1986, Wynne 1990) mutually reinforce the conclusion that thinking is a practical activity that is strongly context-dependent and is adjusted to meet the demands presented by a particular situation. Collectively, these studies present a powerful assault upon the claim that school science education offers skills, insights and understandings that can simply be transferred to, and applied within, the world beyond school. Much the same message comes from historical studies of the nature of technological creativity and, somewhat obliquely, from the findings of constructivist psychologists who have explored children's understanding and use of scientific ideas in everyday contexts. The issues involved here have been reviewed by Layton (1991) in a paper that explores aspects of the relationship between science education and praxis. To these issues must be added the problems facing the scientific endeavour, including aspects of the public support for it, at the end of the twentieth century. Some of these problems and their implications for science education have been discussed by Ravetz who concludes that, collectively, they prompt a revision of 'a faith in science that has been important in the determination of social policy for many generations' (Ravetz 1990a, p. 25).

If scholarly and other grounds now exist to prompt a radical reappraisal of school science education (Ravetz 1990b, Jenkins 1992), how might the insights into the nature of science generated by historians, philosophers and sociologists of science contribute to this task? This, it should be noted, is tantamount to asking how science education should respond to scholarship in the history, philosophy and sociology of science, rather than, as has been more common, what HPS should be included within science curricula. There would seem to be at least three broad categories of response.

The first relates to the transformation that has taken place in the role of science in society. Writing of this role, Redner (1987, p.15) has concluded that 'science has changed its ends. It is no longer the old science of the last few centuries . . . Contemporary science is worldly in every sense of the word and quite different in its essential character from the European science of the recent past . . . . these differences are apparent in all dimensions of scientific research, intellectual, instrumental and organizational'. This merger of science with power (Ravetz 1990b), perhaps because its implications for science are not widely appreciated, is an aspect of the scientific enterprise that has not always received the attention it deserves either from historians or from science educators, although there are some significant sociological accounts. If Redner's analysis is valid, there are some important consequences for science education. For example, the scientists of school science texts, Mendeleev, Joule, Rutherford, Maxwell, Newton and Darwin among them, are not just deservedly famous individuals and the subject of detailed scholarship by historians of science. They represent a kind of science that has little correspondence with most of the scientific research undertaken at the end of the twentieth century.

If science education is to nourish the intellectual excitement and adventure that science undoubtedly offers, it must do so in a context that acknowledges that students are growing up in a world that has at its disposal nuclear, chemical and biological weapons and which seems increasingly threatened by new technologies that not only bring unimagined benefits but also new risks and problems, and may be seen to diminish rather than enhance individual freedom and choice. This also means accommodating the political and social dimensions of contemporary science in ways that, at least up to present, have been marginalised within, or excluded from, most science curricula. To put the matter in the form of a blunt question: is school science education to address not only the traditional question of whether science is good science but also the newer question of who benefits and who loses? To those who reply that this is to confuse science with technology, a number of responses might be made. The first is that distinctions between science and technology are often hard to make (Mayr 1976) and are often more apparent than real. The second is that it is hardly surprising if students fail to see, or are unconvinced by, the distinctions with which they are sometimes presented. The third is, that like some of their elders, young people find themselves uncomfortable with the position represented by Robert Oppenheimer's description of the first nuclear explosion as 'technically sweet' or with Bronowski's denial that science could be held responsible for the explosion because it was 'done by good men in good causes' (Ravetz 1990a, p. 20). The point here is not that an either/or position needs to be adopted about science, technology and their social relations. It is simply that young people's perceptions of science as an activity which increasingly shapes the world in which they live may be far ahead of that which underpins much of the science education to which they are exposed at school (George 1981). It is surely part of the task of historians and sociologists of science to analyse and chart the transformation that has taken place in the scientific endeavour, and in the wider perceptions of it, particularly, but not exclusively, during the second half of the twentieth century. Exploring the educational implications of the resulting scholarship is a critical element of Matthews' rapprochement.

The second category of response relates to the nature and status of scientific knowledge itself. In general terms, students need to be helped to understand that there is nothing inevitable about a now standard scientific explanation and that such explanation requires an agreement about what constitutes reliable knowledge. The nature of that agreement also needs to be illustrated using appropriate examples, e.g. the oxygen theory of combustion, the wave nature of light, polywater and cold nuclear fusion. Inevitably, this latter consideration raises the important issue of how science is to be distinguished from non-science and offers the opportunity for discussion of the related notions of risk and reliable knowledge in contexts likely to be of interest to young people, e.g. health care, drug abuse, nuclear power, waste disposal and other environmental issues. It also offers the opportunity to explore the relationships between observations and explanations and, thereby, to incorporate not only a philosophical perspective within the science curriculum but also to expose the dimensions of difficulty of generating understanding about natural phenomena.

Translation of some of these ideas into curriculum practice will not be easy and will require pedagogies unfamiliar, and perhaps unpalatable, to many science teachers. In particular, the role of the *sine qua non* of school science teaching in many countries, laboratory work, will need to be recast (Hodson 1988) and both students and their teachers will have to come to accept at least some learning outcomes that cannot be categorized as either correct or incorrect. It will also be important to have regard to Koertige's argument that there is no single pedagogical strategy that allows a teacher to address the acquisition of scientific knowledge by students and their simultaneous understanding of the processes involved in the generation, validation and accreditation of that knowledge (Koertige 1969).

The final category of response, namely the re-engagement of science education with values, is entailed by the other two. The rhetoric of science and science education as value-free activities raises a number of difficulties, some of which are now so substantial that it can no longer be taken seriously. Any revaluation must, of course, accommodate the constitutive values of science itself, some of which are technical and procedural while others are more obviously aesthetic. It must also acknowledge the industrialization and commercialization of science to which reference has been made above, and the work of scholars who have revealed the complex interaction of ethical, religious, political, ideological and intellectual commitments in negotiating agreed scientific understandings. There may, too, be a claim for attention to be given to more radical feminist perspectives which argue that there is a gender bias in the very epistemology of Western science (Keller 1985).

What, then, might be the distinguishing features of a reconstructed school science education? Two basic premises might first be postulated. The first is that compulsory school science curricula must be concerned with science education 'for all', rather than with a pre-professional scientific training appropriate for only a minority of students. The second is that it must introduce students to what science has to say about some matters of great interest and importance such as the origin of the cosmos or of life itself. In so doing, it will present science as one of the supreme intellectual and imaginative achievements of the human race. However, unlike most contemporary school science education, careful and critical attention will need to be given to the nature of the scientific enterprise that has become such a powerful influence upon material and intellectual life at the end of the twentieth century. The outcome will be a re-assessment of both the nature of scientific knowledge and the political and moral economies of contemporary science. The triumphs of understanding the natural world need to be set alongside a more realistic perception of the nature of the consensibility that has made such understanding possible. The nature of scientific knowledge is to be exposed, not to confirm its fragility, but to provoke a re-assessment of the boundaries of the confidence that can properly be placed in it by illuminating the nature and complexity, including the cognative dimensions, of its genesis. It thus becomes important to ask questions about how some phenomena come to be deemed worthy of study at the expense of others, how some types of evidence come to be favoured and others rejected, and how certain techniques, methods and 'habits of thought' come to be cultivated and established as norms. It is also important to try to shed at least a little light on the dynamics of the intellectual, emotional, aesthetic and moral elements of scientific creativity. There is, of course, a substantial research agenda here for scholars in the history, philosophy and sociology of science and it is important not to confuse the objectives of scholars working in these areas with those of teachers responsible for teaching science in schools. Nonetheless, it seems important, not least in the long-term interests of science itself, to attempt to re-engage science education with values and, thereby, challenge the widespread notion that science exemplifies 'rationality and facticity' (Daston 1991). A successful challenge would both valorise and problematize scientific knowledge, and, to this degree, redefine and redirect school science education. For many students of school science, these dimensions of science are increasingly evident and matters of growing concern to them in the world in which they live. One consequence of an unsuccessful challenge, therefore, may be a further decline in the authority of science and a growing remoteness of school science education from the concerns and interests of young people upon whose benevolence future support for science ultimately depends. Contributing to the development of a new ideology for school science education seems a task that historians, philosophers and sociologists of science are well-equipped to undertake.

NOTES

1. Lakin and Wellington 1991, p. 16.
2. Lakin and Wellington 1991, p. 17.

REFERENCES

Abell, S. K.: 1989, 'The Nature of Science as Portrayed to Preservice Elementary Teachers via Methods Textbooks' in Herget, D. E. (ed.), *The History and Philosophy of Science in Science Teaching,* Florida State University, Tallahassee.

Alberta Ministry of Education.: 1990, *STS Science Education: Unifying the Goals of Science Education,* Ministry of Education, Alberta, Canada.

ASE.: 1982, *Response by the Association for Science Education to the Committee of Inquiry into the Education of Children from Ethnic Minority Groups,* Association for Science Education, Hatfield.

Asimov, I.: 1984, *Nature,* cited in Thomas, G. and Durant, J.: 1987, 'Why should we promote scientific literacy?' In Shortland, M. (ed.) Scientific Literacy Papers, Department of External Studies, Oxford, 1-14.

Brush, S.: 1989, 'History of Science and Science Education', in Shortland, M. and Warwick, A., *Teaching the History of Science,* B.S.H.S./Blackwell, Oxford, pp. 54-66.

Collingridge, D. and Reeve, C.: 1986, *Science Speaks to Power: The role of experts in policy making,* Francis Pinter, London.

Conant, J. B.: 1948, *Harvard Case Histories in Experimental Science,* 2 vols., Harvard U.P., Cambridge, Mass.

Daston, L.: 1991, *The Moral Economy of Science,* paper presented to a conference on Critical Problems and Research Frontiers in History of Science and History of Technology, Madison, WI.

Debus, A. G.: 1971, 'The relationship of science-history to the history of science', *J. Chem. Ed.*, 48, pp. 804-805.

Delamont, S.: 1990, 'A paradigm shift in science education?', *Studies in Science Education*, 18, pp. 153-158.

DES and Welsh Office: 1989, *Science in the National Curriculum*, H.M.S.O., London.

Feyerabend, P.: 1975, *Against Method: an outline of an anarchistic theory of knowledge*, New Left Books, London.

George, D. A.: 1981, *An engineer's view of science education: a discussion paper*, Science Council of Canada, Ottawa.

Herget, D. E.: 1989, *The History and Philosophy of Science in Science Teaching*, Florida State University, Tallahassee.

Herget, D. E.: 1990, *More History and Philosophy of Science in Science Teaching*, Florida State University, Tallahassee.

Hodson, D.: 1988, 'Experiments in Science and Science Teaching', *Ed. Phil. and Theory*, 20 (2), pp. 53-66.

Jelavich, P.: 1989, Reply to a letter by LaCapra (*op.cit.*), *Am. Hist. Rev.*, 94, pp. 1245-1246.

Jenkins, E. W.: 1989 'Scientific Literacy and School Science Education', *Sch. Sci. Rev.*, (71) 256, 43-51.

Jenkins, E. W.: 1990 'History of science in British schools: retrospect and prospect', *Int. J. Sci. Ed.*, 12 (3), 274-281.

Jenkins, E. W.: 1992, 'School Science Education: Towards a Reconstruction', *J. Curr. St.*, in press.

Joseph, Sir K.: 1983, Annex to a letter dated 8 March, 1983, to the Joint Chairman of the Joint Council of GCE and CSE Boards, quoted in Layton, D.: 1986, 'Revaluing Science Education', in Tomlinson, P. and Quinton, M. (eds.): *Values Across the Curriculum*, Falmer Press, London.

Keller, E. F.: 1985, *Reflections on Gender and Science*, Yale U.P., New Haven.

Koulaidis, V. and Ogborn, J.: 1989, 'Philosophy of Science: An empirical study of teachers' views', *Int. J. Sci. Ed.*, (11) 2, 173-184.

Kuhn, T. S.: 1962, *The Structure of Scientific Revolutions*, University of Chicago Press, Chicago.

LaCapra, D.: 1989, Letter to the editor, *Am. Hist. Rev.*, 94, pp. 1244-1245.

Lakin, S. and Wellington, J.: (1991), *Teaching the Nature of Science, A study of teachers' views of science and their implications for science education,* Division of Education, University of Sheffield, Sheffield.

Latour, B. and Woolgar, S.: 1979, *Laboratory Life: The Social Construction of Scientific Facts,* Sage, London.

Lave, J.: 1988, *Cognition in Practice, Mind, mathematics and culture in everyday life,* Cambridge University Press, Cambridge.

Layton, D.: 1991, 'Science Education and Praxis: the relationship of school science to practical action', *Studies in Science Education,* 19, pp. 43-79.

Layton, D., Davey, A. and Jenkins, E.: 1986, 'Science for Specific Social Purposes (SSSP): Perspectives on Adult Scientific Literacy', *Studies in Science Education,* 13, 27-52.

Mason, S.F.: 1953, *A History of the Sciences,* Routledge and Kegan Paul, London.

Matthews, M. R.: 1990, 'History, Philosophy and Science Teaching: A Rapprochement', *Studies in Science Education,* 18, 25-51.

Matthews, M. R. (ed.), 1991, *History, Philosophy and Science Teaching, Selected Readings,* OISE Press/Teachers College Press, Toronto and New York.

Mayr, O.: 1976, 'The science-technology relationship as a historiographic problem', *Technology and Culture,* 17, pp. 663-673.

Millar, R.: 1989, 'Bending the Evidence: The Relationship between Theory and Experiments in Science Education', in Millar, R. (ed.), *Doing Science: Images of Science in Science Education,* Falmer Press, London.

Nersessian, N.: 1991, *The Cognitive Sciences and the History of Science,* paper presented to a conference on Critical Problems and Research Frontiers in History of Science and History of Technology, Madison, WI.

Nickles, T.: 1991, *Philosophy of Science and History of Science,* paper presented to a conference on Critical Problems and Research Frontiers in History of Science and History of Technology, Madison, WI.

Ravetz, J.R.: 1990a, 'Some New Ideas about Science, Relevant to Education, in Jenkins, E. W. (ed.), *Policy Issues and School Science Education,* University of Leeds, Leeds.

Ravetz, J. R.: 1990b, *The Merger of Knowledge with Power,* Mansell, London. Redner, H.: 1987, *The Ends of Science, An Essay in Scientific Authority,* Westview Press, Colorado.

Rowell, J. A. and Cawthron, E.R.: 1982, 'Images of Science: an empirical study', *Eur. J. Sci. Ed.*, (4) 1, 79-94.

Royal Society: 1985, *The public understanding of science*, The Royal Society, London.

Semin, G. R. and Gergen, K. J. (eds.): 1990, *Everyday Understanding, Social and Scientific Implications*, Sage, London.

Shortland, M. and Warwick, A. (eds.) *Teaching the History of Science*, B.S.H.S./Blackwell, Oxford.

Snow, C.P.: 1959, *The Two Cultures and the Scientific Revolution*, C.U.P., Cambridge.

Sorsby, B.: 1991, 'Where's the history? Changes to the National Curriculum for Science', *Education Forum*, 5, 2-3.

Watson, J. D.: 1968, *The Double Helix*, Athenaeum, New York.

Wynne, B.: 1990, *Knowledges in Context*, background paper from five projects presented at a conference on Policies and Publics for Science and Technology, Science Museum, London.

Yager, R.E.: 1983, *Curriculum Report*, quoted in Alberta Ministry of Education 1990, *STS Science Education: Unifying the Goals of Science Education*, Alberta, Canada.

7

Science Education in the Curriculum

MARLOW EDIGER
Truman State University, Kirksville, USA

A quality science curriculum needs to be in evidence in the school/class setting. Each person lives in a world of science. The natural environment with its plants and animals reflects subject matter in science. Inventions and technology to improve the lot of each person truly emphasizes the methods and content of science.

To life effectively in society, students individually need to experience the wonders and contributions of science and scientists. A vital programme of science instruction should be the lot of each student.

The Use of Experiments

A modern programme of elementary school science will have much in the area of experiments that pupils will perform with teacher guidance. This will mean that learners should actually be involved in conducting these experiments whenever possible. Almost all units taught in elementary school science can emphasize experimentation. For example, if pupils are studying a unit on "Magnetism and Electricity," the following objects and items can be placed on a learning center to initiate the unit:

1. Containers which contain shreds of paper, pieces of wood, a piece of plastic, and different kinds of cloth.

2. Nails, paper clips, different size coins, a piece of copper, and other kinds of metals.

Pupils can notice which objects and items on the learning center are attracted and which are not attracted by the use of magnets.

Scientists engage in conducting many experiments. This is a way of gaining new knowledge. It is a way of identifying new problem areas. Once these problems areas have been clearly defined; information can be gathered to solve these problems. A hypothesis or hypotheses are then developed which pertain to an answer or a solution to the problem. The hypothesis or hypotheses are tentative and not final or fixed. Only through testing can elementary school pupils develop some degree of certainty as to the correctness or accuracy of the hypothesis. Too frequently when science experiments are conducted, pupils want to jump to hasty conclusions as to the outcomes. An experiment or experiments are conducted to test a hypothesis or serval hypotheses. In the preceding example pertaining to the unit "Magnetism and Electricity", pupils could hypothesize as to which kinds of objects and items will be attracted by the magnets. This is only a hypothesis and not a fact. The hypothesis, of course, is based on knowledge. Pupils could then test the hypothesis with the actual using of the magnets. Different kinds of magnets should be utilized to test the hypothesis Hypotheses are substantiated, modified, or refuted based on testing. As time goes, on with the further study and thought, new concepts and generalizations may be developed pertaining to previously held conclusions.

Very early in the experiences of elementary school pupils, the concepts of "experimental" and "control groups" should be emphasized. Pupils on the kindergarten level, for example, may be studying a unit on "Plants in Our Community." The questions may arise as to what plants need in order to grow well. On a learning center, two potted plants can be placed. It is important to have these plants as alike as possible in terms in quality. The soil should be as comparable as possible for the two potted plants. The amount of moisture that each potted plant is to receive should be held constant also. In other words, both potted plants should receive the same treatment except for one variable which will be tested. This variable will be that one of these potted plants has a cardboard box placed over it. This plant will represent the experimental groups whereas the other potted plant will be the control group. Pupils can then test their hypothesis as to what will happen to the plant in the experimental group if it receives no sunshine. The plant in the experimental groups can be compared with the plant in the control group at selected intervals. Experiments such as these should be an experimental groups as well as a control group. If the outcomes are always the same in this experiment, pupils can achieve accurate generalizations.

In the unit previously mentioned pertaining to "Plants in Our Community," other variables can be tested also as to what plants need in order to grow. Let us again assume for purposes of discussion that the two potted plants are as similar as possible in terms of quality. They receive the same amount of sunshine due to their location. The soil of these potted plants is similar. The one variable that will now be tested will pertain to amount of moisture that one plant will receive as compared to the other plant. Desert plants would not be involved in this experiment. On of the potted plants will receive no moisture while the other receives a proper amount. Pupils can observe what happens at different intervals when the experiment is being conducted. The plant receiving no moisture for a period of time would be in the experimental groups whereas the plant which is receiving the normal treatment is in the control group. Again, pupils should have ample opportunities to observe what actually happens when the one variable is tested. Another variable that could be tested in the experiment would be the soil that is used the potted plant. All other variables would remain the same. Pupils could use three kinds of soil; sandy soil, clay and loam. Thus, with several experiments such as these, pupils could generalize as to which kind of soil is most beneficial to plants.

Pupils must have opportunities to identify problems and questions; secondly, information or data needs to be gathered; thirdly, a hypothesis or hypotheses are developed; and finally, the hypothesis or hypotheses are tested and subject to revision and modification. These steps may not necessarily be followed rigidly. However, pupils should use the methods of science in conducting experiments so that results are unbiased and objective.

The Importance of Science

More time, no doubt, is devoted to teaching elementary school science than ever before. The writer can well remember attending a five teacher rural elementary school when science was taught once a week on the intermediate and upper grade levels in the 1930's and early 1940's. The science curriculum then consisted largely of reading about science from a specific series of textbooks. The reading was generally done orally with each pupil taking his turn. Many students in graduate and undergraduate classes of the writer attending the elementary school years in the 1930's and 1940's mention similar learning experience learning experiences. The use of experiments in elementary school science has been discussed previously; experimentation should be central in a modern programme of science. The time, of course, devoted to the teachings of science has increased much.

There is much for pupils to learn in science in a scientific age. The space age, jet planes, cars, trucks, buses, ships, refrigerators, rangers, washers, and driers—to mention a few of man's achievements—require that pupils understand and develop major concepts, principles, and generalization of science.

Many elementary schools have adequate time devoted each day to the teaching of science. To be sure, ample time given to teaching a specific curriculum area will not automatically make for optimum achievements on the part of pupils. However, if pupils are to realize carefully selected objectives, the proper amount of time needs to be given to provide for quality learning activities in elementary school science and evaluate if stated goals have achieved.

Thus, society has realized the importance of science for pupils in the elementary school. If learners are to do well in science on the secondary level, they need to experience an excellent science programme on the elementary level. Young children are curious about their natural environment. Selected pupils have come to school late on the kindergarten and first grade levels due to being curious about insects, rocks, plants, snow, puddles of water, and other natural phenomenon while walking of school.

Teacher have been amazed about the items children will bring to school for a science learning center. Little or no coaxing needs to be done here. Pupils voluntary want to bring objects to school pertaining to the curriculum area of science. They may bring rocks, insects in containers, tadpoles in jars, plants magnets of different kinds, and other items related to science. Pupils can raise many important questions on what has been brought for the science learning center. Pupils may reveal their interest by asking questions such as the following:

1. What do insects feed on?
2. How are rocks formed?
3. How do tadpoles change into frogs?
4. What do plants need in order to grow?
5. Why do magnets "pick up" certain things but not other materials?

Pupils with teacher leadership can discuss possible answers to these questions. Research also will need to be done to get need information in solving problem areas. The area of science offers many occasions for pupils to develop interest in and become curious about natural phenomena. It almost appears that pupils are naturally interested in science. Thus, it is not wonder that elementary school science is receiving more emphasis than ever before in the elementary curriculum. Also, in an industrial, automated society, pupils must understand contributions that science has made to improve the quality of living for human beings.

In-Service Education in Science

With more science taught in the elementary school curriculum than ever before, it has become very important to conduct an adequate number of workshops and hold an ample number of faculty meetings to update science in the elementary school.

An elementary school or several elementary schools conducting workshops in the teaching of science must, first of all, determine what facet or facets of the science curriculum need to be emphasized in this approach in in-service education. Cooperatively, then, faculty members should decide upon the theme of the workshop. The theme can be decided upon only by studying trends in elementary school science and evaluating where one's school is presently in this important curriculum area. Thus, a gap will generally exist between where the school is presently and where it should be in elementary school science. The following areas may represent some of these gaps:

1. objectives of elementary school science.
2. selection of unit titles.
3. proper sequence in the science curriculum.
4. conducting experiments.
5. using a science equipment effectively.
6. using a variety of learning activities.
7. assessing pupil achievement effectively.
8. developing a philosophy for teaching science.
9. assisting pupils in reading science content.
10. identifying the scope of the science curriculum.
11. learning by discovery in science.

Committees can be developed based on decisions made in the general session pertaining to problem areas that need solution in the area of elementary school science. It is excellent if each participant in the general session can select the committee he or she wishes most of participate in. Committee members need to sense purpose in work that is done. In other words, if participants can voluntarily select the committee they wish to serve in and sense that purpose is involved in solving problem areas, energy levels should be high for optimum achievement. The following resources should be available for all committee members:

1. knowledgeable resource personnel who can work effectively with people.
2. a professional library from which participants can get needed information.

Thus, members of the different committees involved in working to gain more insight into a effective elementary school science programme should have resources available which will help in gaining quality results from efforts put forth.

It is necessary for participants in workshop to work on problems and area of interest of their very own choosing. This would then provide for individual differences among committee members. It may be that one participant alone has the following problem pertaining to the teaching of elementary school science: assisting pupils in working on committees where responsibility of each member commensurate with ability in evidence (this teacher may have had difficulty in getting certain committee member to do their share of the work). Thus, the individual participant in the science workshop can work in the direction solving a relevant problem in the teaching of science. Consultant help and resources materials would be available to help participants on an individual basis.

Faculty meetings in an elementary school should also be devoted to improving the elementary school science curriculum. An agenda committee composed of three or four faculty members can arrange items for discussion at the next faculty meeting. It is good to rotate the members of this committee provide for a broad base of participation on the part of faculty members of elementary school. Every faculty member should have equal rights to present items to agenda committee for discussion at faculty meetings. The agenda should be in the hands of participants two to three days before the meeting is held. This should give all participants ample opportunities to think about the various alternatives and possibilities when discussing solutions to questions and problem areas. Individuals can volunteer or be assigned to serve on committees to solve selected problem areas. Some of the problems areas that may be identified in faculty meetings pertaining to the teaching of elementary school science could be the following:

1. How can the inquiry approach be utilized when teaching science?
2. How does one write objectives which are behaviourally stated?

3. How can pupil achievement be effectively evaluated when using the problem solving approach?

Much thought, research, and discussion can go into the solving of each of these questions or problems. Some faculty members, no doubt, will need to visit other schools and observe teachers, for example, using the inquiry approach in teaching, as well as observe other innovations.

Developing Curriculum Guides

Each public school system should develop curriculum guides which can be utilized by teachers in teaching the different curriculum areas of the elementary school. Curriculum guides should be used in terms, of providing suggestions for teaching. They should definitely not be prescriptive. In the early history of curriculum guides, it was felt that these were to be followed rigidly. Today, the emphasis definitely is upon selection, in terms of good criteria or standards, as to what will be utilized from a curriculum guide. The curriculum guide, along with other reference sources, can assist the science teacher to do better job of planning of teaching elementary school pupils.

The question arises as to what are the salient parts of good curriculum guide. The format followed in developing these guides may vary from school system to school system. However, there will be some basic agreements as to which essential parts to include in a curriculum guide. The following are important parts of a curriculum guide in terms of the section devoted to elementary school science:

1. statements pertaining to a philosophy of teaching science.
2. suggestions for using for guide.
3. general and specific objectives for teaching different units of study.
4. scope and sequence of science units for each grade in elementary school.
5. suggested learning activities for each science unit.
6. suggested evaluation techniques to use in evaluating pupil achievement.

7. a listing of child growth and development characteristics.
8. suggestions for implementing committee work, and teacher-pupil pupil planning.
9. suggestions for helping pupils learn inductively, use the problem solving approach, and learn through the inquiry approach.
10. a good bibliography listing teacher references and pupil references.

From the preceding parts that could go into the developing of a curriculum guide, it is quite obvious that the teacher can have a valuable source of ideas to use in planning the science curriculum. For example, the teacher can evaluate and selected objectives which pupils should achieve in a specific unit. The teachers also has numerous opportunities to select learnings activities from the curriculum guide which should help a given set of learners achieve to their optimum. The evaluation section of the guide should give the science teacher some new approaches to utilize in effectively evaluating pupil achievement. Again, curriculum guides must be used as guides and not as a holy book which must be followed precisely.

Use of Television in Science

Educational television has made many important contributions in upgrading the science curriculum. Elementary schools that have access to closed circuit television generally will have listings of programmes which teachers will have well in advance of their showing. These programmes will relate directly to ongoing units being taught in science. For each unit of study, guides have been or should be developed pertaining to the different telecasts. For each broadcast, a listing of objectives for pupils to achieve is important. The teacher can sense then what each broadcast will emphasize in terms of objectives. Suggestions for learning activities are presented in the guide which will provide readiness within learners for viewing the telecast. The teacher can them select which activities would do the best job of providing readiness for learning so that adequate background knowledge will be developed within pupils. If pupils do not have the needed concepts, facts, terms and generalizations necessary for understanding the telecast, optimum achievement cannot result. The readiness activities should also assist pupils in developing interest in the broadcast. An inward desire should exist on the part of the learner in wanting to watch the telecast. Certainly, learners should have identified some questions which they would want to have answered when viewing the broadcast.

After the telecast, follow-up activities are necessary so that pupils can use what has been learned. Answers to questions raised before the broadcast can be discussed. Experiments may need to be performed in order that pupils can get needed data in answer to questions. Pupils may volunteer to develop reports on selected topics which relate to the broadcast using science encyclopedias or regular encyclopedias. Taking an excursion may help to answer additional questions raised after the telecast. In other words, there are many learning activities for pupils which will assist them to "branch out" in broadening their thinking and interests after having viewed a telecast.

Using Knowledge of Children

Science teachers who do a poor job of teaching may not be using knowledge pertaining to important child growth and development characteristics. Teachers need to study each of their pupils carefully so that the best quality of learning activities can be provided. Educational psychologists have long emphasized the importance of providing for individual differences in a class. Too frequently, however, little has been done in this area by practitioners. A very clear violation of providing for individual differences exists when science teachers want to kept all pupils "together" by having the whole group study the same thing at the same time. Perhaps, science has become a reading course where pupils spend much time in reading content from a series of elementary school science textbooks. As educators should be well aware of, this activity will be too difficult for some pupils'; for others it is too easy. Very few pupils will find that the content is written on their reading level. Pupils also desire new experiences and want variety in learning activities they are participating in.

Many statements have been written on child growth and development characteristics. Faculty members of an elementary school need to study these contributions written by psychologists and educators realizing that pupils differ from each other in many ways within a class, such as interest, intelligence, abilities, past experience, motivation, appearance, height, and weight.

Variety in Learning Activities

It is important for the science teacher to provide a variety of learning activities for pupils. This would be important for the following reasons:

1. pupils have different learning styles.
2. different levels of achievement in science exist within any class of pupils.
3. not all pupils, of course, benefit equally from the same activity.
4. teachers have different teaching styles.
5. selected learning activities capture the interests of pupils more than do other kinds of experiences.
6. individuals desire new experiences.
7. monotony in activities hinders pupils in developing proper motivation toward learning.

There are many learning activities in elementary school science which would assist pupils in gaining needed concepts, main ideas, facts, and generalizations. These learning activities could help pupils in the area of problem solving. The following, among others, could become purposeful learning activities for pupils in elementary school science: conducting experiments and demonstrations, taking excursions, reading from a series or several series of elementary school science textbooks, getting information from a set or several sets of general encyclopedias and/or science encyclopedias, reading from library books, working at learning centers, using pictures, using transparencies and the overhead projector, constructing objects, making models, utilizing filmstrips and films, listening to tape recordings. Interviewing resource personnel, viewing slides, visiting museums, having discussions, giving oral reports to the class, writing reports. Engaging in dramatic activities, making dioramas, developing friezes, completing murals, making graphs and charts, developing illustrations, and participating in panel discussions. There are many, many kinds of learning activities for pupil in elementary school science; there should basically be no boredom on the part of pupils when this curriculum area is being taught. It is important to select those learning activities which will help pupils to do the very best possible in elementary school science.

Approaches to teaching science can also be varied in terms of using the inductive versus the deductive approach to learning. Much has been written about the advantages of using the inductive approach as compared to the deductive approach. Some of these advantages are the following:

1. pupils have to do much responding so that generalizations and conclusions can truly be discovered.
2. learners reveal where they are presently in achievement when learning by discovery.
3. pupils can become actively involved in ongoing learning activities.
4. it keeps learners "on their toes" when doing much responding in ongoing learning activities.
5. pupils have many opportunities, to do critical and creative thinking.
6. a variety of learning activities can be utilized in the inductive approach.
7. pupils can become more self-directed with less reliance on the teacher dominating the classroom situation.
8. teachers become more flexible in their thinking when less reliance can be placed upon how pupils will respond.
9. learners can work more in the direction of using the methods and approaches of scientists, scientists gain much knowledge and information through discovery.

The science teacher can have pupils develop generalization deductively. For example, in a unit on "Liquids, Solids, and Gases," the teacher could perform an experiment whereby a bottle with a narrow opening would be filled with a few inches of water and placed on a hot plate. A balloon would be stretched over the narrow opening of the bottle before it is placed on the hot plate. Pupils would be encouraged to see what will happen. The balloon, of course, becomes larger. The teachers then proceeds to explain to the class why the balloon became larger and what happens when air is heated.

In the inductive approach utilizing the same experiment, the teacher could have pupils hypothesize freely as to what will happen when this same bottle, containing a few inches of water, with the attached balloon is placed on the hot plate. Reasons for the hypotheses can also be discussed thus giving the teacher much information on where learners are presently in achievement pertaining to the area now being taught in the unit "Liquids, Solids, and Gases." Following the discussion, the hypotheses need to be tested using the experiment. The experiment can be performed more than one so that pupils can sense than the outcomes in the experiment will have the same results. The size of openings of the bottles as well as the size of the balloons can vary when having pupils view the same kind or type of experiment when noticing that the results are similar in terms of generalizations or conclusions realized. Further research can be done using elementary science textbooks. Encyclopedias, films, filmstrips, and other resources to explain conclusions realized from conducting the experiment. In using the inductive approach, the teacher does a very small amount of explaining or lecturing. The teacher sets the stage for learning. Pupils identify problems, gather information, develop hypotheses, test hypotheses, and revise them when necessary. Active involvement on the part of pupils is of utmost importance in ongoing learning activities.

A science teacher could tape record his own teaching and evaluate the quality of experiences pertaining to pupils learning by discovery or using the inductive approach. If a portable video-tape making is available in the elementary school, teaching performance in science could also observe non-verbal facets of communication such as gestures, facial expressions, and body movements in the teaching-learning situation. Valuation feed-back from learners can come from viewing different facets of teaching on video-tape. The teachers can notice such factors as the following:

1. Do pupils appear interested or bored in the ongoing learning activities?
2. Are all learners actively involved in the lesson being presented?
3. Do a few pupils dominate the discussion while others refrain from participating?
4. Do pupils feel free to hypothesize pertaining to possible outcomes of science experiments?
5. Are pupils using variety of reference sources in gathering data to develop and/or test hypotheses?
6. Do pupils reveal curiosity in wanting to learning more about any unit of study in elementary school science?

If the teacher has access to video-taping teaching performance, or if a tape recorder is used only, he can analyze what kind of verbal interaction occurred between pupils and the teacher in a classroom situation. The teacher, for example, can notice the following in teaching-learning situations:

1. Do pupils have ample opportunities to hypothesize?
2. Does the teacher ask many relevant questions of learners pertaining to ongoing units of study in science?
3. Are these questions on the present achievement level of pupils?
4. Do pupils have need background information to develop meaningful hypotheses?
5. Is lecturing minimized much in ongoing learning activities?
6. Is the teacher praising pupils is achieving desired objectives in elementary school science?
7. Do learners identify relevant problem areas?
8. Does is appear that pupils individually are being challenged in developing an inward desire to learning?

9. Does the teacher give pupils adequate time to engage in hypothesizing when being involved in problem solving activities?
10. Does the teacher refrain from scolding or minimizing pupils is the class setting?

Behavioural Objectives in Elementary Science

Elementary school science lends itself very well to having teachers state their objectives behaviorally. Selected educators advocate that objectives be stated precisely. Advantages of behaviourally stated objectives are the following:

1. These objectives very clearly state what learners are to learn.
2. It can definitely be measured if pupils have achieved these objectives.
3. Learning activities can be selected carefully which will guide learners to realize the objectives.
4. Teachers can be held accountable for pupils realizing the objectives.
5. Learners can achieve these objectives at different rates of speed thus providing for individual differences.
6. Parents can notice specifically what their pupils have learned.
7. Principals and supervisors can have better basis for evaluating teacher performance.
8. Teachers could even be paid on the basis of achievement or lack of it in terms of learner performance (this could be a motivating factor for some teachers).
9. Objective criteria are used to assess pupil achievement; these criteria are the behaviourally stated objectives.

As in almost any innovation, there are also disadvantages to behaviourally stated objectives. The following, among others, are some of the disadvantages:

1. Too frequently, the trivial or unimportant is taught since the lowest level of cognitive objective are easiest to write.
2. No one can definitely be sure what pupil actually should learn when stating all objectives precisely prior to teaching.
3. Objectives should come from the learner also and not the teacher only.
4. Affective domain objectives may become minimized if all objectives need to be stated so that it can be measured precisely if pupils have achieved them.
5. Learners become rather passive individuals if all objectives are stated by the teacher prior to teaching.
6. By stating objectives in advance prior to teaching, the teacher is assuming that proper sequence in learning will be in evidence.
7. The teacher should focus more on the learning activity rather than the objectives since it is in this framework that interest and meaning is developed.
8. Behavioural objectives are very time consuming in writing.

The science teacher, the elementary school principal, and the supervisor need to study behavioural objectives carefully to determine if this plan of teacher is really wanted in elementary school science. Workshops and faculty meeting can be devoted to the study and implementation of behavioural objectives. Objectives which pupils are then to achieve should meet the following criteria:

1. they are important or relevant.
2. they stress key ideas or generalizations emphasized by specialists in the different areas or science such as in biology, chemistry, physics, zoology, botany, geology, and astronomy.
3. there is balance among understandings, skill and attitudinal objectives or among cognitive, psychomotor and affective domain objectives.

All behaviourally stated objectives should follow the following standards:

1. the objectives should be clearly written so that little or no room exists in their interpretation.
2. it can definitely by measured if the objectives have been achieved.
3. it states what learners will learn as a result of teaching.

If pupils are studying a unit on "The Solar System", the following objectives may have been identified for pupils to realize:

1. The pupil will list in writing the nine planets in proper sequence from the sun.
2. The pupil will recite orally the names of the largest and the smallest planet.
3. The pupils will write a fifty paper on the possibility of life as we know it on a planet of his own choice (excluding the planet earth).
4. Pupils in their own words will define the meaning of the following concepts: solar system; universe; planet; satellite; asteroids; theory; hypothesis; magnetic pole; rotation; and revolution.
5. The pupil will demonstrate and discuss the causes of the different seasons of the year.
6. Learners will predict what will happen in the future in space exploration.
7. A model of the solar system will be made in committees of three; the model will be evaluated in terms of criteria discussed in class.

The first and second behaviourally stated objectives require recall of information which is the lowest level of cognition. Pupils would recall the names of the nine known planets in proper order, and be able to name the largest and smallest of these planets. The third objective may also involve simple recall of what has been learned previously by pupils. Pupils could recall from a discussion if there is or is not life as we know it on one of the planets and write on the selected topic. Pupils individually, however, could also be quite creative when writing a paper of at least fifty words peitaining to the possibilities of life existing on a planet which he chooses to write on. The paper could involve unique, novel, original, and constructive ideas which would involve synthesizing of knowledge. The fourth objective goes beyond recall of knowledge. It is true that the child would need to think of definitions he has heard of previously pertaining to such words so solar system, universe, planet, satellite, asteroids, theory, hypothesis, magnetic pole, constellation, rotation, and revolution. The learner, however, would need to reveal his understanding of these concepts by giving definitions in his own words. Comprehension of the meaning of these concepts would be important to pupils when achieving this objective. The fifth objective would generally involve applying what has been learned previously. The knowledge and information the child has developed previously is now utilized in demonstrating the causes of the different seasons of the year. The pupil could use a large globe to represent the earth and flashlight to represent the sun. The learner could also make drawings on the chalkboard and/or use pictures in clarifying the various causes for the different seasons for the year. In the sixth objective, creative thinking based on much knowledge is involved. Pupils would need to have considerable background information to make predictions as to what will happen in the future as far as space exploration is concerned. The last objective involves a psychomotor domain objective in that a construction activity is involved requiring the use of the muscles. To be sure, much thought and research will go into the making of an accurate model of the solar system. Pupils will need to check the accuracy of their model in terms of standards or criteria developed in class. The latter part of this objective (objective number seven) can involve a very complex level of thinking. Definite criteria will need to be developed in class so that the model of the solar system can be effectively evaluated in terms of these guidelines.

Thus, behaviourally stated objectives can be used effectively in a modern programme of elementary school science. It is important when emphasizing these kinds of objectives that teachers have pupils go beyond the level of recall of information.

The science teacher also needs to think terms of some kind of rational balance among cognitive, psychomotor, and affective domain objectives. Never should one category of objectives dominate teacher-learning situations. One category of objectives does affect the other category of categories.

Adjusting the Science Curriculum to the Child

Too frequently, the teacher has objectives for pupils to achieve which are expressively complex. The science teacher may have felt that this is a way of setting high standards in a specific curriculum area. Many pupils then cannot achieve these objectives and develop feelings of an inadequate self. Pupil achievement goes downhill in situations such as these. Learners think and feel that they cannot do well in elementary school science and this becomes a reality. If pupils perceive that they cannot do well in science, this is the way that learners will behave. The teachers needs to have some kind of pretest in a new science unit to determine where learners are presently in achievement. Once this has been determined, objectives can be developed which are attainable. If objectives are attainable, learners can feel successful and develop feelings of an adequate self. The curriculum is then adjusted to where pupils are presently in achievement in different units of study in elementary school science.

Certainly, there is danger, too, in teaching pupils what they already know in a new unit of study. A pretest can give elementary science teachers data if objectives need to be made more complex. Again, the objectives should be attainable for learners. The science curriculum in this case in again adjusted to present achievement levels of learners.

In Summary

Conducting experiments is a very important type or kind of learning activity in a modern elementary school science programme. Balance among the different curriculum areas in the elementary school must be stressed in teaching-learning situation. In-service education for teachers, principals, and supervisors is important to update the science curriculum. Curriculum guides can be a valuable source to utilize when selecting objectives, learning experiences, and evaluation techniques in a modern programme of elementary school science. A variety of learning experiences should be provided for pupils in the elementary school. The science curriculum must be adjusted to the present achievement level of each learner. Inductive approaches should be emphasized by the teacher in teaching-learning situations; critical and creative thinking as well as problem solving should be emphasized. Attitudinal objectives are important for pupils to achieve. There must be proper balance among the following kinds of objectives for pupils to achieve.

1. understanding, skills, and attitudes or
2. cognitive, affective, and psychomotor domains.

Adequate emphasis needs to be placed upon microcomputer instruction in the curriculum. Wright and Forcier list the following general criteria in selecting computer courseware:

1. Content is accurate.
2. Content is appropriate.
3. Presentation is clear.
4. Screen display is highly readable.
5. The computer's capabilities are effectively employed.
6. Programme executes reliably.
7. Programme is cost effective.
8. Programme is easy to use.
9. Support materials are effective.
10. No racial or sexual discrimination implied.

REFERENCES

1. Edward B. Wright and Richard E. Forcier, The Computer: A Tool for the Teacher, Belmont, California: Wadsworth Publishing Company, 1985, page 158.

8

Excellence in the Science Curriculum

MARLOW EDIGER
Truman State University, USA

Each person lives in a world of science. The natural environment affects all of us. It operates in terms of scientific theories, principles, and laws. Pupils in the public school setting need to achieve relevant goals in science. These goals should be attainable, meaningful, and possess purpose for the learner. The *Show Me Standards* (1996) list the following science objectives for pupil achievement in Missouri schools:

In science, students in Missouri public schools will acquire a solid foundation which includes knowledge of

1. properties and principles of matter and energy
2. properties and principles of force and motion
3. characteristics and interactions of living organisms.
4. changes in ecosystems and interactions of organisms with their environment
5. processes (such as plate movement, water cycle, air flow) and interactions of Earth's biosphere, atmosphere, lithosphere, and hydrosphere
6. composition and structure of the universe and the motions of objects within it

7. processes of scientific inquiry (such as formulating and testing hypotheses)
8. impact of science, technology and human activity on resources and the environment.

Each of the above named objectives should be emphasized within a related, designated unit of study. The objectives might also be written more precisely, if desired, so that it can be measured if a pupil has/has not achieve each stated end of instruction. There are states in the United States that mandate measurably stated objectives. Other states have a more open-ended approach in allowing leeway in writing objectives. I recommend that objectives not be written so precisely that facts only are emphasized on tests to appraise pupil achievement. The following objective stresses pupils memorizing facts: the pupil will list in writing the names of ten arthropods. Then too, objectives can be so broadly stated that they become meaningless such as "The pupil will learn science." This objective certainly lacks clarity in terms of what will be taught and evaluated to determine pupil achievement.

To improve the quality of life for each person, a problem solving approach should be emphasized in ongoing lessons and units in science. With problem solving, change occurs from what is to what should be in science.

Diverse schools of philosophical thought will be discussed and how each might relate to improve the science curriculum.

Realism in the Science Curriculum

A science teacher who is a realist emphasizes that one can know the real world, in whole or in part, as it truly is. The mind then does not modify or change what is being perceived. Tillman, Berofsky, and O'Connor (1971) wrote, "Most people when they think about the objects of perception, would say that they perceive a world of objects which is external to them and which exists independently of their perception of it. This view is called realism."

Since the external world is perceived the way it is in actuality, specific objective of instruction can be determined by scientists and science educators for pupils to achieve. Each objective must be relevant and is a part of the whole that can be known by the learner. Thus in geology, biology, chemistry, physics, and astronomy, among other academic disciplines, measurably stated objectives of instruction need to be emphasized in teaching and learning in the science curriculum. With quality learning opportunities selected by the science teacher, pupils either achieve or do not achieve the specific objective (s) as a result of instruction. Measuring pupil achievement in learning stresses what pupils have learned what was stated in each objective. Realists desire observable results in learning from pupils. The results are verifiable regardless of which teacher is appraising learner progress. The verification principle is very important to teachers of science who adhere to realism as a philosophy of instruction.

Skinner (1979) was a leading advocate in stressing precise objectives for pupil attainment. Reinforcement is emphasized to reward correct/good responses in learning. Observable, measurable results are obtained from what pupils have achieved. Guesswork is not involved, but per cents, standard deviations, quartile deviations, grade equivalents, and percentile ranks emphasize how well each pupil is doing in the area of science instruction. Numerical results of pupil achievement in science is wanted by the realist teacher. Scores from tests; objective evaluations of science experiments and demonstrations performed by pupils; ratings given to learner performance as well as responses to questions, oral reports, portfolios and related papers written in which interobserver reliability is in evidence, present data as to how well pupils are achieving. These procedures qualify as objective means of apparaising learner progress.

Mager (1972) stressed the importance of writing objectives so they are operationalized. Objectives are then specific and clear to teachers, pupils, and other interested persons. Learning opportunities may be chosen and aligned with the stated objectives. Appraisal procedures used to determine pupil achievement are also aligned with the objectives. Quality validity and reliability are then in the offing. A pupil reveals if he/she attained or did not attain a stated objective. The realist science teacher wishes to know if pupils individually are or are not achieving objectives of instruction. The results may then be reported to parents in a very precise way.

Prior to instruction, the teachers may announce to pupils which objectives will be emphasized in the science lesson or unit. The pupil knows exactly what will be expected in terms of knowledge or skills to be obtained. The involved pupil should have more confidence in learning when realizing what the instructor's expectations are. The science teacher might desire to arrange the objectives in an ascending order of complexity. A logical sequence follows since the teacher sequences objectives in science for the pupil to achieve.

Advantages given for emphasizing realism as a philosophy of instruction are the following:

1. teachers may realize how successful they are in teaching since results form pupil learning are clear and observable.

2. objectives, learning activities, and evaluation procedures are interrelated in that the learning activities and the evaluation procedures must harmonize with the stated objectives. Thus, for example, it becomes easier to choose learning activities than otherwise would be the case due to the harmony needed between these activities and the stated objectives.

3. effective schools research states that pupils achieve better if there is a clear relationship between the learning activities and the evaluation procedures with that of the objectives of science instruction (Edmonds 1982).

Disadvantages given for emphasizing realism as a philosophy of education stress the fragmented knowledge that pupils may learn since each objective achieved emphasizes parts of a whole. The teacher controls the science curriculum since he/she determines the objectives, learning opportunities, and evaluation procedures; pupils are not involved here in decision making. The products of instruction in science are emphasized, leaving little room for processes such as abstract thinking which is rather difficult to measure.

Examples of precise objectives for pupils to achieve in science are the following:

1. The pupil will write a paragraph indicating seven animals involved in a food chain.
2. The pupil will make a drawing showing ten animals in a forest food web and their interactions.
3. The pupil will list in writing the names of five parasites and their respective hosts.
4. The pupil will define each of the following: producers, consumers, decomposers, symbiosis, and an aquatic/ land community.

Experimentalism in the Science Curriculum

Experimentalists stress a problem solving approach in the curriculum. They emphasize that individuals cannot know the real world as it truly is. Individuals, however, obtain experiences of this reality. With experiences, changes occur in one's thinking and believing. A changing world makes for problematic situations. Problems need identification and solutions sought. In the science curriculum, pupils with teacher guidance select a problem within an ongoing lesson or unit of study. The problem needs to be adequately delimited so that meaning and understanding is involved. An hypothesis is developed directly related to the stated problem. Information from a variety of sources is used by learners to arrive at a tentative solution. Experimentalists believe all knowledge to be tentative, not absolute.

The result might well involve changing and modifying the original hypotheses. The new hypothesis is then tried out in a concrete situation (Geiger 1955). Problem solving may be used in all curriculum areas and in life itself. Knowledge here is used to solve problems and is not an end in and of itself. The practical and the utilitarian are emphasized within the framework of problem solving: knowledge secured from a variety of sources has an application dimension. Knowledge then in useful to solve problems in a changing world, sciences included (Ediger 1955).

Experimentalists emphasize that school and society are one, not separate entities. Since groups in society select and solve problems, pupils in committees also need to be involved in cooperative learning stressing problem solving. School and society are one, not separate entities. Dewey (1915) is still very widely recognized as a leading advocate of experimentalism in teaching and learning. In integrating the learner with the self as well as with the societal arena, he advocated four characteristics of pupils which have wide implications for the teaching of science. These are that pupils possess the social impulse in that they desire to work together with others in the curriculum; the constructive impulse in which learners like to learn by doing, not being passive individuals; the investigative and experimentation inclination whereby pupils desire to learn by discovery rather than being told and lectured; and the creative or expressive impulse, rather than have rigid formal expectations for achievement.

Advantages given in emphasizing experimentalism as a philosophy of teaching science are the following:

1. pupil interest in science becomes paramount when they with teacher assistance identify problem areas. Interest in learning makes for effort in achieving.

2. very young pupils in early primary grades may be involved in problem solving experiences (Ediger 1994).

3. problem solving is useful in all curriculum areas and in life itself when problems are selected and solutions sought.

Disadvantages of using experimentalism as a philosophy of education include problem selection being too difficult as well as problem solving may not be a favourite style and way of learning for a few pupils. Also motivation may be lacking for some pupils to identify and solve problems.

The following are examples of possible problems for pupils to solve:

1. How do animals adapt to their natural environment?

2. How do cells differ in size and shape to fulfil their unique functions? How are cells similar in features possessed?

3. How do unicellular and multicellular organisms differ from each other?
4. Which life processes do all living things perform?

Pertaining to John Dewey's philosophy of experimentalism, Meyer (1949) wrote:

> All of this, of course, depends upon in no small way on thinking. For Dewey, however, thinking becomes significant only when applied to life situations. It is, he had said, "an instrumentality used by man in adjusting himself to the practical situations in life." Or to phrase it more simply, human beings think in order to live. Because of this stimulus, which has its basis in biology and sociology, it is impossible—it is absurd—to interpret life in a systematic and abstract way. Since, moreover, Dwey holds that life is in constant flux, it is impossible to solve problems with any degree of finality for the problems of tomorrow will be different from those of today.
>
> As for the problem of knowledge, Dewey believes that knowledge and true experience is functional. What is this thing for? What is its use? Is a coal mine a physical deposit or does it have function? and if so, what is it? Such are the questions that help to give meaning to one's experience; but such questions cannot be answered without antecedent action. Action must precede knowledge. Whatever knowledge we possess has resulted from our activities, our efforts to survive, to obtain food, shelter, and clothing. Only that which has been organized into our disposition so as to enable us to adapt to our environment to meet our needs and to adapt our aims and desires to the situation in which we exist is really knowledge.

Idealism in the Science Curriculum

Idealists believe that one can receive ideas about the real world only. Thus one cannot know the real world as it truly is independent of the observer. Mental development in idealism becomes of utmost importance since an idea centered world is in evidence. Mind is real and needs development. As a leading idealist still quoted widely presently, Horne (1932) stressed the importance of the use of reason and rational thought in arriving at truth. Concepts and generalizations or universals such as justice, truth, goodness, ethics, and beauty have always existed and can be discovered by human beings. These universals are a prior, to an idealist, in that they have existed prior to human experience.

A subject centered curriculum in science is of paramount importance. In science lessons and units of study, pupils should achieve vital concepts, and generalizations. Depth teaching is needed to cultivate the intellect in guiding pupils achievement in science. A multimedia approach in leaning is needed to assist pupils to achieve abstract ideas in science. The abstract to an idealist is superior to the concrete and semiconcrete in learning. The concrete and semiconcrete facets of learning in science are salient to the degree that learners attain the abstract such as vital facts, concepts, and generalizations in ongoing lessons and units of study. Since reading and writing, in particular, stress abstract learnings, they should not be minimized in the science curriculum.

To emphasize a subject centered curriculum as idealists recommend, an academically inclined teacher needs to teach in a scholarly way so that objectives stressing intellectual goals are attained by pupils. Blanchard (1964) wrote:

> The aim of thought from its very beginning, we saw, was at understanding. To understand anything meant to apprehend it in a system that rendered it necessary. The ideal of complete understanding would be achieved only when the system that rendered it necessary was not a system that itself was fragmentary and therefore contingent, but one that was all-inclusive and so organized internally that every part was linked to every other by intelligible necessity.

Advantages given for emphasizing idealism as a philosophy of teaching science include the following:

1. pupils are to achieve significant subject matter. Idealism emphasizes the acquisition of vital content in science that pupils need to attain. Uses made of knowledge in science need to emphasize what is just to all, what is truthful, what is good in its application, what will truly stress ethical dimensions, and that which has beauty in its aesthetical areas.

2. many pupils may be motivated to learn when an academic approach to learn science is stressed. This might be especially appealing to the gifted and talented learners in science. All pupils need motivation to achieve and learn in science.

3. the abstract in idealism is preferred to the concrete and semiconcrete; relevant concepts, and generalizations, and other universals emphasize abstract goals in science teaching. Idealist advocate wholeness in knowledge, not fragmentation. Knowledge is related in all of its manifestations.

Disadvantages given for idealism as a philosophy in teaching and learning include minimizing a hands on approach in learning science since the focal point of teaching is to have pupils develop well intellectually; placing emphasis upon universals much more so than specifics—the latter is salient in pupils arriving at conclusions such as in science experiments; and integrating of knowledge to the point where science as a discipline is not as clearly defined as it might be. Idealists tend to stress that which goes beyond the five senses. Thus metaphysics and the a prior are salient to an idealist.

Quality sequence in science might be slighted when abstract phases of learning are more prized more highly than the concrete and semiconcrete. Most educators presently recommend a sequence of concrete, semiconcrete, to the abstract in teaching-learning situations. Quite similar in sequence, Bruner (1968) advocated using manipulative materials such as objects and items; followed by iconic materials such as audiovisual materials which are one step removed from the manipulative phase; and then symbolic activities which stresses the abstract including reading and writing.

Objectives in science, according to idealism as a philosophy of education, might well stress the following universal topics:

1. monerans such as bacteria and blue green algae. Monerans are prokaryotes in that they have no true nucleus. They consist of producers, consumers, and decomposers. A few move around whereas others are stationary.

2. protists, such as paramecium, euglenas, diatoms, and cribaria. Protists are unicellular and have a true nucleus. With a true nucleus, protists are eukaryotes, and are producers as well as consumers.

3. fungi, such as mushrooms and bread molds. Most fungi are multicellular. Since fungi do not contain chlorophyll, most are decomposers with a few being consumers.
4. plants, such as mosses, liverworts, ferns, and seed plants. Plants are eukaryotes and are producers. Plants do not move from one place to another.

Pertaining to idealism, Bigge (1982) wrote:

> The heart of idealism is the belief that basic reality consists of ideas, thoughts, minds, or substantive selves, not physical matter. Since priority is given to minds, minds have bodies, but bodies do not have minds. Idealism carries with its view the idea of subsistence (the superexistence) of God, who also is basically mind or self. The universe is an expression of intelligence and will, its order is due to an eternal, spiritual reality. For idealists, people are good-active substantive minds; they are absolutely real selves endowed with free will or genuine moral choice. This philosophy has ancient roots; it dates back to Socrates (469-399 BC) and Plato (427-347 BC).
>
> Idealism really is idea-ism. The source of this title is based on Platonic thought. For Plato, ideas only are genuinely real; they consisted of immaterial essences. That which people perceive is a shadow of reality; each thing that they perceive gets its existence from its Thingness; an idea. A book is a book because of its being more or less an imperfect replica of Bookness, a woman is a woman because she is a replica of Womanness. Plato's assumed world of "eternal varieties" consisted of the True, the Good, and the Beautiful.
>
> We can trace the development of idealism by listing some of the leading philosophers who have contributed to this position and stating a leading idea that each has contributed to this philosophy. Socrates believed that children are born with knowledge already in their minds, but they needed help to recall this innate knowledge. Plato contributed to the idea of Ideas, which are the universal forms of all existing things and are the essence of reality. St. Augustine (350-430) held a dualistic (mind-body) force of goodness.

Existentialism and the Science Curriculum

Existentialists believe that one exists first and then finds his/her purposes in life; there are no standards to guide human beings other than those developed by the human race. Most existentialists advocate that people are condemned to be free with no a priori standards in life. Individuals then make or break themselves due to the kind of society wanted. Each person chooses and makes choices continually. To be human is to choose. If a person permits the self to have someone else makes one's own decisions, then the individual ceases to be human.

Combs (1972) stresses that the way individuals perceive a situation will assist in determining how the individual will behave. Perception is unique to the individual. Each person decides upon what is true, judges what is good, and decides upon plans of action. The science curriculum then must provide opportunities for pupils individually to decide what to learn, that is the objectives of instruction. The pupil needs to be heavily involved in selecting learning opportunities as well as methods of determining progress. The teacher is a guide and encourages pupil learning. The teacher, however, does not lecture nor determine the science curriculum for the individual pupil. A learning centres approach in teaching science may then be emphasized. Here, there are an adequate number of centers with quality tasks for learners at each center. There needs to be more tasks than what a pupil can complete so that individual sequential choices may truly be made. A psychological, no logical, science curriculum is then in evidence. Each pupil may select tasks based on personal needs, interests, and purposes. The choice to be made is up to the individual pupil. If tasks do not meet personal needs of the involved nearner, he/she might plan with the teacher what has merit and value to the pupil. A contract system might also be implemented in which the pupil with teacher guidance selects tasks to put into a contract for completion. The learner himself/herself is responsible for choices made. The individual perceives what is good and has quality. Knowledge is subjective, not objective to the existentialist. For example, in a values clarification session, the pupil determines what is moral in terms of uses made of science and technology; the teacher has a difficult position as a stimulator and of one who encourages pupil learning. Being humane in an absurd environment is a major goal for pupil achievement in existentialist through and thinking.

Within an existentialist science curriculum, through pupil/

teacher planning a learner may select topics such as the following to pursue:

1. How do pesticides and herbicides help or hinder the natural environment? This question pertains to curbing insets and weed growth for the raising of farm crops versus possible contamination of soil and water.
2. How does one deal with animals in a humane way? This question stresses what to do with surplus dogs and cats roaming an area, as well as using animals for food and for scientific experiments.
3. How can the natural environment be used for development so that adequate numbers of jobs are available for workers versus the destruction of natural habitats for wildlife?
4. How can the needs of individuals be met as well as those in the societal arenas? This raises the question of the individual versus the larger group in a community, state, nation, and the world.

Alston and Brandt (1978) write the following direct quote of Jean Paul Sartre, a late leading existentialist:

> Man is nothing else but what he makes of himself. Such is the first principle of existentialism. It is also what is called subjectivity, the name we are labelled with when charges are brought against us. But what do we mean by this, if not that man has a greater dignity than a stone or table? For we mean that man first exists, that is, that man first of all is the being who hurls himself into the future and who is conscious of imagining himself being in the future. Man is at the start a plan which is aware of itself, rather than a patch of moss, a piece of garbage, or a cauliflower; nothing exists prior to this plan; there is nothing in heaven; man will be what he will have planned to be. Not what he will want to be. Because by the word "will" we generally mean a conscious decision, run on which is subsequent to what we have made of ourselves. I may want to belong to a political party, write a book, get married; but all that is only a manifestation of an earlier, more spontaneous choice that is called "will." But if existence really precedes essence, man is responsible for what be is. Thus, existentialism's first move is too make every man aware of what he is and to make the full responsibility of his existence

rest upon him. And when we say that a man is responsible for individuality, but that he is responsible for all men.

The Psychology of Education

Principles of learning from the psychology of learning give direction to the science teacher in teaching-learning situations in ongoing lessons and units of study. Ediger (1994) lists the following criteria upon which education psychologists agree should be followed by teachers:

1. meaningful learning experiences should be provided pupils in the curriculum.
2. interesting content and skills should be offered in lessons and units of study.
3. purpose needs to be established within pupils for learning.
4. quality sequence for pupil learning is a must.
5. attional balance among knowledge, skills, and attitudinal objectives is important in the instructional arena.

In Summary

Science teachers need to select tenets form the philosophy of education which stress pupils attaining vital content, abilities, and attitudes. In reviewing the different philosophies of education discussed in this paper, the following is salient from each philosophy:

1. clarity in objectives of science instruction, carefully selected, as recommended by realists. However, it is important to avoid fragmenting knowledge obtained by pupils.
2. problem solving procedures as recommended by experimentalist. Life in society emphasizes the importance of being able to solve personal and social problems.
3. major concepts and generalizations, as universals in science, advocated by idealists.

4. decision making opportunities in science as recommended by existentialists. Each person needs to learn to make decisions.

We believe that a problem solving philosophy encompasses the other three philosophies. We recommend problem solving as a major philosophy of education to emphasize in teaching science due to its relevance in the curriculum and in life itself. Problems abound and need solutions. Knowledge acquired then in instrumental or useful in problems to be solved which are selected by pupils with teacher guidance.

Ediger and Rao (1996) wrote the following in summarizing different psychologies of teaching:

Comparisons were made among the following models in teaching science:

1. problem solving with teacher guidance.
2. behaviourism with its predetermined precise objectives for student attainment.
3. humanism and its emphasis upon students selecting sequential activities from among alternatives.
4. the structure of knowledge with key concepts and generalizations identified by academicians in their respective areas of specialization. Science teachers assist students to achieve these structural ideas inductively using methods and procedures of scientists in a science laboratory setting.
5. stimulus-response learning of students in which a specific response is associated with a precise stimulus.

The writers advocate a problem solving approach be utilized in teaching science. From a stimulating learning environment in science, students with teacher guidance identify and solve vital problems. Problem solving skills are useful in all academic areas, as well as in the societal arena. Behaviourism, humanism, the structure of knowledge, and stimulus-response learning may be emphasized within the framework of problem solving situations. Subject matter in science may then be utilized in the problem solving science curriculum.

REFERENCES

Alston, William P., and Richard W. Brandt (1978). *The Problems of Philosophy,* third edition. Boston: Allyn and Bacon, Inc., pp. 257-258.

Bigge, Morris (1982). *Educational Philosophies for Teachers.* Columbus, Ohio: Charles E. Merrill Publishing Company, pp. 25-26.

Blanchard, Brand (1964). *The Nature of Thought.* New York: Humanities Press, 492-517.

Bruner, Jerome (1968). *Toward A Theory of Instruction.* Cambridge, Massachusetts: Harvard University Press.

Combs, Arthur (1972). *Educational Objectives: Beyond Behavionural Objectives.* Washington, DC: Asosciation for Supervision and Curriculum Development.

Dewey, John (1915). *School and Society.* Chicago: University of Chicago Press.

Ediger, Marlow (1995). Demonstration Teaching in the Schools. *Education,* 114, 371-372.

Ediger, Marlow (1994). Mathematics, problem Solving, and the Young Learner. *The Primary Teacher,* 19, 34-37.

Ediger, Marlow. Early Field Experiences in Teacher Education. *College Student Journal,* 28, 302-306.

Ediger, Marlow, and D. Bhaskara Rao. *Science Curriculum,* New Delhi, India: Discovery Publishing House, page 117.

Edmonds, Ron (1982). Programs of School Improvement: An Overview. *Educational Leadership.* December, Volume 4.

Geiger, George W. (1955). An Experimentalist Approach to Education. *Modern Philosophies and Education. Chicago,* Illinois: National Society for the Study of Education, 54, 137-174.

Horne, Horman Harrell (1932). *The Demoncratic Philosophy of Education.* New York: The Macmillan Company, 325-340.

Mager, Robert F. (1972). *Goal Analysis.* Belmont, California: Fearon Publishers.

Missouri Department of Elementary and Secondary Education (1996), *Show Me Standards,* Jefferson City, Missouri.

Meyer, Adolph E. (1949). *The Development of Education in the Twentieth Century.* Englewood Cliffs, New Jersey: Prentice-Hall, Inc., pages 42-43.

Skinner, B. F. (1979). *Beyond Freedom and Dignity.* New York: Alfred Knopf, Inc.

Tillman. Frank A., and others (1971). *Introductory Philosophy.* New York: Harper and Row, p. 550.

9

Writing and the Pupil in the Science Curriculum

MARLOW EDIGER
Truman State University, USA.

Pupils need to become quality communicators of content in writing. Why? Scientists in a laboratory setting must be able to write their findings in an accurate, objective approach so that effective communication among experts, as well as others, is in evidence. Not being able to communicate effectively in writing would greatly hinders scientific achievement in sequence on a continuing basis. Thus, in poorly developed written communication, scientists could not benefit from each other's research and findings. It behooves the teacher to encourage, assist, and motivate each pupil to do as well as possible in writing in ongoing science units of study.

Pupils may engage in writing on an individual or committee basis. Pertaining to committee or cooperative learning endeavours, Ediger (1997) write:

> Cooperative learning is receiving considerable emphasis in curriculum development. It is difficult to say how cooperative learning is different from the earlier term "committee endeavours" stressed in curriculum development. Presently, it appears that most writers and speakers in education recommend using cooperative learning rather heavily in the classroom. Thus, pupils in a class work cooperatively in projects, activities, and experiences. The teacher becomes a guide or assistant to help

learners achieve as much as possible. It is important here to emphasize that pupils work as a unit, not separately. Quality group dynamics becomes salient in cooperative learning. Learners then need to achieve goals and be goal centered. Competition among individuals in deemphasized and cooperation is salient. Individuals may work on different tasks in a team setting; however, these endeavours should represent cooperation in goal attainment.

Why is cooperative learning important? Presently, as well as in the future work place, individuals will be asked to work harmoniously with others. The individual who cannot work well with others will be handicapped. There are people from diverse cultures and abilities in any work place. Thus a pupil presently should be able to work with children of different values and talents. Being able to accept others is of utmost importance. Pupils individually need to be responsible to contribute optimally in cooperative endeavours. They need to think of themselves as a part of a group, not as competitive individuals. At issue here is how much time should be placed upon cooperative learning as compared to individual achievement. To think about individual endeavors in the curriculum, one must admit this is also important. Each person interacts with others and yet also needs to be able to use spare time wisely on an individual basis. A person is not a member of a group always but is also a person who has unique interests, needs, and purposes.

Writing and the Pupil

The science teacher needs to determine where each pupil is presently in achievement in writing. At this starting point, the teacher must guide learners on an individual basis to attain optimally and in a sequential manner.

A. Writing Experience Charts in Science

Early primary grade pupils tend to enjoy writing experience charts. A cooperative teacher who supervised a student teacher of mine taught a unit on *Animals in Our Lives.* She had three goldfish in an aquarium, tadpoles in a jar, a frog in a terrarium, a small garter snake in a different terrarium, and a pet canary in a bird cage. Pupils observed the goldfish carefully as they swam in the aquarium. Pupils were then asked to present ideas on what they saw to the teacher who in return recorded in writing observations presented. The following sentences, among others, were given in which first grade learners could see talk written down and experience writing:

1. The gold fish swam rapidly.
2. The bright colours mixed with the sunlight.
3. Water in the aquarium has bubbles inside of it.
4. Fish come up to breathe air.
5. It is fun to watch the fish being fed.

The numerals were then removed from the above experience chart and pupils read the content with teacher guidance. The teacher pointed to the words as the young learners orally read the content together with the teacher. There were numerous pupils who could not read the subject matter initially, but developed confidence to do so as the teacher patiently pronounced the words sequentially in the group exercise using the experience chart. The experience chart was saved and posted on the wall. Pupils could then view the chart as the need arose. A week later, the teacher again read the contents of the chart with the children involved. Several asked to read it individually to the entire class. This developed considerable enthusiasm. The teacher announced to the class that anyone wishing to read the contents off the chart to her (the teacher) should do so at any time. At this point and stage of achievement, most of these first grade pupils read the subject matter on the chart, making very few errors. This chart and later ones developed were saved for learners to reread at their own convenience.

With the use of the experience chart approach in teaching writing, pupils can see talk written down. Thus what is said orally can be printed with the use of abstract symbols in grapheme-phoneme relationships. The experience chart concept of teaching reading is based upon learners having a personal experience. In this situation, the experience was to look at goldfish. Later experience charts would be based upon pupils seeing tadpoles, frogs, a snake, and a canary. This brought to the attention of pupils, fish, amphibians, reptiles, and birds as sequential classification of animals with backbones. Still later, the teacher brought her pet cat to class to show a mammel.

With concrete experiences of viewing lifelike, real animals, pupils began to use language to describe what was viewed. The use of oral communication was then inherent. Pupils listened to the ideas presented by others. The content that resulted was printed in neat, manuscript letters by the teacher. Learners than read the content orally with teacher guidance as the latter pointed to the words and phrases within each sentence. Thus oral communication, listening, writing, and reading were experienced by each learner. The four language arts areas then become an inherent part of the science unit currently being studied.

When pupils are ready, they should write their own experience charts. This activity can be appropriate on any grade level.

Art work may well be related to writing experiences for pupils. Ediger and Rao (1996, pp. 91-92) wrote:

Learning activities involving art work can do much to enrich the elementary school science curriculum. Thus, the science teacher must provide a variety of learning experiences involving art in the science programme.

1. *Developing murals.* Pupils in a committee may plan and develop a mural pertaining to an ongoing unit of study in science. Thus, if pupils, for example, are studying a unit on "Animals with Backbones," they may decide upon scenes involving—

(a) diverse kinds of fish.

(b) amphibians, e.g. toads and frogs.

(c) reptiles, e.g. snakes and turtles.

(d) various kinds of birds.

(e) mammals, e.g. human beings, monkeys, chimpanzees, gorillas.

2. *Developing friezes.* A series of pictures developed by a committee of pupils is inherent in cooperative planning and implementing the frieze concept in art work. A variety of media should be available to pupils when working on a frieze. Thus, crayons, coloured chalk, water colours, coloured pencils and

finger paints should be readily accessible at the frieze center. If pupils, for example, are studying a unit on "Animals Without Backbones," they may develop a series of illustrations (a frieze) on—

(a) protozoans, e.g., the amoeba, the paramecium, and the euglena.

(b) porifera (sponges).

(c) coelenteratas, e.g. hydras, jellyfish, coral, and sea anemones.

(d) platyhelminthes (flatworms) e.g. planarian, flukes, and tapeworms.

(e) aschelminthes (roundworms), e.g. hookworms, ascaris, and the trichinella.

(f) annelida (segmented worms) e.g. earthworm and sandworm.

(g) echinodermata (spiny animals) e.g. star fish, the sea urchin, the sea cucumber, and the sand dollar.

(h) molusca (shellfish) e.g. clams, scallops, oysters, snails, and slugs.

(i) arthropods, e.g. shrimp, lobsters, crayfish, and crabs. Insects are also members of this phylum—praying mantis, grasshopper, walking stick, dragonflies, ladybugs, and potato beetles.

B. Outlining Content in Science

Outlining content read from the basal or other reference source might well assist pupils to be able to organize information better in terms of sequence. A quality outline should possess the following parts:

1. The title.
2. Roman numerals to show the main ideas or divisions.
3. Capitol letters under each main idea to show the relationship of these subdivisions with the main idea.
4. Details with ordered numerals under each subdivision to show relationships between the subdivision and the related details.

In outlining content, such as from the basal textbook in science, pupils may perceive the relationship of subordinate ideas to the main idea, the details to the subordinate idea, and the general sequence of subject matter. A pupil that focuses too much upon isolated facts tends to forget content sooner as compared to those who perceive that broader ides exist such as subordinate and main ideas. Then too, broader ideas tend to become a part of the general repertoire of the learner sooner as compared to the acquisition of isolated facts. Thus, there is a structure of knowledge in science for the learner when he/she perceives that key ideas can be selected and subordinate content and details can be related rather readily to the main ideas. I recommend that when pupils are ready, not before, they experience practice in outlining subject matter, not for the sake of doing so, but to perceive knowledge as being related.

A quality outline on a purposeful topic provides the learner with an excellent tool to present an oral report to others in the classroom setting. The pupil should never read ideas from an outline, but use the ideas therein to present well organized subject matter to listeners. Thus, if the learner forgets sequential content in the report, he/she may then refer to the outline. Quality organization of content assists the listener to acquire what is being presented. If an oral report contains randomly presented ideas, the chances are that comprehension by listeners will be difficult.

Pupils may receive practice in reading content in science that is poorly organized and rearrange the sentences so that coherence is in evidence. Noticing the differences between the two is important.

Writing Results from Science Experiments

A very useful writing experience for pupils is to write up science experiments that have been or will be performed in ongoing units of study. I believe that a plan developed by the teacher with pupil involvement will aid in writing that which is clear and distinct. First of all, the experiment needs to have a title which is meaningful to readers. If pupils are studying a unit or partial unit on water erosion of soil, a science experiment that is salient might well be entitled "Water and Soil Erosion." A problem then needs to be stated. The problem should be written clearly so that related information may be located as solutions. Hazy problem areas do not lend themselves to finding needed answers. A clearly worded problem might be the following: How does rainfall affect the soil in our schoolyard? Learners might then brainstorm answers to this question. No value judgment should be made of contributions of individual pupils. Respect for the thinking of others is necessary to generate ideas. The answers proposed in brainstorming should be recorded on the chalkboard to avoid unnecessary duplications. Higher levels of cognition are involved when pupils continue to offer answers. Initially, it probably is relatively easy to offer answers to the identified problem or question. After brainstorming, pupils need to ascertain which answers are acceptable and which are not. Science experiments should be performed in the classroom to determine the affects of water upon soil as well as observing in the out-of-doors what happens to soil with different levels of intensity of falling rain. As many variables as possible must be observed too, such as the slope of the land, the covering (grass) of the soil, and the kind of soil (clay, sandy, loam, among others). Inside the classroom, two boxes of equivalent soil with equal slope may be used initially. A similar amount of water should be poured over each box containing the soil. The only variable tested here is that one box has a grass covering over the soil whereas the other box does not. The amount of runoff of the soil for each box may be determined with a small container as broad as each box at the base to catch the eroded soil. Other variables to test for include different cover crops, different kinds of soil, as well as different amounts of water with variable intensity poured over each box.

These activities can also be used in testing the different answers given in brainstorming:

1. reading from diverse sources which shed light on water erosion of soil.
2. viewing audiovisual aids on causes and prevention of erosion of soil.
3. listening to qualified resource persons.
4. doing additional experiments and observing demonstrations.

5. making models of soil preservation including terracing, strip cropping, and trees/vegetative coverings to prevent erosion in its diverse forms.

Answers to questions should be viewed as tentative with chances of making necessary modifications as the need arises. Each step discussed above should be written with clarity and precision. Thus the problem or question, the brainstormed ideas, the data gathering, and needed modifications sections should be written with meaning and comprehension. Quality writing assists in communicating ideas more effectively.

A long standing debate has been in evidence in the teaching of science as to should it stress processes or products. A very popular approach in teaching science is *Science—A Process Approach* (SAPA) developed by the American Association for the Advancement of Science (no date given); their advocated objectives are the following processes:

1. observing
2. recognizing and using number relations
3. measuring
4. recognizing and using space time relations
5. classifying
6. communicating
7. inferring
8. predicting
9. defining operationally
10. formulating hypotheses
11. interpreting data
12. controlling variables
13. experimenting

The science teacher may stress the above named SAPA with or without using their materials of instruction. For example, objective number one above which is observing is very important in all science units of study. Here, the teacher may emphasize pupils observing a science experiment and all the sequential steps therein. The teacher may then appraise if pupils are observing carefully. This may be determined by teachers viewing attentiveness of learners during an experiment. Pupils might reveal their observational skills by writing up what happened sequentially in the ongoing experiment.

D. Writing Book Reports

Summarizing what has been read from a library book directly related to an ongoing science unit can be highly educational for pupils. The learner should have had the opportunity to choose his/her own book to read, from among others, at a reading center. There are several kinds of writing activities that can be implemented here. The pupil needs to select which procedure to use when writing about subject matter read from a library book. Thus, the pupils may choose from among the following:

1. writing a certain number of main ideas covered in the chosen book.
2. writing what was perceived to be the most interesting content contained in the reading material.
3. writing one or more paragraphs pertaining to the central idea contained in the library book.
4. writing questions that remain unanswered pertaining to the content.
5. writing a different beginning or ending if the contents of the library book are highly creative, such as the book *Miss Pickerel on Mars*.

Writing summaries pertaining to content read from library books should encourage, not destroy interest, in reading and writing content in science. The teacher should evaluate achievement here and in all writing experiences based on the following criteria:

1. use standards that assist the learner to notice that which needs to be improved upon.
2. have reasonable standards for each pupil, not excessively difficult nor at too low a level of achievement.

3. do not emphasize too many corrections for any one pupil to make, lest the involved child is overwhelmed with corrections that need to be made.
4. focus upon ideas in the written product, not exclusively upon the mechanics of writing such as spelling, punctuation, and grammar.
5. emphasize clarity of ideas expressed, not quantity in content written.

It is important for teachers to have conferences with pupils, one on one, too assist learners to improve over previous attempts at written work. The conference should stress caring for the pupil in becoming a better writer. Negative criticism must be avoided in the conference setting. A positive attitude toward the learner and his/her ability to improve in writing in all school endeavours is a must. Ediger (1996) wrote:

Relevant principles of psychology in teaching and learning must be followed when pupils engage in ongoing units of study . . . in the science curriculum. Thus, experiences for pupils should follow these standards or criteria:

1. learning activities should be interesting and meaningful.
2. pupils must have needed background information and possess adequate readiness for new units of study.
3. learners should perceive purpose in learning in ongoing units of study.
4. each pupil should be guided to achieve optimal development in understandings, skills, an attitudinal objectives.
5. learner progress must be continuously evaluated to determine progress in achieving stated objectives.

E. Journal Writing in Science

Pupils need to be given time to engage in journal writing. This provides opportunities for learners to reflect upon what has been learned in ongoing science units and lessons. Journal entries may be dated. What is written in the journal is up to the pupil. A pupil may then write what transpired in a science experiment or demonstration. The learner may wish to focus upon salient ideas discussed in a committee setting. With reflection, the involved learner will remember better what has been learned due to thinking upon key ideas or concepts stressed in science. The pupil might desire to write about attitudes and interests developed in science as a result of teaching and learning experiences.

Should the teacher appraise the quality of these journal entries? If not, how does a teacher know if the time devoted to journal writing is worthwhile and assists the learner to attain relevant objectives? If the teacher appraises the quality of journal writing, should the contents be graded? These and other vital questions need careful consideration.

We would suggest that teachers encourage pupils to share their writings. This can be done by sharing content written with the teacher on a voluntary basis. Pupils might also meet in committees to share what has been written. It is best if pupils are not coerced to show what was written in the journal. However, a pupils may waste time and pretend he/she is writing, but is day dreaming or writing irrelevant content. We believe the teacher can and must observe pupils to notice that achievement is taking place in all learning opportunities. A general overview in observing learner achievement may suffice in appraising pupil progress in writing journal entries. The teacher needs to be a,good observer and use quality criteria to appraise pupil progress. A listing of criteria may assist the teacher to make justifiable decisions pertaining to pupil journal writing. Among others, these include the following:

1. time on task is vital.
2. conscientious and judicious statements are a must.
3. proper order of written subject matter is salient.
4. clarity of content is necessary.
5. accurate mechanics in writing are needed to the degree it makes the written content more meaningful.

There should be a variety of kinds of learning opportunities in writing so that pupils feel that written work is utilitarian and purposeful.

F. Writing Diary Entries

Pupils individually or in committees need to have ample opportunities to write on a day to day basis what was learned in a science lesson. Each entry should be dated. By writing what was learned on a daily basis in science, writers review previously acquired information. With review, subject matter learned will be retained for a longer period of time than would otherwise be the case. Pupils should participate on a rotating basis in writing these diary entries. The following are examples of diary entries written by a committee of learners:

October One. The teacher explained to us the differences between sheet and gulley erosion. Emphasis was also placed upon the amount of top soil lost each year due to erosion. Farm crop yields decrease when rich top soil is not available for the growing of wheat, soybeans, and corn, among other grains. Marginal and tilled hilly land, in particular, are subject to increased erosion.

October Two. We went outdoors to notice gulley erosion beginnings on our playground. We levelled the soil and seeded grass to avoid erosion. We then came into the classroom to watch a video-tape on "preventing soil Erosion." Before observing the video, we hypothesized on ways to prevent soil erosion. During the video, we were asked to list and describe different ways to prevent or minimize soil erosion as presented in the video. These ways include using terraces, seeding grass and planting trees, as well as emphasizing strip cropping, among others.

The teacher may discuss with the entire class what might be added to each diary entry. These entries should be kept so that pupils might use these for review. Individual or committee members' names may appear on each page of diary entries and bound for future reference. Hopefully, the learning opportunity will increase learner interest, purpose, and meaning for writing in science.

G. Writing Log Entries

Pupils may review and combine the diary entries so that a log may be written. A log covers a longer period of time in terms of lesson content as compared to diary entries. Thus a log may pertain to recording what was learned within a week. The diary entries then become a part of the log. Individuals and committees who record the log entries must read carefully each diary entry so that broader generalizations may be written such as in a log. Log entries should be bound together with the diary entries so that pupils might review and rehearse what had been learned previously. Log entries provide a good basis in reviewing for an oncoming test.

Standards to follow in writing log entries include the following:

1. ideas should be specific enough so that misinterpretation is not possible.
2. quality human relations need to be stressed in any committee endeavors.
3. appropriate order of content is necessary so that sequence is in evidence.
4. correct spelling of words, punctuation, indentation of paragraphs, and grammar should be in evidence in order to communicate effectively. However, the focal point is on ideas in the logs, not the mechanics of writing.
5. log writing must encourage an increased desire to write rather than writing being perceived as a chore.

If pupils are to become good writers, writing should be emphasized across the curriculum. The curriculum area of science provides its many opportunities for pupils to become good writers. The are numerous purposes in writing in science. The author here recommends that pupils participate actively and fully in written work in ongoing lessons and units of study in science.

Using Word Processors

One of the greatest boon to writing has been the use of the word processor. The word processor indeed eliminates much drudgery attached to writing. The mistakes made in typing can quickly be corrected on the monitor before a final copy is sent through the printer. One can secure the desired copy, reading it on the monitor, before printing occurs. A perfect copy may then result even if a person's typing is not the best. A spell check programme eliminates spelling errors in a hurry without retyping any part of the document. There are limitations here in that the computer does not catch errors in homonyms nor in selected other kinds of errors such as in punctuation or capitalization. The user of the word processor still needs to be able to proof read typed content carefully and oh so carefully. However, spelling errors can all be taken care of in a very short time indeed with a spell check programme. Typing errors can be taken care of quickly be looking to see what is on the monitor and making needed revisions when proofing. I find it enjoyable to use a word processor in typing manuscript content each day. One can make much headway in typing with a personal computer that is very user friendly. A person who can type using the old typewriter can learn very quickly to use a word processor and be amazed at its capabilities!

Pupils who use word processors, when ready, feel ownership of the tasks involved thereon. The pupil with teacher assistance determines the content to be put into the computer. He/she sequences the content to be typed. Revisions are made in terms of the writer's goals. When changes need to be made such as rearrangement of ideas in the typing, this can be done quickly. No longer does a writer need to start all over in typing a page if a single error has been made. Whiteout does not need to be used in making corrections as was true of typewriter use. The writing curriculum must be updated so that each learner can benefit from modern technology and its applications. With word processors, the following conclusions may well be emphasized:

1. writing tends to be more enjoyable since errors made can quickly and conveniently be corrected with user friendly technology.

2. the rearrangement of ideas for quality sequence can be rapidly implemented, making it unnecessary to start over again in the typing process.

3. pupils may feel that what is done using the word processor is completely in their hands. The pupil gives the commands to the computer and completely controls

what will follow in terms of content and the mechanics of writing.

4. content typed can involve diverse purposes such as formal and creative writing. Each of the purposes discussed throughout this manuscript pertaining to writing may be emphasized using the word processor.

5. pupils individually or in dyads may write using the word processor depending upon goals stressed in writing in science. Goals may stress individual as well as group or committee endeavours in the curriculum.

In Closing

The science teacher needs to provide a variety of writing activities for pupils. This is necessary to provide for individual differences. Pupils should be guided to become increasingly proficient in writing. One cannot expect a pupil to blossom immediately into becoming a good writer. Rather, sequentially, each pupil can build a repertoire of writing skills. By comparing a pupil's past written product with his preset written work, the teacher can notice the degree to which a learner is achieving more fully. Writing is a basic in the curriculum. The science teacher should incorporate writing experiences when it assists pupils to acquire more subject matter content. Acquisition of facts, concepts, generalizations, principles, and laws of science are vital. So too must skills objectives be emphasized in teaching-learning situations. Thus writing for a variety of purposes in science is salient. The science teacher needs to notice if quality attitudes are a byproduct of subject matter and skills stressed in the science curriculum. Each pupil is unique in achievement and needs adequate provision so that continuous progress is possible in science. Pertaining to stressing a variety of writing activities in science, Ediger and Rao (1996, pages 86-90) summarized the following:

1. develop an outline. Each pupil with teacher guidance may develop an outline pertaining to content that has been read relating to an ongoing unit of study . . .

2. develop a written report. The content of the outline may be used to develop a written report. Written reports may deal with—

(a) summaries of experiments conducted in ongoing units of study in science,

(b) diary entries kept by pupils on a daily basis pertaining to understandings, skills, and attitudes acquired. Members on a committee may be rotated in writing these diary entries . . .

3. write poetry such as haiku, free verse, couplets, triplets, and quatrains . . .

4. Other forms of written work such as writing plays, announcements, and notices, as well as writing biographies of famous scientists.

A variety of kinds of written work should be emphasized so that pupils learn to communicate clearly and accurately in science.

SELECTED REFERENCES

American Association for the Advancement of Science (no date given). *Science a Process Approach*. Washington, DC: Ginn and Company.

Ediger, Marlow (1997). *The Modern Elementary School*. Kirksville, Missouri: Simpson Publishing Company, p. 63.

Ediger, Marlow (1996), "The Pupil, Geology, and the Science Curriculum, *School Science*, Vol. 34, No. 34, p. 26.

Ediger, Marlow and D. Bhaskara Rao (1996). *Science Curriculum*. New Delhi, India: Discovery Publishing House, pp. 90-91.

Ediger, Marlow, and D. Bhaskara Rao (1996). *Science Curriculum*. New Delhi, India: Discovery Publishing House, pp. 91-92.

10

Restructuring the High School Science Curriculum

(A PUBLIC DEBATE)

MARLOW EDIGER
Truman State University, USA

The purpose of this research paper in the form of a public debate is to indicate diversities of thought in terms of what makes for quality in the high school science curriculum.

Setting. A public debate is being held to determine what should be done to change the present high school science curriculum. There is considerable interest on the part of approximately 500 people attending to change from what is to what should be in the science curriculum. The chairperson has just completed introducing each panel member to the audience. Panel members come from nearby universitites and have considerable expertise in the development of innovative high school curricula. Panel member sign of number 1 is ready to present his/her presentation and findings to the audience participants.

Panel member #1. We need to emphasize a high school science curriculum in which all objectives for the different classes are stated precisely. In other words, these objectives have been chosen with utmost care and are then stated in *measurable terms.* There are two criteria I have mentioned as being of utmost importance and that is to select worthwhile objectives and then write them in measurable terms. Do not settle for anything but the most vital objectives possible for each course and academic area. Make sure the resulting objective is stated so precisely that we as teachers and administrators know exactly what will be taught. There is no guesswork then no what pupils are to learn. There is no guesswork either on if pupils have or have not achieved each objective as a result of instruction. This says to us that the evaluation procedures are strictly aligned with each specific objective. Validity and reliability are then in evidence for testing to notice if any pupil has been successful in goal attainment. Why would validity be preset? We have taught with learning opportunities so that the pupil will achieve the objective. Then we have evaluated if the objective has been achieved. Thus the learning opportunities were valid in terms of guiding pupils to attain each objective. Then too, the evaluation procedure(s) were aligned with the stated objective. Reliability should be there in that a pupil achieves the same evaluation results in that the objectives are highly precise and the evaluation procedure specifically measures if the objective was achieved. Certainly each pupil will receive the same test results after instruction should he/she take the test over again. We may even try it one time to notice if this is not the case. Test and measurement specialists continually stress that evaluation must be valid and reliable. I truly believe this presents the ideal model for teaching pupils. Effective Schools and Classrooms Research (1985) indicates that pupils do better in achievement if the objectives are highly precise and are announced prior to instruction. Learners then know what is expected of them in terms of learning from ongoing lessons and units of study.

With measurable results, we can clearly communicate with parents numerically how well pupils are achieving. Thus a pupil as a result of testing is on a certain percentile level, a certain standard deviation level, or quartile deviation level. Either a pupil does/does not respond correctly to test items covering what has been taught.

Panel member #2. I disagree with my predecessor here in that stated measurable objectives tend to become minimum levels of pupil achievement in the classroom. Why don't we set our sights higher than that? The trouble with pupil achievement in high school is that we hold pupils to such low levels of learning. We need to set *high standards* for pupils to attain. Minimum levels of pupil achievement are not adequate in the twenty-first century. Now is the acceptable time to raise standards in terms of what pupils are to attain. There are numerous excellent national standards such as Education 2000, established by the National Governor's Conference, which are to be emphasized in the curriculum (1991). Goal four of their standards for pupils to attain states: "By the year 2000, US students will be first in the world in science and mathematics achievement." Those are the kind of high academic standards we need to have our high school pupils achieve. They need to be lofty standards. The following national professional organizations have come out with goals that pupils are to achieve in different academic areas: the National Council Teachers of Mathematics, the National Science Teachers Association, the National Council for the Social Studies, the National Council Teachers of English, and the International Reading Association. High school teachers in their academic area of speciality may benefit from studying the objectives recommended for pupil achievement by each of these national organizations. They need to select high standards for pupil achievement in the high school curriculum.

What happens to the slower learner when high demanding standards of academic achievement are recommended for all? Let me say that all learners benefit from setting high expectations for pupil achievement. The slow learner will obtain sophisticated ideas that the more talented pupils receive. We can provide assistance for slow learners so that they may catch up with other learners. Tutoring of the slow learner provides the assistance necessary for these learners to obtain and achieve high standards in the school curriculum. What happens to pupils in the future if they have achieved low standards in the academic curriculum? Their chances at the good jobs and occupations will be zilch. Can we afford to let any pupil achieve at the thirty or sixty fold of productivity? No we can't. The parable of the sower says that when seed fell upon fertile ground, not on stony soil nor by the wayside, productivity went up one hundred fold. I truly believe with high teacher expectations from each pupil, we can have learners attain optimally in teaching-learning situations. My predecessor quoted Effective School and Classroom Research by stating we need precise objectives of instruction. What was not quoted was the importance here to also stress high expectations from pupils for learning. If our expectations are high from pupils, they will achieve more optimally.

Panel member #3. I disagree with what has been said so far in these panel presentations. Those ideas have been weighed and found wanting. Why focus only upon measurably stated objectives and high academic standards for pupil attainment in this debate? We have left out the main reason as to why we have schools and that is to focus upon the *pupil.* We teach human beings not subject matter. Let us involve pupils in decision making as to which objectives, learning opportunities, and evaluation procedures to emphasize. Pupil/teacher planning in the curriculum is a necessity. Why? It is the pupil that must do the learning. The teacher sets the stage for learning to occur. It is no wonder that we have low pupils achievement. Pupils have been left out of helping to determine the curriculum. And yet, they are the focal point of teaching and learning (Ediger 1995). As a leading educational psychologist, Combs (1972) advocates openended objectives for pupils to achieve in which they have had decision making skills stressed in determining the curriculum. Why minimize or omit the pupil when making curricular choices? We need to emphasize pupil/teacher planning of the curriculum. Learners must have a voice in terms of what will affect them. Democratic tenets stress that cooperatively, the pupil and the teacher need to determine what the former is to learn. There must be choices made by pupils in the high school curriculum as to what the learner desires sequentially to learn. The teacher has a difficult role here in that he/she is a guide, a stimulator, and a helper, not a lecturer and not a dispenser of information.

Panel member #4. My predecessors here have left out an important segment of the population in deciding upon objectives for pupils attainment. I believe strongly that *parents* must be brought into the educational process. Aren't parents tax payers of our schools? Don't parents assume ultimate responsibility for their offspring's welfare and deeds? Parents have much time and money invested in each child. Why omit their wisdom in helping to make decisions pertaining to their child's education?

Much research has been conducted to show how effective pupil learning is if parents are involved in the former's welfare. Epstein (1995), Co-Director of the Center on Families, Communities, Schools, and Children Learning at John Hopkins University at Baltimore, Maryland identifies six levels of parental involvement in education. These are the following: improved parenting through inservice education, conferences to improve school/home communications, parents volunteering in school, information for parents to help their offspring in school homework, decision making for parents in improving the school curriculum, and parents collaborating with the community for the good of the pupil.

It is no wonder that pupils do poorly in school when parents are not invited to assist the pupil and the school to achieve will for the good of all learners. Let us get parents involved in their child's achievement and progress in education. We need to have a needs assessment questionnaire to find out what parents want their offspring to learn. From the results, we can notice how parents have ranked the objectives for learners to attain. Open spaces can be placed on the questionnaire for parents to list additional concerns than those of the listed objectives which they were to rank on a five point scale. Teachers and principals must also rate the objectives and then come up with a final average in terms of what pupils in high school should learn.

Panel member #5. I believe that we need to update the science curriculum so that our pupils might function well in the world of *technology*. Technology is all around us. Hardly can we go into any business without seeing the latest in technology. I am referring here especially to the use of computers, modems, and internet. Any curriculum can become quite outdated unless pupils interact with multimedia.

There are software programmes for pupil interaction such as drill and practice, tutorial, simulation, and games. These programmes can be chosen so that they relate directly to an ongoing lesson or unit being studied by pupils. There are also software packages with related materials for learner interaction that comprise an entire unit of study in any academic or curriculum area. Then too, all pupils should become highly proficient in using the word processor involving a variety of purposes in writing and communicating. Do we want pupils left out of technological literacy? If we do, pupils, as adults, will be left out of the good positions in the work force. Let us educate pupils presently in our high schools whereby they truly are computer literate (Cawalti 1995).

Most teachers believe in the heavy use of technology in the science curriculum, but the funds have not been there to invest in quality materials of instruction. Teachers who believe in tradition may find it threatening to use computers, and other recently developed media, in the classroom. We need good staff development programmes on the many uses of computers, in particular. Teachers need to understand how software can be used to guide pupils to achieve vital objectives. They must understand how learners may work individually as well as in cooperative learning with computer use. In cooperative learning, pupils may challenge each other in wholesome ways as to which are the possible correct responses to items in a programme. A variety of other materials may be used such as video tapes, video disks, films, slides, reading materials, and construction activities for pupils. Learners need to achieve vital goals in the curriculum. They must experience meaning, interest, and purpose in ongoing lessons and units of study. Individual differences should be provided for so that each might attain as optimally as possible. A technological approach in teaching and learning makes it possible for learners to enjoy learning; they may experience learning opportunities that harmonize with individual learning styles. Dunn and Dunn (1979) have indicated how salient it is to make provision among learners for their preferred style of learning. Multi-media approaches to learning provide teachers opportunities to harmonize pupil preferred style of learning with that of the media available. I do believe we miss the point in teaching pupils when stating that measurably stated objectives are the key to better education for all pupils. The same is true if we become dogmatic about setting up high standards for pupil attainment, pupils being heavily involved in curriculum development, as well as a strong role for parents in developing the curriculum. I cannot say I am opposed to what has been said be each panel member. However, my predecessors all sound so traditional in their educational thinking. Technology and its use is the key to an improved education for all pupils. Technology is the wave to the future. Let us not worship at the shrine of tradition.

Panel member #6. I agree we should not worship at the shrine of tradition. We must always look ahead to make for a better world. That is why I believe we need to have a problem solving science curriculum. Pupils with teacher guidance in each curriculum area need to identify relevant problems. These problems are not identified in isolation from the world of experience, but they are chosen by learners in contextual situations. Thus in an ongoing lesson or unit of study, the pupil selects a problem. The teacher is never left out of the teaching-learning situation, but he/she encourages, motivates, and develops pupil interest in learning. After a problem has been selected, the pupil(s) are guided to choose necessary reference sources to secure information. The information comes from a variety of reference sources in an integrated curriculum. Subject matter boundaries lose their borders here in that whatever content is needed will be used to solve the problem. A hypothesis develops as a result and is tested in a life-like situation. The testing is done using a reality based experience. The hypothesis may be accepted, refuted, or modified as the information indicates. When problems are identified and solutions present, we can move on to something better be it in school or in society.

Society expects individuals to be able to select and solve problems, personal and social. We need to have multi-media available in school so that pupils have a variety of materials to secure solutions to different problem areas. This includes technology and other reference sources. A integrated curriculum results. Why? Subject matter is learned for one purpose only and that is to solve problems. Subject matter needed here depends upon what it takes to solve the problem selected. The separate academic disciplines become one in that it is immaterial which academic disciplines are needed to solve problems. No one has spoken so far of vocational education and training. Is vocational education less useful and worthwhile that is academic course work. The answer here is a resounding *no*. All people have problems that need solving. I do not know of one person that doesn't have problems that need vital solutions. Many of these problems are vocational and not academic alone, by any means. Problem solving can be an individual or committee endeavour. Heterogeneous grouping might well be in evidence since in society people of diverse ability levels work with each other. We need to make school as near to reality as possible and that means not separating school from society.

Chairperson. We have certainly had excellent presentations from each panel member. Let us summarize briefly what has been said by each panel member. Panel member #1 emphasized the importance of receiving objective pupil results from learning and that is why measurably stated objectives should be used in teaching. Panel member #2 indicated a need for high standards in science for all pupils to achieve; the teacher at the same time must have high expectations from each pupil. Panel member #3 stressed the importance of pupils planning the science curriculum together with the teacher. Panel member #4 advocated working closely with parents so that each pupil attains optimally in the curriculum. Panel member #5 believes that a modern technological approach in teaching assists pupils to learn as much as possible. Panel member #6, the final presenter, emphasized that problem solving in science is the most useful method of teaching since we all have problems that need identification and solution. Now, are there any questions from the audience. Yes, I see a hand in the back row. Will you speak clearly so all can hear?

Audience member #1. I wish to direct my question to panel member #3. I do not see how pupils can learn well if they are heavily involved in determining the science curriculum. After all, the teacher has had the training, education, and experience to decide what is salient for pupils to learn.

Panel member #3. You must not have heard all that I said. The pupil alone does not decide what to learn. The teacher has a very difficult task here in working harmoniously with learners to assist the latter in deciding upon what will be learned. Pupils learn only if they are interested, perceive purpose, and understand what is to be learned. Pupils do not learn if they are forced to do so, nor when someone from the outside makes them learn. Pupils intrinsically must feel value in what is to be learned that means the pupil must do the learning, not the teacher nor any outside person, external to the curriculum. It is no wonder pupils fail to learn when so much is decided for them.

Audience member #2. I wish to address my question to panel member #4. Aren't you overdoing the role of parents in determining what pupils are to learn in the high school curriculum? Teachers and administrators have long been responsible for developing the curriculum. Parents would not have the training nor the inclination to do so.

Panel member #4. As I indicated, parents pay the bills and place their trust in us to educate their children. Should they not be involved in deciding upon what should be taught in school? I did not indicate that we should go overboard on parental input into the curriculum. After all, teachers and administrators also need to respond to the needs assessment questionnaire. Certainly, parents, teachers, and administrators should be able to develop a quality high school curriculum. One relevant trend we have in education today is school site management. What I am advocating is local input from those involved in teaching pupils. Shouldn't parents, as well as teachers and administrators, be involved in educating pupils in high school? We know what happens to pupil achievement if parents are left out. Pupil achievement in high school goes downhill if parents are shunned in curriculum development.

Audience member #3. I like to ask panel member #5 if technology can solve all the problems in education that were indicated. I am a former high school teacher and find that all learning activities are extremely individual to the learner. Software and other media may not fit in at a specific point in pupil sequence in learning. Also we may not have the media available to emphasize a relevant unit of study. We as teachers then must improvise at either point in the instructional sequence. I know of teachers who are limited, for example, on software that should be available at a specific point within a unit of study.

Then too, there may not be any software for an entire unit of study or even an entire course. Money in the school budget is extremely limited.

Panel member 5. Your questions seemingly missed the point of what I was saying. To be an updated school, high school pupils need to experience the latest in technology. For example, pupils using a typewriter in writing are using a museum piece for composing written discourse. In mathematics, a computer or hand held calculator should be used to take the drudgery out of routine work formerly done by pupils in high school mathematics. The list can go on and on in how technology can bring high school pupils into the twenty-first century. I see too many schools which have pupils use materials of instruction that were used in the nineteenth century. Rote learning as well as drill and practice seem to abound in outdated schools. Rather, we need to emphasize higher levels of cognition in our curriculum. Diverse kinds of thinking may be stressed when technology is brought into and used in teaching-learning situations.

Audience member #4. I would like to direct my question to panel member #1. To the best of my knowledge, it seems as if you would stress memorization in the curriculum. If you have precise objectives of instruction, the chances are factual information will be acquired by pupils. Then the teacher teaches so that pupils learn required facts as stated in the objectives. After which, pupils are appraised if they have secured the facts. I believe that is outdated teaching to say the least.

Panel member #1. I disagree with you completely. Whatever is to be taught must be stated precisely. Otherwise whatever is done in the classroom is OK. There is nothing that says otherwise. Come on. Should we not emphasize the relevant instead? The relevant goes into each behaviourally stated objective. All levels of thinking that are to be emphasized in teaching and learning must be stated precisely so we can measure if pupils have/have not attained any one objective. The tests given to learners will assist us as teachers to know if pupils have achieved the stated objectives. In my teaching, I like to be certain if pupils have/have not attained stated objectives. I dislike guessing what my pupils have learned. When I report pupil progress to parents, I also like to state numerically what each pupil has learned in my classes. I know of no better way of teaching pupils.

Audience member #5. I do not understand how panel member #2 will help each pupil to learn if high standards are to be emphasized for all pupils, regardless of ability and achievement levels. I feel slow learners will be left out of the learning process; the content will be too complex for them to understand. I do not believe that with coaching, the slow learners can attach meaning to complex content taught. I do not like to see pupils fall through the cracks. Toward the opposite end of the continuum. I can see gifted and talented pupils becoming bored with what is taught even though the subject matter is challenging. I am traditional enough to realize that teaches must assist each pupil to learn as much as possible. Differentiating what pupils are to learn is an answer. Thus with slow learners, the same or similar expectations will not be there. Rather, we take each pupil where he/she is in achievement and go on from there. Each pupil needs to attain optimally. Always remember, high expectations for each pupil to achieve more optimally, I believe is a myth.

Panel member #2. You gave a long speech there. I wondered if it would ever end. If we do not have all pupils in each class obtain the sophisticated knowledge they deserve, I am afraid we will have slower achievers leave school with a shameful education. These slow learners in high school need sophisticated knowledge as does the gifted/talented. Why are you so opposed to having slow learners meet up with similar standards as compared to the talented and gifted? Do you want to segregate pupils so that the slow learners receive inferior education and receive the worst teachers? These pupils too long have experienced rote learning, drill and remedial instruction. Learning activities such as these doom pupils to the low end of the totem pole in all academic areas as well as to jobs in society.

Audience member #6. I wish to address my comments to panel member #6. I believe that knowledge can and will be learned for its own sake and not for the solving of problems only. I would recommend, as panel member #3 stated, we should let pupils learn subject matter for the sake of doing so, if this is their wish. Who is to say that content to be learned needs to be used in the solving of problems only?

Panel member #6. I am sorry that I gave the impression that pupils will learn subject matter to solve problems only. My point is this that pupils need to experience a problem solving curriculum throughout the high school years. Why? When these young people get out into the real world of society, they will have the tools to deal with all kinds of situations in life. Problem solving can be applied to whatever dilemma we encounter. Problem solving is useful and utilitarian in all facets of life and living.

Chairperson, Again, I wish to thank our distinguished panel members for taking the time to present their thinking so well in what to do to emphasize a quality high school curriculum. Audience, I wish to thank you for your interest in these presentations. Thank you all for coming!

REFERENCES

Cawalti, Gordan (1995). High School Restructuring: What Are The Critical Elements? *The National Association of Secondary School Principals Bulletin* 79, 1-15.

Combs, Arthur (1972). *Educational Accountability: Beyond Behavioural Objectives.* Washington DC: Association for Supervision and Curriculum Development.

Dewey, John (1916). *Democracy and Education.* New York: Macmillan Company.

Dunn, Rita S., and Kenneth Dunn (1979). Learning Styles/Teaching Styles. *Educational Leadership* 36, 238-244.

Ediger, Marlow (1995). Demonstration Teaching in the Schools. *Education* 115, 371-373.

Epstein, Joyce, (1995). School/ Family/Community Partnerships. *Phi Delta Kappan* 76, 701-712.

National Education Goals Panel (1991). *The National Education Goals Report: Building a Nation of Learners.* Washington DC: National Education Goals Panel.

Squires, David, and others (1985). *Effective Schools and Classrooms: A Research-Based Perspective.* Alexandria, Virginia: ASCD.

11

History of the Invention and Implementation of the Concept of Science Education

J. PRESTON PRATHER
The University of Virginia, USA

The Foundations of Science Education

A. Introduction

From its inception in the early years of ancient Greek civilization, science has been devoted to the quest for a better understanding of nature. Throughout most of history, however, scientific inquiry was neither widely practiced nor prerceived as a potential source of human benefit. Rather, it was more or less an elite, intellectual activity indulged in by a few people whose social position provided the learning and leisure time for such pursuits. That perception prevailed until the latter part of the Renaissance, when a revolutionary new concept of the nature and social relevance of science emerged. That era of history is distinguished as "The Scientific Revolution," which is generally dated from the early 1500s to the publication of Isaac Newton's sweeping theory of nature around 1700 AD.

During that brief period, a concept of natural phenomena developed that resulted in a new scientific outlook and a fundamental redefinition of what constitutes meaningful scientific inquiry. At the same time, an equally revolutionary reinterpretation of the term "history" occurred that drastically changed the cultural concept of what constitutes meaningful historical research. The cultural flux that accompanied these changes generated an unprecedented awareness of a potential social utility of science that changed the concept of human destiny, inspired the invention of public science education, and ushered in the modern era of applied science. Within the context of earlier concepts of science, however, the idea of public science education as it is conceived today would have met with little interest or support.

B. Early Concepts of Science

The history of science is rooted in the Golden Age of Greek philosophy, which probably began around 700-600 BC and culminated in the Aristotlean era three centuries later. During that relatively brief time, science was born of the philosophers' quest to comprehend the orderly workings of a systematic and predictable universe formed by natural processes. As a result of its origins in philosophy, scientific inquiry was commonly referred to as "natural philosophy."

C. The Prescientific Era of Natural History

Before the era of Greek natural philosophy, the notion of objective scientific inquiry would have been generally meaningless. Natural phenomena were perceived as *Thous* rather than objective *its*. "Primitive thought naturally recognized the relationship of cause and effect" (Frankfort et al., 1946, p. 24), but it was conceived as a personal interaction with the phenomenal world. Some ancient thinkers saw the world around them in terms of gods, and others in terms of natural personages. The stone that hurt the foot that stumbled on it, the wind that below off a hat, and other occurrences were not perceived as person-object encounters but as life encountering life. They were seen as affective encounters with a very real, live presence of Nature.

Most ancient societies felt a need to live in harmony with the *Thous* that constituted their environs. Every natural occurrence was considered a sign, and insight into the environment was believed to be open to perceptive persons who could sense the subjective meaning of natural events. Within this pragmatic epistemological framework, nature observation was the primary source of information for survival. Elaborate systems were developed for collecting data on a variety of recurrent phenomena such as the periodic fluctuations of the flow of the Nile River, the seasons of the year, the apparent motion of the stars, volcanic eruptions, and the ocean tides.

The resultant data indicated a high degree of predictability, but the lack of a concept of *natural order* precluded the notion that such events might be reliably predicted. The causes of natural events were conceived in terms of worldly powers with which people "were forced to wrestle, and which they sought to propitiate" (Toulmin and Goodfield, 1962, p. 34). A *Thou* was believed to be unique and could be known "only in so far as it reveals itself" (Frankfort, et al., 1946, p. 13). Tabulation of observational data may reveal a natural history of repetitive patterns; but if Nature could keep secrets, there would always be room for surprise. Ancient history is replete with accounts of humanity's efforts, frequently of a ritualistic nature, to cope with an environment conceived in terms of a host of capricious, potentially malevolent *Thous*.

The ancient Egyptians, for example, knew what to expect of the Nile River on the basis of their vast tabulations; but the river might *choose* to behave differently the next time for any sort of personal reason. If the river failed to rise on schedule "it has *refused* to rise" (Frankfort, et al., 1946, p. 24), possibly because it was offended by those whose needs it affected. In an effort to guard against offending or otherwise alienating a potentially malevolent local natural power, many ancient societies selected and supported individuals whose primary social function was the interpretation of natural phenomena and propitiation. The interpreters, generally called priests, played a major role in the direction of ancient governments; and some of the more successful were enthroned as priest-kings.

Interpretations of meanings of natural events contributed to a growing body of behavioural norms intended to gain the good will of the natural forces that affected their environment. The well-being of society required that those social values be communicated to other generations; and this problem was handled by what is perhaps the oldest strategy of formal, public education: Mythology. Through the facility of mythology, Wells (1961) concluded, a person could be trained to suppress specific attitudes or actions for the common good. Nature was conceived on a personal basis; and within that world view, the idea of an impersonal, natural order that could explain events in terms of general principles or laws was inconceivable. The scientific explanation of the Nile River's flow as related to remote meteoric events, for example, would have been considered *unmythical* and therefore as unsatisfactory to an ancient Egyptian priest as a mythological interpretation would be to a modern scientist.

Temple cultures developed around the priesthood as it gained power, and city states eventually formed around the temples. Ultimately, the Agean priest-kings of ancient Egypt and Mesopotamia established empires among the scattered city states; and the priesthood characterized one of humanity's earliest attempts toward social stability beyond the tribal form of leadership. The priestly government, however, lacked the strength to defend the scattered city states against repeated assaults of invaders from the North.

D. Emergence of Theory-based Scientific Inquiry

Nomadic Greek tribes moved southward into the Balkan peninsula between 1000 and 800 BC. These tribes "conquered and largely destroyed the civilization that preceded their arrival; (and) upon its ashes they built a civilization of their own (Wells, 1961, p. 230). The conquered empires had long traditions of mythopoeic thought and relatively centralized rule through the priests. The early Greeks, however, had a quite different set of social values dictated by the sense of individuality and independence characteristic of its prehistoric nomadic heritage. Through the genius of epic poets such as Homer, the Greeks had maintained their own mythology, but it represented a radically different world view from that of their new Egyptian and Mesopotamian neighbours. That different perspective, along with the Greek sense of independence, was to play an important role in the development of science.

The mythical traditions of the Greeks' predecessors were serious attempts to understand nature, but they were developed without the subject-object correlation characteristic of scientific thought. The systematic collection of large amounts of information through astronomical and fluvial studies, for example, produced an excellent observational data base; but the disciplined collection and study of data does not necessarily constitute scientific inquiry. Rather, scientific inquiry "requires some set of assumptions to tell the researcher what data to collect and then how to interpret it" (Brown, 1977, p. 30). However, such a set of assumptions would have been unacceptable to most pre-Greek cultures. For ancient humanity, Frankfort et al. (1946) observed, mythical representations of nature were not subject to critical analysis and development. Rather, mythological interpretations were built upon the assumption that "one cannot argue about a revelation; it transcends reason" (p. 262). That which Nature had voluntarily revealed to perceptive vewers was considered appropriate knowledge; but prying into the secrets of nature was inappropriate because it might offend some sensitive *Thou,* godly or otherwise. The concept of intellectually conceived theories to guide the collection and interpretation of data would have been an anathema under those conditions. Within the mythopoeic world view, it would have been considered a dangerous enterprise.

As the early Greeks saw it, however, there was no cause for concern. Like other civilizations in early antiquity, they had strong religious traditions; "and the Gods of Olympus were not very different from contemporary Gods in the Middle East" (Toulmin and Goodfield, 1961, pp. 55-56). However, Wells (1961) reported, there was no record of either priest-kings or a temple-state era in the Greek civilization. There was a vaguely defined stratification of Greek society; but whenever a major leader was needed, as in time of warfare, a temporary commander was chosen, generally by democratic processes, as a "leader among his equals"(p. 232). In ancient Greece, there was no priestly tradition to suggest external guidelines for what might be appropriate conduct, intellectual, governmental, or otherwise.

The spirit of independence that fostered the development of ancient science is clearly reflected in Greek mythology. In the poetic account of origins written by Hesiod (sometime in the eighth century, BC), gods and humans sprang from the same parents: Sky and Earth (Frankfort, et al., 1946). Similarly, Thales contended that "cosmos and earth had been formed by a natural process" (Goldstein, 1980, p. 49). Claiming common ancestry with the gods, the ancient Greeks approached questions of naturalistic enquiry with much less reserve than their peers; and it was in this unrestrained intellectual arena that the concept of *theory* was invented.

Their sense of secular freedom and personal independence enabled the ancient natural philosophers to "look at the world in cheerful reliance on their senses, in easy companionship with the gods" (Goldstein, 1980, p. 47). Their religious beliefs did not hamper their quest for a rational explanation of the cosmos, and "their curiosity was as live as it was unhampered by dogma" (Frankfort et al., 1946, p. 251). As nomads, they had sensed that their own destiny was largely dependent upon their own physical and intellectual resourcefulness. The risk of accepting information from any source without careful examination was a sensitive issue, and they placed much emphasis on the value of critical analysis to weigh their interpretations. As a result, their scientific speculations were deeply rooted in a highly systematic system of logic.

"We may think of Greek science as the first systematic and inclusive attempt to explain the entire natural cosmos" (Goldstein, 1989, p. 47). Like their neighbours to the East, the ancient Greek philosophers sensed an apparent cause-effect relationship in the events around them, but they did not conceive cause as originating in incomprehensible mythological personages. After all, in the Greek world view, both people and gods lived among natural phenomena that could be described in terms of general relationships. For them, there was more to nature than the emotions generated by their encounters with natural events. Things had properties and values independent of human experience.

Rather than seeking the subjective meanings of experiences, the Greeks sought rational explanations in the sense of comprehensible *first-causes* or sustaining principles that were subject to critical intellectual judgement. Though they associated gods with all things, they attempted "to understand the coherence of the *things*" (Frankfort, et al., 1946, p. 253). This bold new perspective laid the basis for objective observations and theoretical speculations of natural relationships.

> This change of viewpoint is breath-taking. It transfers the problems of [humanity] in nature from the realm of faith and poetic intuition to the intellectual sphere . . . . These men proceeded, with preposterous boldness on an entirely unproven assumption. They held that the universe is an intelligible whole. In other words, they presumed that a single order underlies the chaos of our perceptions and, furthermore, that we are able to comprehend that order.[1]

Implicit in that viewpoint is a metaphysical question of fundamental importance for the philosopher of science and scientist alike: "What must the world be like in order that man may know it?" (Kuhn, 1970, p. 173). That question, which may be appropriately called the *First Problem of Science,* "is as old as science itself, and it remains unanswered" (p. 173). Clearly, that fact does not proscribe scientific inquiry, as the history of science indicates, and it certainly did not intimidate the early Greeks. "Neither their basic assumption—that the world is an intelligible whole—nor . . . any of their other theses can be proved by logic or by experiment or by observation," Frankfort, et al. (1946) concluded; but "with conviction they propounded theories which resulted from intuitive insight and which were elaborated by deductive reasoning" (pp. 261-262). Reason, for the ancient Greeks, was the highest authority.

The early Greek scientists or natural philosophers—Toulmin and Goodfield (1961) declared the terms synonymous—believed that natural phenomena could be explained in terms of an intellectual *natural order* that would ensue independently of an observer. In their search for the principles of that order, they raised the study of nature "from a level of scattered empirical observations to the order of a consistent natural philosophy" (Goldstein, 1980, p.46). "The Greeks were the effective forerunners of modern science, not in their particular answers and theories, but rather in the new *questions* they put into circulation . . . . To them belongs the glory of having invented the very idea of a scientific theory" (Toulmin and Goodfield, 1961, p. 59). For their concept of natural order, their perception of objectivity in the relation of cause and effect, and the invention of theory, the ancient Greek philosophers deserve the honour of recognition for the *invention of science.*

It is important to note, however, that even in the heyday of Greek natural philosophy, science was never a widespread activity; and it was not perceived as having practical social utility. Rather, scientific inquiry was a purely intellectual activity indulged in by only a few Greeks, and they were generally "men of leisure" (Toulmin and Goodfield, 1961, p. 57).

> Critical speculation about the powers of Nature was in fact an unpopular, minority activity even in Athens . . . .all in all, in the five centuries following 650 BC, the number of people who contributed actively to "Greek Science" can have been only a few dozen; and the number of their compatriots who read or listened to their teachings with any real understanding probably amounted to no more that a few hundred.[2]

Apparently, unlike their mythopoeic predecessors, the ancient Greeks saw no need to promote a public knowledge of the fruits of their naturalistic speculations. The concept of public science education that emerged nearly 2,000 years later, in the latter part of the Renaissance, would have been considered meaningless in the ancient Greek culture.

E. The Eclipse of Ancient Science

The conditions that nurtured the development of ancient science continued into the early years of the Hellenistic culture, which grew from the consolidation of the previously independent Greek city-states into the empire of Philip of Macedonia (382-336 BC) and his son Alexander the Great (356-323 BC). Aristotle (384-322 BC) had been Alexander's teacher. From that unique position at the interface of the Greek and Hellenistic cultures, Aristotle projected the powerful heritage of Greek natural philosophy into the centrally governed, cosmopolitan civilization that characterized the Alexandrian empire. "On the face of it," Toulmin and Goodfield (1961) declared, "there was no reason why Greek science should not expand to embrace all aspects of the natural world and all sorts of problems" (p. 128).

> But over the next 500 years things took a new, and in some ways a paradoxical turn. After 250 BC the intellectual Centre of the Greek world shifted to Alexandria, and there the opportunities for scientific work were in many ways more favourable than they had been earlier in Athens. Yet science gradually lost its

momentum, and scientists lost faith in their methods. New sorts of questions were rarely asked; urgent but intractable problems were shelved.[3]

The crucial problem, Santillana (1961) declared, was "the lack of an applied science"(p. 282). The problem stated by Santillana highlights an obscure but important distinction between ancient and modern science. "'Nature,' Aristotle declared, 'refuses to be badly administered'" (p. 284). Greek science assumed a *Teleological* universe wherein "everything in nature has a purpose and is animated by a soul fitted to its purpose" (Toulmin and Goodfield, 1961, p. 109). In that cosmology, the universe was linked into a systematic, operational unity in which all things were essentially interrelated. The goal of Greek science was "an intellectual grasp based not just on bare theories, but on a new vision of nature—a new harmony of the reason and the senses"(p. 46).

"The relationship of Greek thought to nature remains fundamentally different from ours: it is not a search for the point of attack from which to attempt a break-through, but a quest for . . . an over-all order to which to adjust" (Santillana, 1961, p. 283). Science could illuminate the principles of nature for the Greeks, but it was inconceivable that science could be systematically applied or made to behave for social benefit. The Greeks conceived an operable universe; but it was operated from a sphere far above the realm of social necessity, with each entity functioning according to a purposive, natural, *Soul*. Humanity was a part of nature; and, nature, in the Greek system, simply could not be subverted to the purposes of one of its parts.

Perhaps largely because of the Greeks' world view, technology and science developed independently of each other. Technological and engineering know-how were valued for the building of roads, cities, aqueducts, and weapons. The craft of mixing or rearranging stones, clays, metals, and liquids was one thing—but the idea of exploiting the very principles of nature to effect the purposes of society was unthinkable. Greek scientists occasionally cited the ancient crafts as evidence for their theories, Toulmin and Goodfield (1962) noted, but there was no direct relationship of ancient science and technology. Greek philosophers sought to understand the order of nature, but not for purposes of reordering nature. If nature were administered from a higher order as the Aristotelians presupposed, then one could "hardly think of questioning them by way of an experiment" (Santillana, 1961, p. 285).

The modern science concepts of non-purposive laws of nature, experimental scientific methodology, and application of science to the resolution of societal problems were unknown in ancient science. Consequently, the idea that science might significantly effect the destiny of society was not a onceivable option for dealing with the turbulent social conditions associated with the Alexandrian and Roman empires. "Science . . . was not undertaken with any technological end in view" (Toulmin and Goodfield, 1961, p. 61). The inventions of Archimedes (c. 287-212 BC) were notable exceptions but, according to the Greek biographer Plutarch, Archimedes and his peers perceived such machines" not as matters of any importance but as mere amusements in geometry" (Santillana, 1961, p. 237). Three centuries later, Heron of Alexandria established a school of engineering and systematically applied his scientific knowledge to the invention of complex steam and water-driven machines. He openly advocated the practical uses of such machines, but his work drew little attention. His creations, like those of Archimedes, were perceived as toys for the entertainment and edification of aristocrats and rulers.

Natural philosophy, and philosophy in general, had been on the defensive in ancient Rome from about 100 BC. Most of the Romans' attention was focused on technological and religious concerns, according to Toulmin and Goodfield (1961), and scientific speculation was not perceived as necessary to either enterprise. Had the concept of a social utility of science occurred in the Golden Age of Natural Philosophy, or even during the later Hellenistic era, the destinies of ancient science and society might have been dramatically different. However, only conjecture can issue from consideration of the potential of science for the ancient Greco-Roman civilization. Some day, historians can reveal with authority the worth of applied science for the modern world, but never for antiquity.

Science was not rejected as an option by ancient society. Rather science simply was never recognized as possessing possible social significance. The prevailing world view would not accommodate such an idea. It is as inappropriate to fault ancient scientists for not attempting to apply their scientific knowledge to pressing social problems of their time as it would be to decry a modern scientist's lack of interest in applying science to basic religious problems. Within the context of their relative traditions, neither consideration is an appropriate scientific objective. Consequently, the modern concept of public science education was unheard of and, if known, would have been considered absurd in ancient Greek and Roman societies.

Greek science, however, did not perish. Largely due to the influence of Alexander's teacher, Aristotle, natural philosophy was established and subsidized as a component of the programme of the Alexandrian museum and library (Toulmin and Goodfield, 1961). This centralization of natural philosophy in that great center of learning established an ancient equivalent of a modern think-tank, but without a technology for communicating with the rest of the world. The Alexandrian museum and library "were a centre of light," Wells (1961, p. 304) observed, "but it was light in a dark lantern hidden from the general world." Greek science was institutionalized, respectably cloistered in a splendid, isolated, self-nurturing environment. It buttered no bread for a practical society preoccupied with building a stable socio-political system. Still it was subsidized, or kept, in case it could be morally uplifting or entertaining to the ruling class. Ancient science was thus established as the exclusive domain of "a new type of human being, . . . the Scholarly Man" (Wells, 1961, p. 305). So encumbered, the Golden Age of Natural Philosophy came to an end.

The isolation of the intellectual community eventually took its toll, and the interests of Alexandrian philosophers turned inward from the remote world of nature toward theological and occult issues that concerned their patrons. Throughout the early years of Greek thought, humanity had been perceived as an integral part of nature. Now the tie was severed, and the natural philosopher "consoled himself by saying in very beautiful and elaborate forms that the world was illusion and that there was in him something quintessential and sublime, outside and above the world" (Wells, 1961, p. 305). Thus fell the early Greeks' confidence in the intelligibility of nature and, along with it, the basis of future development in Greek science. By tome of Ptolemy (about 150 AD), "cosmology, physics, and mathematical astronomy, brought together by Aristotle, had fallen apart again; and the science of the sky had become once more only a collection of mathematical techniques" (Toulmin and Goodfield, 1961, p. 128). Basic questions about the nature of causes of things were simply ignored in Ptolemy's theory of the universe. Ptolemy's system, however, could provide an accurate description and prediction of astronomical events; and it was widely acclaimed for these purposes. Apparently, ancient society had come full circle and was once again satisfied with the predictive power of natural history—as people had been long before the invention of science. As the fascination with an explanation of *why* things happened waned, the essence of Greek science disappeared from the scene.

F. The Era of Medieval Science

Failing confidence in human resourcefulness ultimately set the stage for the onset of the Middle Ages. As marauding barbarian tribes continued to test the Roman Empire's borders, the initial confidence in society's ability to maintain socio-political stability dwindled. A subsequent monarchy failed to produce the desired social stability, and a stronger form of military rule was sought. Military government also proved inadequate; and finally, divinity was ascribed to the monarch, or Caesar, who was thereby expected to outperform a mere human being. Even a divine ruler was not enough to provide protection from external invasion, however; and a supernatural liaison was effected in an effort to save the State. In 325 AD, Christianity was established as the official state religion of the Roman Empire; but even this new approach was insufficient to unify a disillusioned citizenry.

Ancient Western civilizations finally succumbed to a long series of invasions by the Germanic, Oriental, and Arabic tribes that swarmed its borders. "The breakdown of ancient civilization had played brutal havoc with the cosmic imagination of Western man," Goldstein (1980, p. 55) declared. By about 450 AD a civilization which was on confident of its ability to sense its nature and to establish a stable society had relinquished control of all human affairs—intellectual, political, or otherwise—to non-sensible, supernatural authority. The atmosphere in Rome became so intolerant, Toulmin and Goodfield (1961) noted, until "unorthodox views ran the risk of condemnation . . . as treason" (p. 154). The center of natural philosophy migrated Eastward across the frontiers into Persia and beyond as philosophers sought "a more favourable atmosphere for their work" (p. 133). Science and the physical world were largely forgotten in most of Europe as medieval society reckoned with theocratic rule. With this, systematic naturalistic inquiry faded from Western tradition, and science became a non-entity in the land of its creation.

All was not lost for science in the Middle Ages, however. An interest in nature was maintained in the Middle-Eastern intellectual centers to which many natural philosophers had migrated. As they travelled Eastward seeking refuge for their ideas in the relative intellectual freedom of Persia, many natural philosophers carried with them manuscripts of the works of Aristotle, Archimedes, and others from the prime of Greek science. Early in the seventh century AD, the Middle East was overrun by the emerging Muslim Empire, a theocracy based on the new religion of Islam founded in Arabic around 630 AD. Fortunately, Toulmin and Goodfield (1961) noted, "the conditions for intellectual life remained good, owing to the religious tolerance of early Islam" (p. 155).

Within 150 years of its founding, the Islamic Empire had established its domain over a 4,000 mile arc that extended from the Atlantic coast of Southern Spain across North Africa and the Middle East to the Ganges River in India. As it spread, it became heir to the intellectual traditions of many ancient civilizations, including numerous manuscripts of ancient Greek science through its encounters with scattered colonies of Hellenistic scholars in Persia and elsewhere. Other scientific traditions had developed quasi-independently from the seeds of Greek science that were spread as far eastward as India during Alexander the Great's military campaigns a thousand years earlier. Those traditions also enriched the Islamic culture as it expanded its conquests.

In 762 AD, Baghdad was founded near the site of the ancient city of Babylon, and the new city became the cultural center of the thriving Islamic civilization. An Arabic university was established at Baghdad, and many ancient manuscripts were sent there to be translated into Arabic. Islamic science resulted from "the natural fusion of all these precious legacies" (Goldstein, 1980, p. 98), and Baghdad succeeded Alexandria as the scholarly center of natural philosophy. For approximately two centuries, natural philosophies enjoyed patronage at Baghdad, and the period from 800 to 1000 AD is recognized as the Golden Age of Islamic science. Within those centuries, the intellectual community at Baghdad had collected and assimilated nearly a thousand years of ancient natural philosophy.

By 1000 AD, natural philosophers at Baghdad had come to the cutting edge of science. Some, such as Avicenna (980-1037 AD), who had conceived a dynamic, natural origin of mountain chains over long periods of time, were beginning to suggest radical hypotheses. Had these been developed, they may have had a profound impact on the history of science, but "these insights were not followed up" (Toulmin and Goodfield, 1965, p. 64). By this time, the political power of Islam was declining, and the disenchantment with natural philosophy that had spelled doom for science in ancient Rome began to repeat itself. The Muslim civilization's concern turned to political stability, and the atmosphere turned to one of religious intolerance. The heyday of the empire was past, and the changes eclipsed the early Islamic tradition of open inquiry. The Golden Age of Muslim science came to an end.

By 1100 AD, the center of Islamic intellectual activity had shifted from Baghdad to the remote outposts of Southern Spain and Sicily. Science was on the run again, this time westward to the volatile border between the antagonistic Spanish Muslims and the Christians of France and Italy. In the end, the tradition of the Islamic scholar was basically one of collection, translation, and refinement of existing knowledge rather that original inquiry or theory production. The science that returned to the West in the twelfth century was therefore essentially a refined version of the same science that Islam had inherited five centuries earlier.

Goldstein attributed the character of Islamic science to a culturally induced disinterest in theoretical scientific pursuits. Inspired by their culture's passion for natural detail, he noted, Muslin scientists produced a profusion of concrete information based on detailed observations, but little in the way of abstract scientific conjecture. Muslim science was motivated by "the pleasurable observation of nature's diversity and the use of its bounty to the enhancement of life" (Goldstein, 1980, p. 99). The Islamic culture looked on the Earth as a lovely garden, he noted, and "it had little concern for establishing the mastery of mind over nature . . . or for proving human power through the relentless technological transformation of the natural environment" (p. 99).

Toulmin and Goodfield attributed the Arabic lack of scientific creativity to the limited duration of intellectual freedom prior to the decline of science in Islam. However, substantial improvements were made in particular areas of science by the Muslims, they noted, notably in medicine and chemistry.

> But in astronomy and dynamics, they had time only to digest and adapt the existing traditions. They developed and greatly improved the astronomical instruments left to them by the Greeks: notably the astrolabe . . . . They made fresh estimates of the size of the earth and the relative distances of the planets . . . but made no fundamental changes in Ptolemy's methods. Certainly they never questioned the central features of his picture: at most they tried to bring it more closely into line with the ideas of Aristotle.[4]

In the medieval Muslim culture, Goldstein (1980) indicated, the appeal of science was primarily related to pragmatic social and commercial interests. There was little incentive to develop natural philosophy as an ideology in its own right. The medieval Arabs were a highly creative and intellectually capable society in their own right, as indicated by their brilliant mathematical achievements; but the traditional objective of Islamic science was concrete detail, and abstract theory was simply not a cultural desideratum. The medieval Muslim civilization valued science primarily as an established body of interesting and useful information about nature. Ultimately, the emphasis was on detailed treatises on nature, or ancient histories, not science. Islamic contributions were therefore primarily in the form of technological innovations and refinements of existing scientific knowledge.

Islam did contribute a radical new perception of science as a practical enterprise. Specific contributions included the application of existing science to practical problems such as navigation and health care. The Muslims also conceived science as a diversified body of specialized knowledge and restored to natural philosophy the early Greek notion of nature as reality, rather than a philosophical idea. The Muslim interest in ancient astronomy and physics resulted in a science-based technology of navigation and a practical union of science and commerce. Trade was central to the Arabic culture, and it was necessary for merchants' camel caravans to travel at night to avoid the devastating daylight heat of the vast deserts that characterized the Islamic empire. Ptolemy's science of astronomy, which was recognized for its accuracy, was highly valued as a means to improved nighttime navigation.

Islam also developed a science of medicine and a comprehensive system of health care, including the world's first network of independently functioning hospitals. The Greeks, whose science Islam inherited, had seen illness as a natural process subject to treatment by natural means; and Islamic physicians built on that tradition. By 1100 AD, Goldstein (1980) observed, Islam possessed a skilled medical profession employing the careful observations of symptoms and the prescription of curative agents or surgical procedures based on centuries of accumulated physiological studies and medical experience.

Islam's perfection of the Arabic numbers system was perhaps its greatest contribution. The system "was able to reduce the cosmos to a system of ten elementary symbols" (Goldstein, 1980, p. 121), and quickly replaced the cumbersome and confusing number systems of the ancient Egyptian, Greek, and Roman systems. It allowed "almost perfect technical efficiency in the manipulation of numbers" (Whitehead, 1941, p. 44). The development of algebra made it possible to manipulate unknown factors and to quickly demonstrate and equate complexly related, abstract quantities of virtually unlimited scope (Goldstein, 1980). Although science emerged from the medieval Islamic era much as it had entered it, the mathematics that emerged in the 12th century was drastically different from that which had characterized the ancient era.

The Arabs employed their new mathematics extensively in business and technology, but the use of the numbers system for purposes of scientific development was virtually unheard of in Islam. Even the reconciliation of Aristotelian physics and Ptolemaic astronomy had proceeded essentially non-mathematical lines. Therefore, the Muslims' developments in mathematics had little effect on the nature of the science they cherished; but the potential of their versatile new system for the scientific enterprise was demonstrated several centuries later with the development of the dynamic theories of Galileo, Newton, and others. Without the progress in Islamic mathematics during the Middle Ages, modern science would not have been possible.

For nearly a thousand years, the interest in the Greek tradition of scientific inquiry had remained dormant throughout most of Europe. Had it not been for the enthusiastic collection and translation of ancient manuscripts by the Islamic invaders, much of the scientific productivity of the ancient Greek scientists might have been lost. In addition to preserving the Greek scientific tradition and giving the world a powerful new system of mathematics, the Muslims also established an unprecedented new tradition of *applied science.* Like the ancient Babylonians and Egyptians who accumulated hundreds of years of observations upon which early Greek scientists could test their theories, Islamic scientists accumulated a tremendous additional reservoir of concrete information about nature upon which Renaissance theorists could ultimately base new concepts. For centuries, scientific inquiry had remained largely document, except for a brief stirring in Baghdad around 800-1000 AD. During that brief time, theoretical inquiry into the workings of nature was on the threshold of a reawakening; but by 1100 AD, that interest had flickered to dormancy. Again science lay asleep, so to speak; and it would not be revived until another era and another culture.

G. The Reawakening of Science in Europe

For nearly a millennium, most of Western Europe had existed in quiescent religious resignation. Theological tradition was the prevalent authority for interpretation of human affairs, and the study of nature was generally valued "only as a source of allegories, which were used to illustrate the virtues and beauties of the spiritual life" (Toulmin and Goodfield, 1961, p. 154). There was simply no place for the scientific point of view in Christendom at the time. The emphasis was wholly on things spiritual; and the senses, which are essential to empirical observations of nature, were not considered reliable sources of knowledge. To question basic principles of the prevailing cosmology on the basis of sensible phenomena probably would have been considered irrational. In such a climate, it is not surprising that the appearance of the Crab Nebula supernova was not recorded by the Europeans.

> We may explain the apparent failure of the Europeans to observe and record the appearance of the Crab Nebula supernova in AD 1054, even though it was apparent to Chinese and American Indian observers, by noting that such an observation implies the nonimmutability of the heavens, contrary to the commonly (European) accepted scriptural cosmology.[5]

That the supernova was not *recorded* by the Europeans is a matter of historical fact. That it was not *observed* (assuming that Saperstein's sense of the term connotes attentive notice for purposes of learning something) illustrates the epistemological significance of cultural tradition. Many Europeans, who were geographically intermediate to the known observers, must have seen and puzzled over the supernova which was visible in daylight for a time. Medieval Christendom was committed to the authority of scripture and Christian tradition, and both indicated that the heavens were unchangeable. Probably, the spectacular supernova was not systematically observed and recorded because it was not perceived as meaningful.

Five hundred years later, when a revolutionary new world view was taking form in Western Europe, the concept of stellar immutability was suspect and a nova that appeared in 1572 was observed as "giving fact that the heavens were alterable" (Orlich, 1964, p. 97). In the emerging cosmology of the 16th century, the condition of the heavens was a major question; and observations of a nova produced meaningful scientific data. In the very different world of the 11th century, however, there was no such question that would given meaning to a supernova.

In all livelihood, the Crab Nebula supernova was viewed with much interest, but a single sensible phenomenon was not enough to shake the religious resolve of a struggling society that, centuries earlier, had denounced the natural world as illusionary. If additional occurrences had been observed, Christendom would have been challenged to question its tradition; but novae that are visible to the unaided eye are very uncommon. Today, extraneous data that cannot be accommodated by the established research tradition are generally not considered appropriate subjects for study with in normal scientific communities (Kuhn, 1970). From this perspective, the intellectuals of medieval Christendom were no more and no less irresponsible than modern scientists in the dismissal of apparently insignificant data that could not be accommodated within their established cosmological tradition.

During the late Middle Ages, however, conditions in Western Europe began to change. By the 12th century, the feudal system of localized government had gradually overcome the perennial threats of invasions from the north, and the declining condition of the Muslim empire had reduced the threat from the South and East. Under the relation peace and social stability that finally prevailed, the trauma of the collapse of Rome was healed and a vibrant new culture emerged. Political expansion occurred as European armies pushed across the collapsing Islamic borders into Southern Spain and Sicily. Trade flourished, and cultural exchange generated by travels of merchants brought new ideas and new things into the West. The once isolated, passive society of Western Europe was undergoing "the first vigorous stirrings of a new cultural vitality, primarily in France" (Goldestein, 1980, p. 58). Manufacturing, trade, and travel continued to increase, and a restless, searching society envisioned "new social realities that were opening tempting glimpses of the here and now, the contemporary, . . . more prosperous world, which was, in turn, opening up a vast prospect to the world of nature" (p. 137). Amidst the excitement of political expansion and prosperity, and the associated increase in leisure time, an atmosphere of enthusiasm and interest in learning developed. As the ancient Greek manuscripts fell into the hands of Westerners, an interest in ancient traditions was generated.

The new society that developed in the towns of Western Europe reflected the energy and vitality of the early Roman civilization, but it "had little in common with the defunct world of Rome, beyond . . . a thin thread of tradition" (Goldstein, 1980, p.58). Prior to that time, interest in nature and natural philosophy had been almost obliterated in Christendom. "In rebuilding the scientific tradition after AD 1000, therefore, men in Western Europe had in effect to start from scratch" (Toulmin and Goodfield, 1961, p. 159). The rejection of the world of nature was quickly coming to an end, however, and the era of cultural flux known as the Renaissance was emerging.

In the early years of the ninth century, Charlemagne (742-814) had prodded the churches and monasteries to open "schools for the general education of boys and girls" (Durant, 1950, p. 913). In the tenth century, the first cathedral school was established at Chartres, France. Soon other schools were established, and these were unique in their concentration on classical studies. Up to this time, Toulmin and Goodfield (1961) observed, learning had been valued only for purposes of improving the soul; but the teachers at Chartres "encouraged learning of all sorts—for its own sake" (p. 158). Other schools and universities encouraged similar programmes, but at first most of the schools had to make do with only a few fragments of ancient literature. The teachers were "quick to take advantage of the new intellectual contacts with the Arabs" (p. 158), and translations of ancient manuscripts were brought to Christendom with enthusiasm akin to that with which the Arabs had collected the original Greek manuscripts centuries earlier.

It was to this receptive atmosphere that science returned, after nearly a thousand years of exile, in Europe. "After 1150, as wealth and leisure grew, and translations began to pour in from Islam, the mind of Western Europe was aroused from its torpor, curiosity flared into eagerness" (Durant, 1950, p. 986). By the early 1300s, "all the important doctrines of antiquity were known" (Toulmin and Goodfield, 1961, p. 165). However, the interest in science was more or less a fad, according to Goldstein (1980): "The study of nature was an intellectual delight, not necessarily a stern and specialized academic pursuit" (p. 128). As was the case in ancient Greece, science was more or less an elite intellectual activity indulged in by a few persistent persons whose social position provided the leisure time and learning for the pursuit of such ideas. Schooling was very limited for most people, and science was still not recognized as an important part of their past, present, or future. It would be another 300 years before a new scientific tradition would be established and the sociocultural benefits of the Islamic concept of applied science would be realized. With the cultural and social changes that opened the door to that new tradition would also come an unprecedented perception of a social utility of scientific inquiry and an equally unprecedented concept of public science education.

The Invention of Science Education

Science did not suddenly explode upon the scene in the Renaissance nor did it lead the cultural flux of the era. Rather, "the Renaissance gave its soul to art, leaving a little for literature, less for philosophy, least for science" (Durant, 1953, p. 529). Science was neither widely known nor recognized as an important part of society's past, present, or future. This soon changed, however; and the history of modern science became inextricably interwoven with the history of Western civilization.

During the early years of the Renaissance, the scientific traditions of the ancient Greeks and medieval Islamics were viewed with increasing interest throughout Europe. Eventually the interest turned to action as an increasingly restless European civilization looked beyond the seclusion of the Middle Ages toward a bigger and more hospitable world. Intrigued by the ancient Greek concept of an Earth surrounded by a navigable ocean sphere, for example, and inspired by Islam's successful use of Ptolemy's astronomy for desert motivation, and encouraged by the invention of the magnetic compass, a few daring European sailors ventured into the unknown seas. Their safe return and fantastic stories of adventure and treasure inspired others; and by AD 1522, the Americas had been discovered and the Earth had been circumnavigated.

The wonders of geographic discovery overwhelmed the European world. Once the contributions of Greek and Hellenistic science to these discoveries were realized, there was a surge of public interest in natural philosophy. By the middle of the 17th century, but still a half century before Isaac Newton formulated the basic principles of modern science, the interest had turned to fervour. Science, still generally known as "natural philosophy," was enthusiastically perceived as the source of "Utopia and the saviour of mankind" (Durant and Durant, 1963, p. 530). Out of the Renaissance came an unprecedented concept of science as having significant social relevance, and with it a received need for a government-supported programme of science education for all citizens. Preceding the full realization of these ideals, however, there were major reinterpretations of both the nature and purposes of history and science.

A. The Reinterpretation of History

By the early 1600s, Francis Bacon (1561-1626) and his peers predicated that science would produce great practical benefits by making society the masters of nature (Durant and Durant, 1961). This was an unprecedented concept—the Islamics had advocated a social utility of existing science information, but neither they nor their Greek predecessors advocated the mastery of nature for human benefit—and it was a highly questionable prediction, considering the world-view that prevailed at the time. Nevertheless, Western society was soon enthralled with the prospects of employing the intellect to take control of nature for purposes of secular human power and social benefit.

That goal was not immediately achieved, however, for a reason that, for many people, rendered it an essentially moot objective. The Renaissance society, although characterized as restless and searching, was slow to change. For more than a thousand years, religious tradition had held that human destiny was fixed between a relatively recent creation and not-too-distant destruction of the world. Humanity, according to Christian tradition, had been divinely created in a perfect state and placed in a perfect garden. Soon, however, the human creature demonstrated an imperfect character and was expelled to a less hospitable environment. In addition, human imperfection was believed to have infected nature itself (Toulmin and Goodfield, 1965). Humanity and the nature it touched were received as degenerating toward a terminal condition, and history was a providential revelation of that decline. Even the great mechanistic genius of Leonardo da Vinci (1452-1519) was eclipsed by the specter of inevitable doom as society looked back upon ancient civilizations and intellectual accomplishments that supposedly could never the equalled, and a deep sense of pessimism settled over the European world.

In his *History of the World* (1602), Sir Walter Raleigh (1552.-1618) reflected the traditional historians' point of view when he calculated that the end of the world would come around 1968. Many, however, saw the end as much more imminent; and some believed that the novel ideas of scientists such as Copernicus (1473-1543), Galileo (1564-1642), and Kepler (1571-1630) were a contributing factor. But most Renaissance thinkers did not attribute such power to the human intellect. They felt that those strange ideas were a symbol, rather than a cause, of the breakdown of the natural order of things (Santillana, 1956).

The World was breaking down, they believed; and the novel things that Galileo and others reported were taken as evidence of its dying spasms. Whereas the Crab Nebula had been dismissed as meaningless five centuries earlier, Tyco Brahe's (1546-1601) sixteenth century observations of a comet and nova were seen as evidence that the degeneration had spread into the heavens. Seeing no hope of a future for humanity, a despondent civilization settled in to contemplate its end on the eve of the Scientific Revolution. History was valued for whatever moral instruction it could provide to a society that was preoccupied with preparing for a spiritual afterlife.

Fortunately, their was a minority point of view regarding history and the destiny of humanity. For example, the English statesman Francis Bacon contended that history should be viewed in terms of cultural development, not degeneration. He had served for 19 years in the British Parliament, and his ideas grew out of a statesman's sincere concern for the social welfare. Francis Bacon viewed books as little "boats with precious cargos launched on the great sea of time" (Eiseley, 1973, p. 30)—and he searched those cargos for insight into the human condition. From that search, Bacon concluded that the past should not be looked upon as perfection nor the future as lost.

Antiquity represented the naive beginning rather than the pinnaçle of civilization, he boldly declared; and history should be considered a chronicle of a maturing civilization from which even further growth might be patterned.

> So Bacon became one of the first true modern historians . . . . he was prepared to treat the men and evens of his own age as significant in their own right. If anything, he argued, the men of modern times had built on the achievements of the ancients and so surpassed them.[6]

The idea of an inevitable end of the world persisted, however, until the 18th-century concept of geological time finally shattered the sacred 6,000 years timetable. So for Bacon and his 17th-century colleagues, the end still loomed near. But while awaiting the inevitable, they saw no reason why society should not attempt to make those last years as comfortable as possible.

A comfortable environment was an intrinsically worthy goal, Bacon concluded, and society was justified in taking control of nature to achieve it. Bacon's radical new point of view, which was published in *The Advancement of Learning* around in 1605, broke completely with Western tradition regarding both the criteria of human progress and the meaning of history. Traditionally, human progress had been perceived in transcendental terms of personal struggle and sacrifice for the edification of the soul. But he conceived it in terms of secular human welfare—and in doing so laid the philosophical groundwork for the modern concept of applied science.

Likewise, history had been interpreted as depicting a fixed human destiny. Bacon, however, saw it as a basis for a systematic study of human options—and in doing so laid the philosophical groundwork for the modern concept of history. All types of societies and governments had flourished and faltered in the past, he observed; and a proper study of history should reveal the causes of their ups and downs. From such a study, he concluded, a plan for a better civilization could be built. That redefinition of history justifies his acclaim as "The Man Who Saw Through Time" (Eiseley, 1973).

Bacon's radical idea of a social utility of history constituted a revolution in the concept of the nature and meaning of history akin, in scope and philosophical significance, to the new ideas of science that characterized and Scientific Revolution.

Renaissance society's interest in the Baconian notion that it could employ history to build a better civilization precipitated a new cultural perception of the value of the study of human events that, for lack of a better term, deserves distinction as *The Historical Revolution*.

B. The Socialization of Science

On the basis of his concept of the meaning of history, Francis Bacon searched the histories of past and present civilizations for those factors that had most affected society's cultural development and strength. Citing benefits of mechanical inventions such as the compass, printing press, and gunpowder, he concluded that technological development showed the greatest potential for building a strong, new world. The modern concept of applied science was finally formalized when he declared that *science* is the tool with which civilization may achieve the end of technological progress.

So for Francis Bacon, science was more than the natural history appreciated by the ancient Mesopotamians or the practical body of knowledge cherished by the medieval Muslims. It was more than the intellectual system the ancient Greeks valued for understanding their place in nature, and it was more than a source of insight into the divine plan for the World as conceived by medieval Christendom. It was also a *work* that could be done to change the world for the better. "The true and lawful goal of the sciences," Bacon wrote," is none other than this: that human life be endowed with new powers and discoveries" (in Jones, editor, 1937, p. 303). He took as his life's goal the task of prescribing a methodology through which society pursue that end.

Because of Aristotle's heavy dependence on deductive logic, Bacon rejected the Aristotelian tradition of science. He proposed an alternative based on inductive generalization from experience (Salmon, 1967). In the *Novum Organum* (published in 1620) and *The New Atlantis* (published in 1624), he described a new philosophy of science that, he confidently predicted, would answer all important scientific questions. His system was based on an inductive methodology, however, that would severely tax—if not overwhelm—today's most advanced data processing capabilities. Ironically, Durant and Durant (1961) noted, Bacon also discounted the works of his contemporary, Galileo. He recognized the advantages of Galileo's use of scientific hypotheses as guides for further observation, but was concerned that some hypothetical conditions might appear so obvious that they, like Aristotle's logic, would cause observers to disregard contrary evidence.

In the end, Bacon had an accurate vision of the future of science, but not its development. He foresaw the modern association of science and technology and the benefits of empiricism, for example, but remained committed to Ptolemy's geocentric concept of the universe. Ultimately, many of his ideas were dismissed as naive. Furthermore, in 1621 Bacon was impeached and banned from public service for accepting gratuities from persons appealing to his office. This indiscretion, and his adherence to the Ptolemaic cosmos (which was not an unreasonable choice at the time, considering the scientific evidence that was available), discredited his works in future years.

Nevertheless, Bacon made several very important contributions to the future development of science. Among the greatest was his optimistic reinterpretation of the nature of history. His new concept of the past appealed to the restless secularism that had been building in Western civilization since the late Middle Ages, and it inspired a social confidence that finally displaced the pessimism that had prevailed in Europe since the collapse of the Roman Empire. This in turn generated a social receptivity to his then-radical ideas of the purposeful application of science to the problems of building a better civilization. The revolutionary concept of the nature and meaning of history also enabled the later development of science. For example, Bacon's non-providential basis of history is inherent in both the mechanistic cosmic systems that characterize Newtonian science and the specialization concepts that undergird Darwin's evolutionary theory of biological development.

C. Justification of the Concept of Science Education

Bacon's enthusiasm for the social utility of science culminated in what may be his greatest contribution—the concept of science education. In *The Advancement of Learning,* published in 1605, he proposed an elaborate plan for the systematic development and dissemination of scientific knowledge. Many of his suggestions are remarkably appropriate nearly four centuries later. For example:

> He calls for the multiplication and support of colleges, libraries, laboratories, biological gardens, museums of science and industry; for the better payment of teachers and researchers; for ampler funds to finance scientific experiments.[7]

In *The New Atlantis*, Bacon advocated an intimate union of science and government to insure the resources needed for technological advancement. He also proposed the classification and application of the sciences to appropriate fields of research. Mass education of scientists and technologists was proposed to staff a large number of specialized, problem-solving laboratories. Each laboratory, much as Thomas Edison's did two and a half centuries later, would produce inventions on a wholesale basis with each invention scientifically fitted to the fulfilment of human need. This called for a new cultural institution: science education. With an effective programme of public science education, Bacon believed, any society could produce many great scientists and advance scientific development. An occasional genius might still come along, he admitted, but the progress of science would no longer be dependent on the sporadic appearance of exceptional individual such as Aristotle.

It is significant that, from the outset, Bacon deemed the education of all citizens to be essential to the appropriate development of science. He saw science as a public, teachable entity with which society could produce a better world; but he clearly declared that it was no panacea. The technological arts may promote as well as prevent human misery, he warned; and scientific development and the new technology it may produce could therefore be either a boon or bane, depending upon the nature of its use or abuse.

The society that would exploit science, he believed, must accept responsibility for its application and accommodate its affect. Perhaps troubled by his own laxity in a position of power, he emphasized that a public programme of liberal education, including literature and philosophy, was necessary to insure wise public judgement in the support of scientific activity. The advancement of science alone was not the key to a better future; rather, it must be accompanied by an equally significant advancement of human character if society is to cope with the social and cultural change produced by scientific and technological development.

On that basis, Bacon conceived three distinct threats to a successful relationship of science and society: an inadequate supply of competent scientists; a lack of public understanding and support of science; and avaricious leadership. The first threat could be handled by building sound programmes for recruiting and training scientists and technologists. The second threat could be lessened by including science as a basic component of an extensive programme of public education. The third could be reduced by placing equal emphasis on studies that would teach essential human values and social ideals as well as science.

Tremendous power will accrue to the society that exploits the potential of applied science, Bacon declared; and an educated citizenry will be essential to insure the reasoned direction of that power. It is therefore essential that science and education be advanced together if society is to maintain the potential for a better life through science and technology. In other words, he believed, the benefits of science are dependent upon an educated society.

Bacon, like Galileo, lived in the dawn of modern science; and both were worldshakers in their own right. As a statesman, bacon dared to look beyond historical tradition in search of a better destiny for civilization. As a natural philosopher, Galileo dared to look beyond scientific tradition for new insight into the nature of things. Had there been Bacon alone, the 17th-century surge of scientific curiosity might have bogged down under the burden of unmanageable methodology and inadequate cosmic theory. But there was Galileo, whose telescopic observations exposed the heavens to detailed scrutiny and whose techniques of experimentation earned him acclaim as *The Inventor of Experimental Science.*

Had there been Galileo alone, his ideas might have languished amidst an apathetic society awaiting the end of the physical world. But there was Bacon, whose radical interpretation of the meaning of history swung society's attention toward visions of a better life—and whose enthusiasm for science as the key to that better life helped to fan the flicker of scientific curiosity into a bonfire of interest. Having justified the potential social value of science, Bacon found himself challenged with the problem of communicating science to the society. He turned with characteristic zeal to the development of a system of public education that would prepare a citizenry with a balanced, interdisciplinary background appropriate for the equitable development and deployment of science. Finally, his eloquent advocacy of general public participation in the scientific enterprise elevated the teaching of science to the level of social necessity; and this justifies his designation as *The Inventor of Science Education.*

Implementation of the Concept of Science Education in the United States of America

In the centuries since Francis Bacon proposed his revolutionary ideas about the role of science in society, history has justified both his enthusiasm and caution. Science and technology have produced benefits beyond his greatest dreams, and both have become essential components of modern culture. There have also been problems reminiscent of Bacon's gravest concerns about the dangers of scientific development outpacing society's ability to cope with change. Practical problems include environmental pollution and the threat of nuclear catastrophe. Cultural issues include changing employment patterns and the influence of science on traditional human values.

Some people have blamed scientific and technological development for our problems, Bybee (1979) noted while others have seen science and technology as the solution to our problems. "Both positions", he declared, "are partially correct and partially wrong."

> It is not science and technology *per se* that cause the problems; rather, it is human ideas and values about scientific development and technological application that have both contributed to our progress and potential collapse.[8]

Bybee's comments reflected Bacon's warning that scientific development must be accompanied by effective public education to produce a scientifically enlightened citizenry. Recognition of the importance of such a populace for the well-being of both science and society has elevated science education to the level of a national priority in the United States of America.

A. Science Education as a National Priority

Science education did not begin to emerge as a major concern in this country until the last half of the 19th century, nearly two and a half centuries after Bacon. By that time, science and technology had become the dominant cultural forces Bacon had envisioned, but science education had not kept pace. Science was receiving increasing attention as a curricular component, but the value of science education was perceived in a variety of ways. A diversity of special interest groups ranging from agricultural and vocational advocates, moral reformers, temperance groups, humane societies, and health groups "demanded that their concerns be incorporated into science education" (Peterson, et al., 1984, p. 17). As a result, the value of science education was perceived in a variety of ways.

Rapid technological change in the late 1800s, for example, created a demand for a more utilitarian emphasis on science per se. This resulted in the *elementary science movement,* which emphasized the contributions of scientific theories to technology and was promoted as a means to fulfilling "the need for skilled labour in the rapidly developing technology" (Underhill, 1941, p. 98). On the other hand, advocates of *object teaching,* which was popular from about 1860 to the 1880s, saw science largely as a source of material for use in mental-discipline exercises. Widespread concern for the emotional development of children in the early years of elementary education contributed to development of a third programme called *nature study,* which, among other things, was promoted as developing children's aesthetic and emotional values. Rivalry between the advocates of the elementary science and nature study movements was often intense from the 1890s into the early years of the twentieth century. However, neither of the programmes achieved its ideals, Underhill concluded, because of "a broad lack of knowledge of science on the part of the teacher" (p. 121).

The Industrial Revolution was in full swing by 1900, and the United States had become a major industrial power.

Technological developments over the previous half century produced a new lifestyle of unprecedented material comfort and convenience. The new lifestyle was accompanied by a marked change in employment patterns, and technical education became increasingly important for competition in the job market. Still, science education was far from a major social force.

World War I (1914-1918) was among the more influential factors that contributed to an increased emphasis on science as a major curricular objective. The United States had emerged from the conflict as an acknowledged world power, and technological capability had played a significant role in the victory The nation came to realize the scientific development could be a critical factor in national defence.

Little more than a quarter-century later, in 1945, the nation merged from World War II as an undisputed superpower and sole possessor of the secret of nuclear energy. The United States was a new wonderland of science; and great scientists migrated to the US with enthusiasm akin to that of the natural philosophers who flocked to ancient Alexandria and medieval Baghdad. A feeling of national pride and security in the power of science prevailed, and no problem seemed too big nor any goal too remote for the resources of modern science and technology.

In 1949, however, just four years into the Atomic Age, Soviet Russia also laid claim to the secret of nuclear power. In 1952, the US reasserted its technological supremacy with the detonation of a hydrogen bomb, but just a year later this time, the Soviets detonated a hydrogen bomb. This created concern among the nation's political and scientific communities; but to the average American citizen, the Soviets were just following the leader. The United States was still the undisputed world leader in science and technology, and most Americans believed it was just a matter of time until another great scientific feat would make that quite clear.

The confidence seemed justified. American technology had produced the first supersonic flight in 1947; and by the early 1950s, engineers were designing a person carrying spacecraft. In 1955, the federal government "published a detailed description of the rockets that would be used to launch a small satellite in late 1957 or early 1958" (Wolfe, 1979, p. 56). These developments generated increased interest in science education; and from 1945 to 1955, "virtually all . . . [secondary students were] exposed to at least two years of general science" (Lacey, 1966, p. 16). From this, it would appear that all was well with science education in the United States—but this was not the case.

Student testing during World War II had revealed weaknesses in the areas of science and mathematics (Lacey, 1966). In response, many studies on the condition of science education were conducted over the next decade. One such study, the "Bush Report" (*Science, the Endless Frontier,* which was published in 1945), had far-reaching implications for science education. The United States had developed an extensive scientific enterprise in World War II, and President Roosevelt asked Vannever Bush to examine ways that the power of science might be redirected to peace-time pursuits. The Bush Report "led to the establishment of the National Science Foundation in 1950 and . . . . [highlighted] the need to improve science instruction at all levels of education" (Buccino, 1983, p. 4).

The Bush Report prompted another study by the American Association for the Advancement of Science (AAAS) in 1946. That study attributed the condition of science education to three major problems—all anticipated by Francis Bacon's concern for the adequate support of science education:

> The American public . . . fails to pay its teaches decently, . . . colleges and universities . . . failed to prepare prospective teachers for the kind of teaching they should do . . . . [and] the high school curriculum needs a thoroughgoing reorganization.[9]

Reaction to the Bush Report and the AAAS study precipitated action. In 1953, the NSF implemented a series of programmes to improve science education. In 1954, the National Science Teachers Association (NSTA) initiated a programme to recognize and award outstanding teachers (Lacey, 1966). Science education had clearly become a matter of national policy, and a determined movement for reform was gathering momentum.

Then something happened that riveted the nation's attention to the issue of science education. In October, 1957, the Soviet

Union placed the world's first artificial satellite in orbit around the Earth. The United States' cherished position of superiority in science and technology was lost as Sputnik beeped overhead, and pressure for reform in science education suddenly intensified to the proportions of a revolution. Whatever the scientific and technological significance of Sputnik, its social and political impact was galvanizing. "The fact that the Soviets had the rocket power to launch Sputnik meant that they now also had the capacity to deliver the bomb on an intercontinental ballistic missile" (Wolfe, 1979, p. 57).

Being second did not come easy to a young civilization accustomed to being first. The nation's ego had been badly bruised and its confidence severely shaken by Sputnik, and the desire to catch up became an obsession. Many who remember those frantic days blush at the recall of the nation's first entries into the space race. Effort after effort to launch a satellite—all televised for the world to see—ended in flaming failure. It was a time of national humiliation and uncertainty, and the crisis rhetoric that characterized the era magnified the public concern. The Soviets continued to dominate in space as they put the first human in orbit. The production of the scientists and engineers needed to catch up with the Soviets became an immediate national priority. With a critical but hopeful eye, a desperate nation turned its attention—and its money—to the support of science education.

B. A Revolution In Science Education

The NSF had already declared a need for reforms in science education, and a reform movement had started in the schools. Soon all eyes were on the schools, and it was there that the blame was laid and the hope was placed. Billions of dollars were devoted to science education—often without question (Yager, 1981), and a new direction in science education soon emerged.

Previously, science education was valued primarily for student-centered purposes such as social and vocational competence. But the curricular reformers of the early 1960s generally adopted Bruner's subject-centered model of education, which placed primary emphasis on "the underlying principles that give structure to . . . [a science] subject" (Bruner, 1960, p. 31). Previously, most school science textbooks had been written by educators; but by the late 1950s, the central involvement of scientists was considered essential to the development of science curricula (Butts, 1982). A new series of NSF-founded programmes was developed along that line; and many are commonly known by the acronyms of their titles, such as BSCS (Biological Science Curriculum Study), SCIS (Science Curriculum Improvement Study), ESS (Elementary Science Study), and SAPA (Science-A Process Approach).

By 1962, a subject-centered emphasis clearly prevailed, and NSTA adopted the position that "science proper . . . should be the primary goal of scientific education" (NSTA, 1962, p. 33) "The [new] curriculum reflected the discipline of the scientist," Butts (1982) observed, "and not the social problems, life, skills, or contextual environmental concerns" (p. 1666) of earlier science education.

Hundreds of new educational programmes were launched in the late 1950s and early 1960s. But some were based on convincing presuppositions that, in retrospect, lacked adequate philosophical justification; and others lacked adequate planning and organization. Four years after Sputnik, the executive director of the NSTA expressed a growing concern:

> All of us are caught up in "the pursuit of excellence," but all too often, the pursuit becomes a mad rush to "do something, even though we are not sure it is right." Reasons for this, perhaps, are that we seldom take time to think and spell out what is meant by excellence.[10]

Nevertheless, interest and enthusiasm for science education were high, and students entering college soon appeared to be better prepared in science (Lacey, 1966). Furthermore, Butts (1982) noted, "by 1970 the goal of a man on the moon was achieved, and internationally our position as 'number one' in science was recaptured" (p. 1669). In many ways it appeared that the 1960s had ushered in a Golden Age for science education in the United States. Several events occurred in the 1960s and 1970s, however, that led to a reorientation of national priorities.

C. Reflections On Educational Priorities

Chief among the events leading to a reorientation of national educational priorities was the struggle for civil rights and human equality in the 1960s and 1970s.

> Just as Sputnik had provided the visible symbol to justify federal support for the improvement of science education, the assassinations of John F. Kennedy, Martin Luther King, and Robert Kennedy provided the visible justification for allocating billions of dollars toward nationally supported economic and educational equity programmes. Thus, without fanfare, the greatest nationally supported reformation in science education was gradually and completely over-shadowed by the human rights movement.[11]

Twice within a decade, the United States had been shocked to the core with the reality of vulnerability. The first shock, Sputnik, represented a clearly identified threat from the outside. The second shock, the assassinations of the nation's president and leading proponents of civil rights and human equality, represented a less clearly defined threat from within. The first threat had focused the American public's attention on the importance of the advancement of science, and the nation responded with a wholehearted commitment of resources. The second threat turned the nation's attention toward the importance of the advancement of human character, and the country responded with an equally wholehearted commitment.

Education was again conceived as the key and society turned once more to its schools for deliverance. This time, as before, there was extensive pressure for curricular change. This time, as before, there was much impulsive action, sometimes without sufficient planning or philosophical justification. Given the country's continuing interest in science for the space race and national defence, it is conceivable that both science education and educational equity would have shared positions of top priority. But there were other influencing factors.

By the late 1960s, the Vietnam War had generated serious public concern regarding the efficacy of advanced military technology in the current arena of international politics. Growing public awareness of such problems as environmental pollution, hazardous waste management, and industrial nuclear accidents raids additional questions about the nation's investment in science and technology. Rapid scientific and technological development also contributed to changing employment patterns. The resulting social stress led some to believe that science caused too much change too fast and that it was insensitive to human needs and values (Etzioni and Nunn, 1974).

Public confidence in science began to decline by the mid 1960s. By the end of the decade, the United States had succeeded in the spectacular and much publicized goal of putting a human on the moon, but even this did not stay the changing public attitude toward science. As the world watched the first human footsteps on the moon, most people were aware of some of the spectacular contributions of science as well some of its undesirable side-effects; but there was little general understanding of either the actual or desirable relationship of science to society. Similarly, there was little public understanding of the nature and purposes of science, or the distinction between science, technology, and engineering. By the 1980s, it was painfully clear that the nation's science education efforts had not kept pace with its scientific and technological development. Educators began to use the term "crisis" to describe the condition of science education in the United States.

Three-and-a-half centuries earlier, Francis Bacon had predicted the need for effective science education to help society accommodate the tremendous change that applied science would produce. Furthermore, he saw the direction of applied science as the responsibility of all the people—not just the scientific community, government agencies, or any other subset of society. Otherwise, the scientific enterprise might perish for lack of public trust and support. Or perhaps even more ominous, the great power of science and technology might be inequitably or irresponsibly deployed to the detriment of civilization. By the mid-1960s, and again in the 1980s, the wisdom of his prediction was confirmed by the declining public attitude toward science in this country; but the problem had been clearly recognized several decades earlier.

In 1934, John Dewey unequivocally declared that the social impact of science requires science education for the masses as well as for would-be scientists. Applied science has clearly produced many benefits for everyone, but it has also created bewildering social problems. To prevent further bewilderment, he prescribed an integrated curricular approach to keep other social institutions from lagging behind science in a rapidly changing world.

In 1947, J. B. Conant pointed out that science-related policy issues must deal with highly technical, scientific considerations. Like Bacon, he concluded that it is very important that those in positions of authority and responsibility, and especially those whose attitudes and actions may influence others, have a basic understanding of science.

However, Conant concluded, it is an oversimplification to assume that the solution to this problem is greater dissemination of factual scientific knowledge among non-scientists. The research scientist approaches problems from a particular point of view, he explained, so information that may be meaningful to a scientist may be quite bewildering to those having no research background with which to interpret it. Therefore, he proposed that the average student would be better served by historical case studies of the basic purposes and methods of science.

These ideas had generated considerable interest in curricular reform by the early 1950s; but in the reforms that followed the Sputnik era, neither Dewey's interdisciplinary ideas nor Conant's historical approach prevailed. The emphasis had suddenly shifted to the production of technical personnel to counter the Soviet threat and a discipline-specific, subject-centered approach was generally accepted as appropriate to that goal. However, the need for a scientifically competent society was neither ignored nor forgotten by the science education community. Many phrases were coined to express the science background needed by the average citizen, and "'scientific literacy' [was] the term most frequently used" (Agin, 1974, p. 405).

D. The Challenge of Scientific Literacy

"Scientific literacy" had a convincing and appealing ring of legitimacy, and it was an immediately popular topic. Unfortunately, Miller (1983) indicated, use of the term became widespread long before a clear concept of its meaning was developed. From the start, science teachers were generally convinced that scientific literacy should be an educational priority; but by the mid-1960s, the futility of attempting to develop a curriculum around an inadequately defined concept had become a prominent topic (Pella, et al., 1966). On the one hand, some educators began to suspect that scientific literacy may be an unrealistic curricular goal for science education. On the other hand, scientific illiteracy was not an acceptable option.

Klopfer (1969) echoed a prevalent concern. "For every man and woman who hopes to function effectively as a citizen of society in the twentieth century, literacy in science is an essential requirement" (p. 88). On that basis, he declared that science education has two main purposes: requisite science training for those few students preparing for careers in science and technology; and training that will contribute to the scientific literacy of all students.

As 1970 approached, the science education community became increasingly concerned that it was not accomplishing that important second purpose. The reforms of the 1950s and 1960s had provided the sorely needed advancement of science, but the nation still lacked a citizenry that could understand and accommodate applied science. "Science and technology have come close to providing us the world mankind has been seeking for thousands of years," Hurd (1970) wrote; "however, we have not been successful in teaching man how to live successfully in the new world" (p. 14).

Over the thousands of years alluded to by Hurd, humanity had interpreted the "good life" in a number of ways ranging from the intellectual independence of ancient Greece to the materialism of the Roman Empire to the spiritual self-denial of the Middle Ages. Over those same years, humanity sought better living from many means, including mythology, mysticism, magic, and a multitude of religious and political systems—and recently, applied science. The latter had produced the greatest promise of a good life for humanity in modern times.

All this came to a head for the United States in the science education issues that have characterized the era from the 1960s through the 1980s. Now that American society had brought the long-sought better world closer through the power of applied science, it was faced with the problem of educating itself to accommodate and maintain that new world—or risk losing it as more and more people have second thoughts about the benefits and risks of science and technology.

Some educators and scientist expressed alarm at the relative lack of public concern over the problem outside the scientific and educational communities. The explosion of scientific knowledge has outstripped the public's ability to assimilate it, T.P. Evans (1970) concluded, and "as a result, the average citizen has disassociated himself intellectually from science" (p. 83). This attitude, he lamented, is a deterrent to scientific literacy that, unless overcome, will prevent the realization of that goal.

Beginning in the 1960s, however, several major public policy issues had emerged, however, that eventually helped to sensitive other groups to the immediate threat of scientific illiteracy. Many environmentalists and conservationists became alarmed that the general public lacked the basic scientific knowledge needed to understand policy debates about pollution. Government and business leaders became concerned that important projects might be stymied by unfounded public fear of possible deleterious side effects of science and technology. There was also increasing concern that serious problems might result from the lack of sufficient science backgrounds among key decision-makers involved in science-related programmes or activities in government, business and industry.

Though still undefined in meaningful educational terms, "scientific literacy" was suddenly catapulted to the status of major national issue. Pressure for curricular change multiplied. Some educators called for drastic reforms to shift the curricular focus from science-centered to a student-centered emphasis. Evans (1970), for example, suggested avoiding the specialized language of the scientist so science could be "presented to the general public in terms it can understand" (p. 83). In an effort to clarify the issue, NSTA conducted a survey of science educators and convened several conferences to develop a position statement in the goals of science education in the 1970s. That statement, released in July 1971, established the long-standing consensus that "the major goal of science education is to develop scientifically literate and personally concerned individuals with a high competency of rational thought and action" (NSTA, 1971, p. 47).

By the late 1980s, there was general concern that major reforms were needed in science education. The tremendous outpouring of energy in the 1960s had apparently been futile—an exercise devoid of philosophical direction. The literature of the 1970s echoed the struggles and confusion of the 1960s as writers continued to ask "what is meant by the term 'scientific literacy'?" (N. Smith, 1974, p. 34). Brovey (1980) declared that the current practices in science education were producing a nation of scientifically *aware* but scientifically *illiterate* people. Surveys commissioned by NSF during the late 1970s indicated that less than five per cent of citizens outside the scientifically involved community could be classified as scientifically literate (Miller, 1983). Hazen and Trefil (1991) challenge the nation that general scientific literacy prevailed even in the scientific community: "Indeed, it has been our experience that working scientists are often illiterate outside their own field of professional expertise" (p. xiii).

There was intense concern over the condition of science education in the 1950s, and it preceded a period of major reform. Again in the 1980s, a strong movement for reform has emerged. Although the science education profession still lacks a clear, philosophically justified definition of its boldly acclaimed goal, "scientific literacy," the struggles of the past three decades have not been fruitless. The profession now has a clear concept of its basic purpose—the dual purpose advocated by Francis Bacon three-and-a-half centuries ago: Training the specialized personnel needed to maintain the current scientific enterprise, and educating the scientifically informed public that must accommodate and direct the application of science and technology to the equitable resolution of society's problems.

The means to accomplish the first dimension of that purpose can be built upon the successful practices of the past two or three decades. The means to the second dimension, however, constitute the supreme challenge to science educators. Programmes such as AAAS's Project 2061 (Rutherford and Ahlgren, 1990) and the National Science Teachers Association's (1990) project, Scope, Sequence, and Coordination of Secondary Science, have implemented field projects to assess options for radical curricular reforms. And the results of those and other studies are anxiously awaited by a concerned public that is acutely aware of the importance of the issues involved.

> By most criteria, science education is not preparing students for their role as citizens who must make informed and responsible decisions about science-related social problems during the next decades. Such problems cannot simply be turned over to scientific "aristocrats," consumer advocates, or corporate enterprises. The democratic process requires public participation, and it is assumed that the public is informed and literate.[12]

More that 350 years earlier, in the dawn of the era of modern science, Francis Bacon had expressed similar concern about the importance of citizen participation in the direction of a nation's scientific enterprise. The history of the relation of science, technology, and society in the United States over the past 150 years further justifies Bacon's contention that a scientifically educated citizenry is an essential counterpart of scientific and technological development. The means to achieve this must be a fundamental research objective of science education, and further study of Bacon's prophetic vision of the role of science and education in a technologically advanced culture is clearly indicated as a source of insight into appropriate goals and objectives for science education in the 1990s and beyond.

NOTES

1. p. 251.
2. p. 57.
3. p. 128.
4. Toulmin and Goodfield, 1961, p. 156.
5. Saperstein, 1982, p. 10.
6. Toulmin and Goodfield, 1965, p. 108.
7. Durant and Durant, 1961, p. 174.
8. Bybee 1979, p. 107.
9. Lacey, 1966, p. 16.
10. Carleton, 1961, p. 4.
11. Peterson, et al., 1984, pp. 20-21.
12. Bybee et al., 1980, p. 393.

REFERENCES

Agin, M. L.: 1974, 'Education for Scientific Literacy: A Conceptual Frame of Reference and Some Applications', *Science Education,* 58 (3), 403-415.

Brown, H.I.: 1977, *'Perception, Theory and Commitment: The New Philosophy of Science'*, The University of Chicago Press, Chicago.

Brovey, D.J.: 1980, 'Science Among Ordinary Citizens,' *Journal of College Science Teaching,* 10(2), 88-91.

Bruner, J. S.: 1960. *The Process of Education,* Harvard University Press, Cambridge, Massachusetts.

Buccino, A.: 1983, November 5, 'Images of Science Education', A paper presented at the Ninth Children's Book International, Boston, Massachusetts.

Butts, D.: 1982, 'Science Education', In H. E. Mitzel (Ed. in Chief), *Encyclopedia of Educational Research (Vol. 4, 5th Ed.).* The Free Press (Div. of MacMillan Publishing Co., Inc., New York, pp. 1665-1675.

Bybee, R.: 1979, 'Science Education and the Emerging Ecological Society', *Science Education,* 63(1), 95-109.

Bybee, R., Harms, N., Ward, B., & Yager, R.: 1980, 'Science, Society and Science Education', *Science Education, 64(3),* 377-395.

Carleton, R.: 1961, 'Editorial', *The Science Teacher,* 28(7), 4.

Conant, J. B.: 1947, *On Understanding Science: An Historical Approach,* Yele University Press, New Haven, Connecticut.

Dewey, J.: 1934, 'The Supreme Intellectual Obligation , *Science Education,* 18(1), 1-4.

Durant, W.: 1950, 'The Age of Faith: A History of Medieval Civilization—Christian, Islamic, and Judaic—From Constantine to Dante: AD 325-1300'. In W. Durant, *The Story of Civilization (Vol. 4),* Simon and Schuster, New York.

Durant, W.: 1953, 'The Renaissance: A History of Civilization in Italy from 1304-1576 AD', In W. Durant, *The Story of Civilization (Vol. 5),* Simon and Schuster, New York.

Durant, W. & Durant, A. 1961, 'The Age of Reason Begins: A History of European Civilization in the Period of Shakespeare, Bacon, Montaigne, Rembrandt, Galileo, and Descartes: 1558-1648', In W. Durant & A. Durant, *The Story of Civilization (Vol. 7),* Simon and Schuster, New York.

Durant, W. & Durant, A.: 1963, 'The Age of Louis XIV: A History of European Civilization in the Period of Pascal, Moliere, Cromwell,

Milton, Peter the Great, Newton, and Spinoza: 1648-1715', In W. Durant & A. Durant, *The Story of Civilization (Vol. 8)*, Simon and Schuster, New York.

Eiseley, L.: 1973, *'The Man Who Saw Through Time'*, Charles Scribner's Sons New York (originally published as *Francis Bacon and the Modern Dilemma*, 1961).

Etzioni, A. & Nunn, C.: 1974, 'The Public Appreciation of Science in Contemporary America, *Daedalus, 103(2)*, 191-205.

Frankfort, H., Frankfort, H.A., Wilson, J., & Jacobsen, T.: 1946, *Before Philosophy: The Intellectual Adventure of Ancient Man*, Penguin Books, Inc., Baltimore, Maryland.

Goldstein, T.: 1980, *Dawn of Modern Science*, Houghton Mifflin Company, Boston.

Hazen, R., & Trefil, J., 1991, *Science Matters: Achieving Scientific Literacy*. Doubleday, New York.

Hurd, P.D.: 1970, 'Scientific Enlightenment for an Age of Science', *The Science Teacher, 37(1)*, 13-15.

Jones, R. F. (Ed.): 1937, *Francis Bacon Essays, Advancement of Learning, New Atlantis, and Other Pieces*, The Odyssey Press, Inc., New York.

Klopfer, L.: 1969, 'The Teaching of Science and the History of Science', *Journal of Research in Science Teaching*, 6, 87-95.

Kuhn, T.S., 1970, *The Structure of Scientific Revolutions (2nd Edition)*, The University of Chicago Press, Chicago.

Lacey, A.L.: 1966, *Guide to Science Teaching*, Wadsworth Publishing Co., Inc., Belmont, California.

Miller, J. D.: 1983, 'Scientific Literacy: A Conceptual and Empirical Review', *Daedalus, 112(2)*, 29-48.

National Science Teachers Association: 1962, 'Curriculum Development in Science', *The Science Teacher*, 29(8), 32-37.

National Science Teachers Association, 1990, May 10, *'Scope, Sequence, and Coordination of Secondary Science: A Rationale (SS&C);*. Position paper available from the National Science Teachers Association, Washington, D.C.

Orlich, D.: 1964, 'The Dawn of Scientific Epistemology: 1564-1964', *Journal of Research in Science Teaching*, 2, 95-99.

Pella, M., O'Hearn, G., & Gale, C.: 1966, 'Scientific Literacy—Its Referents', *The Science Teacher, 33(5)*, 44.

Peterson, R., Bowyer, J., Butts, D., & Bybee, R.: 1984, *Science and Society: A Source Book for Elementary and Junior High School Teachers,* Charles E. Merrill Publishing Company, Columbus, Ohio.

Rutherford, F. J., & Ahlgren, A., 1990, *Science For All Americans.* Oxford University Press, New York.

Salmon, W. C.: 1967, *The Foundations of Scientific Inference,* University of Pittsburgh Press, Pittsburgh, Pennsylvania (original copyright, 1966).

Santillana, G. de.: 1961, *'The Origins of Scientific Thought',* Mentor Books, The New American Library, New York.

Saperstein, A.: 1982, 'Ethics in the Classroom—Morality and the Laws of Thermodynamics', *Journal of College Science Teaching, 12(1),* 10-11.

Toulmin, S. & Goodfield, J.: 1961, *The Fabric of the Heavens: The Development of Astronomy and Dynamics,* Harper Torchbooks, Harper & Row, Publishers, New York.

Toulmin, S. & Goodfield, J.: 1962, *The Architecture of Matter,* University of Chicago Press, Chicago.

Toulmin, S. & Goodfield, J.: 1965, *The Discovery of Time,* University of Chicago Press, Chicago.

Underhill, O.E., 1941, *The Origins and Development of Elementary-School Science,* Scott Foresman and Company, New York.

Wells, H.G.: 1961,. *The Outline of History,* Garden City Books, New York.

Whitehead, A.N; 1941, *Science and Modern World,* The MacMillan company, New York.

Wolfe, T.: 1979, *The Right Stuff,* Bantam Books, New York.

Yager, R.: 1981, 'The Current Situation in Science Education', In Staver, J. R. (Ed.), *An Analysis of the Secondary School Science Curriculum for Action in the 1980s (1982) AETS Yearbook),* Ohio State University, Columbus, Ohio, pp. 15-41. (ERIC Document Reproduction No. SE-03-0-586.)

12

Science Across Cultures: Introducing the Science, Technology & Medicine of Non-Western Cultures into the Classroom

HELEN SELIN
Hampshire College, USA

Introduction

Since the European scientific revolution of the seventeenth and eighteenth centuries, we have come to regard Western science as the only true scientific enterprise. We think of science as objective, truthful, progressive, and free of superstition and the limits of our own culture. In fact, we think of Western science as science. "It has been customary to treat as folly and superstition many . . . past attempts at knowledge of nature or at understanding her phases and processes. It is not uncommon to casually stumble upon some excellent text in the physical sciences or even some erudite modern treatise in the philosophy of science, and read there that science began with Galileo, that the Greek or medieval scholars did not know the meaning of an experiment or of evidence, that people did not know how to count the teeth of a horse . . .—and many more such foibles." (Graubard, 1953)

The Eurocentric view has been challenged in many fields over the past few years. Teachers have begun to restructure the curriculum on all educational levels. They offer classes on African, African American, Native American, Chinese and Latin American history and literature. Or, at the very least, they often include a non-western component. Teachers have also found themselves under pressure from parents and school districts to incorporate multi-ethnic and multi-cultural studies into their classes. Textbooks are being rewritten with the aim of making up for years of oversight in not including the accomplishments of peoples of other cultures. However, even in these rewritings and rethinkings, science is often overlooked. We are quick to recognize the charm and importance and superior ability involved in African painting or sculpture, in Brazilian music, in Indonesian textiles. But we may still look skeptically on their medical and agricultural practices. "Western peoples have simply absorbed only those aspects of Egyptian, Roman and Arab science which appeal to a people with a mechanistic frame of mind. What they do not understand they call magic." (Ezeabasili, 1977)

"If we define science and technology broadly as ways of observing, describing, explaining, predicting and controlling events in the natural world, then it is obvious that each culture has its own characteristic science and technology. The people of different cultures have developed different ways of perceiving and interacting with the natural world, because they have lived in different environments and have sought solutions to different problems. Moreover, the distribution of scientific and technological information; the means of recording, transmitting and disseminating such information; and the social status of scientists and technologists have varied from one culture to the next." (Dugan, 1992)

It is clear that cultural attitudes and ideas have affected the development and application of science throughout history. In comparing scientific traditions, students may discover ways that their own tradition can profitably incorporate insights from others. They can achieve deeper understanding of the relationship between science, its technological applications, and the cultures that benefit from those applications. They can acquire insights into aspects of the intellectual traditions of other cultures which, unlike their artistic, religious, literary or philosophical ones, are often underrepresented in curricula.

In this paper, I hope to dispel the notion of non-Western science as magic, by pointing to a number of scientific and medical accomplishments of other cultures. The paper is meant to be an introduction to the literature in this field, to direct teachers to books, films and video they might use in preparing curricula that include elements of the science of other cultures. I will talk about science in Africa, Asia, the Middle East, and the Americas by exploring some of the scientific achievements of the Chinese, Muslims, Africans and Native Americans. This is just a small sample of what is available. The great civilizations of India and the Pacific, and many other areas, have been excluded, entirely because of space. It is my hope that you will explore further. My book, *Science Across Cultures,* lists over 800 books for scholars and laypeople on the scientific achievements of other cultures. A bibliography of about 100 titles suitable for the high school level and a videography and filmography are appended. The science of other cultures in rich and varied and makes for lively, interesting class projects.

China

"Historians of science have focused more attention on Asia than on any other non-Western region. Based on an ancient scholarly tradition, Asian science and technology was theoretically sophisticated and technologically advanced, and led the world for the fifteen centuries prior to the Scientific Revolution in the West." (Dugan, 1992) China's contributions to science began as far back as the thirteenth century BC, with the invention of lacquer, the first plastic. 3,200 years later, the Europeans followed suit. It is possible to make that sort of comparison in many areas of science, from agriculture and astronomy to technology and medicine. Documents from the sixth century BC demonstrate that the Chinese believed in the circulation of the blood 1,800 years before Harvey made his "discovery". They used the Mercator map projection in the tenth century AD, 600 years before its use in the West. Many engineering feats, such as the suspension bridge, the chain-drive and the essentials of the steam engine, preceded their so-called invention in Europe over a thousand years later. This paper will focus on three inventions and achievements that illustrate

China's impressive science and technology: the seismograph, papermaking, and Chinese medicine.

A. Earthquake Detection

China has always been beset by earthquakes. Often the quake would not just disrupt the earth, but be followed by food riots or outbreaks of rebellion against the government. "The imperial government had every reason to want to know as soon as possible when there had been an earthquake in a distant province. First of all, it would mean that grain shipments would be interrupted, which was relevant since taxes were paid in grain. But it would also mean that both food aid and extra military forces would be needed in the afflicted area." (Temple, 1986, p. 163) Chang Heng, the Astronomer-Royal, in 132 AD, invented an instrument which could indicate when earthquakes had occurred. It was called an earthquake weathercock.

The seismograph was a "bronze vessel, rather like a wine-jar, six feet across, with a domed lid. The outer surface of the vessel was decorated with motifs of mountains, tortoises, birds, animals and antique writing. All around the vessel was a series of eight dragons' heads, equally spaced, holding bronze balls in their mouths. The balls would drop out if the dragons' mouths opened, or if pushed. Round the base of the vessle sat eight corresponding bronze toads, looking upwards, with their mouths wide open. They were positioned directly beneath the dragon mouths, ready to catch the falling balls. Obviously, a bronze ball dropping into a bronze toad would make a great deal of noise; people would be alerted by the resounding clang." (Temple, 1986, p. 164) The actual mechanism inside the vessel consisted of a weighted pendulum or bob that would tilt if there were an earth tremor, causing a ball to move along a slider and drop out of the dragon's mouth. The pendulum also released a hook, which fell and locked the other sliders in place, so that subsequent tremors could not send other balls in other directions, thus making it possible to detect both the time and the direction of the quake. It should be added that the instrument was magnificently crafted, if any of the reproductions surviving today are credible copies.

The first Western seismograph was designed in France in 1703, and the ones we use today began development in 1848.

B. Papermaking

The making of paper is arguably China's greatest contribution to world culture, since paper made possible the preservation and dissemination of knowledge. "Paper was a brand-new type of writing material. Those used before had been tortoise shell, bone, metals, stones, bamboo slips, wooden tablets and silk . . . None of these materials, however, suited the need. Tortoise shell was scarce, metal and stone cumbersome, silk costly and bamboo slips and wooden tablets took up too much space." (Institute, 1983)

The invention of paper is usually credited to Cai Lun, a eunuch who was Inspector of Public Works during the Han dynasty. In 105 AD, he came up with an affordable and easy to make paper, created from vegetable fibres made from hemp, using rope ends, rags and old fishing nets. The fibres were shredded and boiled, and then pounded into a soggy pulp. Then they were placed on a fine mesh screen in a water filled vat. After being strained, the fibres were left to dry, and the smooth dry fibres on the screen became paper. This process is virtually unchanged today, although the materials used have changed through the years. In fact, the Chinese have made paper from bamboo, rice and wheat straw, sandalwood, hibiscus, seaweed, floss silk, rattan, jute, flax and ramie.

There is evidence that the Chinese made use of paper for many reasons besides writing. It was much coarser and stronger than power today, and was used for clothing, lacquerware and even military armour. "So tough was paper then that it was frequently used as a shoe liner. And paper clothing was so very warm and impenetrable by cold winds that people complained that it allowed no circulation of air round the body and was too hot to wear." (Temple, 1986, p. 82) Paper was also used for wall decoration, and it is possible to trace the use of toilet paper in China back to the sixth century AD. And of course, paper for writing became the setting for Chinese, artistry, and led to the development of calligraphy, water colour painting, and block printing.

The movement of papermaking technology to the West was quite slow, travelling from India and West Asia in the seventh and eighth centuries. Eighth century Arabs sold paper to the Europeans, but would not share the secret of its production. An equivalent paper making industry did not thrive in Europe until 1500 years after its invention in China.

C. Medicine

Although it is impossible to summarize Chinese medicine in three paragraphs, I will briefly discuss some of its basic tenets, hoping to give an idea of how extraordinary and complete a system it is. Traditional Chinese medicine is a completely different system from Western biomedicine, and evidence of its practice dates back to the first century AD, with the *Yellow Emperor's Classic*. Acupuncture needles have been found buried in tombs from before the time of Christ.

Traditional Chinese medicine is holistic in its outlook, taking into account the season, weather, environment, family, diet and situation of the unhealthy person, rather than looking at isolated symptoms. Diagnosis is performed by a series of four functions: looking, listening and smelling (interestingly, these two words are the same in the Chinese language), asking, and touching. Another essential part of diagnosis is the reading of the pulse. The physician takes the pulse in many places, looking for signs of disharmony, since the aim of medicine is to restore the body to harmoniousness. An elaborate system of pulse readings was devised, in which different pulses corresponded to different states of ill health. Illness is said to be caused by blockages in the flow of energy through a series of meridians and channels described in Chinese medical anatomy. Illness is also described as an excess in either yin or yang, the two poles that are the basis for much Chinese philosophy. All things and all parts of things are either yin or yang, the way many European languages classify all nouns as either masculine or feminine. Too much of either is said to be the cause of distress, since the body is thrown into imbalance.

There are several means to effect a cure. The Chinese have one of the most advanced systems of pharmacy, using medications derived mostly from plants, but also from minerals and animals. They practiced diet therapy as far back as 200 AD, and in later years recommended special diets for specific deficiency diseases. They may not have named the vitamins the way we have, but their suggestions for dietary improvements are ones we are just getting our own physicians to incorporate in their suggested therapies today. In addition, herbs are often applied to the skin, or burned and inhaled, in a process called moxibustion, which is a non-invasive, natural form of therapy. Moxibustion's partner in the therapeutic world is acupuncture, in which small needles are inserted into specific spots along the meridians and channels, in order to release the flow of energy and wellness. The Western world has been able to accept the efficacy of acupuncture as an anaesthetic, when in fact it is primarily used to cure diseases.

If this sounds magical to your Western ears, or questionably scientific, then you may wonder why it has survived all these years, and why Western doctors have gone to China to observe surgical procedures practiced without chemical anesthesia, and the curing of diseases from malaria to dysentery without using expensive medications produced in a laboratory. The most obvious answer is that it works. Another is that is more easily accessible to a large rural population than Western medicine is. The fact remains that centuries before Europeans began the practice of experimental medicine, the Chinese had a fully developed and effective medical system which was harmonious with its environment, inexpensive, and successful. In a time of growing dissatisfaction with the cost and outcomes of Western medicine, traditional Chinese medicine has great appeal.

The Chinese contributed greatly to our scientific foundations, and there is a vast literature on Chinese science and medicine that is readily available to teachers and their students.

Islamic Science

"The Arabs not only assimilated Greek science but also made themselves masters of its methods and techniques. Their role did not consist merely of handing over to Europe what they had earlier acquired from the ancients; rather, having digested what they learned from their predecessors, they were able to enrich it by new observations, new results, and new techniques." (Hayes, 1983) It seems to me that either would be a mark of outstanding scientific achievement. In the ninth century AD, the

Muslims translated and disseminated many documents from other cultures, and added their own, sparked by Islam's call to its believers to seek knowledge. Scientific knowledge was not limited to scholars, but was available to a large population. This paper will discuss two areas in which Islamic scientists excelled: mechanical engineering and astronomy.

A. Mechanical Engineering

The evidence for remarkable inventive achievement in the Islamic world is contained in a book often translated as *The Book of Ingenious Devices,* written in 850 by the Banu (sons of) Musa bin Shakir. Most of these are trick vessels: pitchers that can pour hot, cold, or mixed water; a basin with a figure of a bull nearby constructed so that when water is poured into the basin the bull makes a thirsty sound, a flask which discharges nothing when poured the first time, but which works the second time; a trough which replenishes itself when animals drink from it. Islamic ingenuity was used not only for playful gadgetry, but for other feats of engineering and technology such as water-raising machines; water and mechanical clocks; roads and bridges; dams; shipbuilding; textile, paper and leather production, and agriculture and food technology. The Banu Musa were said to be the authors of several mathematics texts, including *On the Trisection of an Angle* and *On the Mesurement of Plane and Spherical Figures*. "They lived during the initial stage of translation, but soon moved to a stage of research and innovation. As scientists and engineers they established an observatory at their own home . . . (and) carried out reliable observations." (al-Hassan, 1986)

B. Astronomy

Islamic scientists also made great advances in observational and mathematical astronomy. Many great observatories were established and funded, and Islamic astronomers were able to correct errors derived from calculations based on the belief that the universe was geocentric (revolving around the earth) rather than heliocentric (revolving around the sun). One of the greatest achievements had to do with being able to calculate the direction of Mecca. Muslims have to face Mecca and pay five times a day. One of the greatest Islamic scientists, al-Biruni, was a political prisoner at one point in his life. While he was being transported to a prison in what is now Afghanistan, he attempted to determine the distance from and direction of Mecca. He was quite successful, and his operations led to the exploration of many related scientific areas such as terrestrial latitude and equinox observations.

In 1007, Ibn Yunus composed "a masterpiece of observational astronomy in which many constants have been measured anew and in which extensive use is made of trigonometry for the solution of astronomical problems. Ibn Yunus was also the first person to make a serious study of the oscillatory motion of a pendulum, which finally led to the invention of the mechanical clock." (Nasr, 1976, p. 101)

The Muslims were also superior crafters of astronomical instruments, and their skill in the construction of astrolabes, instruments for measuring angles in the changing position of the stars and thereby charting their courses, was enormous.

It should also be mentioned that astronomy was often employed in conjunction with a sister science, astrology. In fact, in Arabic, the two words could be used interchangeably. "Although there were some authorities who accepted astronomy and condemned astrology, by and large the two inter-mingled and there was never in Islam the clear distinction that exists in the West today between astronomy considered as a science and astrology as a pseudo-science (with the embarrassing consequence that the supposedly pseudo-science seems to be attracting more Westerners than the science of astronomy itself in this supposedly most rational age of human history.)" (Nasr, 1976, p. 105)

"The Arabic-writing cultures of the medieval Islamic societies supported scientific work more widely and more intensively than any of the societies which preceded them. Many of the findings of their scientists were transmitted to other regions and contributed directly to the further advance of the subject. Other Arabic discoveries were lost, to reappear elsewhere independently. In the centuries that followed the ninth century translation movement, Islamic scientists made significant contributions in all the fields they cultivated, and until the rise of modern science they were the best of their age." (Dallal, 1992)

Literature on Islamic science and technology is also abundant and easy to incorporate into lessons on multi-cultural scientific achievements.

Africa

We all known that the remains of the earliest humans have been found in Africa. Evidence of ancient African science also exists. A bone found in what is now Zaire, in Central Africa, bears markings that indicate it was probably used as a record of months and lunar phases. The bone has been dated from between 9000 and 6500 BC. And we are also all aware that the flooding of the Nile was responsible for the first intensive agricultural schemes. Metallurgy, including the mining and smelting of copper, was practiced in Africa as far back at 4000 BC, and in the next millennium Egyptians developed the system of hieroglyphic writing as well as the use of papyrus to write on. The science of architecture reached new heights with the building of the pyramids, which were amazing accomplishments both in terms of construction and of the mathematical and astronomical knowledge necessary to build and situate them. And, in the years between 3000 and 2500 BC, a calendar and numeration system were developed and a carefully defined medical system was established under the guidance of Imhotep, an African physician and architect.

This section will focus on two aspects of African science: mathematics and medicine. I will discuss the Ishango bone and the African calendar, and surgery and medication in the Egyptian papyri. For those of you who may be unaware of this scholarly debate, I should point out that for many years Egypt was given a place of its own as the source of "civilization." Egypt is, of course, geographically a part of Africa; the Rift valley that begins in Egypt extends to South Africa. And we now know that Egypt was racially a part of Africa as well; examination of papyri and paintings clearly reveals that many Egyptians were black Africans. So Africa has reclaimed Egypt as its own.

A. Mathematics and the Calendar

The markings on the Ishango bone consist of three columns of sets of notches arranged in distinct patterns. "One column has four groups composed of eleven, thirteen, seventeen and nineteen notches; these are the prime numbers between ten and twenty. In another column the groups consists of eleven, twenty-one, nineteen and nine notches, in that order. The pattern here may be 10+1, 20+1, 20–1, and 10–1." (Zaslavsky, 1973) The third column is arranged in a way that suggests a doubling operation. One can conclude from this that the people who made these notations used a base ten number system, knew how to double and were familiar with prime numbers. Besides indicating a system of notation and counting, the bone shows early Africans were marking time. Alexander Marshack, in *The Roots of Civilization,* plotted the marks against a lunar model, and concluded that there was a "close tally between the groups of marks and the astronomical lunar periods." (Marshack, 1972) The Ishango bone provides evidence that 8000 years ago, African people were plotting sequential notation on the basis of a Lunar calendar.

Many ancient cultures counted time. The Egyptian calendar was the first to use a 365 day year. "This calendar is indeed the only intelligent calendar which ever existed in human history." (Neugebauer, 1962) The Egyptians were helped in establishing their calendar by several geographical factors. One is that the Nile floods at the same time every year, and that occurs at the same time that Sirius, the Dog Star, and one of the brightest in the heavens, rises at the same time as the sun. Thus they were able to recognize that day as the start of the new year. They divided the year into three seasons of four months each: flooding, seeding and harvesting. This system based on the lunar cycle would have been fine, except that we know that the year is actually a little more than 5 hours more than 365 days. At first, the priests just added an extra month every few years. But this proved too chaotic, and finally a civil calendar was created which was based on a solar year divided into 12 months of 30 days each, with an extra 5 days tacked on at the beginning. This orderly, easy calendar predated the Aztec calendar by about 3000 years.

Another African contribution to mathematics and the calendar was a correct calculation of the length of the day. In this case, Egyptians were aided by the fact that, because of Egypt's proximity to the Equator, night and day are of equal length, so sun rise and set are very predictable, and the Egyptians were able to make this calculation easily.

B. Surgery and Gynecology

Egyptians were responsible for many medical innovations. In addition to developing an elaborate herbal tradition and many methods of clinical therapy, they devised a code of medical ethics, urging physicians to treat the poor, to take little for themselves, and to live well in order to be able to pass their skills on to their progeny. This section will focus on three areas of medical science: contraception, aborting and circumcision.

"The oldest of all the surviving medical papyri, the Kahun gynaecological Papyrus, which was compiled around 1900 BC during the Middle Kingdom, lists several recipes for contraceptives to be inserted into the vagina. They included pessaries made of honey with a pinch of natron, of crocodile dung in sour milk, or sour milk alone, or of acacia gum. Recently the latter has been recognized as spermatocidal in the presence of vaginal lactic acid, and it is conceivable that sour milk, too, might be an effective spermatocide." (Estes, 1989, p. 58) Celery was also used as a contraceptive. Mixed with equal parts of oil and sweet beer, boiled and taken for four mornings, it was said to prevent conception. A large dose of this mixture was said to induce abortion. (Manniche, 1989) "Dates, Onions and the Fruit-of-the-Acanthus, were crushed in a vessel with Honey, sprinkled on a cloth, and applied to the Vulva. It ensured abortion either in the first, second or third period." (Bryan, 1974) Most societies have tried to find ways of preventing, encouraging, and stopping birth. The Egyptians used plants whose scientific validity has been proven by modern biomedical methods 4000 years later.

The Egyptians were also among the first to practice surgery. Many societies used surgical techniques for ornament (ear piercing) and medicine (bone setting, etc.). The Egyptians were among the first to circumcise men. "It was a ritual performed by priests, probably on large groups of adolescents or young men (but not infants). During the Old Kingdom only royalty, nobility and priests were circumcised routinely. In later centuries the rite may have become obligatory for all pubertal males, perhaps as a precondition of marriage, but it may have been optional or even unavailable for some young men. Regardless of the extent to which circumcision was practiced, it seems to have grown out of the priests' concern for bodily cleanliness and, hence, purity . . . The world's oldest portrayal of circumcision—in fact, the first known picture of any surgical technique—was carved on the wall of a Dynasty VI tomb about 250 years after Imhotep's death. The priest performing the ritual tells his assistant to hold the young man so he won't faint, and tries to make him comfortable. However, it was probably impossible to console a boy about to be circumcised with a stone knife." (Estes, 1989, p. 55)

Native Americans

As a result of recent archaeological findings, many of our ideas about Native American culture and science have changed. The image of nomadic hunter-gatherers has been replaced by that of "budding technocrats who adapted to environmental conditions in quite resourceful ways, carried on extensive trade and intertribal relations over great distances, and developed considerable artistic and technical skills." (Cornell, 1981, pp. 149-50) This paper will focus on two areas of Native American scientific achievement: astronomy and agriculture. I should add that there are many different Native American people, and what holds true for one may not be identical in another culture. However, for our purposes here, we will treat Native Americans as one, and presume that their were enough similarities in astronomical and agricultural practices to make this intellectually acceptable.

A. Astronomy and Architecture

Like some other early cultures, the Aŋasazi situated their dwellings and buildings in accordance with astronomical knowledge. For example, the Pueblo Bonito settlement is arranged in the shape of a D. It has been suggested that "the shape and layout were deliberately conceived to make maximum use of solar energy. The great semicircular shape open to the south is an effective solar collector, with the high northern walls both reflecting the sun's rays into the central plaza in winter and protecting it from the prevailing northwest winds." (Cornell, 1981, pp. 155-6) Other buildings, or sometimes boulders, were assembled in a way that supplies information about the sun's motion, in order to produce a calendar. "Their interactions with light from the rising sun served both ritual and calendrical purposes for the Anasazi who placed them there. The patterns of light and shadow that play along the panel, when watched carefully for a sufficient time, are capable of allowing one to devise a calendar suitable for planting and harvesting. In fact, I believe it would be possible, by watching the forms of the streaks of light several weeks prior to the solstice, to anticipate the arrival of the solstice with an accuracy of within two or three days." (Williamson, 1983)

Other sites were designed so that certain astronomical phenomena, such as equinoxes, were made obvious by the movement of light through holes or windows. At certain times of the year, the light enters a specially placed window and reflects on an altar or other ceremonial spot. This marking of the divisions of the solar year by means of the midday sun, rather than by the rising and setting of the sun, is evidence of an advanced astronomical system.

B. Agriculture

We practice a very advanced form of agricultural technology. Our farms are enormous and highly mechanized. Yield is very high. And yet we find ourselves destroying the land and having to make use of more and more chemicals to fight off insects and keep the soil productive. We do this often at the expense of the workers who produce the food and of the land that supplies it. Native Americans practiced forms of agriculture that were harmonious with the land (even in arid or forested areas) and still highly productive. The system was self-supporting and self-renewing, as the best cultivars were selected and recorded and re-used. Fertilizers were natural, gathered from animals that inhabited the region. "The traditional agricultural system of North and Central America centered on the small field called a *milpa,* which was not cultivated by plowing or planting in neat rows. The Indian farmer made a field of small mounds on which to plant the corn. In contrast to plowed rows, the small mound loses less soil to rain runoff and thus helps to stabilize the soil. While farmers in America adopted the practice, known as killing, and followed it consistently from early colonial times until the 1930s. Since the United States abandoned hilling in favour of dense planting, erosion has increased remarkably." (Weatherford, 1988)

Another area in which Native Americans showed agricultural superiority was in intercropping. We tend to practice monoculture—one field devoted to one crop. They created plots of mixed crops, usually beans, corn and squash. What may look chaotic to our eyes is in fact a wise and sensible polyculture system. The wide leaves from the corn plant protect the beans from the sun; the hardy stalk serves as a stake for the squash and bean vines to grow. The vines provide good ground cover, reducing the need for weeding and helping to keep the soil moist and protect wind and water erosion. The beans in their turn are nitrogen fixers, which encourages the growth of the corn and squash. We would have to provide cover and stakes for the beans, and fill the soil with artificially produced nitrogen and week killers to achieve the same result.

Native American farmers tended to plant seed rather than sow it. Most of the New World crops, such as beans and corn, had large seeds that could not be broadcast, but had to be placed in the earth. This required extensive knowledge of the seed itself, as farmers knew that certain seeds needed to be placed near others in order to increase cross-pollinization and fertilization. Our own biotechnological studies are beginning to reveal what these agricultural scientists knew long before we came. It should also be mentioned that many of the plants cultivated by Native Americans have become staples in the world's diet: corn, beans, potatoes, maple syrup and chocolate.

Conclusion

We think of ourselves as the most scientifically and technologically advanced people ever. In some ways we are. And yet all our science is based on that which came before, often thousands of years before, it was developed in the West. Some systems have expanded and improved on ancient science, and in some cases the ancients appear to have had a more humane and harmonious system that is equally efficient. This paper examined a few of the scientific accomplishments of a few civilizations, in China, Africa, the Middle East and the New

World. It is possible to match each of these with equally astonishing achivements of the Polynesians, Indians, South Americans or Koreans. The world of science is vast and limitless, and every culture has produced its own science, which is a unique reflection of its world view and philosophy. To limit ourselves and our students to the study of one way of looking at medicine, or mathematics, or astronomy, is to deny a world of knowledge that is rich and fascinating. As the Bantu proverb says, "He who never goes visiting thinks mother is the only cook."

REFERENCES

al-Hassan, A.Y., and Hill, D. R.: 1986, *Islamic technology: an illustrated history*, Cambridge University Press, New York, p. 14.

Bryan, C.P.: 1974, *Ancient Egyptian medicine: the Papyrus Ebers*, Ares, Chicago, p. 83.

Cornell, J.: 1981, *The first stargazers: an introduction to the origins of astronomy*. Charles Scribner's Sons, New York, pp. 149-150.

Dallal, A.: 1992 "Islamic science", in Selin, H., *Science across cultures: a bibliography of books on non-Western science and medicine*, Garland Press, New York, in press.

Dugan, K.: 1992, in Selin, H., *Science across cultures: a bibliography of books on non-Western science and medicine*, Garland Press, New York, in press.

Estes, J.W.: 1989, *The medical skills of ancient Egypt*, Science History Publications/USA, Canton, MA, p. 58.

Ezeabasili, N.: 1977, *African science: myth or reality*, Vantage, New York.

Graubard, M.: 1953, *Astrology and alchemy*, Philosophical Library, New York, p. vii.

Hayes, J.R., ed.: 1983, *The genius of Arab civilization: source of Renaissance*, Second edition, MIT Press, Cambridge, MA, p. 163.

Institute of the History of Natural Sciences, China Academy of Sciences, 1983, *Ancient China's technology and science*, Foreign Languages Press, Beijing, p. 176.

Manniche, L.: 1989, *An ancient Egyptian herbal*, University of Texas Press, Austin, p. 76.

Marshack, A.: 1972, *The roots of civilization*, McGraw-Hill, New York, p. 30.

Nasr, S.H.: 1976, *Islamic science: an illustrated study,* World of Islam Festival Publishing Company, p. 101.

Neugebauer, O.: 1962, *The exact sciences in antiquity,* Harper, New York, p. 81.

Temple, R.: 1986, *The genius of China: 3,000 years of science, discovery and invention,* Simon and Schuster, New York.

Weatherford, J. M.: 1988, *Indian givers: how the Indians of the Americas transformed the world.* Crown, New York, p. 82.

Williamson, R.A.: 1983, "Light and shadow, ritual, and astronomy in Anasazi structures", in Carlson, J.B. and Judge, W.J., eds., *Astronomy and ceremony in the prehistoric Southewest,* Maxwell Museum of Anthropology, University of New Mexico, Albuquerque p. 111. (Papers of the Maxwell Museum of Anthropology, number 2).

Zaslavsky, C.: *Africa counts: number and pattern in African culture,* Prindle, Weber & Schmidt, Boston, p. 18.

13

An Issue of Cultural Diversity in Science

ALOK KUMAR & PATRICK KENEALY
Califormia State University, USA

Introduction

Today the North American continent appears to be undergoing new waves of immigration that may pose major problems if enclaves of various cultures are isolated from each other's viewpoints, roots, and contributions. An idea of "tolerance of diversity" when interpreted as "enduring differences" is thin and fragile. A much more solid foundation for a diverse society is respect and appreciation for the achievements of many cultures. This latter attitude is often the *raison d'etre* of the recent push for the establishment of university courses that have "a multicultural component". So far, these additions or modifications seem to have taken place primarily in the liberal arts, with little effect so far appearent in science-related courses.

Every race and culture in the past has found intellectual satisfaction, pride, and material benefits in attempting to understand the world's physical and biological phenomena and the place of humans in the universe. Each culture may have a distinctive method of recognizing, approaching, and transmitting knowledge in science and technology. Further, each may have used a distinctive way to solve to their satisfaction the issues that arise. Modern science certainly did not spring into existence full grown with the Renaissance in Europe. Influences came from all parts of the world like a thousand capillary vanules joining to form the vena cave magna.

We propose that history and philosophy of science courses, whether already established or newly formed, use a significant fraction of semester time to explore multi-cultural contributions. As part of his effort, we wish to discuss some details of the contributions of the Indus Valley Civilization, namely, India, to science.

Neglected Chapters in the History of Science

One of the general orientations of science-history books in our culture is to place the origins of scientific thought in the ancient Greek tradition, and then trace their development in Medieval Europe. Greek philosophers are considered directly responsible for the initiation of many scientific theories. In the development of mathematics and astronomy, Greece was likely indebted to Mesopotamia and Egypt, Islam to India, Greece, Iran, and Western Europe to Islam. Most of the work of the Greeks entered Europe via Spain by means of Arabic, not Latin, manuscripts. From science texts, one generally gets the impression that experimental science started in Europe, perhaps with Galileo about 400 years back. Hardly any scientific thought has its origin assigned to other civilizations of the past. Arab cultures has escaped from this list of the absent due to the Arab presence in Medieval Europe.

In what follows we cannot and do not wish in any sense to establish claims of priority of any culture on workable ideas of science that have persisted to become more fully developed in the modern era. The ideas of physical and biological science, of mathematics, of astronomy and the physical place of humans in the universe are articulated in many cultures in qualitative and quantitative ways.

As part of our contributions to a multicultural sense of scientific knowledge, we wish to look in particular at information available from India about some ideas that often receive heavy emphasis in current texts on the history of science. India has produced and articulated significant contributions in mathematics, astronomy, medicine, and philosophy. The place-value system of numbers, trigonometry, a well evolved system of medicine, detailed anatomical knowledge of human body, circulation of blood, and similarities of living plants, animals, and humans were generally known in India much before these concepts were introduced in the western world.

On the contribution of the ancient Indians, the noted philosopher-scientist Henry Margenau writes (1978, p. XXX): "[A] connection with philosophy is evident . . . in the sacred literature of the East, where we find Rig-veda [Rig-Veda] . . . replete with discoveries and views regarding the physical world . . . which are usually ignored in American course on the history of science."

Margenau mentions several topics: the spherical shape of the earth, the seven colours of sunlight, the earth is suspended in space, the sun never sets or rises, the moon reflects sunlight, and other concepts in the Rig-Veda. Margenau further points out that one of ". . . the most remarkable features which I have never seen in American text books on the history of science, is the atomic theory of philosopher Kanada (about 500 BC)." (1978, p. XXX). We will say a little more about these topics later in this paper.

In what follows we will first give a few general citations regarding the contributions of early Indian science and mathematics. Then we will discuss a perhaps unexpected kind of connection between religion and science, and the source of a major way of transmitting knowledge that allowed information to exist in a way that even allowed Indian libraries to be restored after the destruction of their contents. We also briefly describe the organization of Indian literature to provide some context for how the information was handled. We then briefly cite various sources on some specific topics in astronomy, in mathematics and trigonometry, in medicine, and about Kanada's notion of atoms.

Finally, we will also refer to a recent English translation (Salem and Kumar, 1991) of a medieval Arabic manuscript on the history of science, *Science in the Medieval World,* from a manuscript Ṭabaqāt al-Umam, by Ṣā'id al-Andalusī, an eleventh-century Islamic natural philosopher in Spain, as a source of information about some of the contributions of various cultures to science. Ṣā'id refers to the science of India, Persia, Chaldea, Egypt, Greece, the Arab-Orient, Spain, and some other countries.

General Comments

It is important to have some knowledge of the chronology of various civilizations. The main philosophical contributions from Greece started mainly with the work of Thales or Pythagoras during the sixth century BC. Indian traditions have their roots in the manuscript of Rig-Veda that is about 3500 years old or earlier. Keith appropriately writes (1925, p. 601):

> It is not to be thought that the early philosophy of Greece exercised any influence on the philosophy of India. Apart from every other consideration, it is clear that the rise of philosophy in Greece was long subsequent to the beginnings of Indian philosophy in the hymns of Rigveda [Rig-Veda], and from those hymns the history of that philosophy presents itself in the light of an ordered development . . . The only question, therefore, which can arise is whether the early schools of Greek philosophy were effected by the tenets of the schools of the Brahmans.

Such a view is shared by many other philosophers of antiquity who were conversant with the Indian literature. Here were some observations from some philosophers of the first millennium:

Beginning at the beginning, al-Jāḥiz (AD c.776-868), a 9th-century Arab philosopher-scientist from Baghdad writes (Pellat, 1969, p. 198), "When Adam descended from Paradise, it was to their land [India] that he made his way." Sebokht, a Christian bishop at Qinnesrin in North Syria/Iraq was of the opinion that many cultures had contribution in the Arab scientific pool. Seobkht, in the year AD 662, writes (Dutta and Singh, 1938, vol.I, p. 96, Clark, 1929, p. 220):

> I will omit all discussion of the science of the Hindus [Indians], a people not the smae as Syrians, their subtle discoveries in the science of astronomy, discoveries which are more ingenious than those of the Greeks and the Babylonians; their valuable method of calculation; their computing that surpasses discription. I wish only to say that this computation is done by means of nine signs. If those who believe because they speak Greek, that they have

reached the limits of science should know these things, they would be convinced that there are also others who know something.

Ṣā'id al-Andalusī, the 11th-century Islamic natural philosopher of Spain, writes (Salem and Kumar, 1991, p. 11):

> The first nation (to have cultivated science) is India. These is a powerful nation having a large population, and a rich kingdom (possession). India is known for the wisdom of its people. Over many centuries, all the kings of the past have recognized the ability of the Indians in all branches of knowledge, . . . The Indians to all nations for many centuries, are the metal (essence) of wisdom, the source of fairness and objectivity. They are peoples of sublime pensiveness, universal apologues, and useful and rare inventions.

A Coalition of Religion and Science

There is an interesting, and perhaps unexpected, connection between religion and science in India. Ancient Indian science is an essential and integral part of Indian religions. The growth in science has never been a hindrance to a spiritual growth in the history of India. That is in contrast to several other regions where the people had to make a choice between science and religion. In Indian traditions, secular knowledge (Aar-a-vidy-a) is considered to be helpful to spiritual knowledge (Par-a-vidy-a), as advised in Munkaka-Upanishad (1: 1: 3-5) (Hume, 1989, p. 366). In ancient Indian literature, knowledge is procured by "tark" (logic), "anubhuti" (intuition), and "anubhav" (experience) that are common to religion and science. The understanding of phenomena is the primary task. Most ancient Indian religion, like the modern science, is a dynamic system rather than a static one; it changes and evolves. al-Mas'-ud-i, a tenth-century Islamic historian from Baghdad, considers India as a country where science and technology is without the aid of prophets. In India, in his opinion, "the wise men could deduce the principles without the benefit of the revealed laws." al-Mas'-ud-i considers India as the land of "virtue and wisdom" (Khalidi, 1975, p. 102-106).

Ch-andogya-Upanishad (VII: 1:2,4) (Hume, 1989, p. 250), a holy book of the Hindus, cities an episode where the vagabond-deity, N-arada, approaches another sage Sanatkum-ara to learn ultimate knowledge. Sanatkum-ara asks for the various arts and sciences that N-arada has already mastered. In his list, Narada points out astronomy (Naksatra-vidy-a), mathematics (r-asi-vidy-a), logic, history (itih-asa-Pur-aṇa), grammar (vedn-am vedam), and fine arts, along with the four veda. Thus, natural science is considered an important knowledge to be learned for balanced spiritual growth.

Aryahaṭṭa I (born AD 476), a noted astronomer in India, known for his heliocentric theory of solar system, in his book Ārybhaṭiya, writes (Clark, 1930, p. 20): "whoever knows Dasgitika Sutra [a section in his book] which describes the movements of the Earth and the planets in the sphere of the asterisms [stars] passes through the paths of the planets and asterisms and go to the higher brāhman [God]."

In India, religious literature is not just moral codes or the discription of a heaven and hell. In understanding the nature of the physical world, these scriptures do not use an approach which appeals to design or purpose. For example, such a non-teleological approach is evident in the theory of creation described in Rig-Veda (X: 7: 2,3).

> These heavenly bodies were produced with blast and smelting, like a smith. Existence, in the earlier age of Gods, came from non-existence . . . Who verily knows and who can declare it, whence it [the world] was born? The Gods are later than this world's production. Who knows then whence it first came? He [God], the first origin of this creation, whether He formed it all or did not form it, Whose eye controls this world in the highest heaven, *He verily knows it—or perhaps He knows not.*

This expression has a modern favour, as noted in a comment by the physicist, Carl Sagan: "The Hindu holy book, the Rigveda (X:129) has a much more realistic view of the matter [Theory of Creation]."

Mathematics in India may have evolved in observing religious ritualistic practices. India festivals are observed on dates and time determined by using an astronomical map that requires rigorous mathematical calculations and a sound knowledge of the motion of celestial objects. The rising and setting of the sun, the moon, and the planets are needed for various religious observances that can only be predicted with the knowledge of arithmetic, algebra, geometry, and trigonometry along with astronomical observations. The Sanskrit word for mathematics is "Ganiita"—the science of calculation. However, Cajori (1980, p. 83) writes: "Of the development of Indian mathematics we know but little. A few manuscripts bear testimony that the Hindus had climbed to a lofty height, but thier path of ascent is no longer traceable." The process of acquiring knowledge might indeed be obscure but the Indian manuscripts clearly establish that the well developed mathematical tools were available to ancient Indians.

We have mentioned the Rig-Veda and an Upanishad. Since much of historical Indian science is embedded in Indian literature, we will again be referring to various classical documents. It would perhaps be useful to briefly outline Indian literature and establish a rough chronology. Table 13.1 provides some information.

In the remainder of this part of the paper on ancient Indian science and mathematics, we will briefly discuss some specific topics as reflected in the Indian literature. We mention first the use of poetry and codes in mathematics.

Poetic Mathematics

Indian mathematical results were often put into verses, clothed in obscure and mystical language that, though well adapted to aid the memory or those who already understood the subject, is often unintelligible to the uninitiated. These mathematical formulae, written in religious verses, can only be understood with an expertise in mathematics and Sanskrit language.

In ancient Indian tradition, disciples lived with the teacher to acquire knowledge. The attitude was that sacred knowledge should not be shared with an uninitiated person, an attitude similar to Pythagorean tradition. This was not to make learning a privilege, but an attempt to avoid the ridicule of a person not trained in their system of knowledge. Also, books tended to use elaborate secret codes, with symbols and inflexions that made no sense to someone not trained in the particular coded system of the author. This encryption of ideas has been frequently used in Indian literature. For example, Cāṇakya, in his book

Table 13.1: A Brief Outline and Rough Chronology of Indian Literature

The commonly called "vedas" were written in the sequence given to the right. Vedas are extremely rich in their poetic essence; they describe the splendor of the dawn and dusk, the beauty and grace of women, the appreciation of nature, and the mysteries of nature. The vedic hymns unite the imagery and melody of human fascination into a complete whole.	**"Vedas"** 1. Rig-Veda, 2. Sām-Veda, 3. Yajur-Veda, and 4. Atharva-Veda.
Next in chronology in the Indian literature are Brāhmanias that extend philosophical discussions on vedic doctrines. During the same period, a sacred book of Buddhism, Lalitivistara, was written that describes an established number system and large numbers.	The main **Brāhmanias** are: Aitareya, Satpatha, Taittiriya, Kaushitiki, and Gopatha.
Upanishads were generally written after Brāhmanas, and are, in general, the commentaries by various scholars on vedas. There are some 250 Upanishads, of which roughly 100 are more popularly known. Fourteen are called principal Upanishads, and are given to the right.	**Principal Upanishads** Isa, Māndukya, Svetāsvatara, Kena, Taittiriya, Kaushitaki, Kathā, Àitareya, Mahānārāyna, Mundaka, Chāndogya, Maitri, Parasana, Brihad-āranyaka.
Purānas are last in order, and embraces the whole Indian mythology, comprising eighteen books.	**Purāṇas:** Matsya, Mārkandeya, Bhaviśya, Bhāgvata, Brahmanda, Brahmavairta, Brahma, Vāmana, Varāha, Visnu, Vāyu, Agni, Nārada, Padma, Linga, Garāda, Kurma, and Skanda.

Arthsāstra, advocates that a king should be trained in cryptography to communicate secret messages to avoid any leak.

The poetic form of mathematical formulae has rather severe interpretive limitations; it is difficult to a person who is not trained in the Indian poetic tradition to grasp the meaning. One can take a crash programme in the German, Russian, or French languages to understand the scientific literature, but the same crash programme may not help at all with German, Russian, or French poetry. It can be difficult to understand a hidden meaning in a poem even after a long familiarity with the language.

al-Birūnī mentions how Indians have learned the abstract thoughts with joy and passion from their rhythmic poetry (Sachau, 1964, vol. I, p. 137):

> By composing their books in meters they [Indians] intend to facilitate their being learned by heart, and to prevent people in all questions of science ever recurring [referring] to a written text, save in case of bare necessity. For they think that the mind of man sympathizes with everything in which there is symmetry and order, and has an aversion to everything in which their is no order. Therefore most Hindus are passionately fond of their verses, and always desirous of reciting them, even it they do not understand the meaning of words, and the audience will snap their fingers in token of joy and applause.

Accustomed to put history and even astronomy and mathematics into verse, several alternative ways were developed, for the sake of rhythm in chanting, of giving the numbers that were involved in the verses. A detailed list of such words is compiled by Datta and Singh (1938, vol. I, p. 55). In this system, along with various words for numerals, the Sanskrit alphabets are used to depict a mathematical formula or a number. The rules of conversions from Sanskrit alphabets to mathematical number are well defined, and are known in many cases. Karpinski (1965, p. 42) has given a good analogy of such a system. He uses, in his analogical system, the consonants of the English language as follows:

b	c	d	f	g	h	j	k	l	m	n	p	q	r	s	t	v	w	x	y	z
1	2	3	4	5	6	7	8	9	0	1	2	3	4	5	6	7	8	9	0	1

The vowels help in forming the words, and are not associated with any number. For example, the number 1492 can be depicted by choosing various possible consonants for 1, 4, 9, 2, and inserting the vowels to complete the word. Thus "near lace" or "be real ice" can represent the number 1492 in this system. This is a cumbersome task despite a larger number of consonants and vowels in Sanskrit language. Karpinski points out the limitation of poetic approach to mathematics (1965, p. 42), saying the following: "Apparently those Indians who used this system had a great deal of time to spend on thinking up the words."

"This is likely to be true. Vedas and other Indian scriptures were generally memorized by scholars, as practice which has an unexpected dividend. Even today, vadas and other Indian literature are learned by heart by millions of devoted Indians as they did long before the invasion of Alexander. Indian literature could be restored from the lips of religious teachers in its original form if every manuscript or printed copy of them were destroyed. While the Egyptians, with the burning of Alexandrian library, lost much precious knowledge, Indians have managed to keep their cultural heritage and scientific knowledge intact for several centuries despite dominating and suppression by foreign-rulers. Many times in the history of India, libraries were burned and then were able to be reproduced. I-tsing, the Chinese traveller who visited India during seventh century AD, witnessed persons who could recite 100,000 verses of vedas (Takakusu, 1966, p. 182).

On Indian Numerals

Georges Ifrah in his book, From One to Zero, on the history of numeration, writes (1985, p. 428):

> "Our modern written numeration, of Indian origin, seems so obvious to us that it is difficult for us to realize its profundity and importance. Our civilization uses it unthinkably, so to speak, and as a result we tend to be unaware of its merits. But no one who consdiers the history of numerical notations can fail to be struck by the ingenuity of our system, because its use of the zero concept and the place-value principle gives it an enormous advantage over most of the other systems that have been devised through the centuries."

The invention of numerals, with its place-value notation, was a milestone in the growth of abstract mathematics and its extension to the physical world, a connection between "a priori" and "posteriori world." Nicholas Copernicus (AD 1473-1543), the Polish astronomer who gave us the heliocentric model of the solar system, writes on the usefulness of Indian numerals (Rosen, 1978, p. 27), saying: "This [Indian] numeral notation certainly surpasses every other, whether Greek or Latin, in lending itself to computations with exceptional speed. For this reason I have accepted [them]." Copernicus also used the Indian numeral system in his calculations on the heliocentric model of our solar system.

On Trigonometry

Trigonometry is a branch of science which deals with specific functions of angles and their application to calculations in geometry. Such studies unite other disciplines of arithmetic, algebra, geometry, and astronomy.

The origin of the word "sine" is not often ascribed to India, but in fact it can be traced to Sanskrit. The word "sine" is called "*jyā*" in Sanskrit language, transformed from the Sanskrit word "jīvā" indicating the chord of an arc. Arabs distorted the pronunciation to the word "jaib" that means a lace fold or pocket used in Arabic clothes of the time. It was called "sinus" in Latin as a literal translation from Arabic. From the Encyclopedia Brittanica (1989, vol. 23, p. 605) comes the following coment:

> "The most significant contribution of India to medieval mathematics is in trigonometry. For a circle of unit radius the length of an arc is a measure of the angle it subtends at the centre of the circle. The Greeks, to felicitate calculations in geometry, tabulated values of the chord of arcs. This method was replaced by Indian mathematicians with half chord of an arc, known as sine of the angle . . . No influence on the West was exerted by the development in India . . . Thus methods had been known in India were not rediscovered until 1624 by the French mathematician Claude-Gaspar Bachet, sieur de Meziriac."

Āryabhaṭṭa I (born AD 476), gives the table of sines of the angles, and explains various properties related to it (Clark, 1930). Paṁca-Siddhanta of Varāha-Mihira (c. AD 505) explains the nature of sine and cosine functions (Sūrya-siddānta, II: 34-37).

A detailed list of values can be found in Srinivasiengar (1967, p. 48).

On Antronomy

Colebrooke writes (1817, p. XXII):

> the Hindus [Indians] had undoubtedly made some progress at an early period in the astronomy cultivated by them for the regulation of time. Their calendar, both civil and religious, was governed chiefly, not exclusively, by the moon and sun: and the motions of these luminaries were carefully observed by them: and with success, that their determination of the moon's synodical revolution, which was what they were principally concerned with, is a much more correct one than the Greeks ever achieved. They had a division of the ecliptic into twenty-seven and twenty-eight parts, suggested evidently by the moon's period in days: and seemingly their own: it was certainly borrowed by the Arabians.

Arabic literature indicates that significant roots of astronomical ideas can be found in the literature from the Indus Valley civilization. For astronomical observations, rules of geometry were defined and astrolabes were constructed. al-Jāhiz (AD 776-868) writes (Pellet, 1969, p. 198) that the Indians "were the originators of . . . astronomical reckoning, subsequently adopted by rest of the world."

From the early Christian era, Arab merchants visited India for trade. The second Abbāsid Caliph, al-Munstūr (AD 712-775) brought an Indian astronomer, in AD 773, to the Arab world, and Indian works that include astronomical treatises were translated into Arabic, and called Sindhind. In the words of Ṣā'id al-Andalusī (Salem and Kumar, 1991, p. 46): "al-Manṣūr ordered that the book be translated into Arabic so that it could be used by Arab astronomers as the foundation for understanding celestial motions. Muhammad ibn Ibrahim al-Fazārī accepted the charge and extracted from it the book that astronomers called al-Sindhind."

The Sindhind system played an important role in the Medieval world. In fact, the famous Toledan astronomical tables were compiled by Azzarqali, a student of Ṣā'id al-Andalusī in 11th-century Spain, and were based on the Sindhind system. Many Arab scholars such as Khwarizmi and al-Fazāri studied it and compiled their own tables, based on Sindhind system.

On the Shape of Earth

al-Birūnī writes (Sachau, 1964, vol. 1, p. 233): "According to the religious traditions of Hindus [Indians] the earth is on which we live is round." He then quotes Varāhmihir (fifth century), an Indian astronomer, to indicate the spherical shape of earth (Sachau, 1964, vol. 1, p. 272):

> Mountains, seas, trees, cities, men, and angels, all are around the globe of the earth. And if Yamakoti [or Yavakoti, eastern part of Java, Indonesia] and Rum [Rome] are opposite to each other, one could not say the one is low in its relation to the other, since the low does not exist . . . *all of them are around the globe like the blossoms springing on the branches of Kadamba-tree.* They encircle it on all sides, but each individual blossom has the same position as the other, neither the one hanging downward nor the standing upright. For the earth attracts that which is upon her, for it [the earth] is the below towards all directions, and heaven is the above towards all directions.

Varāhmihir was certainly not the first person to compare the shape of earth with Kādamba flower. Āryabhaṭṭa I (born AD 476) uses a similarly analogy of kādamba flower and earth (Clark, 1930, Gola, 5-7).

> Half of the sphere of the earth, the planets, and the asterisms [stars] is darkend by their shadows, and half, being turned toward the sun, is lighted according to their size . . . The sphere of the earth, being quite round, situated in the center of space, in the middle of the circle of asterisms, surrounded by the orbits of the planets, consist of water, earth, fire, and air . . . *Just as the ball formed by a kadamba flower is surrounded on all sides by blossoms just so the earth is surrounded on all sides by all creatures terrestrial and aquatic."*

On a Heliocentric Universe

Despite the apparent contradiction between the statement that the round Earth is "situated in the center of space", Āryabhatta I (Clark, 1930, Dagitika, 1-2) seems to explain the motion of Mercury and Venus as in a heliocentric model and not in a geocentric model, at least according to a detailed analysis given by Van der Waerden (King and Saliba, 1987, p. 525). Van der Waerden notes that Āryabhatta's assignment of a rotating Earth is not needed in a geocentric model, and argues that the geometrical constructions in the given geocentric model are possible derived from a heliocentric model. He cites "traces" of numbers and constructions that have little meaning without reference to a heliocentric theory. Van der Waerden writes (King and Saliba 1987, p. 534): "It is highly probable that the system of Āryabhata was derived from a heliocentric theory by setting the center of the earth at rest." The reason for this kind of torturous path in Āryabhatta's work is only indicated vaguely by Van der Waerden as perhaps due to an overwhelming tendency among all early astronomers and their students "to get away from the idea of a motion of the Earth."

On the Movement and Rotation of the Earth

Regarding the motion of earth in his heliocentric model, Aryabhaṭṭa I writes (Clark, 1930, Gola 9) that Earth is moving in axial rotation and the heaven is at rest. It is an illusion that we notice the motion of the stars. To explain the apparent motion of sun, Āryabhatta I [born AD 476] uses an analogy of a boat in a river." As a man in a boat going forward sees a stationary object moving backward just so a Laṁka [Sri-Lankal] man sees the stationary asterisms moving backward in a straight line." He depicts the Earth as rotating eastward.

al-Birīnī (AD 973-1050), when he visited India some six hundred years after Āryabhaṭṭa I, criticized Indian philosophers for a heliocentric universe theory. al-Birīnī refers to the 5th-century the work of Varāhmihir (Pamcasiddhānta XII: 67) to support his idea of geocentric universe (Sachau, 1964, vol. I, p. 276). Varāhmihir said that "If that [eastward motion or rotation] were the case, a bird would not return to its nest as soon as it had flown away from it towards the west," and (p. 277) "stones and trees would fall." A similar argument was used by Aristotel (384-322 BC) to favour his theory of the geocentric universe.

On Atoms

Kanada wrote a book, Vaiśeṣika-Sūtra (Sinha, 1911), in which he proposed that matter is made up of small particles, called parmāṇa (atom). Kanada's description is based on the impossibility of infinite division of matter. A parmāṇu is not visible; the non-perception of atoms disappears when they mass together to form a combination of three double-atoms, a combination which does assume visibility (Vaiśeṣika-Sūtra, IV: 1: 4). The shape of atom is spherical (Vaiśeṣika-Sūtra, VII: 1: 20). Cyril Bailey compares the Indian description of atoms with the Greek description, and writes (1964, p. 64):

> It is interesting to realize that at an early date Indian philosophers had arrived at an atomic explanation of the universe. The doctrines of this school were expounded by Vaicesika Sūtra [Vaiśeṣika-Sūtra] and interpreted by the aphorisms of Kanada. . . Kanada works out the idea of their combinations in a detailed system, which reminds us at once of the Pythagoreans and in some respect of modern science, holding that two atoms combined in a binary compound and three of these binaries in a traid which would be of a size to be perceptible to senses.

On Medicine

Indian medicinal herbs, compounds, and medical knowledge are mentioned in numerous places in the historical literature. Aelianus, Calusius, second century Romans who served Emperor Hadrian, writes (1958, IV: 41): "So let us compare Indian and Egyptian drug and see which of the two was to be preferred. On the one hand the Egyptian drug repelled and suppresed sorrow for a day, whereas the Indian drug caused a man to forget his trouble for ever." It is unclear exactly what this last phrase meant. Athenaeus tells us that Hindu king, Chandragupta Maurya (Sandrocottus), sent aphrodisiac Indian herbs to the Greek Emperor for sexual arousal and retention (Deipnosophists: 18). Ṣā'id al-Andalusī writes (Salem and Kumar, 1991, p. 12): "They [Indians] have surpassed all the other peoples in their knowledge of medical science and the strength of various drugs, the characteristics of compounds and the peculiarities of substances."

Arab medicine laid the guiding principles for the European medicine till the seventeenth century and name of "Caraka" is repeatedly mentioned in medieval-Latin, Arabic, and Persian literature on medicine (Weber, 1961, p. 271; Royle, 1837, p. 153). Caraka-Saṁhitā is a treatise of medicine from India. An Arabic translation of Caraka-Saṁhitā is mentioned by al-Birūnī (AD 973-1050) (Sachau, 1964, p. XXVIII).

Filliozat, an authority on the history of medicine, asserts on the presence of the Indian ayurvedic system in Hipppocratic writings indicating a communication between Indian and Greece. Filliozat writes (1964, p. 253):

> Indices furnished by chance positively tell us on the other hand that Indian data in medicine had been received in the Greek medical circles where an hippocratic manual namely 'On woman's Diseases' had been elaborated; this manual being quite generally considered as Cnidian [Cnidus, an ancient city in Asia Minor].

Human, animals, and plants, in Indian literature, are considered as different stages of a same life form; the assumed kinship of humans with plants and animals is evident in Indian literature. Brahadāranyaka-Upanishad compares man with a tree (III: 9: 28; Hume, 1989, p. 126). To modern ears, it seems more metaphorical than was probably intended by its author.

> A man is indeed like a mighty tree; his hairs are like his leaves and his skin is its outer bark. The blood follows from the skin (of a man), so does the sap from the skin (of a tree). Thus blood flows from a wounded man in the same manner as sap from the tree that is struck. His flesh (corresponds to what is) within the inner bark, this nerves are as though the inner fibres (of a tree). His bones lie behind his flesh as the wood lies behind the soft tissues. Marrow (of a human bone) resembles the pith (of a tree)."

The Indians perceived a common connection between plants, animals and humans, and the importance of trees for human life. This is a major reason that it became a religious code to preserve plant-life. An unnecessary cutting of a tree was against social and religious doctrines. Asoka, a king in India known for his Mayura empire and the propagation of Buddhism, made a strict law against a demolition of trees.

On Some Other Cultures Mentioned By Ṣā'id Al-Andalusī in Tabaqāt Al-Umam

We will just provide a few comments by Ṣā'id al-Andalusī on the other cultures he considered in his survey of science in the medieval world. According to Ṣā'id, most of the contributions to science were made by the seven nations: India, Persia, Chaldea, Greece, Egypt, Arab-Orient, and Spain. Ṣā'id further subdivided the scientific contributions of Greece into the contributions of Greeks and Romans. Similarly, he divided the contributions of Chaldea into the race of the Chaldeans, the Arabs, and the Hebrews.

Ṣā'id dealt with practically all aspects of human knowledge; the book discusses philosophy, religion, political science, geometry, mathematics, natural sciences, the arts, poetry, geography, climate, languages, and human behaviour. He collectively called them 'ulum (sciences). This is typical of the Middle Ages. A servant was not valued for his/her detailed knowledge in any specialized field, but for his/her complete mastery of culture in encyclopedic proportions.

Ṣā'id placed India first in his list of ordering nations in their contribution to science. In specifics, he mentions of India's contributions to philosophy, medicine, mathematics, and astronomy. He provides detailed information on how Indian astronomical system, Sindhind, made impact on scholars in Arabia and Spain.

All quotations below are from Salem and Kumar, 1991. In the words of Ṣā'id (p.16), "the most noted traits of the Persians are the following: their great interest in the study of medicine and their profound knowledge of the positions of stars and the effect of the stars on the lower world (astrology). They had ancient observatories to study the planets and they had devised various systems to describe their motions." Ṣā'id specifically mentions the work of Abū Ma'shar.

For the Chaldeans, Ṣā'id writes (p.18): "There were many great scholars and well established servants who contributed generously to all the branches of human knowledge, especially mathematics and theology. They had particular interest in the observations of planets and carefully searched through the secrets of the skies. They had well-established knowledge in the nature of the stars and their influence. They knew of the properties and strength of the various [chemical] compounds." He placed Hermes of Babylon to be the best-known and the noblest Chaldean scholar.

Ṣā'id placed Greek language as "one of the richest and noblest of all languages." (p. 21) In his view (p. 21), "the Greek philosophers are the highest tabaqat [class] of people and the most respected among the people of knowledge; this is because of the true care that they have demonstrated in cultiviting all branches of knowledge, including mathematical sciences, logic, natural philosophy, and theology, as well as the political sciences, logic, natural philosophy, and theology, as well as the political sciences, logic, national philosophy, and theology." He considered Pythagoras, Empedocles, Plato, and Aristotle to be the most noted philosophers of Greece.

On Egypt, Ṣā'id divides the history in two parts: before the flood and after the flood. According to him, Hermes the First was the most noted scientist before the flood. Hermes, in Ṣā'id's opinion, is the person who built the great pyramids. "On the walls of the pyramids he (Hermes) drew all forms of technical equipment and devices and described all aspects of science, intending to preserve them for future generations, because he was afraid they might be lost to the world." (p. 36)

After the flood, in the words of Ṣā'id (p. 36), Egyptian scientists "were knowledgeable in all aspects of science and philosophy, including mathematics, the physical sciences, and theology. They (Egyptians) excelled in the composition of talismans, Fiteh charms, burning mirrors, chemistry, and others." Ṣā'id also mentioned the fact that Pythagoras went to Egypt to learn philosophy (p. 21). Ṣā'id mentioned the contributions of the Arab-Orient with an emphasis on the contributions of Abbāsid dynasty. These contributions are related to astronomy, mathematics, philosophy, medicine, geometry, and genetics.

Being born and raised in Spain, Ṣā'id provided an excellent account on the scientific activities in Muslim Spain. Spain was a center of learning during the Middle Ages. Ṣā'id mentioned the good quality astronomical instruments and astronomical tables compiled by Spanish philosophers, based on the Sindhind system. In his views (p. 71), "none of the scientists of al-Andalus (Spain) paid much attention to the study of natural sciences or theology . . . . Similarly, medical science was not well understood by the people of al-Andalus and none of its scientists progressed to lead in this field."

Finally, in a modern context, we have said nothing of the contributions of the native peoples of North and South America. The scientific knowledge of ancient and medieval America is still being established; the research is relatively new. We confess our own ignorance of much detailed knowledge those topics, and hope to improve that in the future. Once again, although we have focused on our special interest in speaking of ancient India, we want to reiterate that we have not wished in any sense to establish claims of priority of any culture on workable ideas of science, but simply to call attention to neglected areas in education on the history of science, at least as they are reflected in current university coursework.

REFERENCES

Aelianus, Claudius: 1958, On the *Characteristics of Animals,* Trans. A. F. Scholfield, Harvard University Press.

Bailey, C.: 1964, *The Greek Atomists and Epicurus,* Russell and Russell, New York.

Cajori, F.:1980, A History of Mathematics, Chelsea Publishing Company, New York.

Clark, W.E.: 1929, *Indian Studies in the honor of Charles Rockwell,* Harvard University Press.

Clark, W.E.: 1930, The Āryabhatia of Āryabhata, The University of Chicago Press, Illinois.

Colebrook, H.T. (trans.): 1817, *Algebra with Arithmetic and Mensuration from the Sanscrit of Brahemegupta and Bhascara,* John Murray, London.

Dutta, B.B. and A.N. Singh: 1938, *History of Hindu Mathematics,* Asia Publishing House, New York. 2 vols.

Filliozat, J.: 1964, *The Classical Doctrines of Indian Medicine,* Munshirm Manoharlal, New Delhi.

Hume, R.E.: 1989, *The Thirteen Principal Upanishads,* Oxford University Press, Bombay.

Ifrah, G.: 1985, *From One to Zero,* Viking Penguin Inc., New York.

Karpinski, L.C.: 1978, The History of Arithmetic, Russell and Russell, New York.

Keith, A.B.: 1925, reprinted 1917, *The Religion and Philosophy of the Veda and Upanishads,* Greenwood Press, Connecticut.

Khalidi, T.: 1975, *Islamic Historiography,* State University of New York, Albany.

King, D.A. and G. Saliba: 1987, From Deferent to Equant, *Annals of the New York Academy of Sciences,* volume 500, New York Academy of Sciences, New York.

Margenau, H.: 1978, *Physics and Philosophy*, D. Reidel Publishing Company, London.

Pellat, C.: 1969, The Life and Works of Jahiz, University of California Press, Los Angeles.

Rosen, E. (trans.): 1978, *On the Revolutions by Nicholas Copernicus*, The Johns Hopkins University Press, Baltimore. (Original title: De Revolutionibus Orbium Coelestium).

Royle, J.F.: 1837, Antiquity of Hindoo Medicine, W.H. Allen and Company, London.

Sachau, E.C.: 1964, Alberuni's India, S. Chand and Company, Delhi.

Sagan, Carl: 1979, *Broca's Brain*, Random House, New York.

Salem S.I. and A. Kumar: 1991, *Science in the Medieval World*, University to Texas Press, Austin.

Sinha, N.: 1911, *Vaisesika Sutras of Kanada*, Bhuvaneswari Ashram, Allahabad.

Srinivasiengar, C.N.: 1967, *The History of Ancient Indian Mathematics*, World Press, Calcutta.

Takakusu, J. (trans.): 1966, *The Buddhist Religion by I-tsing*, Munshiram Manoharlal, Delhi.

Weber, A.: 1961, *The History of Indian Literature*, Chowkhamba Sanskrit Series, Varanasi.

14

A Cross-Cultural Comparison of Conceptions of Science

EVA K. SMOLSKA

Introduction

Due to the degree of migration in the world today, almost every science classroom can be considered to have a multicultural population to some extent. This is especially true in urban Western classrooms. At a time when students are apparently turning away from science it may be important to show them that science is not strictly a Western phenomenon, and so may also be relevant to those from a non-Western background. This is one reason for including cross-cultural comparisons of science in science curricula.

Another reason affects all students in the context of science being taught from a science-technology-society (STS) interaction perspective. In this context the history of science in other cultures is an important aspect, for much of Western science is built on foundations established in other contexts. This is especially, but not exclusively, true of Chinese, Islamic and American Indian cultures. Not only is it important to examine specific contributions of these cultures in terms of scientific and technical advancements, but even more importantly it is necessary to examine their concepts and ethos of science especially as they relate to "man's" position in relationship to nature. To observe how certain problems are approached and solved in other cultures may offer alternate solutions to our own present day STS dilemmas.

The purpose of this paper, therefore, is to begin to explore some of these issues and to provide a starting point for teachers who also see the need for incorporating historical and cross-cultural aspects into their science classrooms.

In such a beginning exploration, the dilemma presents itself as to whether one should provide a survey of science in a variety of cultures, or whether one should examine one case study in depth, a dilemma which arises in any comparative research. While it is perhaps a way to avoiding the dilemma this paper will to some extent do both. The intent is to present a brief overview of science in Chinese and Hindu cultures, and then to concentrate in a little more depth on science in Islamic culture, which was influenced by the other as well as Greek culture and may be considered the bridge to modern science.

Comparative Science

While some may argue that it is inappropriate to speak in terms of Chinese science, Hindu science, Greek science and Islamic science (e.g. Storer, 1974), it is now accepted terminology in the history of science, and to a lesser extent in the philosophy and sociology of science, although the latter tends to concentrate on Western science. In the very process of identifying science as Western science there is tacit acknowledgement of the existence of non-Western science. One of the earliest major projects to study non-Western science culminated in Needham's (1954) 7 volume work *Science and Civilization in China*.

Needham (1981), himself, related that when he started the project most of his friends did not think he would find anything interesting. Furthermore, there was a question of where to house the project for neither the department of oriental studies nor the department of the history of science seemed to be interested.

While announcing that there is no discipline called comparative science (Elkana, 1981) is overstating the case, there is no doubt that science has not been treated similarly to art, music, religion or literature, histories of which have often been taken to represent the history of a particular culture. Elkana argues that "science is rarely considered as much of a totality of human culture as is art or religion, because it is seen as something different, unique, apart" (1981, p. 6). Perhaps the reason for this is the previous misrepresentation of science as a cultural and value-free in the Western tradition. While this perception is changing among the academic community as a result of work by philosophers, sociologists, historians and anthropologists of science, it is not yet apparent that this is the case among scientists, science teachers and the general public.

In an effort to strengthen his case for an anthropology of science, Elkana provides an analytical framework for those who take up his call. He argues that knowledge grows by the interaction of three factors: the body of knowledge, the socially determined images of knowledge; and the values and norms included in ideologies which do not directly depend on the images of knowledge. In this growth, there is a continuous critical dialogue between competing total world-views or research programmes. Furthermore, images of knowledge determine for each culture eight issues: (1) sources of knowledge; (2) legitimization of knowledge; (3) audience or public of knowledge; (4) location on the sacred-secular continuum; (5) location of some of the aspects on a time-scale continuum; (6) degree of consciousness; (7) relatedness to prevailling norms, values, ideologies; (8) translatability into statements about nature. Each of these may then also be broken down into further detail. For example, sources of knowledge "can be sense-experience, ratiocination, revelation, authority, tradition, analogy, competence, originality, novelty, beauty, and many others" (1981, p. 16). There is a hierarchy of sources of knowledge which change on a time-scale and no knowledge, whether religious or scientific, rests on only one source. It is through this framework that the issues identified in this paper will be examined. The basic assumption, which will not be defended here, is that science is a cultural system like any other.

In taking a comparative, anthropological approach to science, two questions almost immediately present themselves: (1) is there a difference in thinking (both content and form) within Western and non-Western science? and (2) why is it that science as we know it appeared in the West (and supposedly only in the West)? The answer to the first is provided by Elkana, following Horton's (1967) classic treatment of the question:

> There is in short no 'great divide between Western science and traditional thought. There are no fundamental characteristics of the one which are totally absent in the other, no sources of knowledge unknown to either, no aims of knowledge acceptable to one of them only. Yet there are real and significant differences. These are, however, relative and quantitative, not absolute and qualitative.[1]

Holzner et al. concur and start to provide an answer to the second question:

> There have indeed been many developments in the intellectual life and in scholarly inquiry in China, India, Islamic civilization, and so on that pointed in the direction of universal validity. However, in most cases, the long-range institutionalization of validity-enhancing intellectual activity did not occur as forcefully as it occurred in the scientific revolution of the West.[2]

The rest of this paper, guided by Elkana's framework will investigate these two questions in more detail. A cautionary note is necessary at this point. While we speak of Western science or Islamic science, it should be kept in mind that there are variations within these traditions: The generalizations are maintained for simplification in examining over all patterns. Where significant variations exist, these will be identified.

Chinese Science

While some of the technological accomplishments of China have been recognized for a long time, it was not until fairly recently and probably due in large part to the work of Needham (1954) that the extent of China's contributions to science and technology have been recognized. It should be acknowledge that many of the developments occurred essentially in isolation (although there was limited cross-fertilization with India), predating, often by many centuries, the same developments in Europe, which often had the benefit of Greek and Arabic writings as background influences.

Comparing the effect of some of those developments on Chinese society and on European society might provide an interesting study of the science-technology-society interaction.

The discoveries of printing, gunpowder and magnetism (9th, 9th and 1st century AD respectively, 500 and 1000 years later in Europe), for example, did not have the major impact on Chinese society that they did in Europe (Marks, 1983). This may be due to the different structures of the societies.

There are records of Chinese civilization dating to 1500 BC By about 200 BC, at the beginning of the Han dynasty, China took on the traditional structure that lasted for about 2000 years without major changes. It was based on the philosophy of Confucius who lived at roughly the same time (551-479 BC) as Pythagoras and Socrates in Greece. The empire was essentially ruled by an imperial civil service made up of Mandarins who were experts in the writings of Confucius, whose principles permeated the society and were used in making decisions in lieu of a system of written laws. While Confucian philosophy was very important in China, other philosophical writings were also influential. With respect to science, a book called *Ta Hsueh,* probably written by Yochang K'O a pupil of Mencius about 260 AD, became a classic. It contained the statement: "The attainment of knowledge lies in the investigation of things" which became the watchword of Chinese naturalists and scientific thinkers all through the ages (Needham, 1981, p. 107).

Several other discoveries made within this social context may be highlighted. In the area of astronomy, for example, in addition to the development of a number of astronomical instruments and clocks, the Chinese mapped the stars with great thoroughness and kept detailed records of eclipses, comets, novae and meteors that are still used today. They used the same celestial coordinates as modern astronomers, based on the pole star and celestial equator, in contrast to the ecliptic used by the Greeks (Marks, 1983). In physics, apart from work on magnetism (Chinese compasses point south, by the way), they made contributions in optics and acoustics. This contrasts with the focus on mechanics and dynamics of early European physicists. Also, they were more partial to the wave theory of matter than to the atomic theory. In methematics the focus was on algebra rather than geometry as in Greece, however that did not preclude engineering feats, especially in hydraulics for which they were famous, and inventions such as a clock toward built in 1088. It was preceded by a theoretical treatise on gears, and the mechanics were worked out from first principles. Expertise in iron, steel, porcelain and ceramics must also be acknowledged.

Biology and medicine were also quite advanced. Apart from acupuncture (where the concept of circulation existed long before Harvey's demonstrations), the Chinese used a variety of mineral, animal and botanical remedies. These included fumigation of homes against insects and libraries against bookworm, as well as the use of insects to keep down insects, and biological protection of plants. While the alchemical traditions in the West (Greece and Alexandria) were often focussed on aurifaction (making gold from other substances), Chinese alchemists were much more interested in macrobiotics—the art of long life—and the search for an elixir, a concept that later reached Europe through the mediation of the Arabs. In medicine, while the focus was on natural healing of the body and the concept of disease as a malfunction or imbalance in the body, there was also treatment against external agents. In the West we use the natural healing process only when we don't know what the problem or pathogen is, and the concept of balance/imbalance is starting to be accepted with modern endocrinology.

Needham (1981) describes the philosophy that underpined these scientific and technological advances as an organic naturalism, in contrast to a mechanical view evident in the West, or a metaphysical idealism evident in Buddhism for example. In this organicist conception, every phenomenon was connected with every other according to a hierarchical order. This view was universal among Chinese thinkers. They were also a priori inclined to field theories where action occurred at a distance (e.g. tides). Time was considered real and important, so that in the *Book of Changes* (I Ching) one reads that "change is the only thing in the universe that is unchanging". Such a concept of time is very important for an appreciation of causality, so basic to science. While a linear time-consciousness was the predominant view, cyclical time was also accepted, especially by the early Taoist philosophers. Neo-Confucian thought included concepts of cosmic, biological and social evolution.

While there were many philosophical influences in Chinese thought, including Buddhism to a small extent, the two main influences were Confucianism and Taoism. The former, as mentioned above was the philosophy of social organization, of common sense and practical knowledge. The latter was concerned with the careful observation of nature and the discovery (also through intuition) of its Way or Tao. The "Tao is the cosmic process in which all things are involved; the world is seen as a continuous flow and change" (Capra, 1972, p. 117). This change is considered cyclic and moves from opposite poles called *yin* and *yang*. In the body, the balance between these is maintained by a continuous flow of energy. Whenever the flow is blocked, the body falls ill, and acupuncture restores the flow. Capra (1972) contends that advances in modern physics have led theorists back to concepts that fit in very nicely with Taoist philosophy. The Tao might be considered the universal (unifying) theory for which physicists have been searching.

Within the philosophical context described above and the social context described earlier, slow, steady progress was made in Chinese science over the centuries (in some cases, even with the scientific revolution, the West has not caught up). There was no equivalent in China of the Dark Ages found in Europe. The question arises again, therefore, as to why there was no equivalent of the European scientific revolution in China (assuming, as most Westerners do, that it was a positive event). Capra suggests that while the Taoist attitude was essentially scientific, "only their deep mistrust in the analytic prevented them from constructing proper scientific theories" (1972, p. 126).

Marks (1983) summarizes some of the other arguments that have been presented:

> Some have argued that mathematics was the key factor in the scientific revolution. They claim that Chinese science was hampered because Chinese mathematics was largely algebraic and lacked anything comparable to the Euclidean geometry of classical Greece. Others suggest that the complex Chinese language inhibited science since it tends to be imprecise and allusive and so is not well adapted to precise logical expression. Another suggestion is that the absence in traditional Chinese philosophy of anything resembling a divine law-giver made it less likely for men to seek for universal laws of nature. Or it has been claimed that the centralised bureaucratic structure of traditional Chinese society restricted the development of independent centres of

thought and of power, while at the same time given stability to that society when it was faced with major technological changes.[3]

Needham elaborates on this last point by suggesting that the difference was the different types of feudalism in Chinese and European society.

No easy answer will be found, no matter how such speculation continues. What should be acknowledged, it seems to me, is that both in traditional Chinese society and during the scientific revolution in Europe, the science and technology that existed served the needs of the society at the time.

Indian Science

It might be easier to find the answer to why modern science did not develop in India, for India did experience the equivalent of the Dark Ages in Europe, and they lasted a lot longer than in the Europe, in fact almost 1000 years. The period of decay set in when knowledge was no longer the result of questioning experience, but accepted on authority (Ranganadhananda, 1978). This probably arose during the medieval period when modern Indian languages broke away from Sanskrit, access to the ancient texts was lost, and the caste system became dominant (Machwe, 1979).

It is from the ancient texts that one learns not only about India's contributions to science, but also the philosophical underpinnings of those discoveries. In the *Vadas* (3 books dating from before 1500 BC) there are references to numbers, mathematics, gambling and dice; it was accepted that the earth was round and without support; the moon, sun, Jupiter, Venus and eclipses are mentioned; as is a 12 month calendar. Our numbers, the decimal value system, and the concept of "0" were invented by Hindus and transmitted to us by the Arabs. Prior to and during the Vedic period advances were made in pottery (including the use of the wheel), furnaces for glazing, fermented drinks, soldering, metal-tipped arrows, mortar made of gypsum, lime and sand, etc. (Machwe, 1979).

In the area of biology and medicine also there were many early contributions: 260 names of animals (including 170 species of snake) with their habits are described; domestication of a variety of animals (not including dogs and cats); surgery, for fractures and even plastic surgery; psychiatric therapy; healing plants; sanitation systems; and of course the study of breathing and breath control important in Yoga.

Machwe (1979) goes on to describe a myriad of such developments, making an interesting case for the importance of Hinduism to modern civilization, though he does not share the "revivalists' absurd belief that for every new invention and discovery in Western science, there was always a counterpart or parallel in ancient India" (p. 6). Moreover, by about 500 AD there appeared to be a great deal of cross-fertilization among Mesopotamia, Greece, the Arab world, and perhaps to a lesser extent, China. As a result, it is more difficult to clearly accord credit to any one of these cultures for some scientific and technological advancements.

Even though Greek culture interacted with Indian culture and the philosophies, science and technology to the two contemporary civilizations were very much in touch with each other, the Greek distinction between science as 'knowing' and art as 'doing' did not dominate in ancient Indian thought. Science, like most other Western terms, including culture, has no exact equivalent in Indian languages.

> The Indian view of science is not exclusive. It is synchretic and in India metaphysics is not divorced from ethics, as logic is not mere linguistic analysis, or philology is not bereft of meaning and mere structuralism. Every science in India was related to a life and its requirements . . . The worldly and other-worldly were balanced.[4]

As mentioned above, the philosophical and spiritual underpinnings of Hinduism and the context for ancient Indian science lie in the ancient texts called *Vadas* of which there were four. The oldest parts contain hymns and prayers, the most significant being the *Upanishads,* which elaborate the philosophical and practical content of the texts. While Hinduism is a complex socio-religious system, consisting of innumerable sects, cults and philosophies (including influences from Buddhism, Jainism and Islam), the basis of all Hinduism

> is the idea that the multitude of things and events around us are but different manifestation of the same ultimate reality. This reality, called *Brahman,* is the unifying concept which gives

> Hinduism its essentially monastic character in spite of the worship of numerous goods and gooddesses.[5]

In this view, all forms are fluid, ever-changing, and the active force of change, the total universe in action is called *karma,* although this term has acquired a psychological meaning at the human level different from its cosmic meaning:

> as long as we . . . think that we are separated from our environment and can act independently, we are bound by *karma.* Being free from the bond of *karma* means to realize the unity and harmony of all nature, including ourselves, and to act accordingly . . . to break the bonds of *karma* means to realize that all the phenomena we perceive with our senses are part of the same reality. It means to experience, concretely and personally, that everything, including our own self, is *Brahman.* This experience is called *moksha,* or 'liberation'.[6]

Within this cosmo-centric view of life, every microcosm was a reflection of the macrocosm. Bowing for greeting, for example, was a reflection of the reverence for the divine in the other. This extended to all living creatures including trees and plants. The cow is an object of worship symbolizing the earth. As a result, the attitude towards nature and the environment in India is fundamentally different from that in the West. There is no question of controlling or dominating nature. Nature is the consort of man (Machwe, 1979).

In India all knowledge, including religion, is presided over by one goddess. There is a profound understanding of the unity of all human knowledge. The search for this knowledge is through experience, including induction, deduction and the use of sense data. There is even recognition that the observer is a very important datum in all understanding of the nature of observed data. While Western science ends there, in India there is a further search for the centre of infinite energy in every human being and the most prestigious knowledge (as a result of Buddhist influences) is knowledge of self (Ranganadhananda, 1978).

Islamic Science

The search for knowledge is probably the most fundamental aspect of Islamic culture, which is based on the Quran (Koran). 'Read in the name of Allah', the first revelation that the Prophet received from Allah, makes it obligatory for knowledge to be acquired in the name of, or for the sake of Allah. Furthermore, 'pursuit of knowledge is an incumbent duty of every man and woman', and knowledge is to be acquired from 'birth (cradle) to death (grave)'. In fact, knowledge is more highly valued than piety and good deeds (Qadir, 1988, pp. 15-16). Both revealed knowledge (the Quran) and unrevealed knowledge (sciences) are considered equally important. "The Quran puts so much value on proof and validity that it advises believers not to accept that of which they have no knowledge" (Qadir, 1988, p. 16).

Given this context, therefore, it is not surprising that the Islamic empire experienced something similar to a scientific renaissance. This occurred around the 9th and 10th centuries, referred to as the golden age of Islamic science. The reasons for this period of enormous scientific activity were many.

About a year after the Prophet's death in 632, most of Arabia had joined the Muslim fold and by about 750 the Arab empire stretched from the Pyranees to central Asia (Hill., 1991). This was about the same time that the art of paper-making was captured from the Chinese. In a society where reading was considered so important, access to books by a large segment of the population, especially private citizens, was bound to have an effect.

By the close of the 8th century, Baghdad had become a meeting place for people of different religions and speaking many different languages, all welcome. But the turning point seemed to come as a result of a dream in which Aristotle appeared to the Caliph al-Ma'mun, assuring him there was no conflict between reason and revelation. This eventually led to the establishment by the then ruling dynasty, the Abbasids, of the House of Wisdom in 830. Besides being a centre of intellectual and scientific activity, it was a centre for translation of a myriad of books, among them Greek classics (Lunde, 1982).

It is important to remember that while the translation of Greek classics was a central concern for a period of time, there was a tradition of Islamic science prior to that period, and, after initial translation, there followed a period of original research often leading to major revisions of the received tradition. Most of the writers of this period did not specialize and were extraordinarily prolific. Al-Jahiz (776-868), for example wrote some 200 works, of which only about 30 survive, the most famous of which is his *Book of Animals*. (See Lunde, 1982 for further examples) Many of the books of this period were later translated into Latin by Genard of Cremona in the 12th century.

As mentioned earlier, it is difficult to isolate some of the unique contributions of Islamic scholars due to the myriad of influences, nevertheless there were areas where their contributions were unique. For example, while China and India were significant contributors to algebra, and Greece is credited with geometry, Muslim mathematicians are responsible for contributions to (if not the innovation of) trigonometry. There were also contributions in geography, astronomy, natural history, physics, especially in the area of optics, and chemistry. (See Lunde, 1982; Quadir, 1988; Hill, 1991 for details) But perhaps the most significant contributions were made in medicine. There were hospitals, with attached medical schools, all over the Islamic world, the earliest built in Damascus in 707. Ideas of quarantine sprang from an empirical notion of contagion. Al-Razi (865-925) one of the best known physicians wrote, among other subjects, about 100 books on medicine, including a 20-volume encyclopedia and a monograph on children's disease. Ibn Sina (Avicenna, 980-1037) wrote eight large medical treatises, including an encyclopedic work later used as a textbook in European universities for centuries.

With the sack of Baghdad by the Mongols in 1258, the golden period of Islamic science came to an end. However, it did continue, though not to as great a degree and with more of an emphasis on practical aspects (see Hill, 1991), in other centres such as Spain, and later Persia. While it is easy to blame the end of this period on this event, the decline had already set in. Contrary to the view espoused by some such as Lunde (1982) that the translation of Greek classics was important to the blossoming of Islamic science, it also marked the beginning of the end, for it brought with it pro-deductive and anti-inductive method of searching for knowledge. Sardar (1989) is more explicit:

> it was the perversion of reason which led to the fall of Islamic science. Revelation in Islam is above reasoning, but not above reason. Neither is reason above revelation. This rather subtle relationship was destroyed when Greek thought became

dominant in Muslim societies. The introduction of Greek classics, through translations mainly by Christian Arabs, introduced two alien elements on the Muslim intellectual scene: Greek philosophy and gnosis; both of which were to lead to the suffocation of indigenous thought and the eventual downfall of Islamic science.[7]

Qadir (1988) also suggests that in response to the Greek influence by certain philosophers, the spirit of free enquiry died and conformism set in, so that not only did philosophy and science suffer, but also the entire Muslim world, politically and morally.

While credit for the scientific method is generally given to Bacon, it must be acknowledged that induction was already a powerful tool in Islamic science. The writings of a variety of scholars including Ibn Sina, al-Biruni and al-Haitham in his *Book of Optics* are all testimony to this. Qadir (1988) suggests that:

> Bacon forgot or was ignorant of the fact that the inductive method which he espoused and advocated in the *Novum Organum* had been expounded by the Quran and Muslim scientists and philosophers many centuries before him.[8]

Sardar (1989) is not quite so forgiving and suggests (based on the work of Sezgin) that the medieval Western world diligently imitated, copied and plagiarized the works of Muslim scientists:

> piracy was so common that as early as the twelfth century a decree was issued in Seville, forbidding the sale of scientific writings to Christians because the latter translated the writings and published them under another name[9].

On the other hand, Waddy (1982) reports that Bacon in his *Opus Tertius,* a copy of which was on display in the Bodleian Library in Oxford, sites the philosophers Ibn Sina, Ibn Rushd, al-Farabi, the astronomer al-Zarqali and the physicist al-Haitham. So, perhaps it was the later writers who failed to acknowledge his sources. There is little doubt, however, that "Western historians of science have systematically and consistently played down the contribution of Muslim scientists to civilization" (Sardar, 1989, p. 11).

While induction was important, the essence of Islamic science was that it embodied and encouraged a variety of methods according to the nature of the questions, the way they are formed, and the area of study. This is perhaps best examplified by the work of Al-Biruni (11th century) who produced some 108 works on diverse subjects and measured the circumference of the earth, latitudes and longitudes, and the specific density of several metals and procious stones with remarkable accuracy. Where necessary, he used deduction, observation and experimentation, induction, intellectual intuition, and of course, revelation (Qadir, 1988; Sardar, 1989). The philosophical underpinnings of this approach are found, as mentioned earlier, in the Quran, where people are commanded to contemplate the heavens and the earth and all that is enclosed within so that life could be lived in harmony with the natural world.

> Muslim scientists sought to understand, not to dominate the object of their study. Their respect for which was almost reverential. Bacon's dictum that 'nature yields her secrets under torture' would have sent shudders down al-Biruni's spine! Humility, recognition of the limitations of the scientific method, respect for the object of study: these primary lessons can be adopted at the very start of the journey to rediscover the heritage and contemporary meaning of Islamic science. And this, in essence, is also the message of Islamic science to the world.[10]

Conclusions

From the brief, and intentionally simplified, treatment of the history and philosophy of science in ancient China, India, and the Islamic empire, certain lessons can be learned. Perhaps the most obvious one is the threat to the scientific spirit and enterprise of a climate that does not support inquiry and the search for knowledge. This should be a warning to Western society, especially North America, where, ironically at a time when information is considered a source of power, the search for knowledge is not highly valued. This search for knowledge should not, however, be divorced from the context of the everyday, and should be available to a wide segment of the population. It could be argued that this condition, also, is not met in present day Western science.

It should be recognized that the search for knowledge, including self-knowledge can take on many forms and methods and that science (and the various methods included in the scientific activity) is but one source, albeit an important one, and useful for answering only certain questions. In each of the cultures examined, science was not divorced from other aspects of the culture, especially philosophy and religion. The integrated approach, both in the study of scientific questions and day to day living, was a characteristic of these cultures, as was the recognition of humanity as part of nature, not its master. The lack of reductionism in the study of nature was also characteristic of these cultures.

It has been suggested in this discussion that Western societies can learn from the way science was practised in these cultures in an attempt to solve some of our own problems or to recognize danger signals. That, of course, in an oversimplification of the issue. What may be a more useful lesson, is an examination of how these same cultures, having had an indigenous science with a particular philosophy for a number of centuries, now struggle to bring science back into their world view. That science is now different, however, being of Western origin. The struggle to incorporate modern science into societies that stress balance, harmony and a respect for nature has already begun in India, parts of the Islamic world, and to a lesser extent in China, where free inquiry had not really gained a foothold yet. An examination of how they are progressing is left for another discussion. However, if they are successful, there is hope for us yet.

NOTES

1. Elkana, 1981, p. 31.
2. 1985, p. 309.
3. pp. 237-238.
4. Machwe, 1979, p. 8.
5. Capra, 1972, p. 99.
6. Capra, 1972, p. 101.
7. p. 13.
8. p. 19.
9. p. 10.
10. Sardar, 1989, p. 27.

REFERENCES

Alavi, R.: 1985, 'Science and Society in Perisan Civilization', *Knowledge: Creation, Diffusion, Utilization*, 6, 329-349.

Capra, F.: 1972, *The Tao of Physics*, Flamingo Fontana Paperbacks, London.

Elkana, Y.: 1981, 'A Programmatic Attempt at an Anthropology of Knowledge', in E. Mendelsohn and Y. Elkana (eds.), *Sciences and Cultures*, D. Reidel Publishing Company, Dordrecht, Holland, pp. 1-70.

Hill, D.R.: 1991, 'Mechanical Engineering in the Medieval Near East', *Scientific American*, May, 100-105.

Holzner, B., Cambell, D.T. Shahidullah, M.: 1985, 'Introduction', *Knowledge: Creation, Diffusion, Utilization*, 6, 307-328.

Horton, R.: 1967, 'African Traditional Thought and Western Science', *Africa*, 37, 1-2.

Lunde, P.: 1982, 'Science: The Islamic Legacy', *Aramco World Magazine*, 33, 3-28.

Machwe, P.: 1979, *Hinduism—Its Contribution to Science and Civilization*, Vikas Publishing House Pvt. Ltd., New Delhi.

Marks, J.: 1983, *Science and the Making of the Modern World*, Heinemann, Oxford.

Nanda, J. N.: 1986, *Science and Technology in India's Transformation*, Concept Publishing Company, New Delhi.

Needham, J.: 1981, *Science of Traditional China: A Comparative Perspective*, Chinese University Press, Hong Kong.

Needham, J.: 1954, *Science and Civilization in China* (7 vols.) Cambridge University Press, Cambridge.

Qadir, C.A.: 1988, *Philosophy and Science in the Islamic World*, Routledge, London.

Ranganadhananda, S.: 1978, *Religious and Scientific Culture of India*, Andhra University Press, Visakhapatnam, India.

Ravetz, J.R.V. 1991, 'Prospects for an Islamic Science', *Futures*, April, 262-272.

Sardar, Z.: 1989, *Explorations in Islamic Science*, Mansell, London.

Storer, N.W.: 1974, 'The Internationality of Science', in Restivo, S.P., Venderpool, C.K. (eds), *Comparative Studies in Science and Society*, Merrill Publishing Co., Colombus, Ohio, pp. 444-460.

Waddy C.: 1982, 'The Bodleian Remembers', Aramco World Magazine, 33, 29-32.

Weatherford, J.: 1988, *Indian Givers*, Fawcett Columbine, New York.

15

Current Events in Science and the Pupil

MARLOW EDIGER
Truman State University, Kirksville, USA

Pupils desire to experience relevant content in science. The content then needs to be based on the interests and needs of learners. Who determines these interests and needs? The pupil should be in the best position to determine what is relevant. He/she decides what is useful and has application values. One way of approaching the problem of ascertaining relevancy is for the teacher to develop and provide learning stations for pupils whereby each pupil may select that task or learning activity which has the greatest value when enagaging in sequential learning experiences. There should be enough tasks at the different stations so that learners may omit what does not possess perceived relevancy and yet have plenty of work to do.

A second approach in teaching is to use teacher-pupil planning within the framework of a thematic unit of study. The science teacher then plans with the pupil that which the latter wishes to learn. There may be large class, collaborative experiences within committees, as well as individual study activities. Thus, the teacher assists pupils to determine objectives, learning opportunities, and evaluation procedures that possess relevancy.

A third approach in deciding upon relevant topics for pupils to pursue in the science curriculum is for teachers, principals, and supervisors to study, analyze, and accept thematic units of study involving consensus thinking. This might well incorporate state mandated objectives as well as the National Science Teachers Association standards for learners to achieve in the science curriculum. Clearly written objectives, quality learning opportunities for pupils to attain the objectives, as well as valid/reliable evaluation procedures to ascertain if pupils have attained the stated objectives of instruction must then be in the offing.

I would like to suggest a fourth approach which emphasizes a current events procedure. Fupils may hear news items in the home setting pertaining to what is happening currently in the natural environment. Current events indicate that the happening is occurring at the present time and is of concern to many people.

Current Events in Science

What is transpiring presently has many natural phenomena for pupil study. At this writing, there are devastating floods in Oregon and to some extent in Washington. Annual floods occur in different areas around the world. People lose homes, lives, cars, furniture, and other property in flood waters. Floods carry much energy with the damage that these high waters can do. Learners then find floods to be a natural phenomenon that occur frequently. It is a very worth topic and theme to study if human being wish to do something to deter the devastating happenings that result from floods. Newspapers, TV and radio news reports, newsmagazines, newspapers written for pupils such as *My Weekly Reader*, video tapes, multiple series basal texts, science encyclopedias, computer packages, internet, and videodisks, among other materials of instruction, might well provide appropriate content for pupils to use in problem solving such as:

1. identifying and answering questions involving "What causes floods to occur?"
2. securing information in problem solving activities.
3. developing a hypothesis or tentative answer to the question/problem.

4. testing the hypothesis when reading and acquiring information to approve or refute the hypothesis.
5. revising the hypothesis if necessary as a result of the test.

When studying about floods, pupils should also learn what human beings do to try to alleviate the suffering that occurs from these problematic situations. Social studies here becomes a part of the science curriculum. An integrated, interdisciplinary curriculum results. Pupils then need to learn about the work of the Red Cross, relief organizations which provide cleanup crews with no costs involved, as well as state, country, and federal efforts working toward remedying problems involving flooding.

A second natural disaster which occurred two weeks ago, at this writing, was freezing rain in the southeastern states of the US. North Carolina, an entire state, dismissed schools and business workdays for one day due to electric wires being down, roads being slick and unsafe, and tree limbs blocking areas for driving. Freezing rain which damages electrical lines and makes roads slick occurs when the temperature reading goes below thirty-two degrees Fahrenheit land moisture falls in the form of rain. The coasts of freezing rain might well run into the billions of dollars and cause many accidents and deaths from slick road surfaces.

Pupils need to learn about causes for freezing rain. They should learn about hazards that occur and why. Safety should be discussed and taught when freezing rain comes about. Goals of instruction pertaining to the phenomenon of freezing rain should be relevant and important for pupils. Learners need to have opportunities to work individually and collaboratively in problems identified pertaining to learning about freezing rain. A variety of materials need to be used by pupils in finding answers to problems. Depth teaching should be in emphasis. Intensive learning about freezing rain and its consequences should be an end result.

Sequence in learning may follow a logical approach whereby the science teacher sequences or orders the learning opportunities for pupils. At other times a psychological sequence may be followed in that learners with teacher guidance may order experiences and activities. Methods of teaching should involve induction, deduction, guided instruction by the teacher, as well as pupils with teacher guidance planning the ongoing lessons and units of study pertaining to natural disasters.

Three years ago at this writing, California had a series of earthquakes with its accompanying after shocks. China, Japan, Russia, the Ukraine, and Iran, among other nations on the planet earth, experience rather frequent problems pertaining to earthquakes as a natural phenomena. Property and road damage can be high indeed depending upon the severity of the quake as measured by the Richter scale. Destruction to buildings might well depend, in part, upon how these were built and which materials were used. Pertaining to earthquakes online, Butler, et al. (1996) wrote:

> Earthquakes provide a perfect interdisciplinary teaching opportunity to involve students in highly motivational real-world experiences. Access to information regarding earthquakes is available from several sources on the internet, but the primary source is the National Earthquake Information Service (NEIS) in Golden, Colorado. This service is provided by the US Geological Survey . . . The site gives near-real-time international information on earthquakes. For each earthquake, the following data are provided: the time in Universal Time, the latitude and longitude of the epicenter, the depth in kilometres to the focus, the magnitude, and the general location.
>
> To implement the earthquake project, access to a computer with a modem, a printer, and an Internet account is necessary. In addition to the hardware, the real ingredient necessary for a successful project is a group of motivated teachers. In our district this mix of material and personnel was located at Canton Middle School, Las Vegas, Nevada. The lead teacher was a science teacher, who was supported by a geography teacher and a mathematics teacher.
>
> This science teacher, who has the Internet connection in the classroom, introduced students to the Internet. On the first day of the programme, one student from each class period was trained to use the computer and modem to access NEIS's earthquake reporting site. The following day, students who had been trained each trained another student . . . In the weeks that followed, each student became a trainee and a trainer in turn . . .

> A large Mercator projection map of the Earth was posted on a bulletin board in the science classroom. Each day as information was gathered, groups of students located the epicenter of each earthquake reported on the map using pushpins colour coded according to earthquake magnitude. . .

Objectives for instruction should be developed cooperatively by teachers with supervisor assistance. Careful evaluation of each objective is a must. The learning activities for pupils to attain vital objectives need to be conducive to helping pupils attain as optimally as possible. Pupil interests, needs, purposes, and attitudes need proper provision so that quality achievement in these areas are in evidence. Appraisal procedures to determine pupil attainment of goals need to be varied so that each facet of achievement is evaluated. Teacher developed, norm referenced, as well as criterion referenced tests may be used to ascertain pupil achievement of vital objective. Anecdotal records, journal writing, teacher observation, pupil self evaluation, learner products of instruction, class participation, videotapes, and snapshots of learner achievement need to be in the offing to reveal and indicate the quality of pupil achievement. Thus a variety of procedures should be used in determine how much pupils have learned planet to natural disasters on the planet earth.

Four years ago, several of the plains states were hit by tornadoes. One tornado in central Kanasas uprooted evergreen trees ten feet tall and eleven inches in diameter. A half mile away, a newly built sturdy brick house had just been completed as a dream house for a retired couple. This durable structure was completely demolished by the 150 miles per hour winds in the tornado. Houses in the path of the tornado that remained standing were damaged to the point where they were later torn down. The path of the tornado could be followed easily in terms of where devastating destruction had occurred. Farm houses and barns, directly adjacent, were unharmed. There is tremendous energy in the force of tornadoes.

Pupils with teacher guidance then need to

1. identify relevant problems areas to solve.
2. choose subject matter content which supplies needed answers.

3. select from the acquired subject matter that which provides tentative answers to the question.
4. check the accuracy of the answer(s) through additional study.
5. notice additional problem areas pertaining to tornadoes that would be relevant to solve.

Cyclones and hurricanes may be incorporated into the study of tornadoes. Pupils also need to view each natural disaster in terms of what human beings can do to minimize its destructive forces as well as what can be done to alleviate human suffering.

Lightning strikes buildings and kills human beings, perhaps not to the extent that the previously discussed natural disasters do. A barn or shed filled with hay bales and farm implements may be struck by a bolt of lightning causing the property to be completely destroyed. Millions of dollars worth of labour and property burn ferociously, even with fire departments out in full force in rural areas. It is costly to remove the remains such as bulldozers dozing the concrete floors and slabs, from the destroyed buildings, to be hauled away by trucks. Trash from the burning property needs to be disposed of using bulldozers to load the contents onto trucks. Thus the hauling away of trash after lightning has hit a building is labour intensive and expensive.

The science teacher needs to identify key structural ideas that pupils should achieve pertaining to lightning and its affects on people and the environment. Forests, among other areas, can be damaged much due to being hit by lightning. This is easy to observe when travelling through any wooded area, small or large.

Drouth, as another natural disaster, keeps farm crops from producing or makes water scarce for livestock and other rural needs. Farmers and ranchers can be bankrupted when drouth hits an area. Livestock has to be sold cheaply since no one can afford to care for these animals when feed costs become very high due to scarcity and greed. It has an opposite affect as compared to farm crops being destroyed due to floods or excessive rain. Drouth has as a consequence a lack of water in cities for watering the lawn or washing the car, luxuries perhaps.

When farm land has drouth and strong winds are in evidence, erosion of soil can well be an end result. Erosion of top soil is difficult to restore. The farmer can minimize erosion through terracing, strip cropping, as well as growing grass and trees on farm land. All of these measures to control soil erosion are costly and tend to bring in minimal farm income. For example, quality hay, baled from excellent grassland, will not provide the income to farmers as compared to cultivated land where wheat, corn and soybeans are grown. Generally an inch of eroded top soil takes 100 to 500 years to rejuvenate.

Pertaining to drouth as a natural disaster, I recommend the following questions and issues for pupils to pursue using a variety of learning opportunities:

1. How can a balance be established between farmers making a living from farming as compared to using proper methods of preventing soil erosion?
2. Should there be federal and state government payments to farmers to prevent soil erosion, wetlands protection, as well as other means of protecting soil in the natural environment?
3. How can the natural environment best be protected, especially in the area of soil protection?

The use of pesticides and herbicides has become increasingly common to control harmful insects and weeds. If pesticides were not used, the chances are that our food supply would be greatly reduced due to sharing more and more of it with insects and other pests. Apple damage from moths can indeed by extensive. The corn borer, as well as smut, can greatly minimize yields in corn production. The Colorado potato beetle, in larva stage, can strip an otherwise good crop of potatoes in a matter of two to three days. A hoard of grasshoppers can cause extensive damage, in a few days, to growing soybean plants. The reasons for using pesticides is quite obvious. Farmers may experience huge financial losses from insects and other pests in a short time of hours a or few days.

Weeds also can do much damage to farm crops in a few days. Cockleburs, for example, can crowd out soybean plants, in a week, from securing needed moisture and sunlight.

Herbicides when used may completely destroy all cocklebsurs in a matter of hours. Gardeners realize that foxtail weeds might well take all the moisture away from growing garden crops. How to minimize weed damage in the growing of farm crops as well as to prevent damage to ornamental plants can indeed be a problem. Pesticides and herbicides can control insect populations and weed growth. Increasingly, there are more resistant strains of insects and weeds to pesticides and herbicides. When DDT first came out in 1944, there was much optimism about its future in controlling flies, mosquitoes, and other pests that hinder livestock production. DDT initially was very successful in curbing flies, insects, and other pests, particularly in livestock production. It did not take long, twenty years in general, when there were insects that became increasingly resistant to DDT. DDT also had its affects upon pollution of land, water supplies, and bodies of water until its use was banned.

I recently attended a science teachers convention in which a speaker stated how beneficial earthworns are to soil such as in providing natural fertilizer from body wastes, aeration of the soil, and richness of the soil. The speaker perceived the situation from one perception only and that was the negative effects of using pesticides and herbicides which kill many, many earthworms. The earthworm certainly provides soil with its numerous benefits to be sure. However, the income factor for farmers is also involved in that pests and weeds destroy domesticated plants. A highly complex problem is involved. With adequate background information, pupils with teacher guidance may brainstorm possible solutions to the dilemma of using agricultural chemicals to destroy pests and weeds as compared to using other procedures to minimize yield damage to farm crops. Other procedures might include the use of insects which feed upon pests that destroy farm crops. To control weeds, brightly coloured flowers which attract pests have been used by gardeners, thus protecting valuable garden crops for human consumption. However, efforts so far in controlling pests and weeds have been only successful in a minor way.

To vary procedures of instruction mentioned in this manuscript, a learning stations approach may be used in the curriculum on natural disasters. An adequate, number of stations need to be in the offing. Each station has concute, semiconcrete, and abstract learning activities from which learners may choose sequentially to pursue. There are more tasks at the different stations than what any one learner can complete. Those tasks not possessing perceived purpose by the pupil may be omitted. The pupil is the chooser. The teacher assists and helps each pupil to accomplish as much as possible. The tasks at each station should be meaningful, interesting, emphasize a balance between individual and group endeavours, as well as possess challenge. Learners sequence or order their very own activities and experiences. An activity centered curriculum in science is an end result.

Ediger and Rao (1996) stress the importance of having a variety of learning opportunities in teaching science for the following reasons:

1. pupils have different learning styles.
2. different levels of achievement in science exist within any class of pupils.
3. not all pupils, of course, benefit equally from the same activity.
4. teachers have different teaching styles.
5. selected learning activities capture the interests of pupils more than do other kinds of experiences.
6. individuals desire new experiences.
7. monotony in activities hinders pupils in developing motivation toward learning.

Philosophy of Science Education

A study of diverse philosophies of education might well assist teachers to make quality decisions pertaining to current events in the sciences curriculum. Ediger (1995) wrote:

> Diverse philosophical schools of thought in science are in evidence to develop and implement lessons plans and units in science. Experimentalism emphasizes the use of problem solving experiences for pupil. Flexible steps in problems solving involve

1. Identifying the problem.
2. Gathering data to solve the identified problem.
3. Developing a hypothesis, directly based to the obtained data and in answer to the problem.
4. Testing the hypothesis.
5. Revising the hopothesis, if evidence warrants.

Experimentalism emphasizes that real live problems be identified by pupils. The problems come directly from society. In society, earthquakes, hurricanes, tornadoes, volcanic eruptions, among other natural phenomena occur. Out of these scenes and situations, problems arise and are identified, such as "What makes for the happening of earthquakes?" Information needs to be gathered to answer the problem or question. An answer, tentative in nature, is then developed. The answer, a hypothesis, is then checked against further content, secured form a variety of reference sources. Modification of the original answer or hypotheses may then be needed.

Idealism, as a philosophy of education, emphasizes an idea centered curriculum. Science then becomes a part of the general education curriculum. A subject centered, not an activity centered philosophy, is then in evidence. Diverse academic disciplines such as zoology, botany, physics, astronomy, biology, chemistry, and geology provide subject matter for ongoing units of study. Textbooks, workbooks, worksheets, and a few selected audiovisual aids provide content for pupils. Universal ideas or generalizations in science units need to be achieved by pupils. The teacher needs to be a true academician and scholar to stimulate pupil learning.

Realism, as a third philosophy of education, advocates the use of precise, measurable objectives. Realist believe the real world can be known in whole or part as it truly is. What pupils achieve in each science unit can be measured. The real world of natural phenomena can be stated in precise, measurable objectives. A variety of concrete learning activities, in particular, should be provided for pupils to attain the precise ends. Semiconcrete as well as abstract experiences also should be in the offing. After instruction, it is observable and measurable if an objective has been achieved by pupils.

Existentialism, as a fourth philosophy of education, emphasizes the learner, himself or herself, being heavily involved in deciding what (the objectives) to learn, as well as the means (learning activities) in ongoing science units of study. Thus, a learning centres philosophy may be emphasized. More centres and tasks for learners to pursue are in evidence then what can be completed. Each pupil may then sequentially choose which tasks to complete, as well as which to omit. Pupils individually are involved in making these decisions. The teacher develops the centres for learner interaction. Better yet, pupil/teacher planning may be used to develop the centres and their inherent tasks.

In supervising student teachers and cooperating teachers in the public schools, I have observed the following current events items in science emphasized in each of the above named philosophies:

1. *Experimentalism*: In an ongoing lesson, pupils identified problems such as (a) Why did Iran experience a major earthquake this past weekend? (b) How is the strength of earthquakes measured?

2. *Idealism*: A teacher determined topic for discussion with pupil involvement stressing in an ongoing unit (a) the causes of hurricanes and their after affects. (b) the differences between huricanes and tornadoes.

3. *Realism*: The science teacher stating prior to implementing the lesson on the following two precise objectives pupils are to achieve: (a) The pupil will list in writing three causes of major floods in the environment. (b) The pupil will write a fifty word paragraph on ways of preventing flood damage.

4. *Existentialism*: Pupils choosing what to study in a unit through teacher/learner planning. These areas, for example, might include (a) What may be done to help people care for which other when a natural disaster such as a cyclone occurs. (b) How might the United States annual budget be changed so that the needs of people are met in times of emergency when destruction from natural forces occur?

My recommendations here are that current events in science emphasize problem solving. Experimentalism then should hold sway. Thus subject matter acquired when stressing idealism, content achieved from attaining measurably stated objectives (realism), and pupil/teacher planning procedures (existentialism) may all be used to identify and solve problems. Why is problem solving important? In life's situations, people face problems which need identification and necessary solutions. Each solution appears to be tentative and will need revisions as evidence indicates. In everyday situations then, individuals and groups experience problems continually which need some kind of answer.

There are current events papers written expecially for the grade level pupils are in presently. These present items pertaining to natural disasters, among other human related factors. I recommend the following current events papers for pupils to be considered:

My Weekly Reader (grades kindergarten through grade six)
P.O. Box 16673
Columbus, Ohio 43216

Let's find Out (kindergarten level)
News Pilot (grade one)
News Ranger (grade two)
News Trails (grade three)
News Explorer (grade four)
Newstime (grades five and six)
The above are published by
Scholastic Magazines
750 Broadway
New York, NY 10003

Penny Power (for all grades)
(by the editors of Consumer Reports)
256 Washington Street
Mt. Vernon, NY 10053

Ranger Rick (grades one-six)
National Wild Life Federation
1412 16th Street, NW
Washington DC 20036

National Geographic World
(grades three through six)
17th and M streets, NW
Washington DC 20036

Newspapers written for pupils have an intended audience and that is the learner himself/herself. Many problems in word recognition have been taken care of when a child centered paper has been written, but to provide for individual needs, selected learners will still need assistance in identifying unknown words. A few pupils will also need guidance in understanding the meaning of important words. Current events papers can have much appeal to learners providing that the teacher assists pupils in achieving background information prior to reading these weekly/monthly newspapers.

To assist pupil learning in discussions after having read the current events items, the following guidelines need to be stressed by teachers:

1. Each pupil needs to stay on the topic being discussed and not digress to other information.
2. Learners must respect the thinking of each discussion participant.
3. It is important to listen carefully to the ideas of others in the group.
4. All should be actively engaged in the discussion, but on one dominate the interactions.
5. Content presented should be evaluated in an atmosphere of respect and trust.
6. Participants need to speak clearly and accurately in terms of concepts, generalizations, main ideas, and facts presented.
7. Valid and reliable conclusions should be drawn from each discussion.
8. Chairpersons may be chosen by the teacher with rotation procedures. Leadership might also emerge within a group without a chairperson.

Group/committee endeavours may follow listening to a radio news broadcast on natural catastrophes in the environment. These may be cassette recorded by the teacher in the home setting so that only relevant information is played to pupils. The teacher may also videotape, with a VCR, vital current events items from TV broadcasts in the home setting. These may be played in the classroom with proper readiness provided by the science teacher. Daily newspaper items as well as weekly news items from reputable magazines might well provide relevant information on natural disasters and means used to prevent these occurrences from doing damage. The latest data sources should also be heavily used and involved in the science curriculum such as Internet and computer packages. To achieve optimally in science current events, pupils need to experience quality reference sources using a hands-on approach.

Organization of the Science Current Events Curriculum

There are several approaches that may be used by the teacher to organize the current events programme in science. First, the teacher may take time at the beginning of each class session to discuss news articles that pupils have brought in for discussion. Thus, a pupil might, for example, have brought in a news item about an avalanche that caused much destruction in a village in Switzerland. The temperature readings there were much warmer for that season than usual causing the snow and ice to melt above on the mountains. The result was a massive amount of snow and ice that came crashing down onto houses in the village. Or a pupil brought to the class a news clipping about the flooding of the Ohio River causing home evacuations and much property damage due to the mighty force of the rushing flood waters. A third pupil brought into the classroom and reported on a volcanic eruption in the Philippines. These happenings occurred simultaneously. There are enough natural disasters occurring which could provide an entire unit in science for pupils to study. These occurrences may be placed around a world man with a coloured piece of yarn connecting the place of the geographical location with the news clipping. Geography and the science curriculum are then correlated and taught as being related. Several of my student teachers and their cooperating teachers whom I have supervised in the public schools believe very strongly in bringing in humanitarian efforts used to alleviate the resulting human suffering from natural disasters. Historical efforts in assisting the unfortunate during times of natural disasters bring in a study of history integrated with the science curriculum. With the above examples given an entire science unit may be taught entitled "Natural Disasters and Their Consequences."

A second approach in organizing the science current events curriculum is to discuss with pupils news items as they relate to the ongoing unit of study. Thus, if pupils, for example, are studying a unit on "Preserving Wildlife," current events items may emphasize sanctuaries for bald eagles, an endangered species. Also recently, wolves from Alaska were realised into a designated area in the state of Wyoming. Wolves formerly had a niche in that state but had become extinct until a new pack from Alaska was released in Wyoming. An issue that can provide for higher levels of cognition which might be discussed here is the point of view of cattle ranchers in Wyoming versus those of wildlife advocates in restoring an area to its original state. I have observed pupils with teacher guidance doing much research from a variety of reference sources to understand opposing sides in a dispute. Intrinsic motivation seems to be in evidence here.

A third approach in organizing the current events is to stress the separate subjects curriculum. Here, pupils are encouraged to bring news items to class if they related to the ongoing unit in science or not. There are excellent reasons for emphasizing the separate subjects procedure in organizing the current events programme in science. Thus, there are vital news happenings in the world of science that have no relationship to the ongoing unit of study being taught. Then too, there are not an adequate number of science news items that relate so that an entire unit may be taught. At the same time, the isolated news item brought to class is highly relevant and should receive adequate attention in class as soon as possible. I have observed in different classrooms which have a quality programme of science in the news and yet the items are not related to the present unit being taught. I would like to offer the following suggestions for implementing a good current events programme. These suggestions are the following:

1. pupils should volunteer to bring into the classroom setting news items pertaining to science. If there is a lack of voluntary participation, the science teacher may require pupils to collect and have well in mind relevant news items pertaining to science.

2. the teacher(s) need to reward pupil participation by praising positive efforts.
3. learners should understand and attach meaning to news items presented to classmates.
4. each news item needs to be evaluated using critical and creative thinking as well as problem solving procedures. To think critically, pupils need to separate facts from opinions, fantasy from reality, as well as detect bias. With creative thinking, pupils come up with new, novel ideas when predicting what might happen in the future based on knowledge. Unique ideas are needed in any endeavour since creativity is necessary in response to problem areas. Too frequently, the tried and true are stressed and this may not work in a new situation involving problem solving.
4. pupils should be encouraged to use what has been learned. If knowledge is not used, it might be forgotten. Also, use made of what has been learned makes for relevance in the current events science curriculum.

There are many uses that can be made of any vital current events item studied. The following have been observed in different classrooms and appear to work well:

1. pupils in a committee collaboratively working on a mural to portray content learned. Thus three or four pupils worked on a mural four feet by five feet in dimension. Planning together what to show using a variety of art media stress a problem solving approach. Thus each pupils showed one of the following: plate tectonics in art form; a hurricane with its destructive path; a fault with different layers of rock; and sheet/ gulley erosion.
2. three pupils in a committee made a model volcano using wadded newspaper for the core with a potted empty meat can for the opening at the top of the model volcano. The outside of the volcano was finished with a plaster of paris mix to make for a realistic portrayal. The plaster of paris dries quickly and pupils need to

work quickly to give the model an identifiable lifelike appearance. Tempera paint may be used to give the model a natural like appearance in its final form. Ammonium dichromate crystals may be put into the empty potted meat can. These crystals, obtained from a scientific supply company, should then be ignited. A model volcanic eruption occurs. There needs to be ample ventilation in the classroom when doing this experiment.

3. pupils developing and presenting a simulated radio newscast on recent natural disasters, locally and nationally. Careful writing and editing of the news is important. A pupil playing the role of the reporter may read the news to the class as would be done in regular newscasts on the radio.
4. three pupils in a committee researching and completing a written report on natural disasters in farming. The science teacher assists these learners to secure relevant information on drouth, hail, and excessive rainfall. Oral reports to classmates on each of these disasters may reveal to pupils what happens when there is a lack of moisture for growing crops, when hail destroys farm crops in a minute or two, and when fields are too wet for seeding or for harvesting.
5. pupils may plan and play roles of *Famous Scientists* when studying this science unit. Much background information is needed to develop the creative dramatics activity. Thus, individual pupils may play roles of well known scientists such as Louis Pasteur, Galileo, and Antony Leeuvenhoek. The presentation may be given to classmates and pupils in other classrooms, as well as to parents invited to the classroom.

The above five examples of how to put knowledge of current events in science to use by pupils are given as models. There are numerous other ideas that can be used by teachers to have pupils apply what has been learned. Shepardson and British (1997) favour pupil journal writing as an excellent means of having pupils apply what has been learned:

Children's observations are essential for learning, but unfortunately they are often downplayed in the science teaching process. It is from science observations that the child begins to construct scientific understandings. Children may, however, have difficulties in observing differences, erroneously recording deductions as observations.

To access the quality of these observations, teachers can analyze journals for the following indicators:

1. actual observations versus deductions.
2. level of detail (qualitative and quantitative).
3. notations of similarities and differences.
4. comparions between phenomena in terms of position (spatial) and time (change).
5. and accurate, careful descriptions . . .

To access the quality of children's observations, specific scoring rubrics need to be developed based on the nature of the activity and the importance of the children's observations in the teaching/learning process.

In Closing

There are numerous natural disasters which need to be emphasized in the science curriculum. A key concept here is relevancy when choosing which news items of pursue. An interdisciplinary curriculum incorporates social studies, mathematics, and language arts. Pupils need assistance to understand that knowledge is related. Retention of subject matter learned improves when pupils can perceive that current events is related to diverse academic disciplines. Ample opportunities should be provided for pupil to work collaboratively with others in the school setting. Problem solving and learner decision making need to be stressed science life itself consists of solving problems and choosing from among alternatives to make decisions. Relevant objectives, learning opportunities, and appraisal procedures should be in the offing for all pupils in units pertaining to natural disasters in the environment. A good current events curriculum in science is a must.

Pertaining to current events, Schuncke (1988) wrote:

There are four basic questions that should be considered in a current events discussion:

1. What does the news item say? Here, your job is to determine that the children are aware of the basic message contained in the news item. You'll want to insure that they know the facts surrounding an event, the who, what, when, where, why, and possibly how.
2. What does it mean? Knowing the facts... does not necessarily mean that the children understand it. Therefore, you will next need to determine their level of comprehension, how they interpret the item, and what inferences they can make about it. You'll want to make certain they have, at least, a basic understanding of what's going on.
3. Why is it important? The question, or a related one, should be used to help children probe the effect of an event—in the children themselves, on others, and on the world.
4. How does it relate to me? Here children can be assisted to examine their roles as citizens—of a community, state, nation, and world—to determine if the importance of an event requires some action on theii part. Often the question can lead to decision making, valuing, and social action in their part.

REFERENCES

Butler, Gene, et. al. (1996). "Earthquakes Online," *The Science Teacher*, Vol. 63, No. 9, pp. 31-32.

Ediger, Marlow, and D. Baskara Rao (1996). *Science Curriculum*. New Delhi: Discovery Publishing House, pp. 40-41.

Ediger, Marlow (1995). "Designing Science Units of Study," *School Science*, Vol. 33, No. 1, pp. 14-15.

Schuncke, George M., *Elementary Social Studies*. New York: The Macmillan Publishing, p. 72.

Shepardson, Daniel P., and Susan J. Britsch (1997). "Children's Science Journals: Tools for Teaching, Learning and Assessing," *Science and Children*, Vol. 34, No. 5, p. 17.

16

Teaching Science As Inquiry

MARLOW EDIGER
Truman State University, USA

Science teaching must reflect change within a curriculum that stresses assisting pupils to attain optimally. Objectives, learning opportunities, and appraisal procedures in science need to be relevant and updated to incorporate National and state standards. Units of instruction in science should stress inquiry, motivate pupils, and encourage high levels of interest. Educational philosophies and psychologies used in teaching-learning situations by the teacher must guide pupils to develop an inward desire to learn.

Philosophy of Science Teaching

The science teacher needs to have a wide repertoire or means of assisting pupils to achieve optimally. There are diverse educational philosophies for teachers to use that encourage optimal learner achievement.

First, a problem solving approach may be used. Inquiry learning is highly salient here. Ideally, pupils with teacher guidance need to identify a problem within the framework of an ongoing science unit of study. The problem must by clearly stated. Learners might then brain storm possible answers to the problem. Value judgements should not be made on responses given by pupils. The consequences or results of each brainstormed answer must be evaluated after the brainstorming session has been completed. A variety of manipulative, pictorial, and abstract materials should be used here. Science experiments may be at the heart of testing each response or hypothesis. Responses are then modified changed, or refuted as a result of the tests. John Dewey and other experimentalists emphasized problem solving strongly in their philosophy of experimentalism. Committee endeavours and cooperative learning are stressed in the problem solving science curriculum.

Experimentalists believe the science curriculum should be as closely related to the real world of society as possible. School and society are not separate but integrated entities. To emphasize problem solving, the science teacher must provide a learning environment that is stimulating and arouses pupil interests. Hopefully, the interests of learners will lead to problem identification. The goal of the science teacher is to have learners select relevant problems. The teacher becomes a resource person, guide, and helper, rather than one who lectures and presents content deductively to pupils. Thus learners need assistance in brain storming, locating reference sources, and attaining hypotheses as means of inquiry learning.

With pupils being heavily involved in selecting problems and strategies to solve each problem, a psychological curriculum is in evidence science each learner is heavily involved in sequencing or ordering his/her own experiences. The learner himself/herself tends to order experiences in a problem solving approach of teaching, according to educational psychologists. Pertaining to John Dewey's philosophy of experimentalism, Meyer (1949) wrote the following:

> All this, of course, depends in no small way upon thinking. For Dewey, however, thinking becomes significant only when applied to life's situations. It is, he has said, "an instrumentality used by man in adjusting himself to the practical situations in life." Or to phrase it more simply, human beings think in order to live. Because to this stimulus, which has its basis in biology and sociology, it is impossible—it is absurd—to interpret life is in a systematic and abstract way. Since, moreover, Dewey holds that life is in constant flux, it is impossible to solve problems with any degree of finality for the problems of tomorrow will be different from those of today.

> As for the problem of knowledge, Dewey believes that knowledge is experience and that true experience is functional. What is this thing for? What is its use? Is a coal mine a physical deposit or does it have function? And if so, what is it? Such are the questions that help give meaning to one's experience; but such questions cannot be answered without antecedent action. Action must precede knowledge. Whatever knowledge we possess has resulted from our activities, our efforts to survive, to obtain food, shelter, and clothing. Only that which has been organized into our disposition so as to enable us to adapt our environment to our needs and to adapt our aims and desires to the situation in which we exist is really knowledge.

A second philosophy of education to stress is a subject centered science curriculum. Here, the science teacher must select and teach vital facts, concepts, and generalizations to pupils. Inquiry learning emphasizing critical and creative thinking, explanations, and vital discussions are methods of instruction used to teach learners. Intellectual development is a major objective of science instruction. Mind is real and needs challenging subject matter to encourage mental development. Cognitive objective should be emphasized primarily. However, effective goals are also salient as they assist pupils to attain cognitive ends of science instruction. It is important to secure pupils interest in science, but each learner must also will to learn. Tasks in life are interesting as well as those that do not stress interest. Thus, the pupil must develop a will to achieve, attain, and develop well intellectually.

Subject centered approaches in teaching science emphasize the abstract instead of the concrete and semiconcrete facets of learning. The concrete (use or real objects, excursions, realia, and experiments), and the semiconcrete (illustrations, video-tapes, videodiscs, computers with diverse capabilities, among other audiovisual aids) should be used as learning opportunities to assist pupils to achieve the abstract. Thus objectives in teaching science need to stress the abstract in subject matter to be acquired as well as higher levels of cognition in ongoing units of study in science. The teacher largely determines which objectives and learning activities pupils are to pursue sequentially. Thus a logical science curriculum is being emphasized, according to educational psychologists. Ediger (1995) wrote:

Idealists are very academic and rigorous in the teaching of subject matter. They emphasize cognitive objectives much more so than affective (attitudinal) or psychcmotor (using of muscles and eye-hand coordination) in teaching-learning situations. Meaning, understanding, and depth learning of subject matter are important to idealists. Vital subject matter, carefully selected, needs to be taught to students. The students in acquiring subject matter in ongoing lessons is to move form the finite (limited) to the Infinite Being. Ideas are important to attain in an idealist's curriculum. The ideal is also salient to achieve in terms of moral standards and values.

The teacher emphasizing idealism as a philosophy of education stresses the selection of subject matter for student achievement which assists forming vital concepts and generalizations. Objectives of instruction need to reflect worthwhile concepts and generalizations. Depth teaching of specifics assists students to form and develop universal ideas. The use of behaviourally stated objectives for instruction would be frowned upon by the idealist teacher. Content would become too fragmented with the realist's position of testing and measuring reflecting measurably stated objectives. Rather, the idealist in emphasizing an idea centered curriculum desires that students relate subject matter acquired so that intense learning transpires. Thus if students are studying causes of World War II, each cause would be studied thoroughly and not merely listed. Causes come in sequence and are complex to appraise. Viewing and analyzing each cause takes time. After analyzing, relating, or synthesizing ideas take time in order to emphasize intensity, not survey teaching. Students are to be evaluated in progress as to how much vital subject matter has been acquired.

The use of the mind or intellect is salient for students to utilize in analyzing and synthesizing subject matter knowledge. Mental development is stressed as students learn, achieve, and develop.

Implications from idealism as a philosophy of education for the curriculum include the following:

1. intellectual, not attitudinal, nor psychomotor, goals come first in teaching-learning situations.

2. quality textbooks, workbooks, and selected audiovisual materials which aid in intellectual development should be used as learning activities to achieve stated goals for students.

3. evaluation techniques should stress appraisal of vital subject matter acquired by students.
4. depth teaching of subject matter is salient to guide learners to attain vital facts, concepts, and generalizations. Survey approaches are not acceptable.
5. the will of the student is needed to attain worthwhile subject matter. Interest of students, alone, is not adequate for students to achieve, attain, and develop well. Students must want to learn.
6. students need to achieve vital subject matter to prepare for the future life of an adult. Education is preparation for adult responsibilities, not present day situations in being a child.
7. learners need to develop from a finite (limited) being toward the Absolute or the Infinite (unlimited being). The Absolute may also be referred to as God.
8. a quality general education programme, consisting of vital content from major academic disciplines, is a must for all students.

A third philosophy of teaching emphasizes pupils being heavily involved in decision making in terms of choosing objectives, learning opportunities, as well as evaluation procedures. The science teacher needs to set up more stations with quality tasks than what any one pupil can complete. The pupil may then select sequential tasks to complete. Those tasks not having perceived purpose may be omitted by the learner. The teacher must choose relevant learning opportunities for pupils to select. Inquiry, problem solving, as well as critical and creative thinking tasks, are vital learning activities for pupils at each station. Careful consideration must be given to the worth of each station and task. The interests of pupils need to be cultivated in the science curriculum. The pupil is the chooser of which tasks to pursue and complete. The science teacher is a guide and stimulator but not a dispenser of information.

The attitudinal dimension is very important to develop within pupils when they select that which is vital to attain. Learners need to learn to make choices and decisions. Life itself consists of making choices within the framework of being openended and possessing freedom. In the science curriculum, pupils too need to make choices in which coercion is kept to a minimum. A decision making philosophy stress the learner being responsible for choices and completions made. Decision making is a skill and an attitude the pupils should learn due to its tremendous value presently and in the future for pupils.

With pupils being heavily involved in choosing sequential tasks to complete, a psychological curriculum is then in evidence due to pupils sequencing their very own activities in the science curriculum.

Pertaining to existentialism and pupil choices in the curriculum, Ozman and Craver (1990) wrote:

> It is interesting that most existentialists and phenomenological philosophers have had lengthy and rigorous educations . . . Most of them taught at one time or another, usually in a university setting. They have been primarily concerned with the humanities and have written exclusively in the genre. Through the humanities the existentialists have tried to awaken modern individuals to the dangers of being swallowed by the magalopolis and runaway technology. This seems to have taken place because the humanities contain greater potential for introspection and the development of self-meaning than other studies.
>
> The humanities loom large in an existentialists curriculum because they deal with the essential aspects of human existence such as the happy, the absurdities as well as meaning. In short, existentialists want to see humankind in its totality—the perverted well as the exalted, the mundane as well as the glorious, the despairing as well as the hopeful, and they feel that the humanities and the arts do this better than the sciences. Existentialists, however do not have any definite rules about what should comprise the curriculum. They believe that the student-in-situation making a choice should be the deciding factor.
>
> Although existential phenomenologists have been interested in understanding the lived experience of the learner than in the specific content to be learned, some of them have given attention to curriculum organization and content. The tendency, however, is to view cirriculum from the standpoint of the learner rather than as a collection of discrete subject matter.

A fourth philosophy of education for science teachers to follow is a criterion referenced (CRT) procedure of instruction. Here the teacher needs to write measurably stated objectives for pupil attainment. These objectives are always written prior to teaching pupils. Each objective is written in as precise a manner as possible. Ideally there is no leeway in interpreting what will be taught when examining any one measurably stated objective. The science teacher can measure after instruction if a learner has or has not achieved as measurably stated objective. The CRT measures against the measurably stated objectives to ascertain pupil achievement.

Science teachers may even announce to pupils what they are to learn as a result of instruction. Learners then might possess security in terms of what they are expected to achieve as a result of teaching and learning. Learning activities selected by the teacher to assist pupils to achieve must be aligned with the measurably stated objectives. These activities must be selected on the basis of guiding each pupil to achieve objectives. A logical curriculum is in evidence if the teacher chooses sequential objectives for pupil attainment as well as learning opportunities that are sequentially arranged so that pupils can experience success in learning.

Since teachers determine the sequence of objectives and learning opportunities for pupils to pursue, a definite logical curriculum is being stressed by science teachers. The teacher then attempts to arrange the order of objectives and activities to guide optimal pupil achievement. Pertaining to realism, Bowyer (1970) wrote the following:

> We have noted that there are different forms of naturalism and of idealism. The same is true of realism, which makes it difficult to define the realist point of view. One element that the various forms of realism do have in common is a rejection of the idealist theory of knowledge that the various qualities of experience depend upon a knower for their existence. Realists believe the universe is composed of real entities that exist in themselves. These entities can be known, and their existence is not dependent upon a knower or perceiver. Although realists can agree on this point, they do not all agree when they attempt to build a metaphysical system. Here, their views range from pluralism to dualism to monism.
>
> The realist epistemological views include epistemological monism where it is held that objects are presented in consciousness, and epistemological dualism where objects are

though to be represented. The monist defines mind as a relation between the organism and an object, while the dualists identify mind more closely with the organisms. Realists do have a tendency to view the world as the mechanism described by the physical sciences, and they generally believe in determinism, in orderliness in the universe, and the objectivity of science. The unifying thesis of realism is that knowledge is thought to have a universal character and comes to man through his sensory capacity. The realists have a confidence in their assertions about reality and value which is most discerning to pragmatists.

Recent Psychologies of Learning

B.F. Skinner (1904-90) was very instrumental in emphasizing S-R theory of instruction. With S-R theory in teaching science, Skinner advocated programmed learning for pupils. Programmed learning can take place either in textbook or computer/software form. Here, pupils move forward very slowly from the simple to that which is gradually more complex. Pupils then respond to a logical sequence developed by the programmer. Thus the pupil reads a small amount of content, responds to a completion item, and checks his/her response what that provided by the programmer. If the learner responded incorrectly, he/she tries a different response. If correct, the learner also moves on to the next sequential item. The sequence is the same each time with read, respond, and check. If the learner is correct, he/she is rewarded and reinforced for giving the correct answer to the completion item as provided by the programmer. Skinner believes that a programmer can always put in another item should the pupil taking the programme in the pilot study miss out in a sequential item. A quality programme should make for a ninety per cent correct pupil response per item for each in the pilot study. The pilot study involves conducting experiments to find out where weaknesses lie in the programme. If too much learners, miss an item, perhaps an additional step needs to be put in where these pupils responded incorrectly. Poorly written items are taken out or modified so that responses can be made based on clarity within that step of learning. I have observed selected well written programmes in science units of study which reflect the making of B.F. Skinner. Pertaining to programmed learning, Harris and Sipay (1985) wrote the following:

Programmed materials are designed so that the user (1) encounters a series of small steps on which success is very likely (2) is involved in the learning process through actively responding (3) receives immediate feedback as to the correctness of each response. In theory, programmed material should greatly facilitate individualized instruction because they allow each student to work almost independently with material suitable for his or her needs, proceeding at a pace commensurate with ability and interest.

Ediger (1997) wrote the following pertaining to programmed instruction:

> The programmer decides upon the objectives for each programme. Also, the sequential activities and appraisal procedures are determined by the programmer. There is basically no input from pupils or from teachers in terms of objectives, learning activities, and evaluation procedures when utilizing programmed materials.

Advantages given for using programmed learning include the following:

1. each learner may pace his/her own optimal speed of learning. No two pupils need to be at the same or similar level of achievement.
2. learners know immediately if they are right or wrong in responses made.
3. rarely do learners make mistakes in quality programmed materials. The error rate is five to ten per cent in field tested programmes.
4. reinforcement is possible in field tested programmed items. Thus an involved learner might experience rather continual progress.
5. sequential progress is made in small steps rather than covering content in terms of a large scope at a time.

Disadvantages given in emphasizing programmed learning include:

1. programmed learning may not harmonize with learning styles of selected pupils.
2. step by step learning—red, respond, and check—does not harmonize with expectations of life in society. Life in society is not programmed.

3. programmed materials tend to deemphasize the utilization of the concrete (reality), and semi-concrete (pictorial form) materials. Abstract content tends to the rather heavily emphasized in programmed materials.

4. selected pupils may not perceive interest and purpose in the programmer choosing objectives, learner activities, and evaluation procedures.

5. small sequential steps in learning may be too finite or limited to meet personal needs of gifted and talented learners.

The influence of programmed learning and the thinking of B.F. Skinner has had wide influence in educational thought. There still are programmed books available on many topics in book form as well as in computer packages. Perhaps, the strongest influence of Dr. Skinner is in the use of behaviourally stated objectives in teaching. These objectives are very precise and are written prior to instruction. A pupil as a result of instruction either does or does not achieve any single objective. Thus, it is possible to measure if a pupil has been successful in goal attainment. Learning activities selected by the teacher align with the stated objectives. The evaluation procedures also are aligned with the measurably stated objectives. Objective results from pupils are in evidence from instruction, regardless of who does the evaluating. Relating B.F. Skinner's thinking and that of the behaviourally stated objectives movement, the following writing will assist in clarifying the two (Morris and Pai, 1976):

> As Skinner pointed out several times, the most important task of the teacher is to arrange the conditions under which desired learning can occur. Considering the fact that teachers are expected to bring about changes in extremely complex behaviour, they should be specialists in human behaviour. Effective and efficient manipulation of the multitude of variables affecting children's intellectual and social behaviours cannot be accomplished by trial and error alone, nor should such work be based solely on the personal experiences of the teacher, since this covers only a limited range of circumstances. Consequently, a scientific study of human behaviour is vital in the improvement of teaching, because it provides us with accurate and reliable knowledge about learning and leads us to the development of new instructional

materials, methods, and techniques. Similarly, an empirical analysis of the teaching process is essential, for it clarifies the teacher's responsibility through a series of small and progressive approximations, thus facilitating a more effective evaluation.

The measurably stated objectives movement, also called behaviourism as a psychology of learning, emphasizes a rather closed system of instruction. The objectives are predetermined and may be announced to pupils for each end to be stressed, as the need progresses, the learning activities and the evaluation techniques harmonize or align. Many educators believe that this alignment optimalize learner achievement in teaching and learning situations.

With this close alignment, little room is left for pupils to raise questions that they deem to be relevant and vital.

Humanism in the Science Curriculum

Toward the other end of the continuum, humanism, as a psychology of learning stresses heavy pupil involvement in selecting objectives, learning opportunities, and appraisal procedures, the pupil here is the focal point of instruction. Learners are to involved in sequencing their own experiences; this emphasizes a psychological science curriculum whereas the behaviourally stated objectives psychology advocated a logical sequence for pupils whereby the teacher orders objectives for pupil attainment. Pertaining to humanism and existentialism, Ediger (1996) wrote:

> Existentialists believe that one exists and then purposes need to be found or developed. The individual self then determines his/her own goals in life. There are no absolutes or guidelines in life to choose what is right and what is good. Each person must select and make decisions. To avoid making decisions is to lack being human. The choice then is to go along with the crowd. However, to be human involves making decisions.
>
> The only broad criterion for existentialists to follow in choosing is to make moral decisions in a complete atmosphere of freedom. Others should definitely not decide one's destiny. One did not ask to be born and yet each person much make authentic decisions.
>
> Moral decisions are difficult to make. An environment of awe exists in making authentic decisions.

> Which objectives, learning activities, and evaluation procedures should be inherent in an existentialist curriculum? Existentialists believe in each person choosing objectives. In the school setting, the goals may be selected by learners with teacher guidance within the framework of an open-ended curriculum. The teacher needs to select ends, means, and evaluation procedures which stress the importance of pupils becoming increasingly responsible for personal freedom. The teacher should definitely not be a policeman. Rather, teachers realize their role as providing for an open environment in order that the learner may select sequential experiences . . .
>
> Each decision made in life involves personal decisions in reaching a goal or goals... Each person makes or breaks himself or herself. No other person or being is responsible for consequence of decisions made. Blaming others for that happened in life is meaningless, according to existentialists. Each person needs to learn to accept responsibilities for thoughts, deeds, and actions.

The humanist or existentialist science curriculum may be implemented in several ways. One approach is to use learning centres in the school/classroom setting. I have observed the following learning centres pertaining to the science unit "The Changing Surface of the Earth," from which pupils may select sequential tasks to complete:

1. a reading center
2. an art center
3. a drama center
4. a writing center
5. an audio-visual center
6. a computer and software center
7. a music center
8. a model making center
9. a problem solving center
10. an experiment center

Each pupil in a classroom may select which center and which task to work on. There are more tasks at each center than what any one child can complete. Learners may then choose what to work on and what to omit in a humanistic science curriculum. The individual pupil determines sequence or order of which tasks to pursue and which to omit. Purpose for learning then reside within the pupil. Examples of which materials will be at a learning center and the kinds of tasks or learning activities that will be in evidence may be illustrated with the first center mentioned above—a reading center. Here, a variety of library books on the unit title and on diverse reading levels need to be in evidence. A pupil chooses a book to read and may complete as many of the following tasks at this center as individual purpose dictates:

1. write a summary covering content read.
2. make a model of inherent subject matter read, such as a model volcano.
3. draw a picture of folding and faulting.
4. write an additional page for the library book read.
5. identify a problem dealing with changes on the earth's surface and use various reference sources to locate information for solving the problem.

Pupils individually make choices sequentially as to what to learn and the means of learning. Tasks can relate to choosing to work by the self or with others. If too many work at one center, the teacher may make a rule as to the optimal number of pupils that may work at any one center. The science teacher here is a guide or motivator of pupils to stay on task and complete satisfactorily what has been selected as learning activities. The pupil may even plan with the teacher what to work on if greater purpose is perceived in working on something else than what is at any of the centers.

Humanists advocate that pupils reveal behaviour, not facades, to be authentic, the pupil needs to reveal more of the real self. Trust in communicating with others is important. Humans have tremendous worth and value. Being authentic and trusting others in a positive relationship is relevant to humanists.

Many studies currently made stress the importance of multiple intelligences. Sternberg (1997) emphasizes that in a Yale

University study, intelligence has analytical, creative, and practical aspects. He presets the following model for science in four categories:

> Memory—name the four types of bacteria.
>
> Analysis—analyze the means the immune system uses to fight bacterial infections.
>
> Creativity—suggest ways to cope with the increasing immunity bacteria are showing to antibiotic drugs.
>
> Practicality—suggest three steps that individuals might take to reduce the likelihood of bacterial infection.

In any lesson and unit of study, the science teacher may emphasize these four categories of instruction. Pupils need to achieve at higher levels of cognition than the memory level. Learners will then reveal in different ways what has been learned in the analysis, creativity, and practicality levels. Intelligence then is not a single score nor a single way of indicating what has been learned. Sternberg (1997) goes on to say:

> By exposing students to instruction emphasizing each type of ability, we enable them to capitalize on their strengths while developing and improving new skills. This appraoch is also important because students need to learn that the world cannot always provide them with activities that suit their preferences. At the same time, if students are never presented with activities that suit them, they will never experience a sense of success and accomplishment. As a result, they may tune out and never achieve their full potential . . .
>
> Success in today's job market often requires creativity, flexibility, and a readiness to see things in new ways. Furthermore, students who graduate with A's but cannot apply what they have learned may find themselves failing on the job.
>
> Creativity, in particular, has become even more important over time, just as other abilities have become less valuable. For example, with the advent of computers and calculators, both penmanship and arithmetic skills have diminished in importance, some standardized ability tests, such as the SAT, even allow students to use calculators. With the increasing availability of massive, rapid data retrieval systems, the ability to memorize information will become even less important. . .

> This is not to say that that memory and analytical abilities are not important. Students need to learn and remember the core content of the curriculum, and they need to be able to analyze—to think critically about—the material. But the importance of these abilities should not be allowed to obfuscate what else is important.
>
> In a pluralistic society, we cannot afford to have a monolithic conception of intelligence and schooling, it's simply a waste of talent. And as I unexpectedly found in my study, it's no random waste. The more we teach and assess students based on a broader set of abilities, the more racially, ethnically, and socioeconomically diverse our achievers will be. We can easily change our closed system—and we should. We must take a more balanced approach to education to reach all of our students.

Sternberg believes strongly that pupils individually are not permitted to indicate what has been learned in diverse ways. It is true that pupils so often are asked to show achievement through testing, generally through pupils taking multiple choice tests. Thus verbal approaches are used to ascertain what pupils individually have learned. This is limiting in that there are many other means of revealing achievement. Dr. Howard Gardner (1995) has determined there are at least seven intelligences, according to his research; these are verbal-linguistic, interpersonal, intrapersonal, musical, spatial, bodily-kinesthetic, and logical mathematics. Pupils may show similar strengths, but not necessarily in the same ways or to the same extent over time. With multiple intelligences, pupils learn in diverse ways and are interested in different subject matter in the academic arena. Learners than reveal their strengths and weaknesses in what has been learned in a variety of ways, not one way only such as in verbal testing using multiple choice items. Thus, the pupil who is strong in the verbal arena will reveal differently what has been learned as compared to the one endowed with musical intelligence. Too frequently, the emphasis has been upon verbal approaches to assessing pupil achievement and yet there are numerous other ways to indicate intelligence, as Dr. Gardner has indicated in multiple intelligences theory. Hatch (1997) wrote:

> Such a view of intelligence is reflected in programs and practices that seek to determine which areas young children show the greatest strengths. Children who do well on tasks in a particular

area—storytelling or reporting, athletics or dance, drawing or building—are broadly labelled as having strengths in linguistics, bodily-kinesthetic, or spatial realms, respectively.

Such an approach, however, implies that children have a reservoir of talent in a variety of activities, shown consistently over a period of time. It suggests that there are more intelligences, but does not necessarily call into question assumptions about the nature, display, and development of intelligence.

In Summary

Science teachers need to develop a philosophy and psychology of instruction that optimalize learner attainment. Pupils differ from each other in many ways including methods and procedures of acquiring relevant facts, concepts, and generalizations. A careful study and implementation of a worth -while philosophy and psychology of learning might well assist each pupils to learn as much as possible.

To stress science as inquiry in harmony with National Standards, the writer emphasizes what he believes to be best from each school of thought discussed above. These are

1. a problem solving science curriculum in which pupils with teacher guidance identify and solve relevant lifelike problems.
2. a subject centered science curriculum emphasizing pupils attaining higher levels of cognition in achieving salient facts, concepts, and generalizations.
3. pupil selection from among alternatives of tasks perceived to be purposeful. Tasks at different stations should reflect science as inquiry.
4. measurably stated objectives which reflect National Standards in a predetermined science curriculum. Precise objectives are then selected prior to instruction for learner attainment. A carefully designed science curriculum may then be in evidence. The content obtained should be inherent in science as inquiry teaching and learning.

Pertaining to the psychology of learning in science, pupils should achieve quality sequence. Interest, purpose, and meaning are important concepts to stress in teaching science in ongoing lesson plans and units of study.

With multiple intelligences theory, pupils do learn in different ways and through diverse methods of instruction. Learners individually do possess their favourite means of learning and achieving. There are numerous methods of revealing what has been learned.

The science teacher then needs to have pupils participate in a variety of learning opportunities and have them indicate achievement using diverse procedures to provide for different learning styles possessed. The following learning opportunities are available for pupils in the science curriculum:

1. hands on approaches in learning.
2. experiments and demonstrations.
3. field trips and excursions.
4. problems solving experiences.
5. reading from basal texts, library books, and science encyclopedias.
6. viewing video tapes, video disks, films, and filmstrips.
7. discussing, interviewing, dramatizing, and pantomiming.
8. writing poems, plays, outlines, summaries, diary entries, log entries, journal entries, and stories.
9. making dioramas, collages, bulletin board displays, murals, models, and equipment for science experiments.
10. using technology such as computer packages, the word processor, internet and world wide web, and calculators.

REFERENCES

Bowyer, Carlton (1970). *Philosophical Perspectives for Education*. Glenview, Illinois: Scott, Foresman and Company, p. 17.

Ediger, Marlow (1995). *Philosophy in Curriculum Development* Kirksville, Missouri: Simpson Publishing Company, pp. 22 and 23.

Ediger Marlow (1997). *The Modern Elementary School*.

Kirksville, Missouri: Simpson Publishing Company, pp. 110 and 111.

Ediger, Marlow (1996). *Eassys in School Administration*.

Kirksville, Missouri: Simpson Publishing Company, pp. 58 and 59.

Gardner, Howard (1995). "Reflections on Multiple Intelligences: Myths and Messages," *Phi Delta Kappan* 77, 3:200-203, 206-209.

Harris, Albert J., and Edward R. Sipay (1985). *How to Increase Reading Ability*. White Plains, New York: Longman, p. 71.

Hatch, Thomas (1997). "Getting Specific About Multiple Intelligences," *Educational Leadership*, 54,6:26.

Meyer, Adolph (1949). *The Development of Education in the Twientieth Century*. Englewood Cliffs, New Jersey: Prentice-Hall, Inc., p. 42-43.

Morris, Van Cleve, and Young Pai (1976). *Philosophy and the American School*. Boston: Houghton Mifflin Company, p. 340.

Ozman, Howard A., and Samuel M. Craver (1990). *Philosophical Foundations of Education*. Columbus, Ohio: Merrill Publishing Company, p. 257.

Sternberg, Robert J. (1997), "What Does It Mean to be Smart?" *Educational Leadership*, 22-24.

17

Social Constructivism in Science Learning: Toward A Mind-World Synthesis

GEORGE E. GLASSON & ROSARY V. LALIK
Virginia Polytechnic Institute and State University, USA

Introduction

Until recently, positivist epistemology has profoundly influenced the development of science and constrained thinking about educational practice. The linchpin of this epistemology was Descartes' premise that the mind is an independent entity, distinct from the physical world. This philosophical premise allowed for the development of the positivistic notion of objectivity:

> The positivism that underpinned this period of "modern science" made an implicit distinction between observer and observed or subject and object. Thus objectivity from a positivist perspective implies an unbiased and impartial observer looking for causal explanations of physical (or, indeed, social) phenomena from which successful prediction may arise by examination of the facts "out there" in an external reality.[1]

In the positivistic tradition, theory value independent observation and logic are used to discover phenomena that purportedly exist in the real world.

More recently, both philosophers of science (Garrison, 1986, Kuhn, 1970; Laudan, 1984; Longino, 1990) and sociologists of science (Latour, 1987; Woolgar, 1988) have rejected positivistic assumptions. Instead, these scholars promote the postpositivist view that knowledge is a creative human construction and that any measure or observation is theory-laden. Constructivist learning theories purportedly reflect this emergent post-positivist philosophy. Consistent with the post-positivist epistemology of philosophers, constructivists reject the earlier receptive models of learning and instead describe learning as an active, interpretive process.

Two major traditions exist within constructivism—the Piagetian tradition and the Vygotskian tradition (Clements & Nastasi, 1988). In this paper, we will show how the cognitive constructivist Piagetian tradition dichotomizes and mind and the world, while Vygotskiasn theorists, taking a social constructivist view, describe the mind as dialectically related to the world. Drawing on the work of Lave (1988), a contemporary social constructivist, we will discuss a practice theory of cognition that explicates a mind-world synthesis. We will refer to the work of Kuhn (1970) and Latour (1987) to show how Lave's perspective is consistent with recent descriptions of scientific practice. Finally, we will consider implications of Lave's social constructivist perspective for science education.

Mind-World Dichotomy: Piagetian Tradition

Constructivists within the Piagetian tradition emphasize internal cognition as distinct from the world (Duckworth, 1987; Posner, Strike, Hewson & Gertzog, 1982; Piaget, 1959; Tobin, 1990; von Glasersfeld, 1989). Von Glasersfeld's (1989) description reflects the cognitivist view that knowledge takes the form of internal conceptual structures that individual learners, "given the range of present experience within their tradition of thought and language consider *vible*".[2] The theme of individualistic learning is developed by Duckworth in her description of children's science learning:

> Thoughts are our way of connecting things up for ourselves. If others tell us about the connections they have made, we can only understand them to the extent that we do the work of making these connections ourselves. Making connections must be a personal elaboration, and sometimes a person is simply not capable of making the connections that someone is trying to point out.[3]

For the Piagetian constructivists, individualistic experiential learning is manifested in the development of internal conceptual structures located in the mind of the learner.

The equilibration process is essential to learning from the Piagetian perspective. As part of their actions with the environment, individual learners may experience cognitive disequilibrium:

> Knowledge is never acquired passively, because novelty cannot be handled except through assimilation to a cognitive structure the experiencing subject already has. Indeed, the subject does not perceive an experience as novel until it generates a perturbation relative to some expected result. Only at that point the experience may lead to an accommodation and thus to a novel conceptual structure that re-establishes a relative equilibrium.[4]

In the view of Posner, Strike, Hewson and Gertzog (1982), the individual experiences dissatisfaction in the face of an anomalous situation in which s/he is unable to make sense of experience on the basis of existing conceptual networks.

Piagetian constructivists argue that social interactions are also an important "source of perturbations for the develing cognitive subject" (von Glasersfeld 1989, p. 136). Further, social interactions provide evidence that a learner can use to judge the viability of a conceptual structure:

> Then, if a particular prediction we have made concerning an action or reaction of an other turns out to be corroborated by what the other does, this adds a second level of viability to our scheme; and the second level of viability strengthens the experiential reality we have constructed.[5]

According to Tobin, Briscoe and Holman (1990), internal knowledge frameworks may be altered on the basis of social interaction "when an individual is unable to find 'fit' between his/her constructions and the perceived environment or a 'fit' with others with whom interactions are taking place".[6]

While social interaction may influence developing cognitive structures, the importance of verbal explanation for conceptual development is questioned:

> The analysis of the process of linguistic communication shows that knowledge cannot simply be transferred by means of words.

Verbally explaining a problem does not lead to understanding, unless the concepts the listener has associated with the linguistic components of the explanation are compatible with those the explainer has in mind.[7]

In describing the conceptual development of children, Duckworth (1987) points to the diminished role of language compared to action in learning as children "are making refinements and connections in their actions—'thinking' in their actions—long before there is any use of language".[8] When speech emerges for the child, it is viewed by Piaget as egocentric rather than social "partly because the child speaks only about himself, but chiefly because he does not attempt to place himself at the point of view of the hearer."[9]

For Piagetians, knowledge is an internal individualistic human construction that is separate from the world. This dichotomy is a remnant of the Cartesian dualism that is foundational to positivistic thinking. Although the Piagetians abandoned the positivistic view that the world can be known directly and emphasized, instead, the active and interpretive character of human learning, they continue to describe the mind as an entity separate from the world.

Mind-World Dialectic: Vygotskian Tradition

While constructivists in the Piagetian tradition dichotomize the mind and the world, Vygotskian theorists view the mind as dialectically related to the world. In particular, they emphasize the interplay between speech and action in the development of internal psychological functions; the dialectic between interpersonal and intrapersonal functions; and the notion of an externalized form of mind in which learning can take place (Newman, Griffin & Cole, 1989; Vygotsky, 1978, 1986; Wertsch, 1979).

The importance of language in conceptual development within the Vygotskian tradition stands in sharp contrast to the more limited role described by Piagetians. According to Vygotsky, speech and action interact in psychological functioning:

(1) A child's speech is as important as the role of action in attaining the goal. Children not only speak about what

they are doing, their speech and action are part of *one and the same complex psychological function*, directed toward the solution of the problem at hand.

(2) The more complex the action demanded by the situation and the less direct its solution, the greater the importance played by speech in the operation as a whole. Sometimes speech becomes of such vital importance, if not permitted to use it, young children cannot accomplish the given task.[10]

Unlike Piaget (1959), who characterizes a child's speech as egocentric before it is social, Vygotsky describes a child's speech as social before it is egocentric. In Vygotsky's view, this early socialized form of speech is foundational to thought:

> The relation of thought to word is not a thing but a process, a continual movement back and fourth from thought to word and from word to thought. In that process, the relation of thought to word undergoes changes that themselves may be regarded as development in the functional sense. Thought is not merely expressed in words; it comes into existence through them.[11]

Vygotsky's description of the relationship between thought and language is essential for understanding the mind as part of the world.

For Vygotsky, mental functions first appear externally as interpersonal forms of meaning before transforming into internalized intrapersonal forms. This transformation process "continues to exist and to change as an external form of activity for a long time before definitely turning inward. For many functions, the stage of external signs lasts forever, that is, it is their final stage of development" (Vygotsky 1978, p. 57). These transformations between the external and internal aspects of mind are dialectically related:

> His psychology is not just about the mind nor just about the externally specifiable stimulus-response relations. It is about the dialectic between the inter- and the intra-psychological and the transformations of one into another. Mind becomes externalized by a culture in its tools, such as written language and social institutions.[12]

The existence of an externalized form of mind stands in

contrast to the Piagetian view of knowledge as being exclusively revealed in the internal conceptual structures of the learner.

For Vygotskian theorists, learning takes place within the zone of proximal development, alternatively known as the construction zone, "where the zone is considered both in terms of an individual's developmental history and in terms of the support structure created by the other people and cultural tools in the setting" (Newman et al., p. 61). While the construction zone is an externalized form of mind, its purpose is to support individual and internal cognitive change:

> The internal and external constructive processes are occurring simultaneously. New, more powerful structures may be constructed interpsychologically and the new structure can interact with the child's intrapsychological structures to result in individual cognitive changes.[13]

By emphasizing the notion of individualistic and internal cognitive change as an important component of knowledge development, Vygotskian theorists, like Piagetians, retain a remnant of the Cartesian dualism. Nevertheless, with their development of an interpersonal-intrapersonal dialectic as a foundational process for learning, Vygotskians bridge the gap between the internal mind and the external world.

Toward a Mind-World Synthesis

Unlike other constructivists, Lave (1988) rejects the Cartesian dualism. Instead, she describes cognition as "distributed—stretched over, not divided among—mind, body, activity and culturally organized settings (which include other actors)" (p. 1). Similarly, Lave eschews the idea of individualistic learning focusing instead on people engaged in purposeful activity:

> A more appropriate unit of analysis is the whole person in action, acting with the settings of that activity. This shifts the boundaries of activity well outside the skull and beyond the hypothetical economic actor, to persons engaged with the world for a variety of "reasons;" it also requires a different version of the everyday world.[14]

This view of cognition "implies that thought (embodied and enacted) is situated in socially and culturally structured time and space."[15]

Similar to Vygotsky's zone of proximal development, Lave develops the notion of "fields-of-action" where learning takes place within the context of practice, social relations and their settings. Rather than focusing on internal and individualistic cognitive change, Lave describes internalization as "a less-important mode of contact with the world than action in the world".[16] Lave explains further:

> By arguing that activity, including cognition, is socially organized and quintessentially social in its very existence, its formation, and its ongoing character, we have committed the enterprise to theorizing about the social production of action as well as its cultural character.[17]

From this theoretical perspective, problem-solving processes are contextualized and situated in ongoing activity:

> Problem solvers proceed in action, often integrally engaging body, self, common sensibilities in the setting . . . . Impelled and given meaning by conflicts generated out of the contradictions governing social practice, "problems" are dilemmas to be resolved, rarely problems to be solved.[18]

The social nature of these dilemmas stands in contrast to the individualistic cognitive constructivist view of disequilibration advocated by Piagetian theorists.

The significance of human social action in learning is highly consistent with descriptions of the development of scientific knowledge. Kuhn (1970), for example, developed the notion of community of scientists and portrayed the establishment of a scientific pardigam as a social enterprise:

> At the start a new candidate for a new paradigm may have few supporters, and on occasions the supporters' motives may be suspect. Nevertheless, if they are competent, they will improve it, explore its possibilities, and show what it will be like to the community guided by it. In as that goes on, if the paradigm is one destined to win its fight, the number and strength of the persuasive arguments in its favour will increase. More scientists will be converted and the exploration of the new paradigm will go on. Gradually the number of experiments, instruments, articles, and books based on the paradigm will multiply.[19]

Scientific knowledge is situated within the community's practice rather than within the mind of the individual scientist.

By studying scientists in the processes of conducting their work, Latour (1987) also presented a view of science-in-action that demonstrates its fundamentally social character. As reflected in their laboratory work and in the development of ideas, scientists establish networks of allies to support their positions. Anyone who wishes to present dissenting views, must address the entire network. As Latour explains, "doubting a spokespersons' word, requires a much more strenuous effort however because it is now one person—he dissenter—against a crowd—the author" (p. 72). For Latour, as all ideas do not have an equal opportunity to compete, science is better characterized as a subjective enterprise. The work of Kuhn and Latour demonstrate the inherently social character of science and dispel the myth of a rational individualistic mind operating apart from the world.

Implications For Science Education

Constructivism that focuses on social action in the world rather than the development of individualistic and internal conceptual structures offers particular advantages to science educators. First, it allows for the development of curricula in which students' reciprocal use of language and action within the classroom and community takes on a much more valued role than the development of internal conceptual frameworks. Like practicing scientists, students would collaborate on purposeful activity rather than complete decontextualized individual tasks. Assessment practices can focus on how students act in social settings rather than attempting to measure internal cognitive structures and processes. Consistent with the work of Moll and Greenberg (1990) and Heath (1983), programmes would be developed based on knowledge about the outside-of-school cultural practices of students, thus attracting and supporting the participation in science of minority and female populations. These students would enrich the development of scientific knowledge by contributing their culturally rooted ideas and metaphors (Keller, 1985). By rejecting the schism between mind and body, the social constructivist theory of learning offers new possibilities for the development of transformative and egalitarian communities of scientists and science learners.

NOTES

1. Cleminson (1990), p. 432.
2. von Glasersfeld (1989), p. 124.
3. Duckworth (1987), p. 26.
4. von Glasersfeld (1989), p. 136.
5. von Glasersfeld (1989), p. 131.
6. Tobin, Briscoe and Holman (1990), p 411.
7. von Glasersfeld (1989), p. 136.
8. Duckworth (1987), p. 19.
9. Piaget (1959), p. 9.
10. Vygotsky (1987), pp. 25-36.
11. Vygotsky (1986), p. 218.
12. Newman, Griffin & Cole (1989), p. 60.
13. Newman, Griffin & Cole (1989), p. 68.
14. Lave (1988), pp. 17-18.
15. Lave (1988), p. 171.
16. Lave (1988), pp. 16-17.
17. Lave (1988), p. 177.
18. Lave (1988), p. 20.
19. Kuhn (1970), p. 159.

REFERENCES

Clements, D.H. & B.K. Nastasi: 1988, 'Social and Cognitive Interactions in Educational Computer Environments', *American Educational Research Journal* 25(1), 87-106.

Cleminson, A.: 1990, 'Establishing and Epistemological Base for Science Teaching in the Light of Contemporary Notions of the Nature of Science and How Children Learn Science', *Journal of Research in Science Teaching* 27(5), 429-445.

Duckworth, E.: 1987, *"The Having of Wonderful Ideas" and Other Eassys on Teaching and Learning*, Teachers College Press, New York.

Garrison, J.W.: 1986, 'Some Principles of Postpositivistic Philosophy of Science', *Educational Researcher 15(9)*, 12-18.

Glasersfeld, E. von.: 1989, 'Congnition, Construction of Knowledge, and Teaching', *Syntheses 80(1)*, 121-140.

Heath, S.B.: 1983, *Ways with Words: Language, Life and Work in*

Communities and Classrooms, Cambridge University Press, Cambridge.

Keller, E.F.: 1985, *Reflections on Gender and Science*, Yale University Press, New Haven.

Kuhn, T.: 1970, *The Structure of Scientific Revolutions*, University of Chicago Press, Chicago.

Latour, B.: 1987, *Science in Action*, Harvard University Press, Cambridge.

Laudan, L.: 1984, *Science and Values*, University of California Press, Berkeley.

Lave, J.: 1988, *Cognition in Practice: Mind, Mathematics and Culture in Everyday Life*, Cambridge University Press, New York.

Longino, H.E.: 1990, *Science as Knowledge: Values and Objectivity in Scientific Inquiry*, Princeton University Press, New Jersey.

Moll, L.C. & J.B. Greenberg: 1990, 'Creating Zones of Possibilities: Combining Social Contexts for Instruction', in L. Moll (eds.), *Vygotsky and Education: Instructional Implications and Applications of Sociohistorical Psychology*, Cambridge University Press, Cambridge, 319-347.

Newman, D., P. Griffin & M. Cole: 1989, *The Construction Zone: Working for Cognitive Change in School*, Cambridge University Press, New York.

Piaget, J.: 1959, *The Language and Thought of the Child*, Routledge & Kegan Paul, London.

Posner, G.J., J.A. Strike, P.W. Hewson & W.A. Gertzog: 1982, 'Accommodation of a Scientific Conception: Toward a Theory of Conceptual Change', *Science Education* 66(2), 211-227.

Tobin, K., C. Briscoe & J.R. Holman: 1990, 'Overcoming Constraints to Effective Elementary Science Teaching', *Science Education* 74(4), 409-420.

Vygotsky, L.S.: 1978, *Mind in Society*, Harvard University Press, Cambridge.

Vygotsky, L.S.: 1986, *Thought and Language*, MIT Press, Cambridge.

Wertch, J.V.: 1979, 'From Social Interaction to Higher Psychological Processes: A Clarification and Application of Vygotsky's Theory', *Human Development* 22, 1-22.

Woolgar, S.: 1988, *Science: The Very Idea*, Tavistock Publications, London.

18

Scientific Literacy: For Whose Benefit?

JAMES W. GARRISON & KENNETH S. LAWWILL
Virginia Polytechnic Institute and State University USA

Introduction

Maxine Greene (1988) begins her book *The Dialectic of Freedom* by remarking: "Talk of the free world today is intertwined with talks of economic competitiveness, technology, and power".[1] A few pages later she further notes that in talks of educational reform: "The dominate watchwords remain 'effectiveness', 'proficiency', 'efficiency', and an ill-defined, one dimensional 'excellence'. Reforms or no, teachers are asked to teach to the *end* of 'economic competitiveness' for the nation".[2] With notable exceptions much of the current call to reform science education and achieve something called "scientific literacy" seems directed toward this *end*. We are not suggesting that global economic competitiveness should not be a concern. One has only to took at the current economic conditions in Eastern Europe and the conditions of the former Soviet states to see the sad consequences of not being economically competitive. Still, we have strong reservations about making this need *the* end or even a very prominent end of science education. First, we feel that the aim of science education is to free the individual and collective intelligence, imagination and have to engage in disciplined inquiry, an inquiry that we have argued elsewhere[3] is inherently open and democratic when done well. We are concerned that emphasis on economic competition could systematically distort democratic dialogue in and about science education. Further, we are worried that using science education, or more specifically, the students that are educated, as a means to some self-alienating end comes very close to violating the widely shared Kantian imperative that says: "*So act as to treat humanity, whether in your own person or any other, always at the same time as an end, and never merely as a means*".[4] Finally, and ironically, we suggest that to harness science education to the production function in the way recommended by the current economically driven reform movement in the US and elsewhere is not only bad for science education but also a bad way to use students of science to increase ecomonic productivity.

Evidence: The Emphases of Reform Literature

> We must act now to improve our educational system and prove that Americans can still outwork, outproduce, outinvent, and outcompete any nation in the world.[5]

As the current wave of concern for reform was first expressed in the early nineteen-eighties, economic and societal concerns were the focus of many reports. *A Nation At Risk* (1983) noted the decline of achievement in schools. A cursory reread of the document revealed approximately forty-five statements regarding academic performance. However, in comparison, sixty references were made to business and societal needs. With regards to the enhanced development of the individual, but twenty-five statements. Individuals' personal growths are needed for societal and business needs! Focus upon the latter does not imply the former. A better cure for national economy would be schools that focus upon maximizing individuals' abilities, imagination and desires, rather than sorting them and preparing them for a position in now existing industry.

In *Action For Excellence* by the Task Force on Education for Economic Growth (1983) there is obviously a much greater bias towards focusing educational reforms to fit needs of business and industry. The report firmly asserts: "We believe especially that businesses, in their role as employers, such be much more deeply involved in the process of setting goals for education in

America . . ."[6] However, we argue reform should focus primarily on the development of individuals and equity of society, with improved business and industry being a necessary, but subsumed component. Further, improved business and industry means an evolution four the current oppressive schemes of managerial control and restrictive profit sharing. (NBC News reported on Friday, Jan. 3, 1992 that in Japan, CEO's salaries averaged sixteen times their workers average salary. In the USA, the CEO's averaged *one-hundred-and-sixty times their workers!* This is even more unjust as corporate heads continue to receive bonuses during a recession in which their workers are being laid-off!)

While reviewing articles on the topics of science literacy and science education reform, economic consideration are listed as the primary concern in almost all. (Please refer to reference listing.) Several recent publications stress economic concerns while de-emphasizing or not even mentioning aspects of individual development. The co-chair of Phase I of Project 2061 stated: "The goal of science education is to impart a sense of empowerment, technical facility, and motivation to the workers who make up the backbone of our economy—not just the fraction who finish college, or the even smaller fraction who perform professional and managerial jobs, but also the large majority who perform less skilled jobs"[7]. Interestingly, *Project 2061* presents one of the approaches focusing more on individuals. An example of focusing upon national economy while neglecting emphasis upon individuals' development would be *Project LASER* (1990) from NASA. *Learning About Science, Engineering, and Research* lists the following as goals:

1. All children, from all backgrounds, must have a quality education which includes science and mathematics, and an equal opportunity to become a vital part of our science and engineering workforce—as workers, beneficiaries, taxpayers, and voters.

2. Education must be reformed to allow American students—from prekindergarten to grade 12—to enter college as future competitors in the international marketplace.

3. By the year 2000 the number and diversity of American science and engineering graduates must expand to meet the demands for faculty, industry, and government.
4. Because Federal R&D resources strongly influence national science and engineering work, they must be used to help leverage the world's best science and engineering workforce by the year 2000.
5. The Federal government will continue to set the pace in providing accessible, equitable and favourable workplaces for under-represented groups in science and engineering.
6. American culture must change. News and entertainment media, businesses and communities are needed to reverse negative images: "Mad" scientists portrayed in entertainment media; Science and math are "too tough" or "for nerds"; "Only geniuses need apply."

In the accompanying text, eighteen further references are made to employment, and national prestige and security. Only ten other comments concerns individual's growth. We believe the implicit message is "more science, more technology equates to better." But better for whom though? Is it possible the real implication is continued replication of current societal structure? Is it limiting the emphasis of creativity to sci-tech?

There are voices that have objected to the business/ industrial focus of current reform from its beginning. Regarding concerns about loss of international competitiveness, Spring (1987) questioned (in 1984) whether the schools should be blamed. What of decisions made by business and industry and their schemes for profit maximizing? He strongly argues that rather than a lack of educational quality leading to decline, it was the choice of industry in the seventies to use more manpower, then abundant and inexpensive. The lack of capital investments of available technologies then has been a bigger contributing factor to our current situation than our schools. Spring contends that the forty per cent reduction in the number of individuals entering the workforce in the eighties (at the end of the baby boom) was predicted. The resulting more expensive labour could have been anticipated!

> After all, the decision of business not to invest in new plants and equipment in the 1970's and instead reap short-term profits is partly responsible for the presents technological crisis. *The failure of the public schools did not cause the problems.* . . . In fact if the schools continue to be geared to meet the changing needs of US business, we can expect another change in educational policy in the next decade to meet those changing desires. Thus the public school system becomes a captive of the profit motive of US industry. And let me emphasize again, this relationship guarantees neither an improved economy nor a higher standard of living for individuals.[8]

With this the case, why then so much current passion regarding "scientific literacy"? In the concluding article of an issue of *Daedalus* (Spring 1983) devoted to the issue, Stephen Graubard notes:

> . . . the term "scientific literacy" lacks all precision, that there are no generally accepted criteria for determining what an individual needs to known to be called scientifically literate, or why it is vital (or even important) for great numbers of Americans to wish to achieve such literacy. Basic competence in science—another way of defining scientific literacy—is clearly an elusive concept, made all the more so by a fundamental ambiguity, even among educators, about the kinds of scientific knowledge and understanding that is useful for ordinary citizens to command."[9]

Graubard discusses the use of these terms for a very powerful reason. He refers to "the capacity of this generation of Americans to ignore its problems, and when it does trouble itself about them, persistently to seek to resolve them with tactics more appropriate to a war against Hitler than to the world as it is at present constituted."[10] He later explains:

> "why dwell on scientific literacy and illiteracy when such terms have so little specific weight? Because no other words will serve as well; they are deliberately chosen, principally to sound a political tocsin. In a world where illiteracy, like disease, is supposed to be disappearing—particularly in advanced countries—the idea that this is not happening at all in the United States, that the American people remain overwhelmingly illiterate in this vital area, is intended to be a disclosure shocking enough to generate a political reaction."[11]

Graubard simply states that the choice of the term is one to generate fear. An illustration would be from "Action for Excellence"

> We are aware that to define the mission of the schools along narrowly utilitarian lines would be to misperceive the purposes of schooling. But if preparation for work is not the only aim of education, it is nevertheless a very important aim. And surely education for economic growth is a worthwhile goal around which to organize our efforts and to rally the American people in the cause of improving the nation's schools.[12]

And the response; federal and private funds become available to resolve this problem for the good of the country. Hurd (1990) describes that concerns regarding the laypersons understanding of science and potential economic consequences have existed since as long ago as 1620! He also quotes the 1988 President of AAAS, Walter Massey, statement to President Bush.

> Any science advisor who cannot explain to you in language you understand, important scientific and technical issues because they are too technical should immediately be replaced.[13]

Hurd suggests that this is a lame excuse sometimes used in education by teachers and texts. It may also be used by industry to divert responsibility. Perhaps this should be considered when fears of an untrainable workforce or an illiterate populace are being discussed. There will always be levels of understanding above an individuals comprehension. (Is this not where scientists engage themselves?) However, there is always a basis at which any individual can understand. As much as we may desire to raise all individuals' bases for understanding, we more desperately need to empower individuals to question until dialogue is upon a level meaningful for them thus allowing them to participate and reflect. This lifetime practice of asking and reflecting will increase science literacy more than some onetime standard set for high school students.

While considering the nation's dilemma, a fundamental question must be poised: Is there evidence supporting the feared future shortage of scientists and engineers? Daniel S. Greenburg (1991), Editor of 'Science and Government Report', states:

> The reality is that the recognized experts strongly disagree about future supply and demand in these fields. Furthermore the basic statistics on technical manpower are in such a derelict condition that disputes even rage about the number of specialists now in

> the work force, let alone manpower needs in the next century. . . For example, the National Science Foundation puts the count of aerospace engineers at 56,000, whereas the figure from the Bureau of Labour Statistics is 93,000 . . . Throughout the postwar era, many factors have conspired to encourage gloomy manpower assessments, including a natural tendency of scientists and engineers to revere their professions and campaign for more recruits . . .

Greenburg further notes that "science and engineering manpower is mobile and adaptable." They will work where there are openings. Perhaps the degree of expertise or specialization some claim is necessary for employment is indeed exaggerated.

It may also be argued that the need is not for scientific literacy par se, but rather literacy and numeracy in general! (Sizer, 1984). George Bugliarello (1990), President of Polytechnic U., N.Y., implores: . . . how to empower humans in an age of technology?

The Dialectic of Freedom

Wirth (1983) asks: "Do the means help all people get in touch with their powers for creative learning and for experiencing the twin needs for individuality and community?"[14]

> John Dewey believed that if we could clarify the human possibilities present in the values of scientific inquiry, we could free individual intelligence and imagination while balancing the dialectic of the self and society. Dewey thought that the social relations descriptive of science when done well were democratic, and democratic social relations resolved the dialectic. In *Intelligence in the Modern World* Dewey (1939) affirmed the need of freedom, imagination and individuality as well as the collective authority of the community. He wrote: "Science has made it way by releasing. . . the elements of variation, of invention and innovation, of novel creation in individuals . . . who freed themselves from the bounds of tradition".[15] Yet while respecting the freedom of individual inquirers, the warrant for any knowledge claim comes from the larger community: "the contribution of the scientific inquirer makes is collectively tested and developed and, in the measure that it is cooperatively confirmed, becomes part of the common funds of the intellectual Commonwealth".[16]

Freeing Intelligence, Imagination, and Desire

There is a well established dislike of the current science curricula by our students. Schwartz (1988) discusses some of the reasons who this occurs. He discusses what is *not* presently emphasized:

> . . .the goals of science and the humanities are the same—to discover beauty in truth and truth in beauty . . . It is a great tragedy that science is so widely regarded as bereft of the beauty of ambiguity—"antiseptically arrogant" as a student of mine once put it. To a large measure, scientists and science teachers have brought about this misunderstanding by pretending to absolute knowledge where none exists.[17]

Our concern is current reforms with their concern, and therefore support, to today's business and industrial practices, will continue to limit imagination, hide oppression, diffuse passion, and further fortify what the majority need to overcome for their personal freedom and a more equitable society. Ironically, "Highly skilled human capital [which] has always been important to our economy"[18] would be more likely develop with an education emphasis upon the quality of human existence throughout our society rather than just business needs. Rather than emphasizing the effect that industrial well-being has upon ". . . our children's individual well being . . ."[19], let's reconsider which should be 'cause' and which should be 'effect'. An endeavour to oppose the seemingly all-mighty business and the pervasive attitude of materialistic greed, may seem impossible. Fortunately Greene (1983) reminds us: "These obstacles or blocks or impediments are, as it were, artifacts, human creations, not "natural" or objectively existent necessities. When oppression or exploitation or segregation or neglect is perceived as "natural" or a "given," there is little stirring in the name of freedom . . ."[20]. To perpetuate our current situation further, will make rectification and liberation even more difficult in the future.

In *Action For Excellence* (1983) a cautionary note is made: "But we must take care to develop teaching materials aimed at attracting, motivating and establishing competency in every ability group. A concept of curriculum improvement that focuses on cognitive goals but ignores motivation is destined to fail"[21]. Ignoring the labelling implications of "every ability group", let us consider which is more likely a successful motivator. Will rough be more likely to engage because of delayed gratification of a better position in a materialistic hierarchy which they may already despise, or will our youth be more receptive of education oriented towards more immediate progress towards self-fulfilment, self-efficacy and individually more meaningful lifestyle? (Refer to Lawwill & Teates, these proceedings, for further discussion.)

The recent report by the AAAS study group project of liberal education and the sciences, *The Liberal Art of Science: Agenda For Action* (1990) "reaffirms":

> . . . the importance of the natural sciences in the liberal arts curriculum and recommends that the study of natural sciences be multidisciplinary. Cross-disciplining teaching that involves faculty from the humanities the social sciences, and the practical and fine arts is encouraged. The Study Group also recommends teaching science as it is practised. This means incorporating the philosophy, values, and methods of science into instruction in the natural sciences.[22]

This multidisciplinary reaffirmation recognizes the role of science in liberal education. One contribution from including aspects of the history, philosophy and sociology of science and mathematics within science and mathematics education is to make a more liberal education in the traditional sense. A liberal education should be a liberating education, one that frees and disciplines the intellect, imagination and creative passions. While the content (or product) of science can be liberating, the methods (or process) are even more so. The connection to the practical as well as the fine arts is important here. The methods of scientific inquiry and their virtues are or should be, cross disciplinary. The study of science and especially its methods could make other disciplines such as history, philosophy and sociology more liberal. It thus should also contribute to liberalizing society.

Moreover, a multidisciplinary approach that also emphasizes the practical social, political and economic context in which knowledge is created reduces the currently perceived sharp distinction between the epistemic values of scientific inquiry in the various disciplines and the normative values of society at large. When the normative values of economic productivity and global competition alone become preeminent than other worthy normative and possibly epistemic, values become devalued. The virtues of scientific method become distorted towards predetermined and unquestioned ends that close down the creative possibilities and captures the intellect. We come close to desire commodities more than congnition and we become what we desire.

Morality

We hear a great deal these days about improving the quality of "human capital" that is put into the production function in order to maximize efficiency and material output. Frequently educational reform, especially in mathematics and science education, is intended to improve human capital. There is something very chilling about describing human beings who kiss, cuss and cry in such an exclusively quantitative and reductionistic way. Somewhere in the *Republic* Plato defined a slave as anyone who tools the proposes of their conduct from another regardless of their status as a citizen in a free state. Chaining science and science education to the goal of maximizing the economic production function enslaves the thoughts, feelings and actions of our students. It is immoral. It is immoral, as both Plato and Kant indicate, because it treats students as means to the pecuniary end of others.

With a similar sentiment, Greenburg (1986) stated:

> Liberal education (geared towards leadership) and vocational training (geared towards career development) have guided curricula away from the chancy investment in someone's *possible* leadership potential and toward the less speculative *trainability* of a person to fill a slot in a mechanistically materialistic culture.[23]

> As we entered the twentieth century, Dewey argued that the issue was whether we would limit our conception of science to a technical phenomenon, to be put in the service of mindless material gain or, whether we would see science intrinsically as a mode of learning—a mode of inquiry, problem solving, reconstructing of experience including reflections on value choices which could be open to all people—and which encompasses basic human needs for individuality and human community. The moral obligation of a democratic society becomes then to reconstruct

> itself so that it reduces the waste of nature and human resources and explores ways to support the learning of all its members in their daily living.[24]

To gear educational reform to serve the current needs and current purposes of business, industry, and government is the surest guarantee of perpetuating an unquestioned *status quo.* Rather than attempting to maintain a currently perceived "greatness" based upon a century of global economic domination (and global exploitation?), we propose that it is indeed time to discard this facade, redefining greatness in a more equitably and just fashion, by addressing the underlying problems of society and individuals.

Conclusion

A liberal education, a liberalizing science education, should free a democratic population to deliberate about ends as well as means and alter them if they so desire. The people might be moved to completely devalue economic competitiveness; although witnessing the social and political consequence of the failure of some nations of compete economically, it is unlikely. On the other hand it is to be expected that a more liberally educated population would recreate the existing modes and (management) of production in order to enhance productivity on every level from the shop floor to the Senate chambers. Free people are more productive, but because they are free they are not always productive of predetermined ends. So, therefore, those that will profit from their productivity cannot precisely be known in advance, and that is disturbing to those who are currently in control of business, industry, government (and dare we say, science?). There is, we suspect, a subtile but crucial tension in the current call for science education reform. Many of the reformers want scientific content, not method, product not process, scientism not science. Yet they know that free minds can make them (more) money. So the problem for those in control becomes one of providing a liberal education without providing a liberating education—a razors edge to tread.

One author of this paper while engaged in dialogue with the noted social critic of education Michael Apple, paraphrased the current situation:

> It seems that industry desires workers who are sufficiently bright enough to increase their productivity, but *not* sufficiently enough brighter to question advertising and the need of purchasing the goods.

Apple's response was "Yes". A quality science education will provide a more productive population, but a truly liberating science education will not only produce better goods, it will produce novel social goals as well.

NOTES

1. p. 7
2. p. 12, italics added.
3. See Garrison and Lawwill, 1992.
4. see Paton (1950) p. 429.
5. James B. Hunt, 1984 (1987, p. 118).
6. p. 3.
7. MacVicar (1990), p. 39
8. Spring (1987), p. 125.
9. p. 231.
10. p. 232.
11. p. 233.
12. p. 46.
13. p. 135.
14. p. 90.
15. (1939), p. 358.
16. p. 358.
17. pp. 169-170.
18. Task Force (1983), p. 14.
19. p. 18.
20. p. 9.
21. p. 27.
22. p. viii.
23. Wirth (1983) summarized Dewey's perspective.
24. p. 103.

REFERENCES

AAAS: 1990, *The Liberal Art of Science: Agenda for Action,* 1133 H Street, NW, Washington, DC 20005.

Arons, A.B.: 1983, 'Achieving wider scientific literacy', *Daedalus* Spring 1983, 91-121.

Bugliarello, G.: 1990, 'Empowering citizens through technology literacy', *Bull. Sci. Tech. Soc.* 10, 187-190.

Dewey, J.:1916, *Democracy and Education,* Macmillan, New York.

Dewey, J.:1939, *Intelligence in the Modern World,* Modern Library, New York.

Dewey, J.:1954, *The Public and Its Problems,* Swallow Press, Chicago.

Garrison, J.W. and Lawwill, K.S.: 1992, 'Democratic science teaching: a role for the history of science', *The Journal of Education Thought* (In press).

Goodland, J.I.:1984, *A Place Called School,* McGraw-Hill, New York.

Graubard, S.R.: 1983, 'Nothing to fear, much to do', *Daedalus* Spring 1983, 231-238.

Greene, M. :1988, *The Dialectic of Freedom,* Teachers College Press, New York.

Greenberg, D.S.:1991, 'A shortage of scientists and engineers?', Washington Post, Sun. Aug.18, 1991 C7.

Hunt, J.B.:1987, Education for economic growth. In J.W. Noll(Ed.), *Taking Sides: Clashing on Controversial Educational Issues,* 4th ed., Dushkin Publishing Group, Guilford, CN. 116-122.

Hurd, P.D.:1990, 'Historical and philosophical insights on scientific literacy', *Bull.Sci.Tech.Soc.*10, 133-136.

Kintgen, E.R.: 1988, 'Literacy literacy', *Visible Language* 1:2/3, 149-168.

Mayer, V.J.: 1990, 'Teaching from a global point of view', *Science Teacher* 57:1, 47-51.

Miller, J.D.:1983, 'Scientific literacy: a conceptual and empirical review', *Daedalus* Spring 1983, 29-47.

NASA: 1990, Project Laser: Learning About Science, Engineering and Research, produced by Matin Marietta for NASA.

Nation at Risk, Superintendent of Documents, USGPO, Wash. D.C., April 1983.

Paton, H.J.:1950, *The Moral Law or Kant's Groundwork of the Metaphysics of Morals,* London.

Pearson, E.:1990, 'Scientific literacy: what is the role of the science teacher?, *Journal of Negro Education* 59:3, 316-319.

Pool, R.:1991, 'Science literacy: the enemy is us', *Science* 251: 4991, 266-267.

Shorthand, M.:1989, 'Advocating science: literacy and public understanding', *Impact of Science on Society* 38:4, spec iss 152, 305-316.

Spring, J.:1987, 'Education and the sony war, In J.W. Noll(Ed.), *Taking Sides: Clashing on Controversial Educational Issues*, 4th ed., Dushkin Publishing Group, Guilford CN, 123-128.

Tanner, D.:1990, 'The curriculum frontier", *Social Education* 54:4, 195-197.

Task Force on Ed. For Economic Growth: 1983, Action For Excellence, Ed. Comm. of the States, Denver.

Wirth, A.G. 1983, *Productive Work—In Industry and Schools*, University Press of America, Lanham.

Worthy, W.:1989, 'AAAS offers guidelines to combat scientific illiteracy problem', *Chemical and Engineering News* 67:11, 22-24.

19

Contextual Realism in Science and Science Teaching

RON GOOD
Louisiana State University, USA
&
RICHARD SCHLAGEL
George Washington University, USA

The Importance of Context

When the importance of context is recognized in the natural sciences and the social sciences, more accurate and more limited conclusions are usually made. Ignoring or avoiding the complexities of context results in oversimplified, overgeneralized, and less useful knowledge. It is this thesis that we explain and defend in this brief paper.

A. Gaston Bachelard on Context

More than 50 years ago Gaston Bachelard (1884-1962), physical chemist and philosopher of science who held the prestigious chain in the history and philosophy of science at the College of France in Paris during the 1940's and 1950's, stressed the importance of context in history and philosophy of science. In the first chapter of his book on Michel Foucault, Gutting (1989) points out Bachelard's ideas on the importance of context and their influence on Foucault:

> Moreover, Bachelard reminds us that there is strictly speaking, on such thing as the history of science, only various histories of different regions of scientific work. Correspondingly, philosophy cannot hope to uncover a single, unified conception of rationality from its reflection on the history of science; it will find only "regions of rationality."[1]

In The New Scientific Spirit Bachelard (1934) tells us in his own words of the importance of context in science:

> When one looks at science what is immediately striking is that its oft-alleged unity has never been a stable condition, so that it is quite dangerous to assume a unitary epistemology. Not only does the history of science reveal a regular alternation between atomism and energetices, realism and positivism, continuity and discontinuity, rationalism and empiricism; and not only is the psychology of the scientist engaged in active research dominated one day by the unity of scientific laws and the next by the diversity of things; but even more, science is divided, in actuality as well as in principle, in all of its aspects.[2]

According to Patrick Heelan, author of the Foreword in Arthur Goldhammer's translation of Bachelard's The New Scientific Spirit, Bachelard's writings are "comparable in spirit and scope to those of Charles Sanders Peirce, the American founder of pragatism" (p. vii). Heelan suggests that many of Bachelard's ideas anticipated modern themes in Anglo-American philosophy of science, such as observations are theory-laden, science is not value neutral, and science is a community endeavour.

B. No Unitary Epistemology

Bachelard's conclusion of on unitary epistemology is supported by evidence within both the natural sciences and the social sciences. Within the natural sciences the various domains of study called biology, chemistry, geology, physics, and so on are composed of ever more specialized areas of study. Each area of study has certain unique features that set it apart from its neighbours. An example in biology will help to support Bachelard's claim of no unitary epistemology of science.

As Alexander Agassiz Professor of Zoology, Emeritus, Harvard University, Ernst Mayr is one of the greatest living commentators on biology. An evolutionary biologist, Mayer

(1988) argues that biology consists of two quite different fields of study. Proximate causation is studied in functional biology and ultimate causation is studied in evolutionary biology. In Toward A New Philosophy of Biology (1988), Mayr lays the foundation for a philosophy of evolutionary biology that differs from other philosophies of science, especially physics, due to the different methods of inquiry, assumptions, use of prediction and experimentation, and so on. His recognition of the uniqueness of evolutionary biology, especially its methods of making progress, is consistent with Bachelard's position on different regions of scientific work. Mayer (1988) points out that many famous controversies in various fields of biology . . . "have been due to a failure of opponents to realize that one of them was interested in proximate, the other in evolutionary, causes" (p.3).

The domain specificity/regionality/context of the many natural sciences argues against an unitary epistemology/ philosophy of science.

Similar arguments can be extended to the social sciences, including science education. The situated cognition movement in cognitive psychology is just one example of the recognition of the importance and complexity of context in human learning and development studies. In both science and science education, context has been under-emphasized, resulting in the sort of confusion and argumentation that Mayr and Bachelard discussed. However, as we try to show in the section on constructivism, failing to appreciate the importance of context can result also in superficial agreement among parties who ordinarily disagree on many fundamental points.

The next section on contextual realism provides details of Schlagel's (1986) conditional or contextual existence of scientific reality.

Contextual Realism in Modern Science

Perhaps the most basic assumption among natural scientists is stated in clear terms in *Science For All Americans* (Rutherford & Ahlgren, 1990): "Science presumes that the things and events in the universe occur in consistent patterns that are comprehensible through careful, systematic study" (p.3). They go on to say, "Scientists

> assume that even if there is no way to secure complete and absolute truth, increasingly accurate approximations can be made to account for the world and how it works."[3]

It is difficult to avoid linking these and similar statements in Science For All Americans to a form of realism. Contextual realism is our choice of terms and Schlagel (1986) provides an extensive overview of this epistemology of the natural sciences. It is important to explain at the outset that the emphasis on contextual reality allows for Bachelard's argument of no unitary epistemology of science. Also, Mayr's emphasis on different methods of inquiry, assumptions, uses of prediction, and so on among the various natural sciences can be taken into account by Schlagel's contextual realism.

Since Kuhn's (1962) work, relativism has become quite fashionable, with Feyerabend's (1975) position at the extreme, suggesting that the methods of "scientific" creationists, astrologers, and other pseudo-scientists are as scientifically able as the methods of microbiologists, physicists, geologists, and so on. This extreme position leads some philosophers, science educators, and others to conclude that no confirmable or reliable knowledge is possible.

Contextual realism claims that "the universe consists of innumerable contexts of endless varieties of entities and processes which 'really exist' within certain conditions" (Schlagel, 1986, p. 280). Bohm's (1957) position on a real world is similar:

> . . . we assume that the world as a whole is objectively real, and that, as far as we know, it has a somewhat precisely describable and analyzable structure of unlimited complexity.[4]

It is important to recognize that as the context is restricted, knowledge can become more certain. In the social sciences, science education for example, as research methods become more quantitative the context becomes correspondingly restricted and simplified. As knowledge of something becomes more certain it is more trivial, and as knowledge becomes more important it is less certain.

Just as contextual realism is not relativism, neither is it

positivism. Schlagel (1986, pp. 279-280) uses a quote from Popper and Eccles to express the nature of contextual realism:

> For a long time, essentialism had been identified by all parties, including its positivist opponents, with the view that the task of science (and of philosophy) was to reveal the ultimate hidden reality behind the appearances, It has now turned out that although there are such hidden realities, none of them is ultimate; although some are on a deeper level than others.[5]

Thus, both primary (i.e., intrinsic) and secondary (i.e., sensory) qualities are real, depending on the conditions of the investigator and what is being investigated. The conditions under which we investigate nature and the particular level of nature being investigated both determine our understanding of the outcome. Contextual realism takes into account the conditional existence of reality as well the autonomous status within the specific conditions (i.e., context).

Schlagel (1986) closes his summary of contextual realism in this way:

> While this conception of inexhaustible, irreducible contexts or levels will probably be replaced in the future by a more adequate meta-physical model, in the meantime, rather than attempting to collapse reality into one dimension, which invariably blinds the investigator to the significance of other contexts, we should assume that the universe consists of an endless nexus of domains with innumerable structures and features. Experimentation and theory construction have been the most successful means so far in providing partial glimpses of this reality, as refracted through our congnitive-linguistic frames, but we should not assume these means are final.[6]

Contextual Realism and Constructivism

The appeal of constructivism for science educators seems to be strong, even though it is not at all clear how this newest "ism" is to be understood. Good, Wandersee, and St. Julien (in press) have identified at least 15 modifiers of the term constructivism found in the literature, so it is important to understand the potential for confusion. Table 19.1 identifies these modifiers and their dictionary definitions.

Table 19.1: Words used to modify constructivism.

1. *Contextual* (context): 1) The part of a written or spoken statement that surrounds a word or passage and that often specifies its meaning. 2) The circumstances in which a particular event occurs: SITUATION.

2. *Dialectical* (dialectic): 1) The art or practice of arriving at the truth by disclosing the contradictions in an opponent's argument and overwhelming them.

3. *Empirical*: 1) a. Relying upon or gained from experiment or observation< empirical techniques > b. Capable of proof or verification by means of experiment or observation < empirical knowledge.>

4. *Humanistic*: 1) Characterized by kindness, mercy, or compassion.

5. *Information-processing*:

   information: 2. Knowledge derived from study, experience, or instruction.

   Processing (process): 1. A system of operations in producing something.

6. *Methodological* (methodology): 1) The system of principles, procedures, and practices applied to a particular branch of knowledge.

7. *Moderate*: 1) Within limits: RESONABLE 2) Opposed to extreme or radical views or measures.

8. *Piagetian*: (not defined)

9. *Postepistemological* (post; epistemology): After; The division of philosophy that investigates the nature and origin of knowledge.

10. *Pragmatic*: 1) Concerned with causes and effects or needs and results rather than ideas or theories.

11. *Radical*: 1) Arising from or going to a root or source: BASIC. 2) Drastic or sweeping: EXTREME.

12. *Rational*: 1) Having or exercising the ability to reason. 2) Of sound mind: SANE.

13. *Realist*: 1) One inclined to factual truth and pragmatism.
14. *Social*: 1) a. Living together in communities. c. Of or relating to society. 2) Of or relating to the upper classes. 3) Enjoying the company of others.
15. *Socio-historical* (society, historical):

   society: 1) a. The totality of social relationships among human beings. c. The institutions and culture of a distinct self-perpetuating group.

   historical: 2) Based on or concerned with events in history.

How does contextual realism in science relate to constructivism in science education? Among the possible implications that contextual realism in science has for constructivism in science education is to serve as the basis of raising questions about the "postepistemological" claims of the radical constructivists. Matthews (1992) and House (1991) raise questions that are relevant here. Metthews (1992) accuses von Glasersfeld and other radical constructivists of abandoning epistemological questions because of a failure to distinguish between the theoretical objects of science (e.g., Newton's point mass) from the real objects of science (e.g., the physical objects of study). House (1991), using Bhaskar's (1978, 1979) works, points out the common epistemic fallacy of the standard view of research:

> . . . events themselves are not the ultimate focus of scientific analysis. Rather events are to the explained by examining the causal structures that produce the events, and events are produced by complex interactions of a multitude of underlying causal entities. Reality consists not only of what we can see but also of the underlying causal entities that are not always directly discernible. Reality then is stratified. Events are explained by underlying structures, which may be explained eventually by other structures at still deeper levels.[7]

A realistic view of science that takes into account the context of research assumes, as Bohm (1957) has said:

> . . . the world as a whole is objectively real, and that as far as we know, it has a precisely describable and analyzable structure

> of unlimited complexity. This structure must be understood with the aid of a series of progressively more fundamental, more extensive, and more accurate concepts, which series will furnish, so to speak, a better and better set of views of the infinite structure of objective reality. We should, however, never expect to obtain a complete theory of this structure, because there are almost certainly more elements in it than we can possibly be aware of at any particular stage of scientific development . . .[8]

Contextual realism does not abandon important epistemological questions as von Glasersfeld and other constructivists seem to urge.

Contextual Realism in Science Education

The brief overview of contextual realism as a framework for interpreting the nature of the natural sciences is describe in much greater detail in Schlagel (1986). This framework can be used to help science educators and their students better understand the various natures of the natural sciences. Since as Schlagel (1986, p. 273) points out, "all scientific knowledge appears to be conditioned by the method and context of investigation," the various natural sciences should be seen as unique within their respective contexts. "Scientific method" has meaning only when considered within the context of the specific investigation in question. Our earlier examples using the ideas of Gaston Bachelard and Ernst Mayr serve to support our thesis that context is crucial in questions about the nature of science, or more accurately, the many natures of the many natural sciences. And yet, as Schlagel (1986) observes, "The claim that all knowledge is relative to limited conditions and contexts, albeit some more basic and pervasive than others, should not be interpreted to mean that no confirmable truth or reliable knowledge are attainable" (p. 282).

As a framework of the nature of science, contextual realism can help to reduce the pervasiveness of positivism in science teaching, while acknowledging the realistic view of practising scientists, as described by Rutherford and Ahlgren (1990).

Most scientists make research progress in their respective fields by focusing on narrowly-defined problems, so that expertise in science commonly means having detailed personal knowledge about a specific piece of nature. Put another way, the expert research scientist knows a great deal about a very limited part of nature, which results in somewhat of a paradox—scientists are often scientifically "illiterate" outside their specialty. They must rely on the community of scientists to broaden narrow perspectives into webs of knowledge that can provide answers to a broad range of questions. This view of science explains Bachelard's (1934) ideas presented earlier in this paper:

> . . . and not only is the psychology of the scientists engaged in active research dominated one day by the unity of scientific laws and the next by the diversity of things; but even more, science is divided, in actuality as well as in principle, in all of its aspects.[9]

The science educator who takes contextual realism seriously recongnizes that a single conception of scientific method is a myth, just as there is no single nature of science. Of course, we can and do find many general similarities among the many natural sciences and among the many lines of investigation within a given sub-field of science. For most of its history, philosophy of science has tried to determine the ultimate nature of science, with answers taking on names like positivism, pragmatism, realism, relativism, and so on. For reasons that have been described in much more detail than is possible in this paper, Bachelard (1934), Mayr (1988), Schlagel (1986), and others make a convincing case for realism within context in science. Using similar arguments, Good et al. (in press) extend the case into science education. We should not expect a single "nature" of science education any more than we should expect a single nature of science. Depending on the nature of the science, the nature of the learner(s), and the many other facets of context that are likely to be important to science education, we should accept the complexity of the enterprise we call science education by refusing to accept simple, all-encompassing solutions.

More than a decade ago Mishler (1979) argued that the importance of context . . . "has been largely ignored by traditional research approaches in the social and behavioural sciences and in their applications to the field of education (p. 1). As science educators use non-traditional research approaches to explore 'meaning in context', we must continue to consider the nature of science, or more accurately, the many natures of the many natural sciences. To the authors of this paper, contextual realism provides a resonable framework to use as we try to reform our practice of science education.

NOTES

1. p.14.
2. pp.14 & 15.
3. p.4.
4. p.100.
5. 1977, p.193.
6. pp. 294-295.
7. p.4.
8. p.100.
9. pp.14 & 15.

REFERENCES

Bachelard, G. (1934, English translation, 1984). *The New Scientific Spirit*. A. Goldhammer (Trans.). Boston: Beacon.

Bhaskar, R. (1978). *A Realist Theory Of Science*. Sassex: Harvester Press.

Bhasker, R. (1989). *Reclaiming Reality*. London: Verso.

Bohm, D (1957). *Causality And Chance In Modern Physics*. Philadelphia, PA: University of Pennsylvania Press.

Feyerabend, P. (1975). *Against Method*. London: New Left Books.

Good, R., Wandersee, J. and St. Julien, J. (in press). Cautionrary notes on the appeal of the new 'ism' (constructivism) in science education.

Gutting, G. (1989). *Michel Foucault's Archeology Of Scientific Reason*. New York: Cambridge University Press.

House, E. (1991). Realism in research. *Educational Researcher*, 20 (6), 2-9, 25.

Kuhn, T. (1962). *Structure of Scientific Revolutions*. Chicago, IL: Chicago University Press.

Matthews, M. (1992, March). A problem with constructivist epistemology. A paper presented at the 65th annual meeting of the National Association for Research in Science Teaching, Boston, MA.

Mishler, E. (1979). Meaning in context: Is there any other kind? *Harvard Educational Review*, 49, 1-19.

Rutherford, F.J. and Ahlgren, A. (1990). *Science for all Americans.* New York: Oxford.

Schlagel, R. (1986). *Contextual Realism: A Meta-Physical Framework For Modern Science.* New York: Paragon House.

von Glasersfeld, E. (1990). An exposition of constructivism: Why some like it radical. In R. Davis, C. Maher, and N. Noddings (Eds.), *Constructivist Views On The Teaching And Learning Of Mathematics.* Reston, VA: National Council of Teachers of Mathematics.

20

Pupils' Learning to Scientific Construction of Knowledge

DANIEL GIL-PEREZ & JAIME CARRASCOSA-ALIS
Universitat De Valencia, Spain

Introduction

It is frequently said that the reforms in science education which took place during the sixties and the seventies, associated to the "learning by discovery" paradigm, was an attempt to bring science learning closer to scientific practice: "It was intended that children should enjoy science (by more direct engagement in scientific activities), should gain an awareness of what scientists do and should be encouraged to pursue the study of science at an advanced level" (Hodson 1988).

This trend, as most studies have shown, resulted in a genuine fiasco. It is therefore easy to conclude that no attempt should be made to involve pupils in scientific activities as an objective of science education. We shall try to show that, on the contrary, the idea of approaching science learning to the way of doing science is not exclusive to the learning by discovery model but constitutes a permanent feature, although not always explicit, in innovations in science teaching. A thread which has shown to be fruitful, even through its wrong avenues, and that is being reinforced nowadays by the emerging constructivist paradigm (Resnick 1983; Novak 1988; Wheatley 1991) and by the implications of the contemporary philosophy of science in science education (Posner et al 1982; Gil and Carrascosa 1985, 1990; Hodson 1988; Cleminson 1990; Matthews 1990; Cobb, Wood and Yackel 1991; Duschl and Gitomer 1991; Gruender and Tobin 1991; Sequeira and Leite 1991. . .). In this paper we intend to analyse, from this perspective, the main trends in the innovation of science education.

The Learning by Discovery Model: A Failure . . . And a Step Forward

It is not necessary to insist here on the numerous studies which have analyzed the failure of the learning by discovery paradigm (Ausubel 1968; Gil 1983; Hodson 1985; Millar and Driver 1987 . . .). The extreme inductivism in which this model fell into, the lack of attention to content, the wrong insistence on the completely autonomous activity of the pupils, and so on, have been repeatedly indicated, as well as the negative results obtained, both in the field of conceptual learning and in the understanding of the nature of science. Nevertheless, we consider that this criticism, although correct, turns out to be partial and should not justify a complete rejection of this wide movement of science education reform.

We can point out, in the first place, that the idea of introducing science training as a component of the basic education of all citizens has been advanced by outstanding scientists and educators such as Dewey (1902), Langevin (1926) or Piaget (1972).

The learning by discovery trend tried to implement this idea, according to which, pupils should become acquainted with scientific methodology so as to be able to understand scientific results. Moreover, with this involvement of pupils in scientific activities, it was intended to give an open and accessible view of science—in order to foster a more positive attitude towards science learning—and to highlight the specific nature and importance of its methods. And even if the results did not correspond to the aims, this attempt can be considered as the beginning of a systematic process of curricular reform of science education in which we are still immersed.

Meanwhile, the objective of engaging pupils in scientific activities has even gained in importance. As Solomon (1991) states: "for most students, our general objectives might be favourable attitudes towards science and a fell for its method of theory-making". Burbules and Linn (1991), put the question in these terms: "One way to pose the central aim of science education is to ask, what epistemological attitude do we want to foster in students? In other words; what view of knowledge and discovery will best support the kinds of scientific activities we want students to undertake in science classes and in their lives?" From this point of view the results obtained with the learning by discovery paradigm cannot just be interpreted as a failure, but as the origin of subsequent restructuring, that is to say, as an invigorating element of science teaching which remained anchored in uncritically accepted traditions. In fact, the negative results obtained, directed attention towards the science education conceptions underlying the learning model (Leboutet 1973, Host 1978, Giordan 1978), in this way initiating an approach to the contemporary philosophy of science.

The Reception Learning Paradigm: A New Step Forward . . . and A New Failure

The criticism of the learning by discovery model brought about a reappraisal of learning by reception or, in other words, of teaching by verbal transmission. Nevertheless, that did not mean a mere return to the "traditional" model and a consequent half on teaching reform. Neither can it be interpreted as a deviation from the aim of getting pupils acquainted with the scientific way of reasoning, although it could seem so at first sight. It is in effect true, that Ausubel (1968) bases his defense of teaching by verbal transmission on, among other reasons, the lack of capacity of most pupils for discovering all that they need to know, and this can be interpreted as a rejection of the involvement of pupils in scientific activities. But a careful consideration of some of Ausubel's proposals show a grater consistency with the basic theses of contemporary epistemology than the learning by discovery paradigm. As an example, the importance given by Ausubel to the pupils' previous ideas and to the integration of the new knowledge in their conceptual structures, is consistent with the role that theoretical paradigms play in scientific research. In the same sense, enhancing the teachers' guide to facilitate meaningful learning—instead of the sparse acquisitions which produce the incidental discovery of an autonomous pupil's work—Ausubel approaches to an essential characteristic of scientific research: any scientist knows how necessary the discussions with more experienced colleagues are, their feedback and orientation, which show how far removed scientific construction of knowledge is from autonomous work or incidental discovery. In such aspects, the reception learning paradigm is closer to the nature of science than the learning by discovery one. It is, of course, an insufficient approach which, moreover, conflicts other essential characteristics of seientific methodology. But it is interesting to point out that some particularly sound aspects of this paradigm are consistent with the idea of bringing pupils' activity closer to the construction of scientific knowledge. The incompatibilities are, nevertheless, very strong, beginning with the explicit limitation of learning to the reception of concepts, without attempting the pupils' engagement in the construction of knowledge.

On the other hand, although the learning by reception model is explicitly opposed to the inductivism of learning by discovery, we must note that underlying the proposals of an external knowledge already elaborated, we can recognize the inductivist theses, because concepts are till considered as something external to the subject who must "receive" them.

Learning by reception is as we can see, clearly and voluntarily quite distant from today's conceptions about how scientific knowledge is constructed. This could be the reason for its well established ineffectiveness in attaining its quite modest aim of an exclusively conceptual learning, neglecting procedural and axiological aspects. Effectively, research on "misconceptions" and "alternative frameworks" has seriously questioned the effectiveness of this transmission/reception model (Viennot 1976; Driver and Easley 1978; Osborne and Gilbert, 1980; Clough and Driver 1986 . . .). On the other hand, although the model pays attention exclusively to conceptual aspects of science, it transmits, nevertheless, a certain view of how scientific knowledge is constructed and, more generally, of the nature of science. As Hodson (1985) explains, "it is the implicit philosophy of the curriculum (what one might call the 'hidden science curriculum') which carries the important message about what science is and is ultimately responsible for forming children's attitudes and beliefs". So, the reception learning paradigm was not only incapable of achieving a meaningful appropriation of concepts but also transmitted an impoverished view of science, responsible to a great extent for the negative attitudes detected in many pupils towards science learning (Schibeci 1984; James and Smith 1985; Yager and Penick 1986).

The need for a deep restructuring of the science teaching/ learning process was again evident. Yet, the results of both discovery and reception learning models had not just been a waste of time and effort. Now, researchers and curriculum designers had a clearer vision of the difficulties and were prepared for more rigorous approaches, without falling into simplistic disqualification of "traditional teaching". The foundation efforts turned back again to the analogies between scientists and pupils' activities, producing the convergence of cognitive science findings and the contributions of contemporary history and philosophy of science.

The Constructivist Approach and the Understanding of Scientific Work Achieved by the Contemporary Philosophy of Science as two Major and Related Advances in Science Education

We are not going to re-examine here the importance of the constructivist approach in science education (Resnick, 1983; Novak, 1988), which is currently considered as being the most outstanding contribution in this field over the last decades (Gruender and Tobin, 1991). Neither is it necessary to give a full description of the characteristics of the new approach to learning, thoroughly described by several authors (Posner et al, 1982; Driver 1986). Resnick[1] summarized them in three statements:

> Learners construct understanding. They do not simply mirror what they are told or what they read . . . To understand something is to know relationships. . .
>
> Bits of information isolated are forgotten or become inaccessible to memory . . .
>
> All learning depends on prior knowledge . . .

This summary is, of course, a simplification that forgets, as Resnick recognizes, many complexities, but it allows us to notice the undeniable similarity with the contemporary view of the construction of scientific knowledge (Kuhn 1970). This resemblance has been pointed out by many science education researchers (Posner et al, 1982; Gil 1983; Gil and Carrascosa 1985, 1990; Hashwhew 1986; Matthews 1990; Burbules, and Linn 1991, Cobb, Wood and Yackel 1991; Duschl and Gitomar, 1991; Gruender and Tobin, 1991 . . .), and appears as one of the fundamental supports of the new trend. In fact, the constructivist approach has shown a great capacity for incorporating many studies: from the contemporary epistemology (Bachelard, Kuhn, Lakatos, Toulmin, Feyerabend . . .) to the constructivists conceptions of Kelly or the works of Piaget or Vygotsky.

This basic coherence of the results obtained by independent researchers has strengthened, logically, the value of the constructivist approach to science education and has made possible a growing consensus. The old aim of approaching pupils' activity to the characteristics of scientific knowledge construction has thus gained new force, supported by a better understanding of the nature of science and by a serious theoretical foundation. We would like to stress, however, that this advancement has been possible in part, thanks to the previous research, with its "errors" and consequent reorientation. Too frequently we forget this evolutionary relation between different and opposite models, and so science education development seems to be submitted to a hazardous agitation. If we want to reinforce the theoretical character of science education, as a specific and coherent corpus of knowledge, it becomes necessary to take into account the preceding models, their resistance to modification—which is a clear index of a certain consistency and affectiveness—and, most particularly, their contribution—frequently through the analysis of their insufficiencies—to the emergence of new approaches. It is likewise necessary to recognize the basic coincidence—in spite, obviously, of some nuances—of many proposals presented by their authors as different models. That is what happens nowadays with several constructivist teaching strategies (Nussbaum and Novick, 1982; Posner et al, 1982; Osborne and Wittrock 1983, 1985; Driver and Oldham 1986; Hewson and Hewson, 1984; Hodson 1988; Giordan 1989; Pozo 1989 . . .). In all of them we can find—stated in a one way or another—the view of *science learning as a conceptual change* in three basic steps:

An elicitation phase of pupils' ideas, making them conscious of the plausibility and fruitfulness of those ideas.

A restructuring phase creating cognitive conflict, generating pupils' dissatisfaction with their current ideas and preparing them for the introduction of scientific conceptions.

An application phase which gives opportunities for using the new conceptions in different contexts and consolidating them.

The effectiveness of those conceptual change strategies has been supported by many researches undertaken in different fields of science education (Nussbaum and Novick 1982; Anderson and Smith 1983; Hewson and Hewson 1984; Ministrell 1984; Roth 1984; Osborne and Freyberg 1985; Zietsman and Hewson 1986; Viennot and Kamisnky 1991. . .).

Nonetheless, other researches have sown that some alternative conceptions are resistant to instruction, even when teaching is explicitly aimed to produce conceptual changes (Fredette and Lochhead 1981; Clough and Driver 1986; Shuell 1987; Gunstone, White and Freshman, 1988; White and Gunstone 1989; Duschl and Gitamer 1991, etc.). These difficulties and the interest for strengthening the foundation of the constructivist model require, in our opinion, a re-examination of the teaching strategies advanced.

Conceptual Change Versus Conceptual and Methodological Change

A primary and, in our opinion, serious limitation of 'conceptual change' teaching strategies is the insufficient attention to the ways of reasoning associated with the pupils' alternative frameworks. We shall summarize here our point of view on the subject (Gil and Carrascosa, 1985, 1990; Gil, Carrascosa, Furio and Martinez Toregrosa 1991):

There is a certain parallel between the historical evolution of a science in its first steps and the formation of children's intuitive conceptions.[2]

This isomorphism between pupils' intuitive ideas and pre-classical conceptions cannot be accidental and could be the consequence of a similar way of approaching problems. This hypothesis is supported by a comparative study of the characteristics of what can be described as "commonsense physics" (Bachelard 1938; Holton and Roller 1963; Koyre 1981) and the pupils' ways of reasoning. It is easy to show, effectively, that both children and pre-classical works on science, approach problems in a very similar way which we have called the "methodology of superficiality" (Gil and Carrascosa, 1985) and Hashweh (1986) "common sense methodology", characterized by certainty, by absence of doubts or consideration of possible alternative solutions, by quick and very confident answers based on "common sense evidence"; by lack of consistency in the analysis of different situations (Ministrell 1982; Whitaker 1983: Halloun and Hestenses 1985; Hewson 1985; Champagne, Gunstone and Klopfer, 1985); by reasoning which follow a linear causality sequence (Closset 1983; Joshua 1985; Viennot 1989; Viennot and Kaminsky 1991).

Pre-classical conceptions could only be overwhelmed thanks to a new methodology which combines the creativity of divergent thinking and of hypotheses checking, through experiments under controlled conditions and a search for full consistency. We can suppose then, that pupils' conceptual change will not be possible without a similar methodological change (Gil and Carrascosa 1985, 1990; Hashweh 1986; Cleminson 1990; Duschl and Gitomer 1991). Historically, this methodological change, was not at all an easy one, and it is quite logical to think that the same will happen with pupils: only if they are repeatedly put in the situation of applying this methodology (that is to say, in the situation of putting forward hypotheses, designing experiments, carrying them out, analyzing carefully the results with particular attention to the global consistency . . .) will they manage to overcome their commonsense epistemology, thus making possible the deep conceptual changes which the acquisition of scientific knowledge demands.

The preceding considerations imply a first criticism of the teaching strategies oriented to produce conceptual changes. Effectively, these strategies seem to pay attention almost exclusively to concepts. It is true that the conceptual change has its epistemological requirements and must not be considered merely as a change in content (Hewson and Thorley 1989). But, in our opinion more explicit attention to the methodological and epistemological commitments should be necessary, since science teaching is usually centered on declarative knowledge (knowing "what") and forgets the procedural type (knowing "how"). We cannot expect so that to speak of conceptual change leads automatically to paying attention to its methodological and epistemological requirements. On the contrary, we are afraid that, without very explicit insistence, the most creative aspects of scientific work will remain absent from our science lessons.

In the same sense, Duschl and Gitomer (1991), studying carefully the implications of the contemporary philosophy of science, state: "if we are to produce radical restructuring of concepts, the personal correlate of Kuhn's revolutionary science, then it seems that we must also teach the procedural knowledge involved". Duschl and Gitomer criticize the hierarchical view of conceptual change that "assumes that changes in central commitments to a theory of science bring simultaneous changes to other ontological, methodological and axiological commitments within the conceptual framework" and they attribute to this wrong vision of how conceptual changes take place the insufficient study of the nature of procedural knowledge (Duschl, Hamilton and Grandy, 1990) and the partial ineffectiveness of conceptual change teaching strategies.

In fact, although several authors have referred, more or less explicitly, to the relationship between alternative frameworks and ways of reasoning and problem solving (Osborne and Wittrock 1983, 1985; Resnick 1983; Gil and Carrascosa 1985, 1990; Hashweh 1986; Reve et al 1987; Hills 1989; Viennot 1989; Burbules and Linn 1991 . . .) the teaching strategies we are analysing do not seem to approach sufficiently pupils' activity to the characteristics of scientific research, that is to say, of scientific knowledge construction. It is necessary to stress that we are not advocating a return to a "process" or a "discovery" learning approach. As we have already argued those trends give a wrong view (very simplistic and linear) of a scientific treatment of problems. On the contrary, we consider that it is necessary to present scientific work in all its richness and complexity (far from the simplistic views so often empraced by teachers). This is, of course, a very important question which demands a constant attention to avoid the usual disregard, of the most creative aspects of science and the reduction of the scientific treatment of problems to a linear sequence of fixed stages. In figure 1, we summarize an attempt to give a more correct view of scientific methodology which governs our objective of facilitating pupils' acquaintance with the scientific way of constructing knowledge as a requirement for effective conceptual change.

But there is still another aspect of conceptual change strategies which demands, in our opinion, re-examination in the light of the contemporary philosophy of science. We shall dedicate the next section to this point.

Conceptual Change Versus Scientific Treatment of Problematic Situations

The sequence of the teaching strategies oriented to produce conceptual changes consists, basically, in eliciting pupils' ideas, making them conscious of the plausibility and fruitfulness of those ideas and next creating conceptual conflicts to prepare the introduction of the scientific conceptions which higher explicative capacity will make possible the conceptual change. This strategy is close to, as we have already discussed in section 3, the scientific construction of knowledge but, in our opinion, the systematic confrontation of pupils' ideas with the scientific ones, can produce inhibition and a quite logical rejection. That obliges us to question the sense of making pupils conscious of their ideas for immediately putting them into conflict. It is easy to understand that this eliciting plus conflict generation strategy is quite far away from the scientific research process. This research is not undertaken to question ideas, or to produce conceptual changes, but to treat problems which interest scientists, problems which are treated, logically, with the possessed knowledge and with new ideas constructed in a tentative way. During this process the initial conceptions may suffer some changes or even be radically questioned, but this will never be the objective that remains the solution of the problems posed.

From a constructivist point of view it is essential to associate knowledge construction with problems: as Bachelard (1938)

Figure 20.1: Diagram of a Research Cycle: A simplified Scheme of A Complex and Very Rich Process

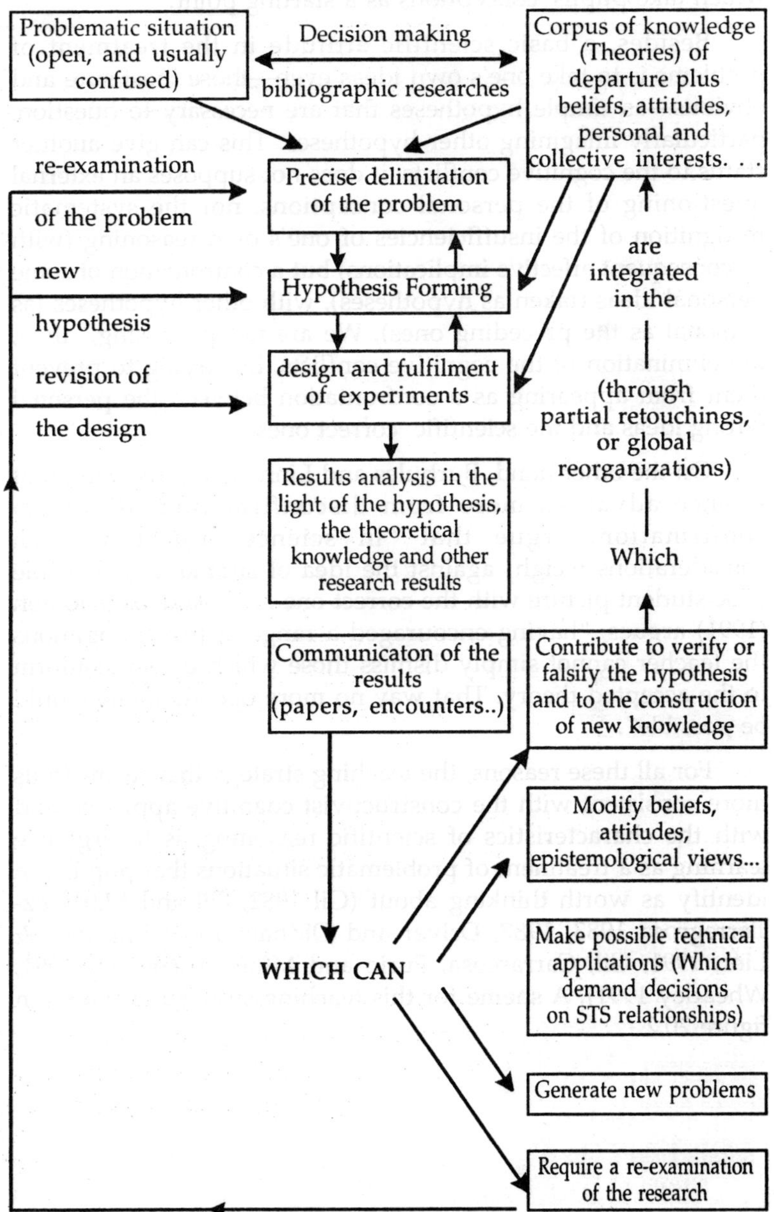

stressed "all knowledge is the answer to a question" and this conflicts radically with the conceptual change teaching strategies which take pupils' conceptions as a starting point.

Besides, a basic scientific attitude in the treatment of problems is to take one's own ideas even—those most sure and obvious—as simple hypotheses that are necessary to question, particularly imagining other hypotheses. This can give another status to the cognitive conflicts: it does not supposes an external questioning of the personal conceptions, nor the systematic recognition of the insufficiencies of one's own reasoning (with its consequent affective implications) but a confrontation of some personal ideas (taken as hypotheses), with other hypotheses (as personal as the preceding ones). We are not proposing, then, the elimination of the cognitive conflicts, but trying to prevent them from appearing as a confrontation between the personal wrong ideas and the scientific correct ones.

On the other hand, Burbules and Linn (1991), recalling that science advances more from disconfirmation than from confirmation, argue that "in science education such considerations weigh against the idea of supplanting a whole false student picture with the correct one . . .". And, as Solomon (1991) argues, "having encouraged a range of private opinions the teacher cannot simply dismiss those which do not conform to the accepted theory. That way no more opendialogue would be possible".

For all these reasons, the teaching strategy that seems to us more consistent with the constructivist cognitive approach and with the characteristics of scientific reasoning, is to organize learning as a treatment of problematic situations that pupils can identify as worth thinking about (Gil 1982; Gil and Martinez-Torregrosa 1983, 1987; Driver and Oldham 1986; Burbules & Linn 1991; Gil, Carrascosa, Furio and Mtnez Torregosa, 1991; Wheatley 1991). A sheme for this teaching strategy is shown in figure 20.2

Figure 20.2: Teaching Strategies For Organizing Learning As A Research Activity
1. Problematic situations that, taking into account the ideas, world view, skills and attitudes of pupils, generate interests and provide a preliminary conception of the task.
2. Propose the qualitative study of the problematic situation, taking decisions to define and delimit concrete problems (an activity during which pupils begin to make their ideas explicit in a functional way).
3. Guide the *scientific treatment of the problems,* which implies, among other things:
— Invention of concepts and forming hypotheses (occasion for using alternative conceptions to make predictions).
— Elaboration of possible strategies for solving the problems, including, where appropriate, experimental designs to check hypotheses in the light of the body of knowledge.
— Carrying out the strategies elaborated, and analysis of the results—checking them with those obtained by other pupils and by the scientific community—that can produce cognitive conflicts between different conceptions (taking all of them as hypotheses), requiring the conception of new hypotheses.
4. Propose the application of the new knowledge in a variety of situations to deepen and consolidate them, putting special emphasis on the S/T/S relationships which frame the scientific development, and leading all this treatment to show the nature of coherent body of knowledge of every science. Favour particularly *synthesis activities* (schemes, reports...) the elaboration of products which help to give sense to the task and increase the interest in it and the conception of new problems.

This strategy aims basically to involve pupils in the construction of knowledge, approaching pupils' activity to the characteristics of the scientific work, giving to scientific treatment of problems the rich and complex view reflected in figure 20.1. But such a strategy—that we can designate as "radically constructivist"—frequently causes reticence among teachers and science education researchers, who express the quite commonsense idea that "it is not sensible to expect pupils to construct by themselves all the knowledge that required so much time and effort from the scientists". Actually, it is difficult to oppose the view that pupils *by themselves* cannot construct *all* the scientific knowledge, and many authors (Pozo, 1987; Burbules and Linn 1991 . . .) have shown in this sense the difficulties of many subjects and the constraints of time and available resources. Nonetheless, that does not mean, in our opinion, that for some subjects it is necessary to make use of teaching by transmission. What is necessary is to clarify the situation we mean to create when we speak about pupils' involvement in the construction of knowledge. We cannot think of pupils as practising scientists working in frontier domains: this metaphor, used by several authors has, of course, many limitations (Burbules and Linn 1991) and cannot give a useful view of how to organize pupils' work. Our metaphor contemplates pupils as *novice researchers* and gives a better appraisal of the learning situation. Effectively, any researcher knows that when someone joins a research team, he or she can catch up quite easily with the standard level of the team. And that does not happen by a verbal transmission, but through the treatment of problems in fields where his or her more experienced colleagues are experts. The situation changes, of course, when problems which are new for every member of the team are treated. In this case, the progress—if there is any—becomes slow and sinuous. The proposal to organize pupils' learning as a knowledge construction corresponds to the first situation, that is to say, to an *oriented research,* in fields very well known by the "research director" (the teacher), and where the partial and embryonic results obtained by pupils can be reinforced, completed or even questioned by those obtained by the "scientific community".

If is not a question, naturally, of "deluding" pupils, making them believe that scientific knowledge has been constructed with the apparent easiness with which they acquire it (Hodson 1985), but of putting them—as it is done with novice researchers—in the situation of replicating researches already carried out by previous scientists, of treating problems well known by those who are directing their work.

The constructivist approach to science learning has to respond to the characteristics of oriented research, a research where results obtained by different teams are steadily compared and where teams count on invaluable feedback and the help of an expert.

We do not believe it necessary to repeat here the well known reasons for advocating small work groups as a way of increasing involvement and creativity in approaching open and unfamiliar situations (Ausubel 1978; Gil 1983; Solomon 1987; Burbules and Linn 1991; Robinson 1991) such as are those aimed at the construction of knowledge. But we want to emphasize the necessity—less frequently stressed—(Gil and Martinez-Torregrosa 1987; Wheatley 1991) of facilitating the interaction between the groups. This constitutes an essential feature of scientific work and can show to the pupils the insufficiency of the ideas and results obtained by a single collective and the need to compare them with those obtained by other groups, with the contribution of the teacher as "spokesman for many other researchers", that is to say, of the knowledge that the scientific community has accepted, as a result of a long and difficult process.

To sum up: against the metaphor which presents pupils as simple receiver and that which views them as autonomous researchers (Pope and Gilbert 1983) or practicing scientists (Burbules and Linn 1991), we propose the metaphor of the "novice researchers" which takes into account the limitations, pointed out by Burbules and Linn, of the "practicing scientists" idea. This metaphor is associated, as we have tried to show, with three basic elements of what we can call a "radical constructivist orientation" for science learning: open problematic situations, scientific work in cooperative groups and interactions between the groups and the "scientific community" represented by the teacher (Gil and Martinez-Torregrosa 1987; Wheatley 1991.)

We shall finish this section stressing that science teaching of the sort that we are proposing requires the transformation of all the activities of science learning—from the introduction of concepts to laboratory work, passing through the paper and pencil problem solving—and not forgetting evaluation. We do not dispose here of the necessary space to undertake even a slight study of these different activities, but our researches in these fields, as much as those of many other researchers, seem to aim at their transformation into open problematic situations to be treated in the creative and rigorous way which characterizes scientific work (Gil, Carrascosa, Furio and Mtnez Torregrosa, 1991; Calatayud, Carrascosa, Gil et al, 1990).

To Conclude: Science Teaching as Research

The science learning paradigm as a research activity that we are proposing here is highly appreciated by the teachers who participate in seminars and courses designed to introduce the new model experientially. Sometimes, however, they put a question which expresses a deep concern: how can a teacher attain all the knowledge this model requires? Let us consider, for instance, the difficulties of translating the curriculum into programmes of activities capable of generating interest and of facilitating pupils' creative and successful work. It is obvious that no teacher can fulfil such a task . . . but, in fact, it is the question itself which does not make sense: effectively, any study on science methodology or epistemology shows requirements for scientific research at least as wide and complex as those we are contemplating here, but no scientist it supposed to possess all the knowledge and skills necessary for the scientific treatment of problems: everybody knows that scientific work is a collective activity. In the same way, the teaching task should not be an isolated activity, nor should any teacher should feel overwhelmed by responsibilities which are, without any doubt beyond the capacities of a human being. It is essential that collective work can take place in all the teaching process—from the curriculum design to evaluation—with teachers involved in open and creative activities of research and curriculum development (Driver and Oldham 1986; Cobb, Wood and Yackel, 1991). From this point of view, the complexity of the strategies proposed can be seen as an invitation to break with monotonous teaching and to allow both pupils and teachers to profit from the potential creativity of the constructivist mode.

NOTES

1. 1983
2. Piaget 1970; Disessa 1982; Clement 1983; McDermott 1984; Saltiel and Viennot 1985; Furio, Hernandez y Harris 1987; Matth ews 1990.

REFERENCES

ANDERSON C.W. and SMITH E.L., 1983, Childrens conceptions of light and color-developing the concept of unseen rays. Annual meeting of the American Educational Research Association, Montreal.

AUSUBEL D, P., 1968. *Educational Psychology. A Cognitive View.* (Holt, Rineheart and Winston, Inc, New York).

BACHELARD, G., 1938. *La formation de l'esprit scientifique.* (Vrin: Paris).

BURBULES N. and LINN M, 1991, Science education and philosophy of science: congruence or contradiction?, *International Journal of Science Education,* 13 (3), 227-241.

CALATAYUD, M, L., CARRASCOSA, J., GIL, D et al, 1990. *La construction de las ciencias fisico-quimicas (Programas guias de trabajo y comentarios para el profesor).* NAU LLIBRES. Periodista Badia 10. Valencia 4610 (Spain).

CHAMPAGNE A, B, GUNSTONE R, F and KLOPFER L,E, (1985). Effecting changes in cognitive structures among physics students. In West L.H.T. and Pines A.L. (Eds). *Cognitive structure and conceptual change.* Orlando. FL: Academic Press.

CLEMINSON A, 1991, Establishing an epistemological base for science teaching in the light of contemporary notions of the nature of science and of how children learn science, *Journal of Research in Science Teaching,* 27 (5), 429-445.

CLEMENT J, 1983, A conceptual model discussed by Galileo and intuitivily used by phisics students, in Genter D and Stevens A. L. (eds), *Mental Models* (Erlbaum, Hilsdalle: N.Y.)

CLOSSET J.L, 1983, D'où proviennent certaines érrèurs rencontrées chez les eleves et les étudiants en électrocinetique . . . .?, *Bulletin de l'Union des physiciens,* 657, 81-102.

CLOUGH, E and DRIVER R, 1986. A study of consistency in the use of students' conceptual frameworks across different task contexts. *Science Education,* 70 (4), 473-496.

COBB P, WOOD T and YACKEL E, 1991, Analogies from the philosophy and sociology of science for understanding classroom life, *Science Education,* 75 (1), 23-44.

DEWEY, J. 1945. *The child and the curriculum.* (The University Chicago Press: Chicago).

DISESSA A.A, 1982, Unlearning Aristotelian Physics: a study of Knowledge-based learning, *Cognitive Science,* 6, 37-75.

DRIVER R, 1986. Psicología cognoscitiva y esquemas conceptuales de los alumnos. *Ensenanza de las Ciencias,* 4 (1), 3-15.

DRIVER R, 1988. Un enfoque constructivista para el desarrollo del curriculo en ciencias. *Ensenanza de las Ciencias,* 6 (2), 109-120.

DRIVER R, and EASLEY 1978, J. (1978). Pupils and paradigms: A review of literature related to concept development in adolescent science students. Studies in Science Education. 10 (37-40).

DRIVER R, and OLDHAM V, 1986. A constructivist approach to curriculum development in science. *Studies in Science Education,* 13, 105-122.

DUSCHUL R y GITOMER D, 1991, Epistemological Perspectives on conceptual change: implications for educational practice, *Journal of Research in Science Teaching,* 28 (9), 839-858.

DUSCHUL R, HAMILTON and GRANDY, 1990. Psychology and Epistemology. Match or mismatch when applied to science education/ International Journal of Science Education, 12 (220-243).

FREDETTE N and LOCHHEAD J, 1981. Students conceptions of electric current. *The Physics Teacher,* vol. 18, 194-198.

FURIO, C; HERNANDEZ, J and HARRIS, H (1987). Parallels between adolescents' conception of gases and the history of Chemistry. *Journal of Chemical Education.* 64 (7), 617-618.

GIL D, 1982. *La investigacion en el aula de Fisica y Quimica.* (Anaya: Madrid).

GIL D, 1983. Tres paradigmas basicos en la ensenanza de las ciencias. *Ensenanza de las Ciencias,* 1 (1), 26-33.

GIL D, and CARRASCOSA J, 1985. Science learning as a conceptual and methodological change. *European Journal of Science Education,* 7 (3), 231-236.

GIL D, and CARRASCOSA J, 1990. What to do about science misconceptions? *Science Educatioin,* 74 (4).

GIL D, CARRASCOSA J. FURIO C and MTNEZ-TORREGROSA J, 1991

La ensenanza de las ciencias en la education secundaria. (Horsori: Barcelona).

GIL D, and MTNEZ-TORREGROSA J, 1983, A model for problem-solving in accordance with scientific methodology, *European Journal of Science Education,* 5(4), 447-455.

GIL D, and MTNEZ-TORREGROSA J, 1987, Los programas-guia de actividades: una concrecion del modelo constructivista de aprendizaje de las ciencias, *Investigacion en la Escuela,* 3, 3-12.

GIORDAN A, 1978. Observation - Experimentation: mais comment les eleves apprennentils/ *Revue Francaise de Pedagogie,* 44, 66-73.

GIORDAN A, 1989. De las concepciones de los alumnos a un modelo de aprendizaje alosterico, Investigacion en la Escuela, 8, 3-14.

GRUENDER C.D. and TOBIN K, 1991, Promise and Prospect, Science Education, 75 (1), 1-8.

HALLOUN I,A and HESTENES D, 1985. Common sense concepts about motion. *American Journal of Science Education,* 7 (3), 231-236.

HASHWEH M, Z, 1986. Towards and explanation of conceptual change. *European Journal of Science Education,* 8 (3), 229-249.

HEWSON P,W. 1985. Epistemological commitments in the learning of science: exemples from dinamics. European Journal of Science Education, 8 (2), 157-171.

HEWSON M, G and HEWSON P, W 1984. Effect of instruction using students prior knowledge and conceptual strategies on science learning. *European Journal of Science Education,* 6 (1), 1-6.

HEWSON P,W and THORLEY N,R 1989. The conditions of conceptual change. *International Journal Science Education.* vol 11, special issue, 541-553.

HILLS G.L, 1989, Students "untotored" beliefs about natural phenomena: primitive science or commonsense?, *Science Education,* 73(2), 155-186.

HODSON D, 1985. Philosophy of science, science and science education. *Studies in Science Education,* 12, 25-57.

HODSON D, 1988. Towards a phylosophicaly more valid science curriculum. *Science Education,* 72 (1), 19-40.

HOLTON G, and ROLLER D, 1963. *Fundamentos de la Fisica Moderna.* (Reverte: Barcelona).

HOST, V., 1978, Procedures d'aprentissage spontanees dans la formation du scientifique, *Revue Francaise de Pedagogie,* 45, 103-110.

JANES R, K and SMITH, S. 1985. Alienation of students from science in grades 4-12. Science Education, 69, pp. 39-45.

JOSHUA 1985. Contribution a la delimitation du contraint et du possible dans l'enseignament de la physique (essai de didactique experimentale). Thèse d'Etat. Aix-Marselle, 2.

KAMINSKI and VIENNOT L, 1989. Optique elementaire. Taller desarrollado en el III Congreso Internacional sobre LA Didáctica de las Ciencias y de las Matemáticas. *Ensenanza de las Ciencias,* número extra, tomo 2, p 230.

KOYRE A, 1981, *Estudios galileanos* (Siglo XXI: Mexico).

KUHN TH, S, 1971. *La estructura de las revoluciones cientificas.* (Fondo de cultura economica: Mexico).

LANGEVIN P, 1926. La valeur educative de l'histoire des sciences. *Bulletin de la Societe Francaise de Pedagogie,* 22. Diciembre de 1926.

LEBOUTET L, 1973, *L'enseignement de la Physique.* (PUF: Paris).

MATTHEWS M,R, 1990. History, Philosophy and Science Teaching: A Rapprochement. *Studies in Science Education,* 18, 25-51.

McDERMOTT L,C, 1984. Research on conceptual understanding in mechanics. *Physics Today.* Julio, 24-34.

MILLAR R and DRIVER R, 1987. Beyond processes. *Studies in Science Education,* 14, 33-62.

MINISTRELL J, 1982. Explaining the "at rest" condition of an object, *Physics Teacher,* 20, 10-14.

MINISTRELL J, 1984, Teaching for the development of understanding of ideas: forces on moving objects. En Anderson C.W. (ed) *Observing science classroom: observing science perspectives from research and practice* (ERIC/SMAC: Columbus, OH).

NOVAK J,D, 1988. Constructivismo humano: un consenso emergente. *Ensenanza de las Ciencias,* 6 (3), 213-223.

NUSBAUM J and NOVICK S, 1982, Alternative frameworks, conceptual conflict and accommodation: towads a principled teaching strategy, *Instructional Science,* 11, 183-200.

OSBORNE R and FREYBERG P, 1985, *Learning in Science* (Heinemann: Postmouth, N.H.).

OSBORNE R and WITTROCK M, 1983. Learning Science: a generative process. *Science Education,* 67, pp. 490-508.

OSBORNE R and WITTROK M, 1985, The generative learning model and its implications for science education, *Studies in Science Education,* 12, 59-87.

PIAGET J, 1970. *La epistemologia genética.* (Redondo: Barcelona).

PIAGET J, 1972. Intellectual evolution from adolescence to adulthood. Human Development, 15 (1-12).

POPE M,L and GILBERT J, 1983. Personal experience and the construction of knowledge in science. *Science Education,* 67, 193-203.

POSNER G,J et al, 1982. Accommodation of a scientific conception: towards a theory of conceptual change. *Science Education,* 66, 211-227.

POZO J,I, 1987. *Aprendizaje de la ciencia y pensamiento causal.* (Visor: Madrid).

POZO, J,I. (1989). *Teorias cognitivas del aprendizaje.* (Morata: Madrid).

RESNICK, L,B, 1983, Mathematics and Science Learning: a new conception. *Science,* 220, 477-478.

REVE R et al, 1987, Everyday and academic thinking: implications for learning and problem solving, *Journal of Curriculum Studies,* 19(2), 123-133.

ROBINSON W.R. and NIAZ M, 1991, Performance based on instruction by lecture or by interaction and its relationship to cognitive variables, *International Journal of Science Education,* 13 (2), 203-215.

ROTH K.J, 1984, Using classroom observations to improve science teaching and curriculum materials. En Anderson C,W (ed) *Observing science classrooms: observing science perspectives from research and practice* (ERIC/SMEAC, OH).

SALTIEL E and VIENNOT L, 1985. Que aprendemos de las semejanzas entre las ideas historicas y el razonamiento espontaneo de los estudiantes? *Ensenanza de las Ciencias,* 3(2), 137-144.

SCHIBECI R,A, 1984. Attitudes to science: an update. *Studies in Science Education,* vol 11, 26-59.

SEQUEIRA M and LEITE L, 1991, Alternative conceptions and history of science in physics teacher education, *Science Education,* 75 (1), 45-56.

SHUELL T,J, 1987. Cognitive psychology and conceptual change: implications for teaching science. *Science Education,* 71 (2), 239-250.

SOLOMON J, 1987. Social influences on the construction of pupils' understanding of science. *Studies in Science Education,* 14, 63-82.

SOLOMON J, 1991, Teaching about the nature of science in the British National Curriculum, *Science Education,* 75 (1), 95-103.

VIENNOT L. 1976, *Le Raisonnement Spontané en Dynamique Elémentaire.* Tesis doctoral. Université Paris 7. (Publicada en 1979 por Herman: Paris).

VIENNOT L, (1989). Obstacle epistemologique et raisonnement en physique. Tendence au contournement des conflicts chez les enseignants. En *Construction des savoirs: obstacles et conflicts* (Agence d'ARC Inc: Ottawa).

VIENNOT L and KAMINSKY W, 1991, Participation des maitres aux modes de raisonnement des eleves, *Ensenanza de las Ciencias,* 9(1), 3-9.

WHEATLEY G.H, 1991, Constructivist perspectives on Science and Mathematics learning, *Science Education,* 75(1), 9-21.

WHITAKER R,J, 1983. Aristotle is not dead: student understanding of trajectory motion. *American Journal of Physics,* 51, 352-357.

WHITE T,R and GUNSTONE F,R, 1989. Metalearning and conceptual change. *International Journal Science Education,* vol 11, 577-586.

YAGER R,E and PENICK J,E, 1986. Perception of four groups towards science classes, teachers and value of science. *Science Education,* 70 (4), 335-363.

ZIETSMAN A. I. and HEWSON P.W., 1986, Effects of instruction using microcomputer simulations and conceptual change strategies on science learning, *Journal of Research in Science Teaching,* 23(1), 27-93.

21

Examining School Science: Using Sociology of Science in the Study of Science Classrooms

ELIZABETH FINKEL
University of Visconsin-Madison, USA

Introduction

Science educators have often looked to other disciplines for ideas to guide the conduct of research and the design of curricula. These other disciplines have included the history and philosophy of science[1], cognitive psychology, as well as other content—specific scientific fields (e.g. biology, geology, chemistry and physics). These disciplines have provided ideas about content and method for science education curriculum designers (e.g. van der Valk, 1989; and, Johnson and Stewart, 1991). For some science education researchers these disciplines have been used to develop models of learning based on ideas derived from the study of change in scientific knowledge (for example, Posner, Strike, Hewson and Gertzog, 1982), and to develop models for studying science education (i.e. Duschl, 1990; Cobb, Wood and Yackel, 1990; and, Stewart and Hafner, 1991).

One discipline which has not had a significant effect on science education, either in terms of curriculum development or research design, is the sociology of science. Although some science educators have referred to differences between current views of the sociology of science and the way science is taught in high schools (e.g. Millar, 1989), and others have discussed the importance of considering social factors in understanding the ways in which students construct meaning in science (e.g. Solomon, 1987), nowhere do science educators suggest that the sociology of science might provide a fruitful source for ideas which can be applied to the study of science classrooms.

This absence may largely result from the fact that what happens in most science classes does not at first resemble what happens in most scientific laboratories, except on a superficial level. Students are commonly engaged in learning science by listening to teachers, whose role it is to present information and then test students to see how well they have memorized it, or by performing laboratory experiments, which more closely resemble recipes than scientific investigations.

Although this view of what happens in high school science classrooms is somewhat exaggerated, it is not completely unrealistic. Most students do leave high school conceiving of science as a body of facts, already complete and well-understood, (at least by teachers and scientists), which they are to memorize for tests given at the end of each unit. This kind of science, called "final form" science by Duschl (1990), does not resemble the practice of science by scientists. As such, may be it is not surprising that the sociology of science, which describes and interprets the growth of, and, changes in, scientific knowledge, has not played a large role in research in science education.

Despite the apparent differences between the practice of science in the research laboratory and the practice of science in classrooms, I am going to argue that, in many classrooms, the sociology of science can provide a useful framework for the study of science teaching and learning. In particular, after reviewing the relevant literature in the sociology of science and examining the kinds of questions that are of interest to sociologists studying science, I will argue that, despite initial appearances, much science learning can be seen as similar to what scientists do, and, I will then propose a framework for research guided by a perspective from the sociology of science that I will argue not only makes sense, but can provide important insights into what students in science classes are doing as they learn.

Background from the Sociology of Science

In developing a sociological framework for the study of science classrooms, it is helpful to recognize that there are several schools within the sociology of science with very different conceptual and methodological approaches to the study of science. Four contrasts within the sociology of science are particularly interesting in the context of studying science in the high school classroom.

The first contrast is one between in "externalist" view of science, in which the focus is on the aspects of society outside the scientific community which affect science, and an "internalist" view, in which the focus is on processes within the scientific community. Sociological studies of science labelled "externalist" focus on discovering and analyzing institutions and practices in society as a whole which influence and/or control the practice of science. These typically include economic or political institutions, funding agencies, and other external forces which may have an effect on both the goals and outcomes of scientific research programmes. An "externalist" study of classroom science would take into account both the larger societal institutions and practices which might effect the construction of science in the classroom, as well as the school itself, an institution which would certainly have an effect on science learning within a particular classroom.

Internalist studies of science have tended to focus on discovering structures or mechanisms within the scientific community (or within specific scientific communities) which control the nature of the science practiced within them. There are two competing schools of thought regarding the nature of these structures, which brings us to the second of the four contrasts, between functionalist studies of science (i.e. Merton, 1957; Hagstrom, 1965), in which sociologists look for aspects of the organization of science (for example, the existence of norms) and interpret them as functioning to enable science to grow and produce knowledge, and "social studies of science", whose proponents (i.e. Woolgar, 1988; Latour and Woolgar, 1986) reject the functionalist approach to interpreting science, not accepting the idea (prevalent in the functionalist school) that science is a privileged way of knowing or gaining knowledge, arguing instead that science and scientific knowledge are socially constructed and are not significantly different from other areas of human endeavour.

For sociologists in the first school (i.e. Merton, 1957; and Hagstrom, 1965), the structures have traditionally been described in terms of functional norms which govern behaviour (i.e. Merton's norms of communism, universalism, disinterestedness, and, organized skepticism; or Hagstrom's norms of independence and service). In both cases, Merton and Hagstrom see norms as functioning to determine behaviour within the scientific community. They both argue that the fact that scientists do not acknowledge the existence of noms is not evidence against their existence, but, as Hagstrom puts it, that this lack of acknowledgement is evidence that "more than overt conformity to norms is demanded, . . . inner conformity is regarded as equally, or more, important" (p. 21).

The use of norms as functioning to control behaviour has been sharply criticized by many sociologists of the second school (i.e. Woolgar, 1990; Latour and Woolgar, 1979/1986; and Mulkay, 1975), who claim that norms are not functional and do not govern behaviour, but are created and used by scientists to explain their behaviour for the benefit of outsiders (nonscientists). The sociologists of the second school reject Merton's and Hagstrom's use of indirect evidence, and prefer to use the scientists' own explanations of their behaviour to explain why they act as they do.

The disagreement here may be even more fundamental than it seems on the surface. According to Woolgar (1990), the Mertonian sociologists, with their focus on the function of norms, and on the "relationships between *scientists* proceeded at the expense of attention to the ways in which different kinds of *scientific knowledge* came to be produced and accredited" (p. 26). He goes on to argue that these sociologists presumed "the actual character of science to be beyond [their] province of inquiry" (p. 26). Woolgar refers to this position as "essentialist", a position from which science is viewed as an object which can be defined (although the defining will be difficult), in contrast to the "nominalist" position, which sees the quest for a definition of science as futile because "science" and the "scientific method" are continually changing, and depend for their definitions not upon some scientific "essence" but upon the practices of scientists themselves (pp. 20-21).

The third contrast is one between macro-studies of science, in which the focus has been on answering large-scale questions about the general form of science and its growth (i.e. Hagstrom, 1965), and microstudies of science where observers spend time in laboratories studying the processes of science (i.e. Latour and Woolgar, 1986; Lynch, 1984). In the former studies the data consist of interviews in which scientists are treated as informants, or surveys where they are counted as respondents (Hagstrom, 1965, p.3), while in the latter studies scientists are seen as participants in a culture foreign to that of the observers, and it is the actions of scientists which are used to construct an understanding of that culture.

This contrast has three implications that are of interest: a methodological change, a change in the kinds of questions asked, and a change in the way in which science is portrayed. Macro-studies are usually based upon large-scale survey and interview—data, and are removed from the everyday practice of science. These studies have "tended . . . to portray science as a world apart" (Latour and Woolgar, 1986, p. 17). Macro-studies of science, with their focus on large scale characteristics of science and on the general characteristics of its growth and organization have tended to see scientists as resources to be mined for information. In these studies, it is not what scientists do that is the subject of study, but what they say about what they do. The data for these studies consist of interviews in which scientists inform researchers and surveys in which they "are counted as respondents" (Hagstrom, 1965, p. 3). Even more importantly, science is not seen as confined to a particular setting; instead, it is seen as generalizable across all settings in which scientists practice.

Micro-studies have tended to be small-scale, observation-based, ethnographic research projects, in which researchers have concentrated on the day to day events within individual scientific laboratories and have attempted to understand the practice of science in such a way that its mysteriousness is reduced instead of enhanced. These studies focus on the practice of science; on what scientists actually do on a daily basis and within particular settings. In these studies, often referred to as ethnographic because of their roots in anthropology and because of the belief, held by many researchers in this school, that science can be seen as a culture, researchers spend time in scientific laboratories observing scientists working at science. The data consist of detailed observational notes, and trascripts of laboratory conversations, as well as interviews with scientists. These micro-studies of science practice focus not on large-scale, general pictures of scientific organization, but on a small scale, specific descriptions of how scientific knowledge is produced in a given context.

The final contrast of interest is that between realism and relativism. This contrast is not confined to studies of the sociology of science, but is also prevalent in philosophy of science. In fact, it might be better termed a conflict, given the heated nature of the discussions engendered by proponents of the two sides. This contrast may be the most fundamental of all, in that it addresses the "realness" of the world sociologists are trying to describe.

Relativists, like Steve Woolgar and Bruno Latour, argue that the traditional (realist) interpretation of the relationship between an object and a representation of that object should be reversed. Rather than a representation reflecting the true nature of the object being represented, "that objects are constituted in virtue of representation" (Woolgar, 1989, p. 56). In other words, objects do not exist independently of their representations. The implications of this world view for science and for the sociology of science are clear. First, scientists have always described their work in terms of the making of discoveries; discoveries that are indeed discoveries—the unmasking of objects that exist somewhere in the world waiting to be found. Instead, Woolgar argues that scientists construct these objects through their representations of them. Objects, according to Woolgar, whether they are countries, or electrons, are socially constructed entities, and do not exist aside from this social construction. Science is therefore *not* the process of finding things that already exist, but the process of creating things that were not there to begin with. It is only thorough a complex social process that a scientific creation becomes socially legitimized as a discovery.

The second implication is equally important, and in some ways more general. If objects do not exist independently of our representations of those objects, then data (defined here as what "anyone" would see if they examined a particular object or situation) "has no meaning outside of an interpretative context". As a result "interpretations normally given in a matter-of-course, taken-for-granted, 'natural' way . . . [must be] . . . suspended" (Collins, 1983, p. 91). And, also according to Collins, this suspension of our common-sense view of science, the view "that gives us certainty about scientists' dealings with nature", leads to relativism: the "radical uncertainty about how things about nature are known"; not ignorance of knowledge production, but the suspension of knowledge and understanding about how we know what we know (p. 91). As a result, "the study of scientific knowledge is primarily seen to involve an investigation of how scientific objects are produced in the laboratory rather than a study of how facts are preserved in scientific statements about nature" (Knorr Cetina, 1983, p. 119).

Studying Science Practice and Science Learning

In attempting to understand how studies from the sociology of science can provide insight into the study of science classrooms, it is necessary to consider how science learning and science practice can be seen as similar. Once those similarities have been delineated, it will be possible to see how science education researchers can benefit from the ideas discussed in the previous section.

From a theoretical perspective, there are important similarities underlying research into the nature of learning and research in the sociology of science. Central to current understanding of the ways in which people learn is the idea that individuals are not passive receptors of knowledge, but that they actively construct knowledge. Of primary interest to constructivists is "how the knowledge that 'enables us to cope' is arrived at" (von Glasersfeld, 1989; p. 125). This interest is shared by sociologists of science who are concerned with the ways in which scientists construct their knowledge of the world (i.e. Latour and Woolgar, 1986).

Originally, ideas about the construction of knowledge focused solely on the ways in which *individuals* construct knowledge, more recently, however focus has shifted towards the role of social *groups* in the development of knowledge. This shift also parallels a concern in the sociology of science with studying the ways in which scientists collaborate to construct scientific knowledge. These similarities between theoretical concerns in the sociology of science and current research into the nature of learning suggest that the theoretical issues of interest to educators and to socioloigists may not be all that different. While the arena for studying the nature of knowledge construction is clearly different, the questions are clearly not.

If one is to argue that methods from the sociology of science can be useful in studying science classrooms, then it is important to show links between science in schools and science in research laboratories. In fact, there are important similarities between science as it is taught and science as it is practiced. Much, if not all, scientific research is conducted collaboratively. It is very rare for a single scientist to claim full responsibility for any new insight; most claims are the result of the combined effort of many scientists working on related problems over a long period of time. Similarly, much classroom science learning is conducted in groups. Although in most classrooms individual students are ultimately responsible for their own understanding, (i.e. they are expected to be able to answer test questions on their own), the use of cooperative groups in science classes is very common. Students often work in small groups to solve problems, to do laboratory work, and to prepare presentations. The recent popularity of, and publicity about, cooperative learning techniques has emphasized a practice that has been common in many science classrooms for years.

The two classes of similarities described above, theoretical similarities addressing concerns with the nature of knowledge construction, and procedural similarities relating to the practice of science in classrooms and in research laboratories, have implications for with aspects of the sociology of science presented in the preceding section are relevant to science educators. Specifically, a concern with the ways in which knowledge is constructed leads one away from a functionalist/essentialist approach to understanding school science, and towards a nominalist approach, in which the focus of research is on what students do as they practice of science in schools. This concern thus focusses research, on questions about the practice of science in schools, and on the day to day activities of students in science classrooms, resulting in a micro-analytic perspective.

Once one acknowledges that there are similarities between the subjects of study, (science as it is practiced in the research laboratory and science as it is learned in science classrooms) and in the theoretical issues of interest (the nature of knowledge construction in individuals and in groups), it becomes clear that studies in the sociology of science can offer considerable insight, in both methodology and theory, for studies in science education.

Sociological Studies of Science—Questions and Methods

According to Karin Knorr-Cetina (1983): "Several laboratory studies refer to the *constructive* nature of scientific activities . . . [an] interpretation which considers the products of science as first and foremost the result of process of (reflexive) fabrication. Accordingly, the study of scientific knowledge is primarily seen to involve an investigation of how scientific objects are produced in the laboratory . . ." (pp. 118-119). Laboratory studies of the sort described by Knorr-Cetina include[2] the work of Latour and Woolgar at the Salk Institute, reported in the book *Laboratory Life: The Construction of Scientific Facts* (1979/1986), the work of Knorr-Cetina on scientists working in a research laboratory at the University of California at Berkeley, reported in several papers (including Knorr-Cetina, 1977; and 1981) and, although completed after Knorr-Cetina's comment above, the work of Gilbert and Mulkay on the ways in which scientists account for discrepancies in research findings, reported in several papers but described most completely in *Opening Pandora's Box: An Analysis of Scientist's Discourse* (Gilbert and Mulkay, 1984). All three of these studies, as well as several other studies not mentioned here, share the constructivist perspective described by Knorr-Cetina.

This shared perspective has resulted in a shared sense of what questions need to be asked about science, and of where and how to look for answers to those questions.

The work of Latour and Woolgar can serve as an illustration of the kinds of questions and methodologies adopted by sociologists within the constructivist school. The central issue for Latour and Woolgar is understanding the ways in which scientific order is constructed out of apparent chaos. This interest stems from two concerns. First, by changing the focus of the study from a more traditional perspective in which one might ask: What sociological features (norms, rules, institutional roles etc.) might be used to explain an action? To a constructivist perspective in which one might ask: How are these sociological features invoked so as to produce order? Latour and Woolgar hoped to alleviate the problem of multiple explanations that occurs because multiple sociological features can be invoked to explain any action. In other words, in any given situation, more than one norm can be invoked to explain why a scientist or group of scientists acted in a particular manner. Second, as observers, the investigators are facing a problem similar to that of the scientists, how to produce an ordered account from seemingly chaotic data. It was hoped that by participating in this process, the researchers could gain "an interesting analytical handle on [their] understanding of scientific practice" (p. 34).

As a result of their interest in the ways in which scientists produce order from chaos, Latour and Woolgar have focused their investigation on the day to day activities of science. Latour and Woolgar focus on the work carried out in one particular laboratory (the Salk Institute). Their approach, which they call "the 'anthropology' of science" (Latour and Woolgar, 1979/1986, p. 27), is designed to "shed light on the nature of 'the soft underbelly of science'" (ibid.). Date collected during this study included "field notes, . . . all literature produced by members of the laboratory, . . . a wide range of documents relevant to the daily activities in the laboratory [including:] drafts of articles in preparation, letters between participants, memoranda, and various data sheets provided by participants, . . . Formal interviews . . . with all members of the laboratory as well as certain other scientists in the field working at other laboratories,

. . . information gleaned during informal discussions, . . . [and] the reflections of the observer . . ." (p. 40).

The two questions which arise from this concern with the construction of order from chaos, and which are central to Latour and Woolgar's investigation are:

1. How are facts constructed in a laboratory, and how can a sociologist account for this construction? and,
2. What, if any, are the differences between the construction of facts and the construction of accounts[3]?

Latour and Woolgar's use of a constructivist framework goes further than their use of the word "construct" in a book title or in the questions they ask. Their questions arise from within the context of a constructivist understanding of the nature of knowledge, and are also informed by ideas from the sociology of science. This dual consideration has a clear influence on the questions asked as well as on the way in which answers are sought.

A constructivist conceptual framework in the sociology of science has permitted researchers to generate questions about the nature of knowledge construction within scientific research groups, and both the nature of the social practices available, as well as the ways in which those practices are used for knowledge construction. The nature of these questions has had implications for the style of research conducted by sociologists, effecting the settings in which data is collected, the kinds of data that are of interest, and the techniques used to gather data. It is my contention that science education researchers working within a constructivist framework can use similar approaches in order to understand the process of knowledge construction in high school settings.

Sociology of Science in Studies of Science Classes

As in the sociological studies discussed in the previous section, it is a constructivist conceptual framework which permits science educators to begin to ask questions about the nature of knowledge construction. However, in science education research, unlike in research in the sociology of science, despite widespread interest (and research) in the idea that students learning science construct (as opposed to accumulate) knowledge, there has been little or no research on the *process* of knowledge construction. It is in this area that ideas from the sociology of science provide a framework which can inform science education researchers.

Using the sociology of science as model, it becomes clear that there is at least one set of questions about science learning that have not begun to be addressed by science education researchers. In particular, once one adopts a sociological perspective for looking at science classrooms, the question of how students construct knowledge becomes one of urgent interest.

There are clearly some important differences between what students do in classrooms and what scientists do in laboratories, (students are typically "re-learning" ready-made science, while scientists are making new science), however, once one accepts that learning (whether by scientists or by students) is a constructive process, the similarities become far more important than the differences.

What kinds of questions, then, might one ask, in a science classroom, if one were to adopt such a sociology of science perspective? What kinds of data would need to be collected, and in what kinds of settings would one look for answers? In the remainder of this section I will provide a brief example of the kinds of questions, the kinds of data, and the kinds of settings required (or more accurately, permitted) by bringing a sociology of science perspective into science education research.

A discussion about questions which arise as the result of seeing science learning through the eyes of sociologist of science can begin with the idea that Latour and Woolgar (1979/1986) saw as central to their research on the construction of science facts: How is scientific order constructed from chaos? Translated for the science classroom, this question begins to sound more like: How do students produce order (usable science knowledge) from chaos (the facts, theories, and concepts that make up the bulk of most science classes)? In addition, Latour and Woolgar (along with other sociologists of science) are interested in the social procedures available for producing such order. Translated for the science classroom, this aspect of the sociology of science perspective begins to sound like: What rules or norms exist, and are used by students, as they construct science knowledge? and, How do students use these norms, or rules, in accounting for their knowledge constructions?

These questions can be addressed in several ways, however, the constructivist sociology of science perspective encourages us to focus on the ways knowledge is constructed by groups of people, rather than individuals. As a result, the focus shifts from individual students constructing knowledge, to groups of students working together as they learn science.

A focus on students working in groups is not foreign to research in science education, however from the sociology of science perspective, rather than simply being a convenient way to get students to talk as they learn, it is an essential factor in gaining an understanding of knowledge construction. Why did Latour and Woolgar (1979/1986) listen to groups of scientists as they practiced science? Because of, in their own words, "the fundamentally social character of the objects, facts and discoveries of science" (p. 275). In the same sense that science itself is "fundamentally social", the process of constructing science is also social, and if we are to understand how students construct science knowledge, we must understand it in a social context. The kinds of data we must gather, and the settings in which we must gather it, are defined by the social nature of scientific knowledge construction. We must listen to students as they work together to construct their knowledge of science.

Bringing a sociology of science perspective into science education research does more than open a new area of inquiry into the process of science learning. It changes to focus of our interest, from individual students to groups of students, and from evaluations, after the fact, of what students *have* learned, to an analysis, during the fact, of what students are doing, and of how they are doing it, as they learn. It is this changed focus, more than anything, that offers such promise for bringing a perspective from the sociology of science into science education research.

An Example

In order to provide a more detailed illustration of the ways in which a sociology of science perspective can influence research in science education, in this section I will describe a research project currently underway in a high school science classroom. The science class in which this research is being conducted is not a typical one, however, it shares many features common to all science classrooms.

The course is an elective genetics class for high school seniors. It has been designed to allow students to learn both about genetics (its conceptual structure, problem—solving strategies, and social implications) and about the nature of science (Johnson and Stewart, 1991). In particular, students are encouraged to develop a picture of genetics (and of science) as a model-building activity in which scientists use, elaborate, and revise existing models (Stewart and Hafner, 1991), and as a practice involving problem-posing, problem-probing and the persuasion of peers; the 3P's of science practice (Peterson and Jungck, 1988).

The problems students encounter in this genetics course are not the kind found in most high school science classes. Instead of solving problems printed at the end of every chapter, with answers provided at the back of the book (or by the teacher), these problems are posed by student researchers in response to data they have generated. As a result, neither a teacher nor a book can provide answers, instead, the solutions are developed by the students and are judged on the basis of how well they enable students to explain existing data and make predictions about new data. Thus, students are engaged in a practice much like the practice of real genetics: posing problems, probing for solutions by elaborating and/or revising models, and eventually persuading peers of the usefulness of those models.

The research questions being addressed in this classroom derive from issues similar to those of interest to Latour and Woolgar (1986) and discussed in previous sections. Beginning with the idea that what is of interest is the process by which students construct models to explain data which does not "fit" already existing models, the first question asks what it is that students are doing as they build models to make sense of previously unexplained data. To focus more specifically on how students make sense, the question is divided into several sub-questions on the nature of the process students engage in as they work. The purpose of these questions is to provide detailed descriptions of the work of sense-making (i.e. can it be described in terms of model-elaboration and/or model revision (Stewart and Hafner, 1991), as well as to investigate the role of the teacher, the role of students' conceptual and procedural knowledge of genetics, and the role of social interactions in sense-making.

Another sub-question focuses on the ways in which students represent both their knowledge (the models they construct) and the process of model construction. This question will provide a way of comparing the process of sense-making with the students' accounts of their work, as well as insights into the ways in which students' representations of problems and genetics' phenomena have changed.

The second set of questions, although also concerned with the work of making sense, deals more specifically with the use of norms as a resource for constructing knowledge in the classroom. In particular, the question focuses on the ways in which norms are constructed or developed in the classroom, and on the ways in which students use norms with reference to:

1. the adequacy of a particular model compared with another,
2. the kind and number of tests a model must undergo, and,
3. when a model is "good enough" to be considered finished.

The kinds of questions being asked in this classroom have also affected the kinds of data that need to be collected. As in studies in the sociology of science, it is important to collect data which can provide a sense of what is happening with in research groups as models are being used, elaborated, and revised. To this end audio recordings are being made of all student research groups as they collaborate to build models. In addition, students are encouraged to record working models, test crosses, and other data in laboratory notebooks provided to each "research team". Students also reflect on the process of model building by responding, in a personal journal, to questions posed by the teacher and the researcher. As a final step students produce accounts of their work, describing the models they have constructed and the process of construction in a paper which will be published in a "journal" distributed to the class. These four sources, audio tapes of research groups' work, laboratory notebooks, personal journals, and published papers, will constitute the data collected for this study.

The sociology of science perspective described in this paper has clearly influenced the nature of the questions being asked in this classroom by providing a focus in which the work that students do becomes the central issue, rather than the products of that work. A focus on science practice rather than science products is not unique to the sociology of science; philosophers of science have suggested a similar emphasis (see, for example, Nickles, 1981), as have researchers in science education influenced by that perspective (i.e. Stewart and Hafner, 1991). The important difference provided by a sociological perspective is the focus on the nature of the work done as students construct science knowledge and on the ways that work contributes to sense-making. This perspective can, therefore, suggest a new way of thinking about science learning and science teaching that leads to a new set of questions to guide research in science education.

Conclusion

Science education researchers have frequently borrowed from other disciplines in their attempts to understand how students learn science and how we can best teach science. In the past, studies have used perspectives from philosophy, psychology, and the cognitive sciences, to name but a few. Strangely enough, although sociology has been valuable for other researchers in education, most science educators have not looked at studies in the sociology of science for inspiration.

This lack may stem from the notion that the differences between science practice and science teaching are so great that studies of science have nothing to contribute to studies of science education. I disagree. Sociology of science can provide at least two kinds of assistance to science educators. First, as I have discussed in this paper, sociological studies of science can provide a framework for the study of science learning in the classroom, one that will bring a new and promising perspective into science education research. And second, sociological studies of science may be able to provide some insight into how to create classrooms in which science learning is related to the practice of science.

NOTES

1. Although the history and philosophy of science have frequently been used to inform science curriculum design, there are some who have suggested that the issue is not so cut and dried. Stephen Brush (1974) has expressed the dilemma clearly when he argues that if one "wants to indoctrinate . . . students in the traditional role of the scientists as a neutral fact finder . . . [one] should not use historical materials of the kind now being prepared by historians of science . . . [however] those teachers who want to counteract the dogmatism of the textbooks and convey some understanding of science as an activity which cannot be divorced from metaphysical or aesthetic considerations may find some stimulation in the new history of science" (p. 1171). Clearly, the role of the history and philosophy of science in science classrooms is by no means uncontroversial.
2. This list of studies within the constructivist school of the sociology of science is by no means exhaustive.
3. Here, "accounts" is used to refer both to the account created by Latour and Woolgar to explain the processes of knowledge construction in the laboratory, as well as to the accounts created by scientists to explain the phenomena of interest.

REFERENCES

Brush, S. (1974). Should the history of science be rated x? *Science,* 183: 1164-1171.

Cobb, P., Wood, T., and Yackel, E., (1991). Analogies from the philosophy and sociology of science for understanding classroom life. *Science Education,* 75(1): 23-44.

Collins, H. M. (1983). An empiricist relativist programme in the sociology of scientific knowledge. In Knorr-Cetina, K.D., and Mulkay, M., (Eds.), *Science Observed,* beverly hills, CA: Sage Publications, p. 85.

Duschl, R., (1990). Restructuring Science Education: The Importance Of Theories And Their Development. New York, NY: Teachers College Press.

Gilbert, G. N., and Mulkay, M., (1984). *Opening Pandora's box: an analysis of scientist's discourse.* Cambridge: Cambridge University Press.

Hagstrom, W. O., (1965). *The Scientific Community.* carbondale, il: southern Illinois University Press.

Johnson, S., and Stewart, J., (1991). Using philosophy of science in curriculum development: An example from high school genetics. *International Journal of Science Education,* 12 (3): 297-307.

Knorr-Cetina, K.D., (1977). Producing and reproducing knowledge: Descriptive or productive? Toward a model of research production. *Social Science Information,* 16: 669-696.

Knorr-Cetina, K.D. (1981). *The Manufacture Of Knowledge: An Essay On The Constuctivist And Contextual Nature Of Science.* Oxford: Pergamon Press.

Knorr-Cetina, K.D., (1983). The ethnographic study of scientific work: Towards a constructivist interpretation of science. In Knorr-Cetina, K.D., and Mulkay, M., (Eds.) *Science Observed.* Beverly Hills, CA: Sage Publications.

Knorr-Cetina, K.D., and Mulkay, M., (Eds.), (1983). *Science Observed.* Beverly Hills, CA: Sage Publications.

Latour, B. and W. and experiment in science education. In Millar, R. (Ed.), *Doing Science: Images Of Science In Science Education.* Philadelphia, PA: The Falmer Press.

Millar, R. (Ed.), *Doing Science: Images Of Science In Science Education.* Philadelphia, PA: The Falmer Press.

Mulkay, M., (1975). Norms and ideology in science. *Social Science Information,* 15 (4/5): 637-656.

Nickels, T., (1981). What is a problem that we may solve it? *Syntheses,* 47: 85-118.

Peterson, N., and Jungck, J., (1988). Problem-posing, Problem-solving and persuasion in biology education. *Academic Computing,* March/ April: 14-17 & 48-50.

Posner, G., Strike, K., Hewson, P., and Gertzog, W. (1982). Accommodation of a scientific conception: Toward a theory of conceptual change. *Science Education,* 66: 211-227.

Solomon, J., (1987). Social influences on the construction of pupils' understanding of science. *Studies in Science Education,* 14: 63-82.

Stewart, J., and Hafner, R. (1991). Extending the conception of "problem" in problem-solving research. *Science Education,* 75 (1): 105-120.

von Glasersfeld, E., (1989). Cognition, construction of knowledge, and teaching. *Synthese,* 80: 121-140.

van der Valk, T., (1989). Waves or particles? The cathode ray debate in the classroom. In Millar, R. (Ed.), *Doing Science: Images Of Science In Science Education.* Philadelphia, pa: the falmer press.

Woolgar, S., (1988). *Science: The Very Idea.* New York, ny: tavistock Publications and Ellis Horwood Limited, in association with Methuen Inc.

22

Sociology of Science Education: Problems and Research Perspectives

PROF. SATYA PAL RUHELA
Jamia Millia Islamia, New Delhi, India

Sociology studies social institutions. Science is also a social institution in modern times, and so it also comes within the purview of sociology. In fact, so much interest has been generated in this direction that a very specialized field of study entitled 'Sociology of Science' has emerged during recent decades to study various aspects of the relationship between society and science. According to Joseph Ben-David the sociology of science studies the way in which scientific research and diffusion of scientific knowledge are influenced by social conditions, which, in turn, influence social behaviour.

Various sociologists like Robert Merton, Sorokin, Bernard Barber, Walter Hirsch, E. Negal, B. Hessen, Joseph Ben-David, Randall Collins, S.N. Eisensteadt, etc. have enriched this field with their contributions. *The Sociology of Science* edited by Bernard Barber and Walter Hirsch (1963) still remains a classic book of readings in this field, although newer contributions are being added to this field by sociologists and educationists of many countries.

The growth of the field of sociology of education can be divided into two periods, the first one starting from the early 1920s to the end of the 1930s, and the second one starting after the World War II and lasting to date.

During 1920-30, the major writing and research interests in this field were: role of science in social change, problem of resistance and suppression, social functions of science, conceptualization of the informal social system of science, and the social history of science and technology in the seventeenth century. The post-War developments in this field have revealed these trends: interactional study of the scientific community, socialization of younger scientists, scientists' interest in philosophical ideas and theories, conceptualization of scientific interaction, influence of class interests, racial origin, political ideology on science, social responsibility of the profession of scientists, institutions of scientific activity, science in totalitarian societies, and very few studies on the social effects of science.

Essentials of the Sociology of Science

1. According to Talcott Parsons, a sociologist, the basic norms of any scientific knowledge are: empirical validity, logical clarity, logical consistency, and generality of the principles involved.
2. German sociologist Max Weber believed that the belief in the value of scientific truth is not derived from nature but it is a product of definite cultures.
3. Robert Merton has demonstrated that there has always been existing a latent and active hostility towards science in many societies which hinders or slows down the pace of development of science in those societies.
4. Scientific research is not conducted in social vacuum.
5. Most institutions demand unqualified faith, but the institution of science makes scepticism a virtue.
6. Dictatorship organizes, centralizes and hence intensifies sources of revolt against science which in a liberal structure remains unorganized, diffuse and often latent.
7. A scientist has to undergo special careeristic stresses. His whole personality is so moulded by his profession that hard work, devotion to duty, fearlessness and sobriety become the very elements of this nature.
8. Any scientific achievement is the result of accumulated

effort of many scientists. Newton's classic statement is worth remembering: If I have seen farther, it is by standing on the shoulders of giants.

9. No modern scientist believes that he will ever be able to make a grand invention by serendipity pattern i.e., by an accidental happening or by just a stroke of luck. Systematic and strenuous research work done by him, taking help from is predecessors and contemporaries, only can produce outstanding inventions or findings.

10. It is in the very ethics of the profession of scientific researchers to stand for truth discovered by them, and to be prepared to sacrifice even their lives for the sake of truth. The long social history of science is full of many such inspiring sacrifices made by scientists of conscience and integrity. That nobel tradition continues in most of the countries even today. The respect of independent scientists and university scientists is definitely greater than bureaucratic scientists, working in governmental and semi-governmental agencies.

11. According to Max Weber, "in the field of science only he who is devoted solely to the work at hand has personality." He further holds "only by strict specialization can the scientific worker become fully conscious, for once and perhaps never again in his life time, that he has achieved something that will endure."

12. The practice of affixing the name of the inventor or discoverer to all or part of what he has found, e.g. Corpernician system, is only the most enduring and perhaps the most prestigious kind of recognition institutionalized in science. Anonymous or mediocre research assistants have no place in this scheme of things.

13. According to Edward Shils, "the freedom of publication and discussion is absolutely central to the tradition of science."

14. Plagiarism and fraud are outside the culture of scientists. A scientist is morally bound to give due credit to other scholars from whose works he has benefited.

15. The applicational aspects of science i.e. technologies of different kinds are of crucial social, cultural, political and economic importance since their basic purpose is to make man's life easy, comfortable and fruitful.
16. Science as an agent of social and cultural change and modernization is very much recognized all over the world.

Sociology of Science Teaching in Schools

In most of our schools there are shortages of labs, tools, materials, dedicated, well trained and innovative teachers, and of the continuance of stale courses and anaemia (normlessness) in the use of science teaching methods. We find many science teachers asking students to read out from science books in classes instead of getting the experiments (even those prescribed in the syllabus and described in the textbooks) actually done by them. The high expectations of our scientists, educationists and leaders usually remain unfulfilled because the science books are written either in difficult. English or Sanskritized Hindi which is even more difficult for the students to understand. Many science teachers are frustrated, apathetic, unenthused, and tuition-hunters. They fail to cross the barrier between the cultures—the culture of science and that of humanities and social sciences. There are schools in which science kits, so enthusiastically sent by UNESCO or NCERT, remain unopened and unused for years and they just lie in the dingy corners of school libraries.

Science Education under the 10 + 2 Scheme

The new curriculum for Classes IX and X, developed by the Central Board of Secondary Education, New Delhi, has envisaged a comprehensive course of general education with provisions for work-experience. A minimum essential core of knowledge for promotion of intellectual capabilities has been provided by teaching subjects like languages, mathematics, sciences and social sciences. The terminal behaviour on the part of the students, in so far as science is concerned, is that the student will have a proper understanding of fundamental concepts of basic laws of nature and their operations, and also be able to have the knowledge of the methodology of applying such knowledge to the solving of everyday problems in a scientific manner.

The curriculum-framers have prescribed several topics in three prominent sciences—physics, chemistry, and life sciences. It is for the subject teachers to tell us now as to how far are these courses suited to our social and cultural contexts. Are they psychologically motivated to the students? Are they full of potentialities for the welfare and enlightenment of our masses? Are they too light or too heavy to discourage the students? Are they really modern courses or just old wine in new bottles? Is it possible to apply new science methods in teaching them?

The author finds that the curriculum-planners have paid scanty attention to the socio-cultural context and the proper methodology of teaching science. At Classes IX and X, the most useful methods would have been the biographical method the observation method, and the experimentation method. The life of a scientist, vividly presented, describing his background, frustration and achievements, etc. should serve as the most effective medium for communicating knowledge, impressions and values of science. The importance of field-observation, nature study, project and experimentation cannot be overlooked.

What types of teachers are needed for teaching science? What personality patterns and competencies should they have? Aren't they going to be grand preceptors teaching every kind of science without having proper qualifications, aptitude and competencies for them?

Research Needs in Science Education

The Regional College of Education, Ajmer, organized on 22-26 March 1976 a workshop on "Research in Science Education", in which research needs in science and mathematics and sociology of science were discussed by the participants. The consensus of the workshop was that research in science education in our country is still very little, almost primitive. There is no research work in the area of sociology of science education. There are no fundamental studies on the pattern of HPP (Harvard Project Physics). There are no studies available on the comparative advantages of new physics versus old physics. The Third Indian Year Book on Education (NCERT,

1968) and A Survey of Research in Education (1974), clearly shows that there is very little of research in India on the sociological aspects of science teaching, and whatever research is there on the teaching and curriculum of science in Indian schools is not creative and functional in the socio-cultural context.

It is necessary to think of evolving research topics in a sociological perspective. Factors like rural-urban social groupings, religion, superstitions, traditions, economy, caste, social class, language, occupations, symbols, public cooperation, opposition, expectations, and needs of the rural masses, politics, bureaucracy, etc. should be closely studied in so far as they affect science education in today's schools. Their impact on TV, radio, journals science comics and fictions, exhibitions, science contests, etc. also deserves to be studied.

The socio-cultural backgrounds career patterns, motivations, frustratation, training, reorientation of science teachers, and the effectiveness and utility of seminars, workshops etc.—all these are vital research priorities in science education. Research is urgently called for in the personality patterns of students who should take up higher science in their college career.

A lot of meaningful research is needed on textbooks, equipment improvisation of tools and procedures, and the pupils' interests, achievements, and difficulties in science subjects being taught to them. How much of science knowledge has, in fact, gone into their daily habits and in the daily life of their relatives in their families as a result of classroom instruction, is yet to be investigated.

The cost-benefit analysis of science tools, methods, laboratories, and the value-conflicts of students teachers and parents are also significant topics for the researchers in science today.

The sum and substance is that we must let our science teachers, their training, their backgrounds, their teaching methods and strategies, science curricula, science books, science laboratories, science clubs, TV lessons on science. TV programmes of SITE for rural transformation, value conflicts arising out of science teaching, mixing up of science and arts teachers etc. i.e.

almost everthing exposed to research without any hesitation what so ever. That is necessary inorder that science education in our schools imbibes the elements of humanism and scientism, and it does not remain ritualistic and mechanical as it is in most of our schools today despite the introduction of many so called innovative practices in science education.

REFERENCES

Barber, Bernard and Walter Hirsch. *The Sociology of Science*, New York: Free Press, 1963.

23

The Innovation "Science, Technology and Society" in Science Education

ANA M. MORAIS
University of Lisbon, Portugal

Introduction

Thus we have a breakdown of certainty in the foundations of scientific knowledge: the possibility of its absolute formal legitimation does not exist (Giannetto, 1985). We must look, hence, at the scientific theories as not simply denotative representations of reality but rather as pragmatic-performative constructions, in the perspective of a general, formal, radical, *"logico-mathematical epistemological constructivism"*. So, apart from other differences, the gap between common knowledge and scientific knowledge can be said to have been reduced as long as there appear many different "schemes of knowledge" at the very formal scientific level and there is a semantical indeterminacy also in formal theories, internal to the exact definitions of the same physico-mathematical concepts (Bell, 1986; Giannetto, 1989, 1990).

Van Fraassen, discussing the problem of the reality of mathematical objects (Van Fraassen, 1984), uses an expression introduced by Beth and speaks of a "galactic system" as the "great semantical model" in which every mathematician or scientist.

The STS—Science, Technology and Society—education has been acquiring at the international level, an increasing importance. The new curricula contain already quite frequently, and implicitly or exploicitly, the idea that the students should be led to understand the relation between science, technology and society. And, as it happened before with other innovations in science education, the STS education emerge as the perspective which was missing, that which will provide the students with a broader and more real understanding of science.

It is the aim of this article to demystify that conception, trying to make clear how the STS education can in nothing contribute to a more real image of science, representing only once again the reproduction of the dominant principles of society, now different. It is also intended to show that are others the dimensions which should be included in science education, in order that science and technology appear in a more correct perspective to the students.

In the analysis and discussion we shall use Bernstein's theory of pedagogic discourse (Bernstein 1977, 1990; Domingos et al, 1986) namely his concept of pedagogic code. His concepts of classification—C (degree of maintenance of boundaries between categories) and framing—F (degree of communication between categories), to refer respectively to power and control relations between discourses, agents and agencies, are therefore crucial to the analysis which we propose to carry out. Concepts related to the production, recontextualizing and reproduction of the pedagogic discourse are also important for the analysis. These conceptual instruments will highlight the points we wish to make.

We shall start by making a brief reference to the differential status which has been attributed in society to the experimental sciences relatively to the social and human sciences. On the basis of the most spread form of transmission of science in science education, we shall analyze and discuss, in terms of variation/change, the sociological meaning of other forms, particularly of the STS perspective.

The Sciences

Let us begin by considering in its two dimensions, the experimental sciences and the social and human sciences. Here a polemic has been raised whether areas of knowledge like sociology or psychology should be considered science. Beyond the question of the different nature of the exact and natural sciences and of the social and human sciences, there is underlying this polemic a question of high status presently recognized to the former, to which the latter wish to ascend and that the experimental sciences want to safeguard.

It is not the objective of this study to enter in that polemic. We shall take both as science and, for purposes of the analysis, we shall start by centre in the experimental sciences, focus of the STS education. Such sciences have developed through time (historical dimension), making use of various methods (philosophical dimension), by people with specific attributes (psychological dimension), interacting with others, inside and outside the academic community (sociological dimension).

History and Philosophy, have constituted themselves as metasciences in the study of the construction and development of science. In fact, if history and especially philosophy have been considered as metasciences, the same has not happened with psychology let alone with sociology (a fact which in itself is sociological). It has been taken for sure that are the former which should fulfil the task of analyzing science in its construction and development. We share with Ziman (1984), the idea that *science is a social institution*, for whose understanding are needed not only the philosophy and the history but also the psychology and especially the sociology. The sociology of science should be considered in its two dimensions: the internal dimension which refers to the relations within the academic community and the external that is the study of its relations with the non-academic community. And this also applies to the construction and development of social and human sciences.

The relations academic community/non-academic community are part of a field in which conflicting forces determine which of those two contexts (discourses agents, agencies) possesses more power in a specific society and in a particular time. The development of present industrialized societies is greatly influenced by science but the development of science depends also to a great extent on the fields of production and of the state. In other words, science influences society and also receives its influence. It may be difficult to say which has more power, the scientific community on one hand or the production and the state on the other. However, the idea which has been promulgated in society at large is the importance and actually the greater power of science.

Science Education

If we intended to lead the students to acquire a real image of science, deep changes had to occur. In fact, if we focus our attention in the history of science education, particularly in the last decades, we can see that emphasis has been given to the history of science—the history of biological concepts, the history of ideas in chemistry and so forth. Attention has also been paid to the philosophy of science although this has been done through a distorted image consubstantiated in the myth of the scientific method. Within a lower degree of emphasis, something similar has happened with the psychology of science which appears in a very restricted and unilateral form, calling the attention of the students to the qualities of the scientist instead to his (her) attributes as a man (or a woman). As far as sociology is concerned it has been virtually absent as a metascience. On the other hand, even when the above aspect are present in the curricula and pedagogic practice they are not evaluated. As a consequence, they appear more as a motivation, a "story" that the students can forget because they not even have the status which deserves evaluation.

If science is a social institution similar to so many other institutions of human endeavour, and as such should be understood by students, an integrating perspective should be introduced in science education which links the experimental sciences to the social and human sciences. This means that the scientific concepts should be integrated with the metascientific concepts of a social and human nature, namely with the sociology of science. Such integration would imply the attenuating of the boundaries between fields of knowledge usually strongly classified that is the experimental sciences, as one hand and the social and human sciences in the other, consequently, in the hierarchy of knowledge, this means a lost of status of the natural sciences relatively to the social sciences and a relative gain of these when compared to the experimental sciences. It also means a tight relation of communication between these two broad areas of knowledge. The relations between discourses would be then characterized by weaker classifications and framings which, in a relative scale, could be defined as $C^+ F^-$. These relations are shown in the diagram of figure 23.1.

The integration we have referred, would have to be evident not only in the process of transmission and learning but also in the evaluation. This means that the understanding and application of the ideas acquired, evidently at a level of abstraction which makes useful their learning, would be done not only at the levels of the biology or physics or chemistry but also at the level of their inter-relation with the social and human sciences. Such perspective causes the raising of the level of abstraction because there are more concepts to be inter-related. However, it carries within itself a better understanding of what science is. We should note that we are not dealing here with the integration of the various experimental sciences which constitutes by itself a different problematic.

Figure 23.1: Inter-relations between experimental and social and human sciences and science education-Integrating perspective.

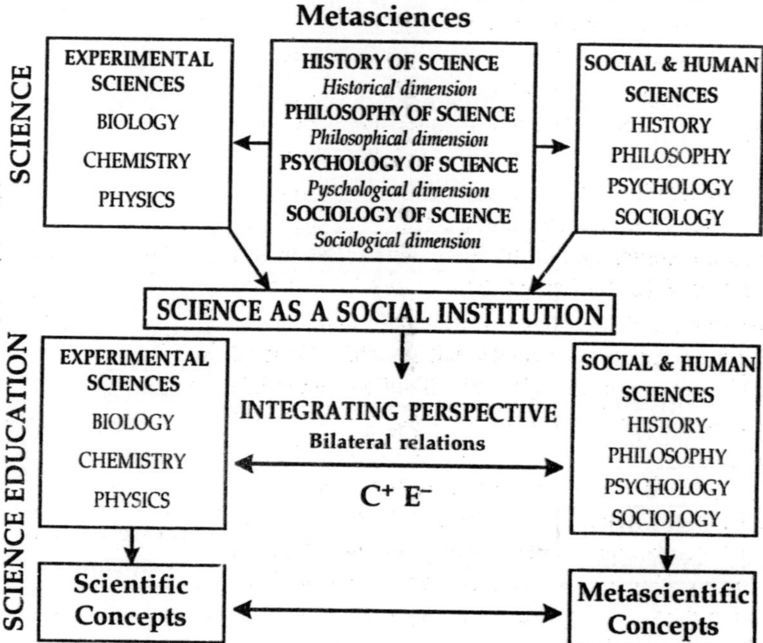

It is important to be aware that the integration we have been talking is far from being total, since a true integration would be much deeper, implicating the complete disappearing of the boundaries between the natural and the social sciences which would appear with equal status. In other words, when we teach, for example, physics and in that teaching are integrated the various dimensions of the construction of science (historical, philosophical, psychological, sociological) in an extent that leads physics to be understood in all which means to be a social institution, boundaries are attenuated but it is the physics which still keeps a higher status. This justifies the classification C^+ . Relations of communication between the categories experimental sciences, in this case the physics, and the social sciences are also established. They are bilateral relations in which the sciences with lower status (the social sciences), in their function of

Figure 23.2: Inter-relations between experimental and social and human sciences and science education - Collection Perspective.

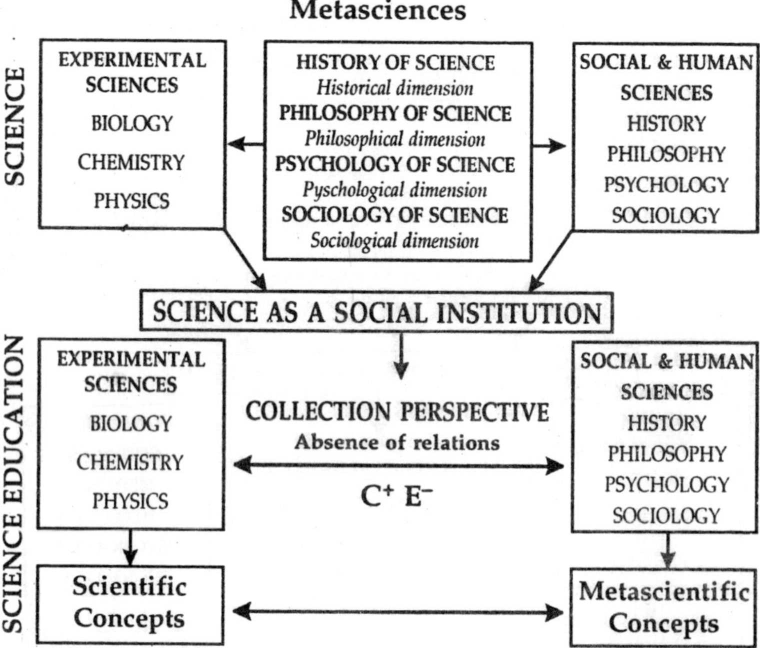

Figure 23.3: Inter-relations between experimental and social and human sciences and science education—STS perspective.

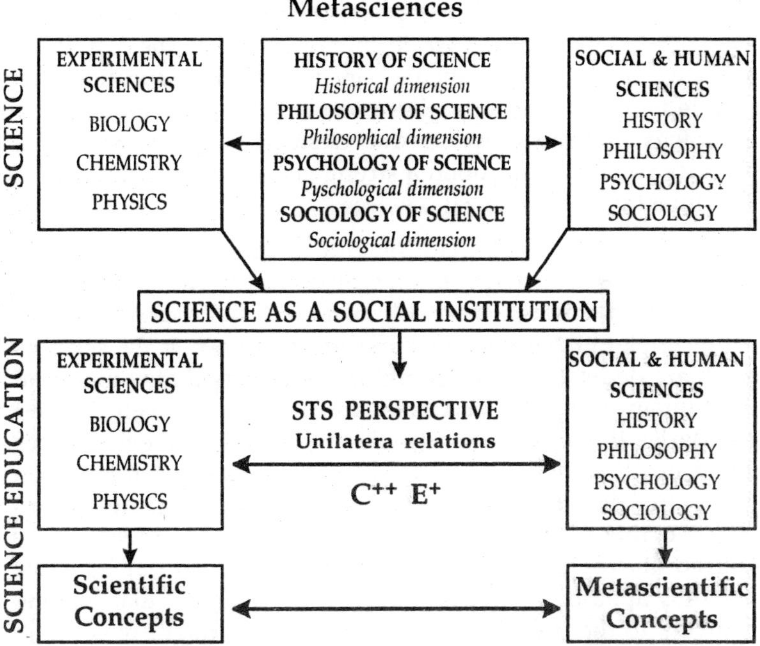

metasciences, demystify the high status and therefore the great power of physics. For that reason we can talk about framing relations characterized by F^-. The psychology of science, but mainly the sociology of science have there a prevalent role. The framing F^- intends to signify that the social sciences have now some control on the discourse physics.

On the other extreme is the traditional perspective in which there are strong boundaries between the experimental sciences and the social sciences (and also within each one of these areas) and an absence of communication between them. We are in face of a curricular perspective of collection. The relations between discourses are then characterized by strong classifications and framings which in a relative scale, as it was done before, could be defined as $C^{++}E^{++}$.

STS Education

The STS education cannot be included in any of the two approaches analyzed. In the perspective which is commonly called STS, relations are established but they are unilateral. Characterized by apparent weak framings between the discourses which we have been analyzing, since with STS education it is intended to tight relations between science and society, the technology appearing as a crucial element in that relation, the STS education is based upon a strong classification between the experimental and the social sciences.

In fact, in the hierarchy of knowledge, the experimental sciences keeps their high status which appears to students still more marked through the study of their importance in society (via technology) and evidently of their influence in the sciences which are dedicated to the study of that society that is the social and human sciences. We are in the presence of well marked boundaries in an hierarchy in which the experimental sciences have a position whose status was never so high. For this reason we can say that the classification is very strong and defined as C^{+++}. To this contributes to a great extent the unilaterallity referred above. In fact, the weak framing pointed out is, as we said, only apparent. There is, in fact, a weakening of that framing relatively to the collection perspective, which might mean that, in relative valued, the social sciences had now more control on the discourse of physics (to use the same example). Paradoxically it is this weak framing which, not being actually weak as in the integrating perspective and originating the unilateral relation referred, establishes relations between experimental and social sciences (which do not exist in the collection perspective) to consubstantiate the high status of the experimental sciences, referred above.

The STS education, with the apparent introduction of the sociology of science (and other metasciences) in science education, is therefore a new modality of control which corresponds to the realization of the power relations between discourses, where it is clear the power of the discourse of science (experimental sciences) although masked by the weaken of framing. The pedagogic code is, in this case, the institutionalization of the school elaborated orientation through classifications extremely strong and framings which, although weaker, are still strong.

For analysis purposes we have been exploring the relationship between discourses. This relationship carries with it and/or is a consequence of the relations between agents (the teachers) and also between agencies (school-other institutions).

A superficial analysis of the discourse of STS education may lead us to foresee deep changes in science education. It is with no doubt a change but it is not deep. STS education makes evident with no ambiguities the power relations between categories (discourses, agents and agencies) legitimizing the reproducing function of the school. The high status and power presently attributed to science and technology in society is now subtly introduced in the school. And the "voice" which is given to social sciences, namely to sociology, inside and outside the school, represents only, as we have said, a new modality of control which permits to make stronger the strength of science and technology.

In face of this change in society there was prompt action in the official recontextualizing field for the introduction of the new relations, evidently ideologically recontextualized. An analysis of the new syllabuses of the new reforms shows how the official pedagogic discourse transmits already to the school this "pedagogic innovation" with progressive characteristics. It is interesting to note how the agents and agencies of the pedagogic recontextualizing field (textbooks authors, university departments of education, private foundations, etc.) are following uncritically the directions contained in the official pedagogic discourse. In fact, although sometimes disagreeing with some aspects of those directions, they are even amplifying the unidirectional and distorted view transmitted by STS education according to which the emphasis is placed on the influence of science and technology on society and the influence of society on science and technology is often virtually ignored. Thus the space of change present in any recontextualizing field is being used for a better reproduction of the dominant principles and relations in society. On their turn teachers will reproduce more this "pedagogic innovation" as they use less the space of change of the school pedagogic practice.

The above considerations lead us directly to teachers' training and also to the education of teachers' trainers. Teachers' trainers, who are located primarily in the pedagogic recontextualizing field but quite often in the official recontextualizing field and even in the field of state, can, in the institutions where they work, influence both the curriculum development and the training of teachers, closely inter-linked. Change *does not occur* through the reproduction of the dominant principles of society which lead to the maintaining of strong boundaries between categories. Is it possible that teachers and especially teachers' trainers, become interested by these issues and mainly come to a position where they want to contribute to a change which corresponds to their own ideological change and which sociologically is of no interest to them? This is a question which so far does not seem to have a positive answer. However, it is from that answer that depends the transformation of the school.

Returning to the STS education, focus of this article, it is urgent that teachers and teachers' trainers consciencialize themselves that science technology and society is not society technology and science and draw from that understanding the appropriate conclusions to their pedagogic practice and/or to the research they develop.

The STS education contains many features and issues which can and should be analyzed. It was not the intention of this article to deal with the whole problematic which surrounds this innovation. The aim of the analysis was to transmit a way of looking at STS education which departs from usual approaches in many crucial aspects. This may constitute a starting point to deeper and more extended analyses of texts and practices through which STS education is realized and also of the assumptions which underlie the new forms of presenting science to the students and which are increasingly being implemented at an international level.

REFERENCES

Domingos, A. M. (now Morais), Barradas, H., Neves, I., Rainha, H. 1986, *A teoria de Bernstein em Sociologia da Educacão,* Lisbon: Fundacao Gulbenkian.

Bernstein, B. 1977, *Class, codes and Control—vol. III—Towards a theory of educational transmissions,* London: Routledge & Kegan Paul.

Bernstein, B. 1990, *Class, codes and control - vol. IV - The structuring of pedagogic discourse,* London: Routledge.

Ziman, J. 1980, *Teaching and learning about science and society,* Cambridge: Cambridge University Press.

Ziman, J. 1984, *An introduction to science studies - The philosophical and social aspects of science and technology,* Cambridge: Cambridge University Press.

24

Science Through Technology and Society: Educating the Teacher Educators

MARGARET RUTHERFORD, JOHN, D. BRADLEY
&
MARIE BRAND
University of the Witwaterstrand, South Africa

Introduction

Science teaching in much of Southern Africa is characterised by what Beeby (1965) would call a stage II development. The teachers have a little trainning but not much, the teaching is teacher centred rather than learner centred with few questions being asked by the teacher and even fewer by the learners. The learners are expected to learn many things by rote and to accept the teacher's word as always correct. There is little opportunity for investigation by learners even in a science subject. The predominant style is therefore at variance with the ethos of scientific enquiry and makes it very difficult for both teachers and learners to be effective scientists even at an elementary level. South Africa is no exception. Although there are some schools with characteristics of a more developed teaching stage, the majority of pupils, almost all black, are taught in this rote learning, non experimental way. Several attempts are being made to change this, for example with an examination emphasis on practical work, but one of the major problems is a shortage of qualified science teachers at all levels. The teachers in the schools rarely have a science background which extends to tertiary level and it is more probable that they will have only matriculation biology if they do indeed have any science at all. An initiative by the education department historically responsible for the education of blacks (the Department of Education and Training (DET), has been to attempt to upgrade the training of science teachers and this is the focus of the present paper.

Teacher Training

If the teaching of science is to change, the induction of teachers into different methods and paradigms must have both an in service and a pre-service thrust. The University of the Witwatersrant (Wits), through the School of Science Education (SoSE), is involved in both of these but we are concerned here with the pre-service training of teachers and with in-service support for the lecturers of these student teachers.

While there are several routes to training as a teacher, in South Africa the majority of teachers are trained in teacher training colleges (a total of +/-70 in the Republic and its satellites). Most of the Colleges are for the training of black teachers.

In several parts of the world, mainly in developed countries, there has been a move to make the science taught in schools more relevant to pupils everyday lives and so to incorporate a social and technological flavour to the topics taught. In general this has been done through initiatives aimed at the pupils and taught by industrially motivated teachers. As far as is known, there has been little attempt worldwide at pre service teacher training institutions to incorporate Science, Technology and Society (STS), into the training programme. In general the initial spur for innovative curricula has come from the school level and the colleges have followed on. In the present programme in the black training colleges in South Africa this has been reversed since the thrust has been towards empowering the teachers during their initial training to initiate syllabus changes. There is little suitable material available for college lecturers, student teachers pupils at present and it is likely that material will have to be produced by these student teachers for their pupils when they enter the teaching profession if they are to teach STS in the classroom. The school syllabus at present is traditional and has no explicit STS content.

History of the Project

In late 1989, members of the SoSE at Wits were asked by the Department of Education responsible for the training of black school teachers (DET), to help design a new syllabus for these training colleges. Whilst a minority of the training colleges fall directly under the control of this Education Department, the majority of them follow the syllabuses laid down by the department and the students sit the same examinations. Prior to this date the students had not been required to take their science content knowledge any further than the school syllabus level (matriculation), and had spent 3 years re-doing the school syllabus with the associated methodology. The new syllabus was to be designed to raise the content level to matriculation + 1.5 or +2 years. From experience it was known that even if these students have nominally studied science at school, their knowledge is at best fragmentary and at worst totally inadequate. However, to repeat the school syllabus when the students considered that they "knew" it seemed likely to be de-motivating. The content could not be ignored since not all the students had taken physical science at school even though this was to be introduced as a nominal requirement for entry to the colleges at the same time as the new syllabus. For this reason, and because of the growing international trend towards STS, a proposal was made that the first year or 1.5 years of study should have an STS flavour where the necessary revision of school content was presented in a new and interesting format. A further reason for the proposal was the feeling that the relevance of science through an emphasis on technology and society was particularly important in a country with first and third world populations in significant proportions. This proposal was greeted enthusiastically if somewhat nervously by the lecturers involved in the working group but has a rather more rocky passage through the Education Department hierachy! However the proposal was accepted by the Education Department at the end of 1989 and this radically new syllabus was scheduled for implementation in January 1990. (Subsequently, in 1991, the

Department of National Education put out a proposal for curricular changes which reflect a learning towards an STS flavour for school science-one of the hoped for results.)

There was no plan to aid the college lecturers and as far as could be ascertained, no materials available for either lecturers or students. The reply to our queries was that the lecturers were expected to cope with the new syllabus on their own. The University staff felt some sort of moral obligation to orientate and to assist the college lecturers and so, with the consent and help of the Department, organised the first of a series of workshops for lecturers in November 1989, the same week as the syllabus was formally approved. The date five workshops have been held with a sixth scheduled for January 1992.

STS and the First Year of Teacher Training

As mentioned previously, the first year of the Secondary Teachers Diploma (STD) or the first one and a half years for the primary Teachers Diploma (PTD) are now based on school science content but in an STS setting. The themes chosen were, Food, Clothing, Shelter, Transport and the Environment. For each theme a team of college lecturers, with the help of the University staff met towards the end of 1989, to design the objectives for the theme. The number of these objectives varied with each theme but overall an attempt was made to balance the physics and chemistry content. An example of a section on the theme "Transport" with its content, objectives and syllabus connections is shown in Figure 24.1 (next page). The syllabus connections are shown in brackets in this figure.

It can be seen that it is difficult to classify some of the objectives as either physics or chemistry and this serves to emphasise the integration of the course content.

In addition to the theoretical content, several skills and process type objectives were built into the syllabus. Traditionally the black schools do little if any practical work and so students arrive at college with no experience of laboratory activities. They are frequently reluctant to try experiments and so the syllabus objectives try to present practical exercises in a novel and interesting way. (There is a separate practical syllabus for the second and third years of the STD course but this is concerned with more 'traditional' laboratory activities.) A survey of the feelings of the college lecturers, conducted after the first workshop (41 responses), indicates that these lecturers felt that the new syllabus was overwhelmingly more related to everyday life and was enough to make pupils aware of technological and scientific developments. A majority of them felt that the changes were essential although few felt confident in teaching such a syllabus. They anticipated problems in implementation and in provision of adequate laboratory facilities.

Figure 24.1: Extract from the STS syllabus theme 'Transport'.

3.2.4 (10)	
Car battery, fuel system, exhaust. [Cells in series and parallel redox reactions, energy conversion, catalysis.]	19. Describe how a car battery is constructed and how it works. 20. Give the equations for the reactions taking place at the electrodes during the charging and discharging cycles. 21. Explain why distilled water has to be added occasionally to the battery. 22. Explain why possible short circuiting of a battery should be avoided. 23. Explain why an open flame should not be brought to the close proximity of the battery. 24. Write down the equation for the combustion of hydrogen. 25. Discuss the advantages of joining cells in a series and in parallel in terms of the car battery. 26. Explain the function of the carburettor and the influence of the composition of the air/fuel mixture on combustion. 27. Describe the composition of petrol and diesel fuels.

A third component of the new syllabus was a requirement that at least 4 visits were to be made by STD students to some industrial and/or commercial venture during their curriculum. It was not possible to be prescriptive about which site or plant should be visited or indeed what type of visit would be appropriate since the colleges are spread throughout South Africa and what was available would depend on the area in which the college was situated. Many lecturers had never themselves visited a chemical plant, or a mine and so in the 5-day workshops a day is always assigned to industrial visits to help the lecturers in planning and running this sort of activity.

Production of STS Materials

Since this was a novel initiative in South Africa, there was no locally-produced material available. A collection of booklets, schemes, pupil worksheets and activities from the U.K. and the U.S.A. was assembled by us from our personal collections and by purchase from the UK and elsewhere. At the first 4 day workshop in November 1989, these materials were shown to the College lecturers and, during working sessions, the possibilities of using some of the ideas was discussed. Whilst the materials are interesting and potentially useful, they are not totally appropriate as they stand for either lecturers or teachers in an African setting. The main problems are in the context and facilities assumed to be available and in the language. This latter is not entirely suitable, not only because of the written word but also because of the implicit assumptions made. An English first language speaker would be expected to understand a phrase such as 'take it with a pinch of salt' whereas an English second language speaker might take in literally and not get the correct understanding.

Lecturers have been encouraged to modify these American and British materials and to write their own but this has not been very productive. To date, (January 1992), one theme—clothing—has received local attention—the cost of writing, production and distribution of a lecturer resource package for this theme has been underwritten by Sough African Nylon Spinners (SANS) and has been produced by Margaret Keogh (SANS) in collaboration with Audrey Ogude (Wits Ph.D. student). Additional material has been produced by some post graduate students in the SoSE at Wits, for example Etienne Mashimbye created a teaching package based on a motor car and relating school physics and chemistry to the starting of the engine, Joseph Dolo one on fertilisers and Malatsi one on glass. Funding has now been secured for employment of a research and development (R&D) officer at Wits for production of more lecturer and student materials.

Workshops

Since 1989, five workshops/courses have been held for the college lecturers. Typically 40-50 lecturers attend each of these courses although, since more than one lecturer from a college may attend, this does not represent 40-50 colleges. The population changes with each course although there is now a sizeable "core" of lecturers who attend regularly. Because of the geographical spread of colleges, some of these lecturers travel 500-1000 km (300-600 miles) to get to Wits.

The workshops/courses have evolved over this period. Initially they were organised in conjunction with the Department of Education and Training and were held either in a College of Education or at a Training Centre. From July 1990 onwards they have, by fairly general consensus, been held on the campus of the University of the Witwatersrand with the exception of that held in July 1991 which was timed to coincide with the Biennial Conference of the South African Association of Teachers of Physical Science in Cape Town. The conference organisers scheduled a strand in the conference for the college lecturers although the sessions were not restricted to this group of people.

The pattern of these workshops has been to concentrate on processes and skills rather than a straight 'how to teach' approach. The lecturers are expected to actively participate and the sessions usually consist of some theoretical input followed by a practical activity and a discussion.

The first workshop was held at a teacher training college and was designed to inform lecturers who had not been part of the working group designing the syllabus of the rationale behind the design. A further aim was to show the lecturers the materials which had been gathered by the Wits team and to put together some sort of initial resource file for each of the themes in the STS part of the syllabus.

The susbsequent workshops each took one or two or the STS themes, worked through some of the ideas with lecturers and had a lecture or workshop led by a representative from industry. For example when the theme was "shelter" the industrial representative was from a cement producing company, when it was transport it was from a car manufacturer. The workshop in January 1990 took the themes 'Clothing' and 'Transport', the July 1990 workshop those of 'Transport, Shelter and the Environment' and in January 1991 the final theme of 'Food' was looked at together with some of the academic physics and chemistry for the second and third years. The January 1990 session was the first at which the lecturers themselves took an active role and helped in both organisation and presentations.

The last workshop to date, held to coincide with the conference in Cape Town in July 1991, took a slightly different approach and looked at some problem areas such as energy—tracing the development of ideas from an historical perspective and looking at problems with the teaching of the concept and, on a different day, performing the same sort of exercise for teaching chemical reactions.

Other participants at the workshops, apart from university personnel, industry representatives and the college lecturers, have been postgraduate students in the School of Science Education (SoSE) at Wits. A number of these students have developed teaching resources as part of their research projects, for example, air pollution, water, gold, coal, and electrochemistry. The emphasis is on problem areas, either identified by the students themselves or by the university academics in the course of their research.

In addition, methods of assessment of students' practical skills have been presented by a post graduate student who is also a college lecturer.

One very healthy development from the workshops has been the enrolment of college lecturers for post graduate degrees in the SoSE. To date eight of the lecturers have enroled for one or other of the post graduate degrees and others have expressed interest. The personal development of the lecturers has therefore been facilitated through the project.

Industrial Visits

It is recognised that a visit to an off campus site is frequently seen by students (and school pupils) as a "day out" when no serious learning takes place. For this reason, the emphasis given to the industrial visits day at the lecturers' workshops is on advance preparation and follow up. The lecturers are prepared for the visit with indications of what they should look for and ideas for using the visit with their students. A follow up session is usually attempted. So far visits have been made to:

- gold mines
- mangnese
- food canning
- fertiliser manufacture
- zinc production
- oil from coal
- S.A. Bureau of Standards
- Council for Scientific and Industrial Research

In January 1992 the visits will be to coal mines coupled with either an electricity generating station or a fertiliser plant or to glass manufacturers.

Whilst some colleges are in remote parts of the country, it is rare that no industrial activity is within the scope of a day's outing. (For example, in the N. Transvaal there are several mines which can be visited).

The rationale for including the industrial visits as a compulsory part of the syllabus is that a course based on STS must show that technology and the people involved in action. That science is not just something to be talked about but is highly relevant to people and part of their lives.

Evaluation of the STS Component

The evaluation which has been done has two components. The first of these relates to lecturer assessment of the syllabus and to the workshops held over the last few years. The second evaluation looks at the students at the Colleges and investigates their changing awareness and knowledge of STS themes and content and their attitudes to physical science.

Lecturer Evaluation of STS and Workshops

Apart from the initial questionnaire (see under STS and the First year of Teacher Training), the lecturers have not been asked to complete a formal evaluation instrument on the STS component of the new syllabuses. However at the end of every workshop those lecturers participating are requested to complete an evaluation questionnaire. Whilst the questionnaires vary in detail, there is always a request for them to rank the activities. Almost invariably the components of the course which receive the highest rank are those dealing with academic content—a reflection may be of the lack of confidence of subject knowledge of these lecturers. It should be emphasised that many of the college lecturers have been at the colleges for several years and, because of the system of appointment and the content of the old syllabus, may well have never taught physical science past school level. Certainly the STS character of the first one or one and a half years in the new College syllabuses is new to them. The next favoured activity in order of rank is usually the industrial visits.

Student Assessment

The lecturers are asked at the end of each January course if they are willing to administer questionnaires to their students. This is an anonymous questionnaire and, because of this, it is not possible to track individual students but only to look at global change. A minority of lecturers have taken part in this research each time so that data is available for their college over a period of time, but more commonly a lecturer will return student questionnaires only once. From the returns it is possible to build student profiles for first and second year students and to see how their knowledge of science content relating to the STS themes changes.

A. Student Profiles

A total of 473 first year students (165 in 1990 and 308 in 1991) have completed the questionnaire. The sample size for second year students was 465 (190 in 1990 and 275 in 1991). (The increase in numbers in 1991 does not necessarily reflect any change in the total numbers of students in teacher training taking physical science. It is because more lecturers administered the qeustionnaire the second time round).

The matriculation marks in physical science of these students are shown in Figures 24.2 (page 379) and 243 (page 380).

Two points need to be made—firstly the large number of PTD students studying science in their second year at college who had not done physical science at school. The corresponding group in 1991 was very small and this reflects a change in admissions policy between the years 1989 and 1990.

The second point is that few students manage to get more than around 40-50% (an 'E' symbol) even though about half of them have taken physical science at standard rather than at higher grade. All students have a very weak background in physical science. Despite this, the vast majority of the students who had taken physical science at school said that they had chosen to take physical science as one of their options: they had not been forced to do so by the College. In the group of second year PTD students, 79% of whom had not taken physical science at school, only 42% had chosen to do physical science. In all groups over 80% of the students would choose to stay with physical science as a teaching subject even if they were given the opportunity to change. In the second year group over 90% were happy with physical science as a subject even if they had not initially chosen it. The last two questions on the questionnaire were difficult to analyse since the students were able to choose more than one option. However it would seem that the majority of them found the science studied at school 'acceptably difficult' with few stating that they had found it very difficult. The second year students were also asked about the science they had studied at college. Once again the tendency was to say that it was acceptably difficult and little differences was seen in the responses of the two second year groups even though the second group surveyed (in 1991) had taken the STS option whereas the first group had been on the old syllabus and had done only junior high school science in that year.

Figure 24.2: Matriculation marks in Physical Science for all students. (Standard and Higher grade examinations combined.)

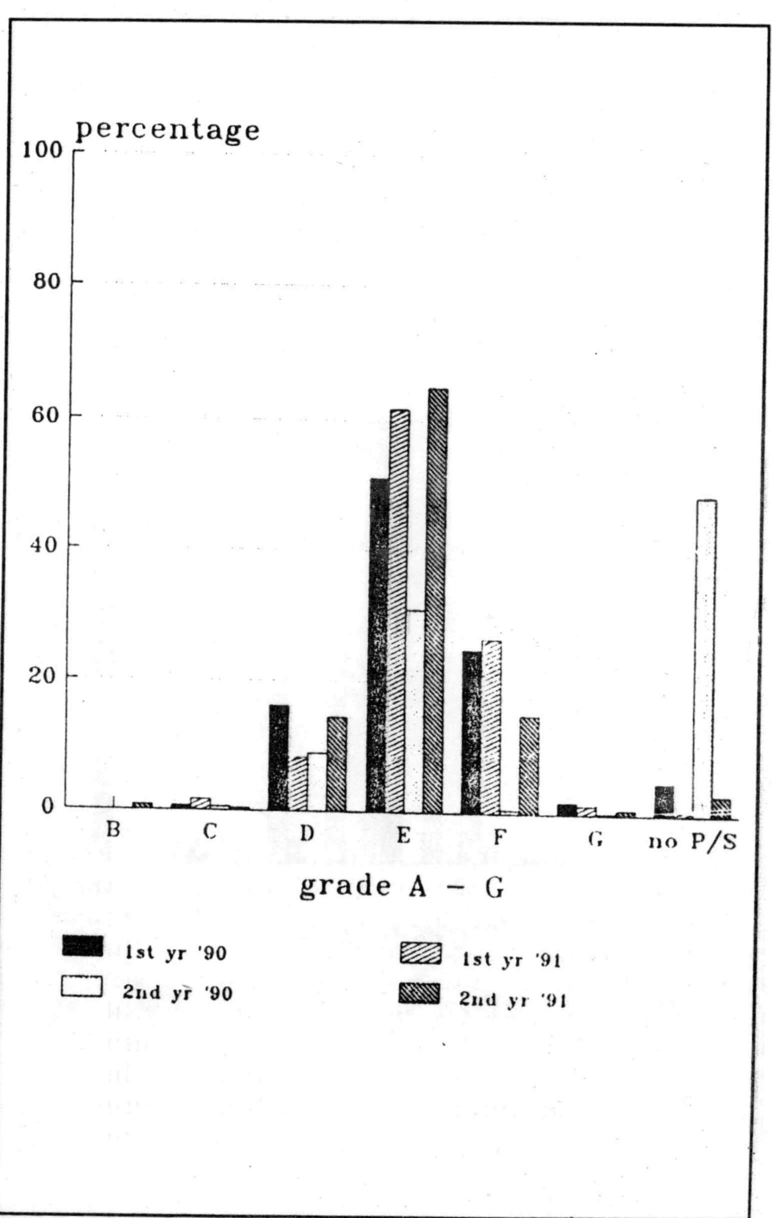

Figure 24.3. Matriculation Marks (second year students only) by course.

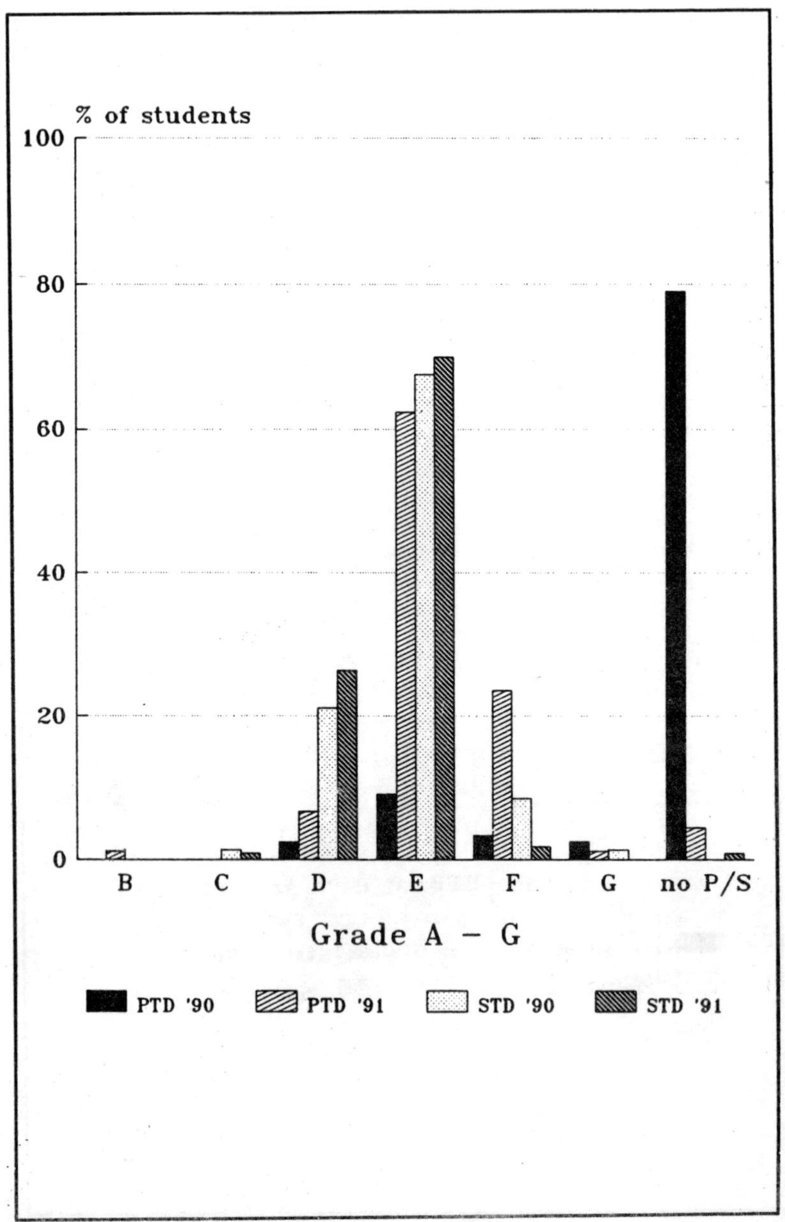

B. STS Knowledge

This section of the questionnaire attempted to sample the students knowledge of what might be termed 'everyday' science. There were 15 questions referring to some STS content which it was believed might be known to the students. The items were compiled by a college lecturer in discussion with the authors of this paper. An example of an item was 'found in a car battery' and there were 21 possible answers given, written in alphabetical order. The students were asked to write the number of the correct response in the space provided. The numbers of students completing the questionnaire are shown in Table 24.1 (below).

Table 24.1 Number of student responses to STS questionnaire

Year	*1st year (STD and PTD)*	2nd Year	
		PTD	*STD*
1990	165	119	71
1991	308	165	110
Total	473	284	181

On entry to the College the first year students over the two samples were very similar. The mean scores were low with a very large range, typically a mean score of five out of fifteen—33% and a range from 0 to 13.

The scores of the second year students in 1990 were similar to those of the 1st year students. These students had not completed an STS course. At the beginning of 1991, second year students scores had improved—the mean of all of these students was now 6.4 although the range was still wide. These students were part of the first STS cohort and it is encouraging that the course, even in its initial "rag-bag" style had had a positive effect on these students' knowledge of these everyday scientific facts. Table 24.2 shows the means and ranges for each of the groups of students.

Table 24.2. Mean scores on STS survey for different cohorts

Group	*Mean (max = 15)*	*Range*
Year 1, 1990	24	0-10
Year 1, 1991	5,04	0-13
Year 2, PTD, 1990	4,03	0-11
Year 2, PTD, 1991	5,7	0-12
Year 2, STD, 1990	5,3	1-11
Year 2, STD, 1991	7,54	2-14

Figures 24.4 (see page 383), 5 (see page 384) and 24.6 show the distribution of marks for different groups and it is encouraging that the second year students who had completed one year of STS (STD 2 91 and PTD 2 91) did in general score higher than the other groups of students. Looking at the individual questions, once again these groups where the students had completed one year of the new course tended to score rather better than the others, despite the year having been disrupted in many areas by class boycotts.

Figure 24.4: Total mark on STS items (max 15) for all first year students.

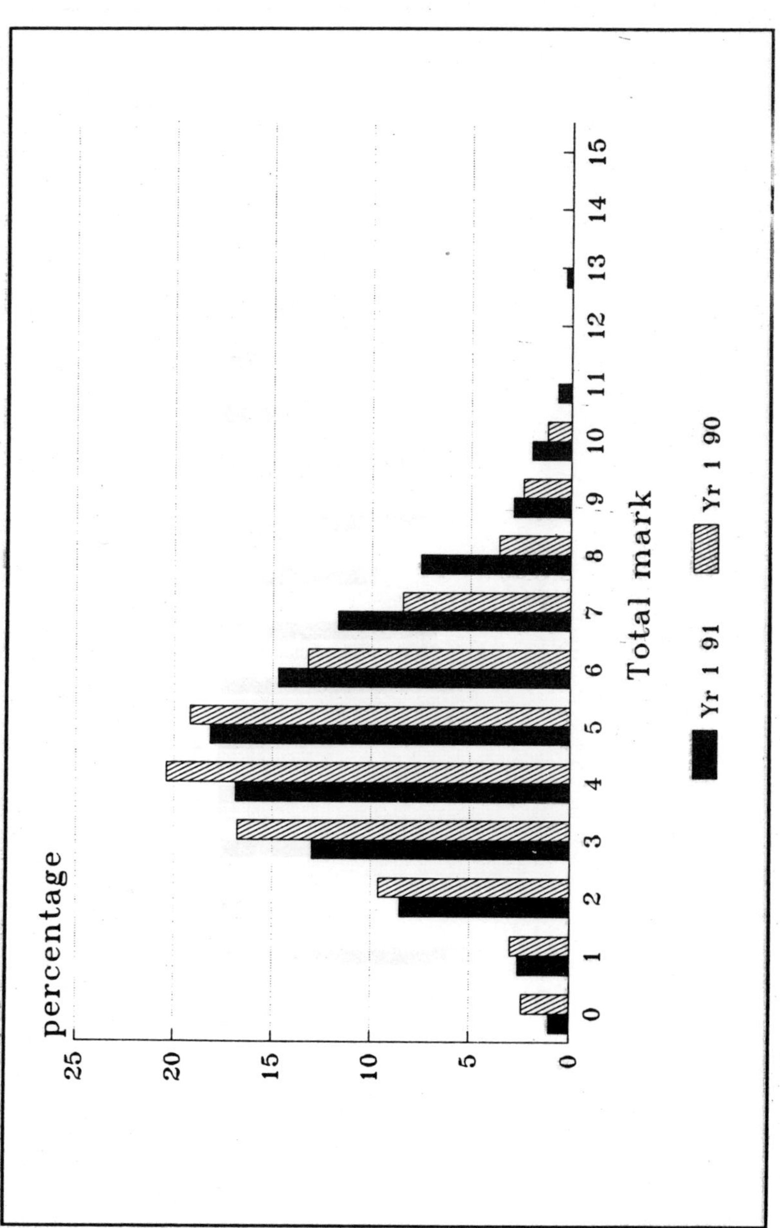

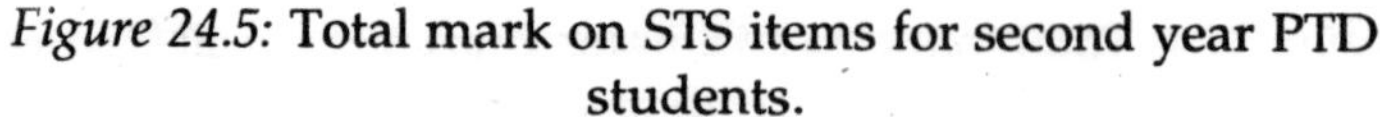

Figure 24.5: Total mark on STS items for second year PTD students.

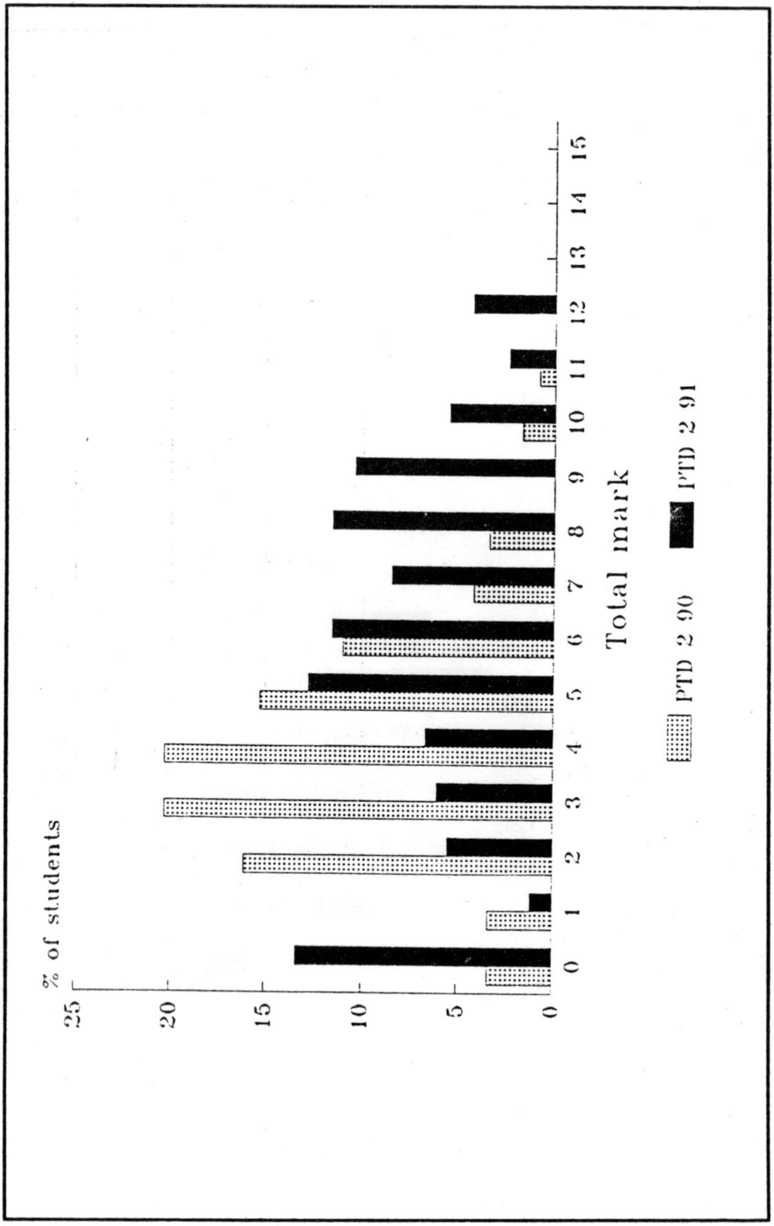

Figure 24.6: Total mark on STS items for second year STS students.

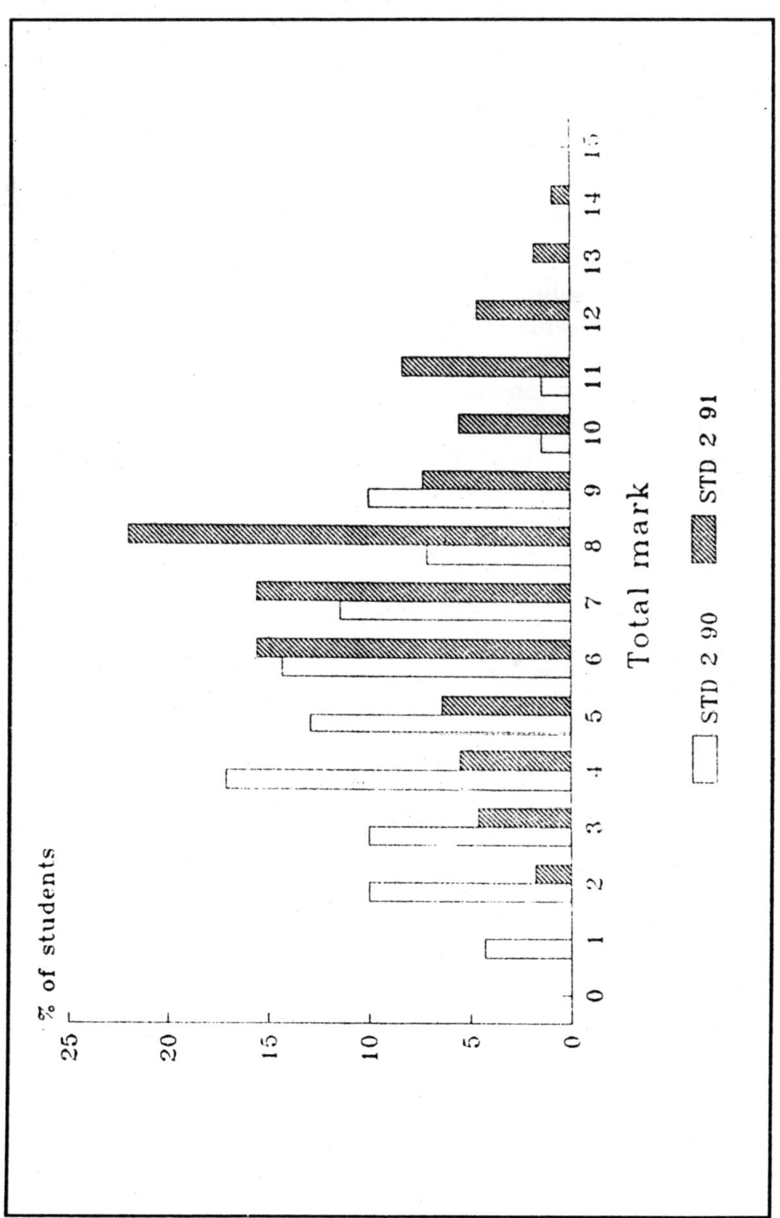

Figure 24.7 (see page 387) shows the percentage of each group getting the correct answer for each of the questions. The items with high scores for all students groups related to motor car transport and to low cost housing—two areas which might be expected to be of particular relevance to students frequently coming from isolated, low income, rural areas where much of transport is by taxi. The item with the lowest score was about food preservation with sulphur dioxide which is a first world technology and possibly not very relevant to these particular students.

A point worthy of note is that the pattern of answers does seem to be the same for all groups—in other words there are certain scientific facts which seem to be learnt by people. The results seem to be consistent across the groups of students.

Figure 24.7: Percentage of students selecting correct answer to STS questions. First and second year groups by year.

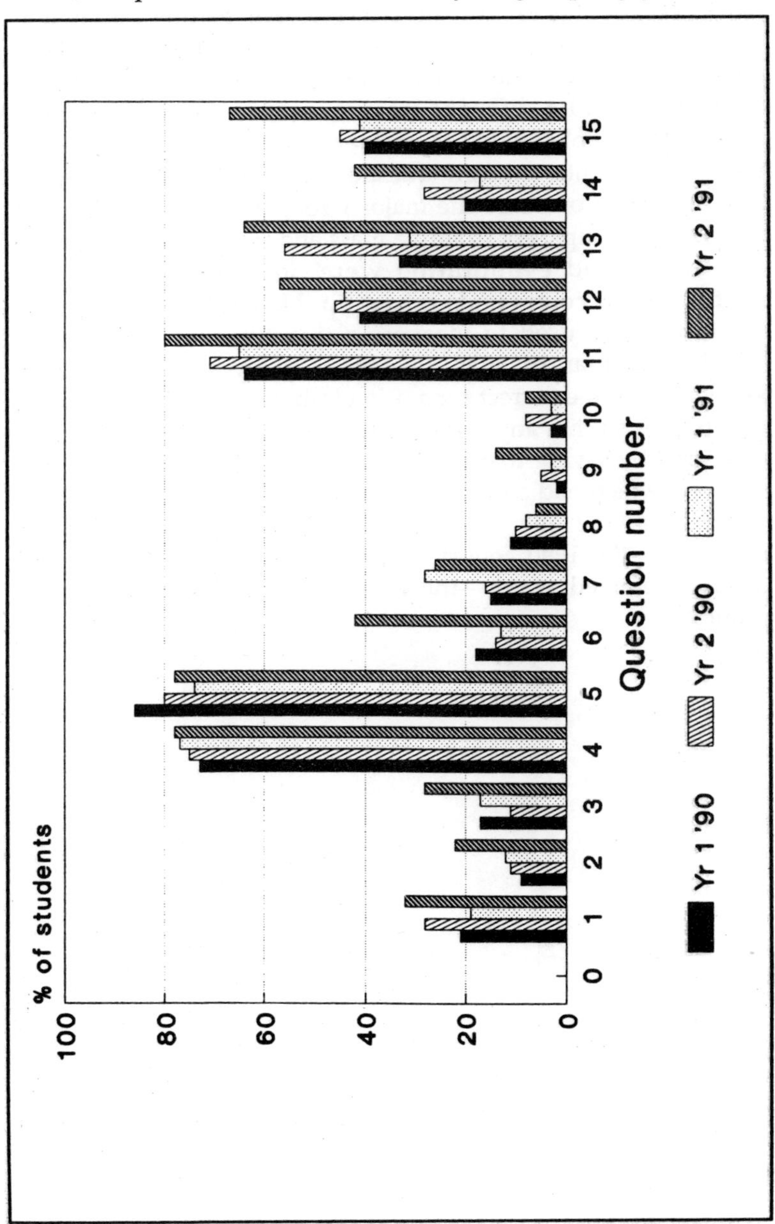

A second part of the questionnaire for second year students sampled their science content knowledge apart from the STS work. Whilst this is not directly relevant to this paper it is interesting to note that the same pattern of knowledge is demonstrated over the two years by the different groups. The STD groups had a different set of questions to the PTD group and, on the whole tended to answer them better. The scores for the STD students on their questionnaire are shown in Figure 24.8. In all but one case the major wrong answer was the same for the two groups. For example mass and weight were confused, convection and evaporation were not differentiated and allotropes and compounds mixed up. Many students confused the instrument used to measure a quantity with the units in which that quantity was measured. Many students had no knowledge of the correct separation technique for different types of mixtures so that any question with 'separate' in the stem was answered by saying that a separating funnel could be used. The question which had a different wrong answer in the two sample groups was the one asking for a non-metal which conducts electricity—the 1990 cohort answered chlorine whilst the 1991 group preferred water—the required answer was or course graphite.

Figure 24.8: Knowledge survey (non STS) for second year STD students.

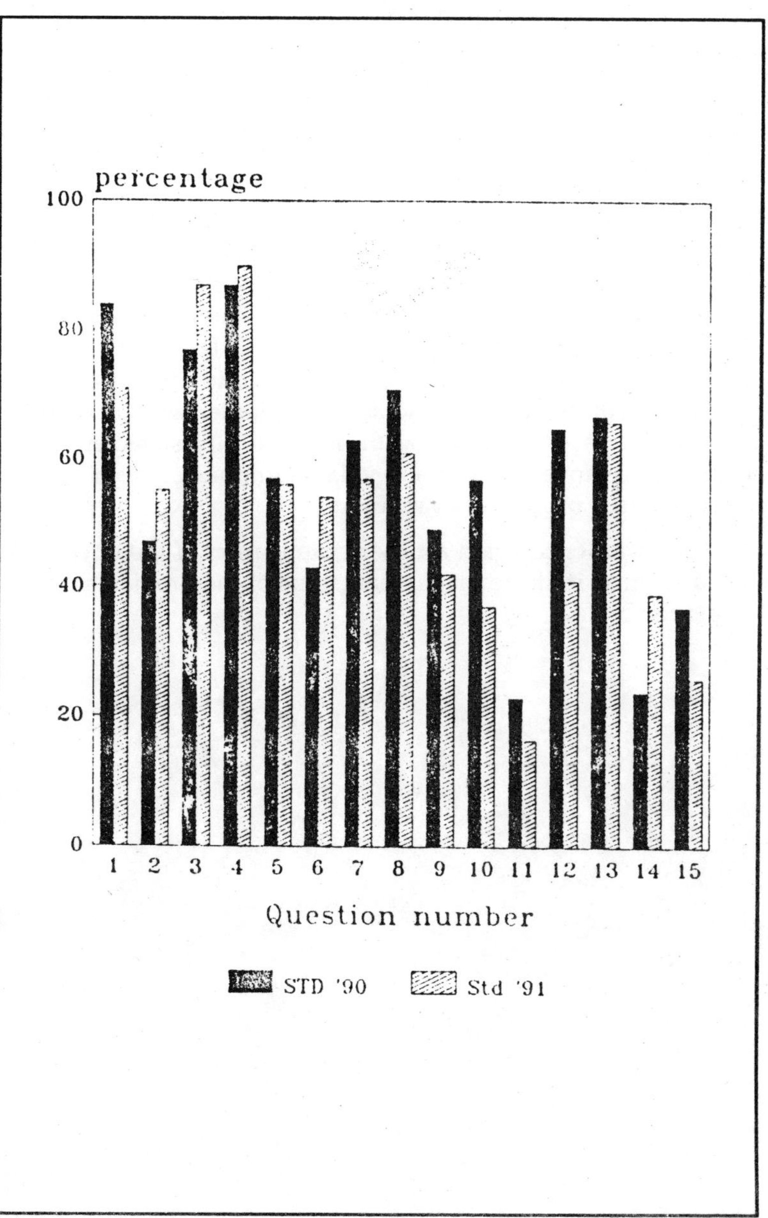

However these results must be treated with caution. Even though the questions were set by an English second language speaker, closer examination of the questions with the responses given reveals some ambiguities which could well have reduced the number of students choosing the correct answer.

The PTD students did not score well on their set of questions (Figure 24.9, next page). The only things which both the 1990 and the 1991 groups knew fairly well were that bacteria cause a bad smell and the rotting of food (Q1), that the sun is a major source of energy (Q6) and that condensation is a change from the gaseous to the liquid phase (Q10). They did not know the common tests for carbon dioxide or for water and confused filtration and distillation. As with the STD survey, many students confused the process with some item possibly associated with the process and seemed happier with a concrete example. Soap was suggested as the match for the statement 'Can be used to remove soluble, non-volatile impurities from water' rather than the process of evaporation.

However, once again a closer examination of the questions would seem to indicate that at least some of the problems might be linguistic.

Figure 24.9: Knowledge survey (non STS) for second year PTD students.

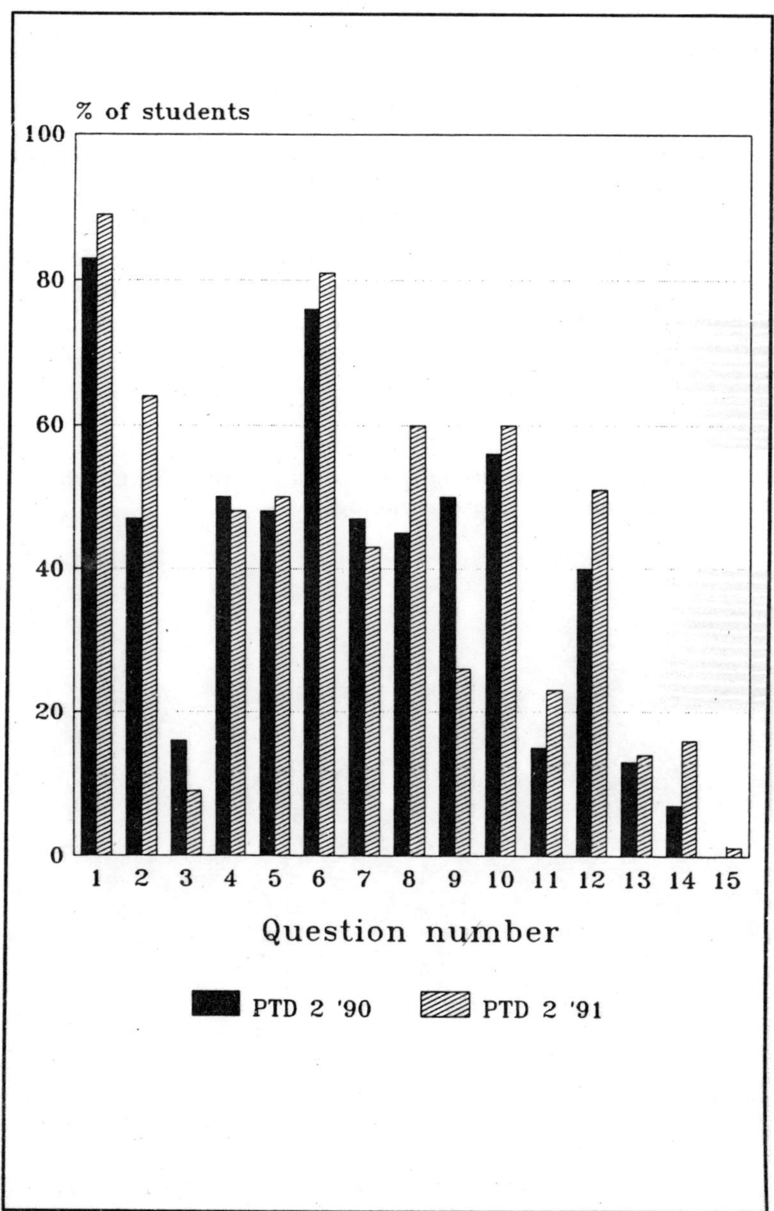

Discussion

This research and development project is still in the early stages. It has now been adopted by the Centre for Research and Development in Mathematics, Science, and Technology Education (RADMASTE) at the University of the Witwatersrand. It would seem that the emphasis on STS has, to a certain extent, improved student teacher's knowledge of the relevance of science to their everyday lives. The next phase is to write resource materials for both lecturers and students which will firmly root the content of the syllabus into a context which is appropriate to Africa, and the same time, to consider the language requirements for non-native speakers of English. This will start at the beginning of 1992 with the appointment of an R&D officer to the project.

REFERENCE

Beeby, C.E.: (1965), *The Quality of Education in Developing Countries*, Harvard University Press, Cambridge, Mass.

25

Science Education and the External Perspective on Science

WILLIAM U. COBERN
Arizona State University, USA

Introduction

Capitalizing on these new developments, Duschl, Hamilton, & Grandy (1990) wrote a compelling argument for the need to have a joint research effort in science education involving the philosophy and history of science along with cognitive psychology. However, the issue of discovery compels the research community go one step further. If the science education community has been guilty of neglecting historical and philosophical issues in science, let it not now be guilty of ignoring sociological issues in science. A collaborative view ought also to include the sociological study of cultural milieu in which scientific ideas arise. In other words, an external sociological perspective on science.

A sociological perspective provides a different view of students. Many students do not deem induction into a scientific paradigm as a thing desirable. This, the presentation of a major scientific concept such as evolution is rather less like two evolutionary biologists debating the fine points of evolutionary theory, and rather more like Darwin presenting the *Origin of Species* to a public who historically had a very different view of origins. Studies in the sociology of knowledge have provided insight into the origins of Darwin's ideas and how those ideas came to be accepted in the scientific community of his day. Shouldn't that same perspective help science educators understand how science is received and understood by their students? The logic of discovery from a sociological point of view implies that conceptual change can also be viewed from a sociological perspective.

Science education has long been grounded in a philosophy of logical positivism which minimizes factors that surround discovery while emphasizing the justification of knowledge. In Kuhnian terms, science education has been a process of inducting students into the reigning paradigms of science. While it may never have been explicit, the goals of science education clearly have been to persuade students that science provides a fairly constant, highly justified, and sufficient understanding of physical phenomena. In 1984, Duschl noted that science education had not kept pace with developments in the history and philosophy of science. Positivism was dethroned years ago and it turns out that factors surrounding discovery are at least as important as the justification of knowledge. Indeed, the entire concept of justification has been drastically changed, so much so that an article was recently published on the "demise of justification" (Eby, 1991, p. 531).

Capitalizing on these new developments, Duschl, Hamilton, & Grandy (1990) wrote a compelling argument for the need to have a joint research effort in science education involving the philosophy and history of science along with cognitive psychology. They point out that cognitive science represents the nature of an individual's knowledge in terms of schemata and that this is analogous to frameworks of knowledge justification in the philosophy of science. Furthermore, they point out the similarity between a cognitive view of learning (i.e., schemata restructuring leading to concerputal change) and scientific discovery as illuminated by philosophers and historians of science (i.e., the logic of discovery). Thus, in theory these three areas ought to be mutually illuminating. I heartily endorse their position, but the historical issue of discovery compels the research community go one step further. Duschl et al. (1990) rightly argue that science education can benefit by examining the cognitive concept of conceptual change in the historical and philosophical lights of discovery and justification. However, what is forgotten is that discovery always takes place in a social and cultural milieu.

Clearly conceptual change in the science classroom takes place, and models of conceptual change (e.g., Posner, Strike, Hewson, & Gertzog, 1982) have helped educators understand and improve learning. The problem is that current thinking about conceptual change is excessively rationalistic and thus limited. In this paper I argue that current thinking needs to be counterbalanced by contextual constructivist ideas (Cobern, in press). As an example of using contextual ideas, I will draw from the social study so science.

The Social Study of Science Education

An external sociological perspective on scientific discovery involves the sociological study of cultural milieu in which scientific ideas arise. If the science education research community has found it helpful to draw upon the history and philosophy of science, I think they will also find it helpful to draw upon the study of cultural issues in the development of science. Without ignoring the achievements of conceptual change research, one can suggest that a cultural perspective [1] on science learning offers additional insight. For example, it may be found that many students resist scientific ideas for reasons similar to those that led many 16th century geocentrists to resist heliocentrism. Bare in mind that one scientist trying to convince a colleague, or even a scientist from another field, is not the same as trying to convince those outside the scientific community. Nor is teaching evolution at the secondary level, for example, anything like a biology professor and graduate students discussing the fine points of evolutionary theory. To the contrary, it is very much like Drawin presenting the *Origin of Species* to a public who historically held a very different view of origins. For the biologist and graduate students the fundamental questions of Drawin's day have long been satisfactorily answered, but not so for the public outside the scientific community including the young science student. It is thus appropriate for the science education researcher to ask about the culture of science classrooms and curricular science *vis-a-vis* the cultures from which students come. It is appropriate to ask about the questions that students deem essential and what those questions mean for science learning.

For some time now, I have been concerned that science education assumes too much about students. I have in mind world view, the "culturally-dependent, implicit, fundamental organization of the mind.... composed of presuppositions or assumptions which predispose on to feel, think, and act in predictable patterns" (Cobern, 1991, p. 19). At a minimum science education appears to assume that students share with scientists particular world view presuppositions about what the world is like, what questions are important, and what methods ought to be used in pursuing answers. Presumably, these shared presuppositions are forged in elementary school. We forget, however, that students live in multiple worlds: the worlds of family, community, peers, and school (Phelan, Davidson, & Cao, 1991). These worlds with their different orientations interact, yet school rarely acts to help students deal with the interactions. As noted by Linn & Songer (1991), students tend to compartmentalize knowledge. The result is that they simply do not deal with the interactions among their worlds, leaving their education permanently impaired. Education for the majority needs to be broadly construed to incorporate students' several worlds, thus facilitating the integration of knowledge.

My point is that while science education researchers are beginning to see that the initial Constructivist views of learning were excessively rationalist, the overall view of science learning as conceptual change is still too narrowly conceived (Strike & Posner, in press). The social study of science education is a young field, but it is here that one finds interesting examples of research on broader views of learning (Bloom, 1991; Cobern, 1991; Gauld, 1989; Kawasaki, 1990; Millar, 1989; Ogawa, 1989; Soiomon, 1989). Another field of interest is Atwater's (1991) multicultural approach to science education. Her focus is more on interpersonal relationship and learning styles as cultural factors than on cognition. Obviously, there are many factors of culture. However, I agree with Ogawa (1991), "the American approach to multicultural science education is problematic. It seems to me that the movement encourages 'universal science for all Americans' without ever considering the possibility of multi-sciences," where multi-science refers to science in various contextualizations. The approach from the social construction of knowledge recognizes that science does not exist disembodied any more than do students. The collaborative effort that joins the history and philosophy of science with cognitive studies is welcomed because of it recognizes the need for a broader approach to science learning—but, it does not yet go far enough.

Conceptual Change

Models of conceptual change are based on the critical elements of prior knowledge and conceptual conflict. As noted by Garrison & Bentley (1990, p. 21), "students' prior, reasonable and highly verified concepts of natural phenomena provide the prior knowledge base for all subsequent learning about such phenomena." When new knowledge and prior knowledge are similar, the student is able to interpret the new knowledge in a way expected by the teacher. The student's knowledge grows smoothly. In Piagetian terms, this is assimilation. It is weak restructuring in cognitive terms.

However, when new knowledge and prior knowledge are quite disssimilar, as is typically the case between commonsense science and formal science, conceptual conflict occurs.

About conceptual conflict there is no doubt, prior knowledge is tenacious and poses a formidable challenge to instruction. The successful interpretation of new knowledge, as per the teacher's intentions, requires accommodating the new knowledge within the prior framework, or in cognitive terms, the radical restructuring of prior knowledge. Models of conceptual change applied to teaching suggest that instruction must accomplish three things for conceptual change to occur. Instruction must enable a student to see that science conceptions are more intelligible, plausible, and fruitful than his or her own priorly held conceptions. What confounds the science teacher is not that some students fail to learn, but that students either remain unconvinced (Lawson & Weser, 1990; Lawson & Worsnop, 1992). Or, they have interpreted a new concept in a fashion unintended by the teacher (Osborne, Bell, & Gilbert, 1983). Even graduate level science students have been shown to hold concepts that vary considerably from what is considered scientific orthodoxy (Clement, 1982). As far back as 1978, Hawkins observed that,

> reasonably patient explanation is no cure . . . we are up against something rather deep in the relation between science and common sense; we are up against a barrier to teaching in the didactic mode which has hardly been recognized, or if recognized has been seen mainly as a challenge to ingenuity in teaching rather than as a challenge to a deeper understanding of human learning.[2]

What is the barrier? Here we are well advised to listen to the radical constructivists' insistence that learning means interpretation (Wheatley, 1989). Learning is not like photography, but like impressionistic artistry. As Ausubel says, the only real learning is meaningful learning. We have learned something when it makes sense to us. If learning occurred by transmission, students would either have the concept or not. What they would not have are idiosyncratic versions of the concept.

Surely an inability to make sense of a concept within the context of one's own background is at least one type of barrier. However, by holding to an exclusively rational perspective on conceptual change, science educators fail to appreciate the role of interpretation and personal meaningfulness. Moreover, the rationalism is exclusive. It is scientific rationalism and nothing else. Excessive scientific rationalism fails to understand that students have different ideas "precisely because the pursuit of scientific knowledge is not the only or even the most important goal [student ideas] subserve" (Hills & McAndrews, 1987, p. 216). Again, insofar as they go models of conceptual change have been helpful (e.g., Clement, 1987). Now, let research push conceptual change into a broader arena.

Internalization vs. Conceptual Change

The science educator is caught on the horns of a dilemma. Those who have acquired a scientific viewpoint find it much easier to understand new scientific concepts because such concepts make sense in light of the person's scientific viewpoint. However, those most in need of learning scientific concepts often lack the very scientific viewpoint that makes scientific concepts meaningful. Of course, as some teachers do, one can always drill students on concepts until they are memorized even without a scientific view point. However, in documents such as the AAAS (1989) Science for All Americans it is evident that educators consider scientific literacy to be much more than the simple acquisition of a minimum number of scientific concepts. Why?

To formulate an answer I want to follow Garrison & Bentley's (1990) example and paraphrase Wittgenstein's (1958) argument against the possibility of anyone ever developing a purely personal language. I begin with the question, what does it mean to understand science? Answer:

> P_1: I can only claim to understand a concept of science when I understand those prior concepts that justify the first concept. In turn, I can only claim to understand the prior concepts when I understand their justification.

Unfortunately, this proposition results in an infinite regress, and as C.S. Lewis (1947, p. 91) so elegantly wrote, "it is simply no use trying to see through first principles . . . If you see through everything, then everything is transparent. But a wholly transparent world is an invisible world. To see through all things is the same as not to see." An infinite regression is the same as "not to see," thus, following the lead of both Lewis and Wittgenstein:

> P_2: Science is more than a system of concept. Science is a set of first principals or presuppositions culturally determined.

> P_3: These presuppositions determine what scientific concepts will be like, and there is nothing prior to those presuppositions.

> P_4: Therefore, an understanding of science is not achieved by acquiring knowledge of a hierarchical set of concepts, but by acquiring the presuppositions that support the hierarchy.

Understanding is made possible by a foundational set of presuppositions—but, these are culturally determined. Thus, science itself is fundamentally an issue of culture. It requires learning to see the world in a new and very different way.

This discussion serves to further clarify the science teacher's dilemma. To break out of the dilemma, Garrison & Bentley (1990) use Kuhn's (1970) explanation of how a scientist becomes a member of a new paradigm. They argue that one cannot learn a new vision, but that one internalizes exemplars of the new way of seeing. For example, motion on an air track can serve as an exemplar in physics, but not as a device for explaining a concept. It is an exemplar to the extent that it helps students visualize motion as Newton visualized it. Internalization of the exemplar is the result of persuasion. Here Garrison & Bentley (1990, p. 30) offer an amusing quote from Wittgenstein on reasoning with someone who has a fundamentally different way of seeing things, "I said I would 'combat' the other man - but wouldn't I give him reasons? Certainly, and how far do they go? At the end of reasons comes persuasion."

Why persuasion? Because, the acquisition of a scientific viewpoint is not at heart an epistemological issue, nor is it a simple matter of rational conceptual change. Models of conceptual change are epistemological models that assume a common starting point, or reference point. Garrison & Bentley (1990) correctly observed that the acquisition of a fundamental viewpoint is an issue of persuasion and internalization, rather than instruction and learning due to the lack of sufficient common ground. In my view, however, Garrison & Bentley (1990) expect too much of exemplars. Exemplars are derived from a culture to represent the same culture. They do not bridge cultures. On the other hand, a metaphor is a language device that presents an exemplar in the language of a different culture precisely for the purpose of bridging the two cultures. There is a classic example in cosmology. Many people find it difficult to visualize the universe expanding in all directions but with no center of expansion. Arthur Eddington suggested a metaphor, the expanding universe is like an expanding balloon. "Pretend that space is two-dimensional and that the stars and galaxies are dots on the surface of an expanding balloon. From the point of view of any one dot, the other dots are moving away from it in all directions, yet no dot is the center" (Lightman, 1989, p. 97). This metaphor is remarkably effective because it uses an ordinary, well known object from one culture to demonstrate a very different way of seeing. A point I wish to emphasize is that Eddington was able to create this metaphor because he was conversant with two cultures. Garrison & Bentley (1990) speak of science as a second culture, but they fail to see that cultures can be bridged. To use Hills' (1989) colorful phrasing, they have not moved from science education as a matter of "domestic affairs" to one of "foreign affairs."

It is not surprising that science education researchers fail to see science education in terms of foreign affairs. The philosophers and historians of science most influential among science educators are philosophers and historians of domestic affairs. For example, Kuhn (1970) acknowledged that science is influenced by factors beyond the community of scientists, but he does not expand upon this influence. Kuhn's,

> scientists are not represented as being influenced by the general conceptions of nature, man, God, society, and history that inform the thought of their age, or as ideologically involved in social or political issues. His scientists confront nature and other scientists.[3]

Once science is viewed in cultural terms as exemplified by Greene's work on Darwin, conceiving of science education as a matter of foreign affairs becomes quite natural. One begins to understand why metaphors can communicate what exemplars alone cannot. This is a rich field for research, however, a thorough discussion of metaphor is beyond the scope of this paper. Instead, I wish to continue with a particular metaphor, foreign affairs.

Two Epistemological Foundations: Creationism[4] and Positivistic[5] Naturalism

A typical biology textbook begins its coverage of evolution with Darwin and his masterpiece, *On the Origin of Species by Means of Natural Selection*. The chapter may include a few historical references, but a typical chapter on evolution will focus on Darwin's observations during his voyage aboard the Beagle and the supporting concepts of "struggle for survival" and "natural selection." The discussion then moves on to evidences for evolution—all in good logic of justification fashion. In the late fifties and early sixties, some scientists and educators grew concerned about the widespread lack of acceptance of evolution by the public. The battle was joined, "A hundred years without

Darwin is enough!" The Biological Sciences Curriculum Study (BSCS) sought not only to increase the amount of evolution taught in high school biology. BSCS sought also to infuse the biology curriculum with evolutionary concepts following Dobzhansky's (1973) dictum "Nothing in biology makes sense except in the light of evolution." The years since have seen the amount of evolution in science curricula go up, then down, and now appears to be on the way back up.[6] On the other hand, the public's attitude toward evolution appears to have remained rather constant.

Regardless the concern that some express over the public's understanding of evolution, one cannot deny that evolutionary theory has had a profound impact on Western thought. We are not the Europeans and Americans of 1859. However, neither are we all evolutionary biologists, let alone scientists in general. Darwin was not then, and is not now, the only influence on Western thought. Though evolutionary theory is not resisted in 1992 the way it was in 1859, we are still interested in many of the same fundamental questions. For example:

1. What is the essence of Nature?
2. How do we account for the fact of life rather than no life at all?
3. What does it mean to be human being?
4. In what sense, and to what extent, are human beings different from other living things?
5. What is society?

The relationship between evolutionary and religious thought has often been stormy. In the wake of creation science challenges to the science curricula of public schools, educators have tried to persuade the public that evolutionary and religious thought are distinct entities that need to be kept separated (e.g. California, 1990).[7] To the contray, I do not believe that evolution can be taught effectively by ignoring significant metaphysical questions. One addresses these issues not by teaching a doctrine, but by looking back historically to the cultural and intellectual milieu of Darwin's day and the great questions over which people struggled.

The Thirty-Year War ended in October, 1648, with the signing of the Peace Treaty of Westphalia. "The supremacy of Christain theology in European life was over. The age of faith, the Middle Ages, had run its course" (Jaki, 1983, p. 11). For centuries, the fundamental questions of life had been answered by a Christian world view, which presented a unified view of knowledge and belief grounded in a theology of creation. The cosmology of the Christian world view was based on the doctrine of the plenary inspiration of Scripture which taught that Nature was the purposeful creation of God. Moreover, people drew from this the inference that Nature was essentially static. The Christian world view had a linear sense of time that had both a beginning and an end. The Biblically based sense of linear time, however, did not necessarily involve the view that the state of human existence was ever progressing (Greene, 1981). The notion of "progress" though based on a linear concept of time was to come much later, and indeed was a notion critical in the development of evolutionary theory.

For the purposes of this paper, even a brief account of the intellectual and cultural history of the Renaissance and reformation is not really needed. Suffice it to say, the religious wars that followed the reformation dealt a crippling blow to the certainty that the Church and Christian world view held for people throughout the Middle Ages- a certainty that was already in a much weakened condition (Cobern, 1992). The 1648 Peace Treaty of Westphalia ended the religious warring, and it also marked the end of the decline into uncertainty. The Christian world view had long been without significant challengers until the skepticism and uncertainty of the 17th century gave birth to positivistic naturalism. In this view, certainty of knowledge could be attained with an empiricism restricted to meansurable characteristics and secondary (or natural) causes. In the words of E.A. Burtt:

> The world that people thought themselves living in—a world rich with colour and sound, redolent with fragrance, filled with gladness, love and beauty, speaking everywhere of purposive harmony and creative ideals—was crowded now into minute corners of the brains of scattered organic beings. The really important world was a world hard, cold, colourless, silent, and dead; a world of quantity, a world of mathmatically computable motions in mechanical regularity.[8]

For those who chose it, positivistic naturalism re-established certainty of knowledge, but one had to accept a diminished view of both religious and humanistic concepts. With the philosophy of Descartes, one sees the beginning of a mortal epistemological struggle between creationism and positivistic naturalism. Early positivists like Descartes were clearly still thinking within a Christian framework. Even Darwin himself as late as 1860, showed the influence of Christian thinking:

> I had no intention to write atheistically. But I own that I cannot see as plainly as others do, and as I should wish to do, evidence of design and beneficence on all sides of us. There seems to me too much misery in the world . . . On the other hand, I cannot anyhow be contented to view this wonderful universe, and especially the nature of man, and to conclude that everything is the result of brute force. I am inclined to look at everything as resulting from designed laws, with details, whether good or bad, left to the working out of what we may call chance.[9]

With the *Descent of Man*, all had changed.

Since Kuhn (1970), the philosophers of science have been saying that theories of science are always underdetermined, and so it was with evolution. It was not enough for Darwin to make the observations he did. For example, there had long been explanations for fossils within the creationist perspective. Without compromising the genius of Darwin, one has to recognize the influence of the intellectual and cultural state of affairs during his lifetime. The West was still dominated by Christian thought. Postitivists shared important elements of creationist epistemology such as the requirements of evidence and experimentation, the canons of proof. The West, however, was no longer a Christian civilization. Darwin was born into an age of transition where long held ideas had been weakened. Of particular significance to Darwin were presuppositions concerning Nature. Newton argued that a static Nature was composed of particulate matter in motion. To others, that was more a description of a changeable Nature than a static one. Herschel demonstrated that the stars were not fixed after all, but moved. By the 1800's, the accepted assumption of a static Nature was not nearly as tenable, as self-evident, as it had been.

By the 1800's, the West had witnessed remarkable scientific progress in providing mechanistic understanding of natural phenomena. Moreover, Darwin's day was a time of unprecedented economic expansion, a time when laissez fair capitalism was the rule of the day. Competition was the ethic of the capitalistic marketplace that provided all the change and progress. In 1850, Joseph Paxton built the Crystal Palace in London to showcase the scientific and technological achievements of modern Europe. This was indeed an age of change and progress, and this was the backdrop for Darwin's accomplishment. Could these ideas of mechanicism, competition, change, and progress be applied to the world of organic life? If only there were a mechanism . . .

I am not saying that these were the literal thoughts that led Darwin to the concept of natural selection or that he even had such thoughts. However, he was not a hermit. This was the environment in which he thought and reasoned. Though what I have written is the barest of descriptions for this rich piece of intellectual and cultural history, it is sufficient to make the point that one can describe Darwin's theories as science, but not his embrace of positivistic naturalism. Yet the first makes no sense without the second. To come again to the classroom, understanding evolution requires no less now then it did for Darwin. To understand evolution one must be able to see the world as it is seen by positivistic naturalists—the world view of evolutionary biologists and of many scientists in general. That is not, however, the world view of many students. Thus, my position is that the teaching of evolution needs to begin with the very metaphysical questions that were so troublesome in Darwin's day: what is the essence of Nature, what is life, what is a human being? How do religion, philosophy, and science inform our view of the world? These questions are not amenable to simple, didactic teaching. One struggles with these questions, and a teacher who desires. To help students must first have an understanding of student views. That is the only way a teacher is able to explain a new way of seeing the world to students accustomed to a very different way of seeing. This returns us to the concept of metaphor and the bridging of cultures. For example, the "two books" metaphor (the book of Scripture and the book of Nature) has long been a powerful device for helping religious students understand the relationship between science and religion (Van Till, 1990). Finally, there is the issue of persuasion. Returning once more to Wittgenstein, "I said I would 'combat' the other man—but wouldn't I give him reasons? Certainly, and how far do they go? At the end of reasons comes persuasion" (quoted in Garrison & Bentley, 1990, p. 30).

Science Education As A Foreign Affair

Studying the cultural history of Darwin's day prepares one to take a contextual or cultural constructivist approach to the teaching of evolution—the foreign affairs approach. Evolution is a good example for a discussion on foreign affairs because it is so widely rejected and misunderstood by the public. It is also very clear that evolution involves a non-commonsense way of looking at nature and human beings. Also, mode is known about Darwin and the intellectual and cultural history surrounding the concept of evolution. However, one can imagine the chemistry teacher saying, "Yes, but my next lesson is on oxidation-reduction equations, so what can this discussion possibly mean for me?" I do not think it means very much if one insists on conceiving of science education as a topic to topic affair. Instead, if one thinks of chemistry in terms of the big ideas that have changed our view of reality, then the discussion means a great deal. In fact, the discussion suggests that attacking a small concept in terms of a superordinant conceptual framework, is a good strategy. One might then adopt the Duschl et al.[10] suggestion concerning the context of discovery:

> A suggestion would be to use the context of justification whenever the development was within normal science and the context of discovery whenever it was revolutionary science. Another suggestion would be to use the context of justification whenever new theory requires only weak restructuring on the part of the student, and the context of discovery when it requires radical restructuring. Perhaps these two suggestions converge, and any historical revolutionary episode corresponds to a radical restructuring on the part of the student, but this remains to be demonstrated.

I share the suspicion that there exists a correspondence between historical revolutionary episodes and conceptual change by radical restructuring, though it has yet to be demonstrated. I am suggesting first that historical revolutionary episodes can provide an effective device for organizing science curricula.

Second, I am suggesting that the history of science alone does not provide an adequate description of such episodes, but that one most in addition look to intellectual and cultural history. In this regard, I am persuaded that one of the best things that could happen in pre-college science education is the elimination of the strict separation of the natural sciences from the social sciences and the humanities—but that is a subject for another paper. Third, one must not fail to take into account the multiple worlds of students and what those worlds mean for how a student sees the world vis-a-vis what the science teacher is trying to teach. This is a contextual constructivist approach to science teaching. It means one should not ignore the cultural context on which a student interprets new knowledge. It means that the social study of science will be at least as helpful to science educators as are the history and philosophy of science. It means that science teachers will have to deal frankly with it.

NOTES

1. My use of the term culture is in reference to "webs of significance" (Geertz 1973, p. 5) which enable one to make sense of the world. I agree with Outram (1990, pp. 327-328), "Even the assumption that culture is relatively coherent is near debate. Contemporary critical theory has now posed a major alternative view: culture as multiple discourses that may occasionally come together in large systemic configurations, but that more often exist together within dynamic fields of interaction and conflict.
2. 1978, pp. 5 & 7; emphases added.
3. Greene, 1981, p. 5
4. In today's climate, the term *creationism* has acquired an incendiary quality. That is unfortunate because the term has a rich history that does not deserve the derision precipitated by its modern relative, creation science. As I have argued elsewhere (Cobern, 1992), creation science is more of a product of the 19th century intellectual tumult caused by two competing views of nature. I use creationism in its historic sense: the earth and its inhabitants are the intentional, purposeful creation of God. This is a superordinant, metaphysical concept which has significant implications for epistemology and science (e.g., Foster, 1934). Creation science, however, is an ill-advised attempt to make creationism a concept within science.
5. Following the example of Gillispie (1979), positivism is not used

here in the restricted sense of the philosophy formally known as logical empiricism or logical positivism.

6. The ups and downs of evolution can be seen in the California science curriculum changes over the last several years.
7. If evolutionary and religious thought have no relationship, one has to wonder what would ever possess an eminent evolutionist such as Gaylord Simpson to write a book titled, This *View of Life: The World of an Evolutionist?*
8. 1967, pp. 238-239
9. quoted in F. Darwin, 1888, vol. 2, pp. 311-312.
10. 1990, p. 234.

REFERENCES

AAAS (1989). *Project 2061: Science for All Americans.* Washington, DC: American Association for the Advancement of Science.

Atwater, M. (1991). Reform in science education assumptions and alternative views: Multicultural science education. A paper presented at the annual meeting of the: National Association for Research in Science Teaching, Lake Geneva, WI.

Bloom, J. W. (1991). Contexts of meaning and the development of knowledge in elementary school children. A paper presented at the annual meeting of the American Educational Research Association, Chicago, IL.

Burtt, E. A. (1967). *The metaphysical foundations of modern physical science.* Lond California (1990). *Science framework for California public schools: Kindergarten through grade twelve.* Sacramento, CA: California State Board of Education.

Clement, J. (1982). Student preconceptions in introductory mechanics. *American Journal of Physics*, 50(1): 6671.

Cobern, W. W. (1991). *World View Theory and Science Education Research, NARST Monograph No. 3.* Cincinnati, OH: National Association for Research in Science Teaching.

Corbern, W.W. (1992). The impact of constructivist epistemology on classroom practice: The problem of knowledge and belief. A paper presented at the annual meeting of the American Educational Research Association, San Francisco, CA.

Darwin, F. Ed. (1888). *The life and letters of Charles Darwin.* London, UK: John Murray.

Dobzhansky, T. (1973). Nothing in biology makes sense except in the light of evolution. *The American Biology Teacher*, 35(3): 125129.

Duschl, R.A. (1984). Science Education and the Philosophy of Science: Twentyfive Years of Mutually Exclusive Development. A paper presented at the annual meeting of the National Association for Research in Science Teaching, New Orleans, LA.

Duschl, R.A., Hamilton, R., Grandy, R.E. (1990). Psychology and epistemology: Match or mismatch when applied to science education. *International Journal of Science Education*, 3(12): 230243.

Eby, L. (1991). Reflections on the philosophy of science: The demise of justificationism. *The World & I*, 6(9): 531545.

Garrison, J.W. Bentley, M.L. (1990). Science education, conceptual change and breading with everyday experience. *Studies in Philosophy and Education*, 10(1): 1935.

Gauld, C. (1989). A Study of Pupil's Responses to Empirical Evidence. In Millar, R. (ed.), *Doing Science: Images of Science in Science Education*. Philadelphia, PA: The Falmer Press.

Geertz, C. (1973). *The Interpretation of Culture*. New York, NY: Basic Books.

Greene, J. C. (1981). *Science, Ideology, and Worldview*. Berkeley, CA: University of California Press.

Hawkins, D. (1978). Critical Barriers to Science Learning. *Outlook*, 3: 325.

Hills, G.L.C. (1989). Students' "Untutored" Beliefs About Natural Phenomena: Primitive Science Or Commonsense? *Science Education*, 73(2): 155186.

Hills, G.L.C. & McAndrews, B. (1987). David Hawkins, Critical Barriers and the Education of Elementary School Science Teachers. In Novak, J.D. (ed.), *Proceedings of the Second International Seminar on Misconceptions in Science and Mathematics*, Ithaca, NY: Cornell University Press.

Jaki, S. L. (1983). *Angels, Apes & Men*. Peru, IL: Sherwood Sugden & Company.

Kawasaki, K. (1990). A Hidden Conflict Between Western and Traditional Concepts of Nature in Science Education in Japan. *Bulletin of the School of Education Okayama University*, 83: 203214.

Kuhn, T.S. (1979). *The Structure of Scienctific Revolutions*. Chicago, IL: The University of Chicago Press.

Lawson, A.E. & Weser, J. (1990). The Rejection of Nonescientific Beliefs About Life: Effects of Instruction and Reasoning Skills. *Journal of Research in Science Teaching*, 27(6): 589606.

Lawson, A.E. & Worsnop, W.A. (1991). Learning About Evolution and Rejecting a Belief in Special Creation: Effects of Reflective Reasoning Skill, Prior Knowledge, Prior Belief and Religious Commitment. *Journal of Research in Science Teaching*, 29(2): 143166.

Lightman, A.P. (1989). Magic on the mind: Physicists' use of metaphor. *The American Scholar*, 58(1): 97-101.

Linn, M. C. & Songer, N. B. (1991). Cognitive and conceptual change in adolescence. *American Journal of Education*, 99(4): 379417.

Millar, R., Ed. (1989). *Doing Science: Images of Science in Science Education*. Philadelphia, PA: The Falmer Press.

Ogawa, M. (1989). Beyond the Tacit Framework of 'science' and 'science education' among Science Educators. *International Journal of Science Education*, 11(3): 247250.

Ogawa, M. (1991). Personal communication.

Osborne, R. J., Bell, B.F., Gilbert, J. K. (1983). Science Teaching and Children's Views of the World. *European Journal of Science Education*, 5(1): 114.

Phelan, P., Davidson, A. L., Cao, H. T. (1991). Students' Multiple Worlds: Negotiating the Boundaries of Family, Peer, and School Cultures. *Anthropology & Education Quarterly*. 22(3): 224249.

Solomon, J. (1989). The Social Construction of School Science. In Millar, R. (ed.), *Doing Science: Images of Science in Science Education*. Philadelphia, PA: The Falmer Press, 126136.

Wheatley, G. H. (1991). Constructivist Perspectives on Science and Mathematics Learning. *Science Education*, 75(1): 9-21.

Van Till, H. J. Ed. (1990). *Portraits of creation: Biblical and scientific perspectives on the world's formation*. Grand Rapids, MI: William B. Eerdmanns.

26

Enhancing the Relevance of Science Teaching and Learning for Community Needs and Development Concerns

VIVIEN M. TALISAYON
University of the Philippines, Philippines

Community development is an old and ongoing concern of governments, private and international agencies. In science education, community development is implied in the widely-accepted goals of national development and scientific literacy for the general populace. It is only recently however that some science educators, particularly biology educators have directly addressed community needs. It is not surprising that biology educators should take the lead since common community concerns like health, sanitation, nutrition, agriculture, and population growth are biological in nature. Community-oriented efforts range from making use of community resources and correspondingly modifying the science curriculum to science-related projects designed to help a community.

This paper describes the community-based projects of the Science Education Center of the University of the Philippines from 1977 to the present. It is hoped that the projects' objectives, approaches and results will point out some strategies and directions for community-oriented science education programmes in other developing countries.

Since farming and fishing are the major means of livelihood in rural Philippines, the community-oriented projects of the Center were conducted in two upland and four lowland farming communities and one fishing village.

Seminars for Farmers

An early community project of the Center was in two rice-producing lowland communities. The objective was to share technology based no the interests of the farmers and their families. Interviewed by school teachers, the farmers indicated strong interests in agriculture, health, and repair of household and farm implements. Seminars were conducted on the following topics:

1. 'Better ways of raising pigs, poultry and cattle';
2. 'Control of rice weeds and rats';
3. 'How to construct a methane gas generator';
4. 'How to prevent communicable diseases';
5. 'What to do for proper rest and sleep';
6. 'How to give first aid for snake and dog bites';
7. 'How to take care of malnourished tots'; and
8. 'How to hold meetings on community problems'.

The farmers were given handouts and taught by actual experience. Those who learned were encouraged to teach others. The project team consisted of science educators, school-teachers, agriculturists and rural health workers. Twenty health modules were among the outputs of the project.

Instructional Materials for Farm Communities

An intensive community study was done in 1978 and 1979 by the Biology Work Group of the Center in two upland villages. Logging and agriculture are the major means of livelihood in these communities.

The primary objective of the project was the development of exemplar materials based on the results of a needs and resource assessment in the community. Some interesting findings obtained through participant observation and informal interviews are as follows:

1. Streams and rivers had gone dry. Some areas flooded during the rainy season and the river dried up during summer months. Before the heavy tree-cutting, the river flowed throughout the year.
2. There was agreement among the farmers not to shoot the hornbill.
3. Illegal logging generated a higher income than agricultural. Transportation for bringing farm produce to the market was inadequate.
4. The people lacked knowledge and confidence in trying new economic activities.

The instructional materials intended for formal or non-formal use were designed to help community members evaluate their environment, develop proper attitudes towards it and make decisions to protect it. The materials developed were on forest ecology: five poems, one *balagtásan* (poetic debate), and 11 fully illustrated articles (comics form). Reflecting the results of the needs and resources assessment, the articles are:

Series	*Article*
1. The forest has life	1. This is my life 2. From a tree 3. The story of a tree
2. Components of the forest and their relationships	1. Soil organisms 2. Camaraderie in the forest 3. Return of the hornbill
3. Economic alternatives in a forest ecosystem	1. The lowly grass 2. Income not only from farming. 3. Other than cows, you can try goats
4. Early benefits from fruit tree	1. Grafting, budding and inarching 2. Marcotting

To reach as many members of the community as possible, the materials were written in Philipino, the national language. The target groups for the materials were elementary school students, youth organizations, and farmers. The project team was composed of science educators, forest scientists, extension workers, biologists, a psychologist, a medical doctor and a nutritionist.

A concept study was undertaken two years later in a Barrio. The responses of two age groups, ages 10 to 16 and ages 19 to 65 to a set of questions about the environment were obtained via interview or questionnaire. The questions dealt with facets of the environment like meaning of conservation of the environment; comparison of the environment now, ten years ago and a decade hence; and effect of population of land distribution in the community a decade hence.

Another study in farming communities confined itself to curriculum materials in elementary science. Undertaken by the Elementary Science Work Group of the Center in 1979 and 1980, the project sites were an abaca-raising community and a coconut-growing community.

The purpose of the study was to generate a list of topics to be developed into instructional materials for elementary schools science appropriate to communities raising abaca and coconuts. The topics were based on interviews with farmers and observations of the health and sanitation conditions of their homes. The farmers were interviewed by school teachers on farm practices and beliefs among other things. Among the major topics to be developed were: 'Abaca propagation and utilization'; 'Coconut propagation and utilization'; and 'Health and nutrition topics like managing intestinal parasitism and prevention and control of communicable diseases'. The curriculum materials to be written will also consider the results of the vocabulary test administered to grades III to VI students in the two communities.

Total Approach in a Fishing Village

The most comprehensive and thorough community project undertaken by the Center was in Barangay San Salvador, Banate, Iloilo in 1977-79. San Salvador, accessible by banca or pumpboat, is half a kilometre from Banate, separated by the sea. Fishing is the major means of livelihood.

In 1977, San Salvador had about 232 families and a population of 1,162. The village had no electricity. The sources of water were a few shallow wells, a large cement tank to catch rain-water, and water brought in by boat from springs in the town of Banate. Prior to the project, sanitation was at a low level. Foul smells greeted visitors stepping out of incoming bancas. Garbage and household sewage were all over the shore and in the backyards of houses. About 87 per cent of the population had not toilet facilities. The nearest clinic was in Banate. The community's only elementary school was rarely visited by school supervisors and extension workers from other ministries. Newspapers, magazines and other reading materials did not reach the village regularly. The adults' main leisure activity was gambling.

The obejctives of the project in San Salvador were to:

1. Extend the reach of science education from the school to the home and community thereby providing closer links between learning in the school and learning at home and in the community;
2. Enrich the home environment of the elementary school pupils by involving parents in some practical and meaningful science-related activities;
3. Enrich the study of science at elementary school level through meaningful home, family and community activities;
4. Use learning situations to encourage individual or family productivity; and
5. Raise the level of scientific consciousness in the individual, family, and community.

A needs and resource assessment was conducted in the community using questionnaires for parents of school children and community leaders; intensive interviews with community members and officials; ocular inspection of the community; and review of documents pertinent to history, education and economic conditions of the community.

The assessment focused on the major and minor occupations of the people; their activities, beliefs and practices related to health and nutrition; the individual's participation in home and community activities; community resources relative to health and sanitation, leisure time activities, cultural and educational facilities; the plant and animal resources, and the productivity of the fishing grounds; and the skills or areas of knowledge the community folk wished to acquire to improve their living conditions.

As a result of matching the needs with the resources and relevant research and development efforts, the project team:

(a) Conducted seminars/workshops on appropriate fishing methods, making encircling gill fish-nets, maintenance and repair of pumpboat engines, communicable diseases, maternal and child-care, preparing nutritious food for the family using local resources, organization of a co-operative;

(b) Organized a co-operative, a sewing circle for mothers, a day care centre, a medicinal garden, a sports team and reading centres;

(c) Assisted the community members in constructing water-sealed toilets and water desalination stills;

(d) Developed science modules and encouraged the use of health modules in classes and reading centres; and

(e) Conducted studies on the students' conceps of health and environment.

The outreach of the project team was total, ranging from changes in the school curriculum with accompanying instructional materials to activities designed to directly improve the living conditions in the community, such as the establishment of a co-operative, construction of water-sealed toilets and a medicinal garden. Table 26.1 shows curriculum implications of some community problems. Table 26.2 lists the science-related modules used in San Salvador classes and reading centres.

The local people, among them the school principal and barangary captain, reported several benefits derived from the project, including improved health and sanitation and increased health consciousness of the people; exposure of fishermen to legal

Table 26.1. Sample analysis of data to identify curriculum needs/non-formal education needs*

Data	Problems	Implications for curriculum	Implications for non-formal education (adult)
A. Analysis of drinking water from all sources revealed infinite number of coli-form bacteria per 100 ml. of water.	Source of drinking water: shallow wells and a few tanks for catching rainwater running off houses with galvanized iron roofs.	Awareness of micro-organisms in the community's water supply. Knowledge about micro-organisms and spread of disease through water-borne organisms. Methods of keeping water safe to drink. Solar distillation of water to demonstrate pure water, water for emergenicies.	Contact National Irrigation Administration to present community's problem. Demonstration of ways of making water potable: boiling, using clean containers. Sanitation activities to keep water from faecal contamination. Results of water examination discussed with adults; implications to health also discussed.
B. Percentage of respondents wanting skills and knolwledge in: 78%— fishing gear, methods 61%— controlling respiratory diseases	Low catch of fish. Small size of fish caught. Idle unrepaired machines. Children frequently ill. Large populations of insects: mosquitoes and other pests.	Comprehension of biology of local fishes (life cycle, habitat). Identification of common fishes of the locality. Methods of fish capture. Awareness of need for preservation of fishing grounds, avoidance of over-fishing.	Seminar workshop on fishing education using local resource persons from government fish extension bureau/projects in nearest city or town. Content of seminar included: improved fishing methods and gear, e.g. making encircling gill nets, out-fitting fishing boat with pump engine for deep-sea fishing.

Source: D.F. Hernandez, "Biological Education and Development in Rural Communities of a Developing Country". *Biological education for community development*, ed. by P. J. Kelly and G. Schaefer. London: Taylor and Francis Ltd., 1980, pp. 180-182.

Table 26.1. *Contd.*

Data	Problems	Implications for curriculum	Implications for non-formal education (adult)
B. 56%— controlling pests and other insects 56%— good water supply		Knowledge of means of preserving fish applicable to locality. Knowledge about parasitic diseases.	Clean-up campaigns of entire community, especially garbage dumps. Seminar on health and nutrition.
C. Use of fine mesh nets by 25% of the respondents.	Illegal fishing.	Knowledge of proper utilization of natural resources (conservation). Knowledge of the ill-effects of illegal methods of fishing.	Demonstration of fish preservation. Introduction of fish farming (putting up a fish pen). Maintenance of fish pen.
D. Twenty-four toilets in a community of 232 families.	Lack of sanitary waste	Awareness of need to dispose human wastes in a snitary way. Knowledge about micro-organisms/parasites causing infectious diseases and parasitism in the poupulation.	Seminar and demonstration on construction and use of water-sealed toilets by R & D team. Encourage use of service from Rural Health Unit personnel (local).
E. There is no doctor in the community.	Inaccessibility of medical service/health care.	Awareness of need to select the right people for health services.	Seminar on health eduction and proper care of sick children (with help of local consultants from

Table 26.1. ***Contd.***

Data	Problems	Implications for curriculum	Implications for non-formal education (adult)
		Knowledge of the use of medicinal plants for simple ailments. Need to maintain a medicinal plant garden in school. Awareness of difficulty of getting proper health care: need to keep oneself healthy.	Ministry of Health and Ministry of Education and Culture).
F. Soil analysis showed that only a few kinds of plants can grow.	Limited vegetable supply and hence no or limited vegetable in the diet, resulting in unbalanced meals and poor nutrition.	Awareness of need for balanced meals for proper nutrition. Knowledge of the importance of vegetales in the diet and good nutrition.	Seminar with mothers on preparation of nutritious foods locally available. Community campaign in vegetable gardening in trench and used containers (plastic, bamboo rafts or pots). Plant malunggay project (fast growing tree, the leaves of which serve as a vegetable).

aspects of fishing methods, training on boat engine repair and better saltmaking procedure; greater awareness of relating community life and school learning; and more functional learning in school and improvement of reading skills.

The success of certain aspects of the project is attributed to the way the adult community problems were dealt with; the economic or other benefits acquired by the participating adults; the utilization of local materials and labour; the encouragement of self-reliance among the community folk; the considration given to constraints in the environment such as geographic and communication, accessibility, and income level; and considration of the human response to introduced technology.

Directions for Community-based Science Education

The community projects of the Center used the following strategies which contributed in a larged measure to the success of the projects:

1. Used the school as an entry point;
2. Identified community needs as perceived by community folk and leaders;

Table 26.2. Titles of science-related modules used in San Salvador, Banate, Iloilo, Philippines

1.	Making a water-sealed toilet
2.	Harmful organisms in water
3.	Keeping water safe to drink
4.	Potable water from sea-water by solar distillation.
5.	Why is sea water salty?
6.	Making and using a solar still
7.	Why do we need drinking water?
8.	Twenty common medicinal plants and how to use them
9.	Vegetables in trenches and pots
10.	Getting to know about fish
11.	Fish conservation and preservation
12.	Fish preservation by dry salting
13.	Salt from sea-water

14. Salt and its importance
15. Making and using a fish pen
16. Milk for Neneng
17. More food for Neneng
18. Food for the family
19. Cleanliness means health
20. Intestinal parasites
21. Respiratory diseases
22. Water and food borne diseases
23. Pulmonary tuberculosis

---

3. Utilized local resources, human and material;
4. Conducted training based on the needs and resource assessment with accompanying instructional materials; and
5. Sought the assistance of other agencies doing community work.

The question arises whether the ordinary science teacher without the resources of a centre can undertake a similar project? Perhaps not too many science teachers realize the benefits accruing from community-oriented teaching. It provides a rich additional resource base that is within the access of the teacher. The approach is likely to appeal to the youth who are increasingly becoming socially-oriented. The social relevance of science will be brought to the fore. More importantly, it is an opportunity for the science teacher to deepen his community consciousness and involvement as well as that of his students.

If school teachers themselves initiate community-based teaching, using the school as an entry point is no longer necessary. Usually respected by community folk, school teachers have already established rapport and trust. As members of the community, the teachers already have some knowledge of the community problems, resources and leadership structure. Science teachers therefore need an increased awareness of the importance of linking school learning with community life, and a systematic approach to such linkage.

Figure 26.1 shows a simple model for community-oriented science teaching.

For additional knowledge about the community, a teacher or group of teachers could interview key community leaders like the barangay captain or town mayor on the goals, problems, resources of the community and how the school can help accomplish certain goals and solve some problems. A community development plan, available in several cities and towns in the Philippines, could replace or supplement the interviews. Such plans typically include (a) characteristics of the community, such as topography, climate and population; and (b) development needs and goals for a specified number of years.

The next phase for the teacher is the integration of identified science-related community needs and resources into the science curriculum. In implementing the curriculum, the teacher can use immediate or long-term strategies. The immediate strategies are easier to implement. A number of teachers occasionally employ these strategies perhaps without being aware of the implications of community-oriented teaching. The long-term strategies will require more time and expertise on the part of the teacher. Co-operation with other community agencies will be a necessity.

Feedback from students and community folk during the implementation phase can be utilized to introduce new modifications into the science curriculum for the next cycle of implementation. The cycle is repeated as many times as needed to improve the linkage of the science curriculum with community life. Over the years a reassessment of community needs and resources will be needed to reflect changes in the community and in its development plans.

Community-oriented teaching will be greatly facilitated if implemented as a school project or objective. Arrangements can be made on an institutional basis and school resources can be fully utilized. Thus, orientation seminars for school administrators are needed to rally their support for community-based teaching.

To equip science teachers with the needed skills and confidence to modify and implement a science curriculum according to the community needs and resurces, teacher-

Figure 26.1. Community-based science education: a classroom approach

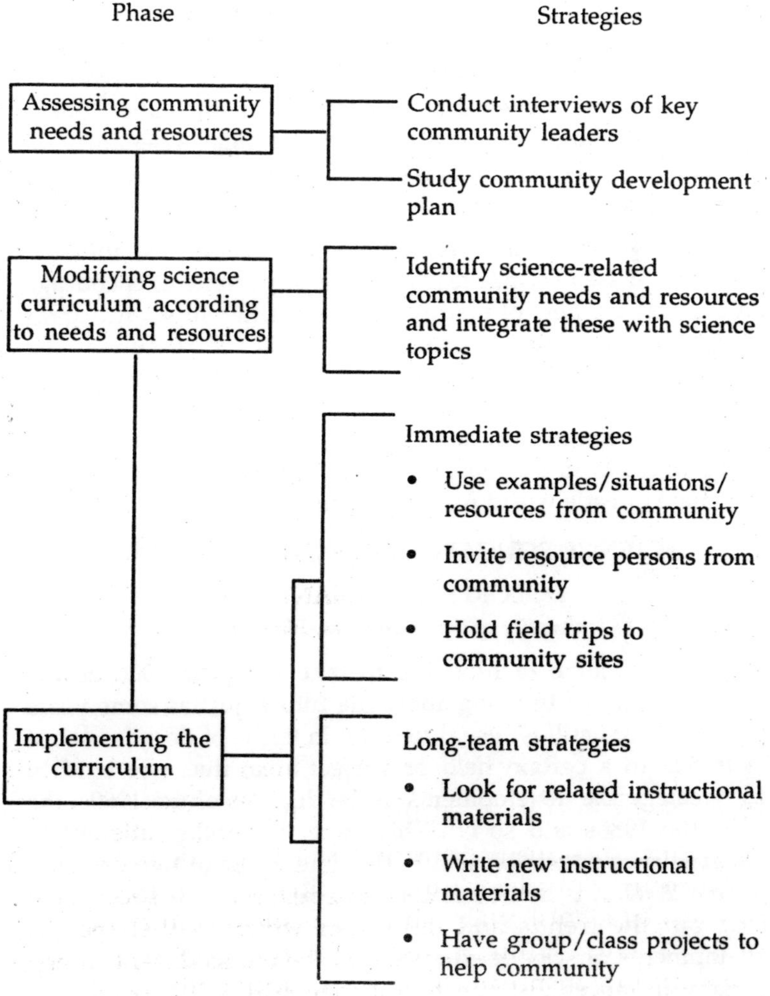

training, in particular a practicum course on community-oriented science teaching, is needed at both pre-service and in-service levels. Graduate students of the author, who are physics teachers, conducted interviews of community leaders and studied community development plans and were able to modify physics syllabi according to the development plan or results of the interviews. Doctoral students in science education who are teachers in physics, chemistry, biology and mathematics took a course under the author and conducted similar assessment of community needs and resources and wrote science lessons in modular form in response to the assessment data.

In many parts of the world, biology educators have initiated community-based science teaching. It is opportune to encourage and support teachers of mathematics and different science areas to orient their teaching to community needs and resources. The ordinary classroom science teacher can begin community teaching even in a limited way. Considering the benefits to the students, the community, and himself, it is time for the science teacher to establish the linkages between school learning and the immediate outside world that is the community.

SCIENCE EDUCATION FOR THE YEAR 2000

DOLORES F. HERNANDEZ
University of the Philippines, Philippines

It has become fashionable to take the year 2000 as the landmark year for thinking about the future, just as some years ago it was (and still is) usual to think in terms of decades about the trends in a certain field or subject area; thus, we tend to neatly categorize developments in the decades of the 1960s, the 1970s, the 1980s and so on. This paper is another attempt to look at science education within the time frame of two decades, the year 2000. It is by no means a forecast; rather it attempts to bring out the trends and the issues which may shape the developments of science education in the not so distant future. In many instances the direction it may take will depend very much on political decisions made by the leaders of a country and to some extent by the expressed will of the people. Yet decisions need to be based on knowledge of what is current and the probabilities of what may yet develop. Hence, looking at what science education may be like in the year 2000 could prove useful for the practitioners, the decision-makers and others who in some way care about what direction it takes.

Science education interacts with and is influenced by many forces; any discussion of what it will be like in the future would need to consider these various interacting factors. The shape of the future, as mentioned earlier, will be determined largely by decisions governments take, which in turn are dependent on the values of society and hence in some measure on the context and process of education.

The first part of this paper considers factors which impinge on science education and may thus influence the directions it may take. The second part deals more specifically with issues and some general considerations rather than outright predictions about science education. These should give us a peep into science education in the year 2000. Science education here refers to education at the pre-university levels and to teacher education for the corresponding levels.

Scenarios for Science Education in the Year 2000

Before considering science education two decades from now, we need to have a reality framework for the science education developments of the year 2000. We need to know the factors that in some way will affect these developments. The context is Asia rather than world-wide. The factors to be considered are those that now exist and from which new areas or developments are emerging.

The assumption is that what will develop two decades from now are generally already here, if not in Asia, in other parts of the world. However, the future will see better or more extensive use of some of these developments, greater understanding of others, more applications of still other ideas and so on.

Biological sciences and education. Many of the issues of the present and the near future are related to biology: food shortages, nutrition, environmental sanitation, health, environmental degradation, pollution, population control, resource management, conservation; in brief, the direction is in the use of knowledge for the advancement of society and for the benefit it brings to the quality of life. In biology, this approach centres on the realities of human life, the realities of society and alternatives for the future of humankind.

From 1978 to the present, the International Union of Biological Sciences, Commission of Biological Education has concentrated on biological education for community development. Three differences have been identified in this current move compared to conventional biology teaching: (1) biological topics that have implications for the community have greater priority for the school curriculum. Such topics would presumably include health, environment (ecology), nutrition, population genetics, behaviour and biological technologies such as those of agriculture, fisheries and medicine; (2) greater emphasis on human biology, and (3) greater emphasis on what might be called issues studies as differentiated from knowledge studies. The former emphasizes problem solving, decision-making, while the latter emphasizes understanding. For example, Mendelian inheritance would be a knowledge topic, genetic engineering an issue topic.

A Unesco sponsored meeting of biology educators in 1980 identified aspects of biology education which are crucial for the secondary school curriculum: environmental aspects of biology education, genetic aspects and health, nutrition and agricultural aspects. For each of these major areas, the pertinent specific concepts and principles, practical experiences for students, teaching/learning strategies, intellectual skills and values were identified. The result of this meeting provides the interested biology educator and curriculum developer with a specific handbook about topics and strategies that Asian educators believe are urgently needed in the education of the secondary school level adolescent now and in the near future.

On a more general and world-wide level, Dr. Paul De Hart Hurd, a well-known science educator, suggested a context for the teaching of biology in the future. Because it bears upon the subject of this paper, the objectives are briefly summarized below: biology (we can substitute the word 'science' and the following will still apply) as part of a liberal education in the future should:

(a) Be taught in a social and human context;

(b) Include values and ethics as goals recognizing that there are moral and aesthetic as well as scientific answers to human problems;

(c) Have courses organized more according to biosocial events and problems rather than on logic of biological discipline;

(d) Consist of subject matter that can serve real life and practical ends;

(e) Be taught from a holistic and integrative point of view;

(f) Ensure that laboratory investigations include individual and laboratory based problems, issues, policies;

(g) Encourage development of skills such as decision-making, valuing, ecological thinking, (self-reliance, social responsibility, use of indigenious and appropriate technology);*

(h) Orient teaching towards the future giving students opportunities to consider alternatives;

(i) Use more individualized and personalized teaching to accommodate learning styles of different students; and

(j) Recognize the role of the biology teacher as an interpreter of biology concepts, an intermediary between scientist and the public.

In the area of ecology and the environment there is concern among ecologists for holistic thanking and approach, for more relevant perceptions of ecology which related it to nationalism and development. Ignacy Sachs of UNEP has provided a concept of ecodevelopment which is very pertinent to current thoughts on this subject among third world countries. Ecodevelopment, he says, is a style of development particularly suited to rural regions of the third world. It calls for specific solutions to particular problems in the light of cultural, ecological data and long term as well as immediate needs.

Our peep into the future should provide some insights on what some Asian countries, the Philippines included, would like to have realized—an agro-bio industrial society. This perception calls for a return to the land—but at the same time it does not reject modern technology. The trend in this type of technology is towards miniaturization, more efficient utilization of materials and energy, recycling and use of 'cleaner' technologies. Agro-bio industry is an integrated system of production of goods and services which tightly links primary production from agriculture, fishery and forestry with the conversion of the raw materials into the complex and more useful. A few examples of the applications of microbiology are: production of power alcohol; syntheses of antibiotics for medical and agricultural use; syntheses of hormones for medical purposes; the transfer of nitrogen-fixing genes to new organisms which associate with non-leguminous plants.

The extent to which some of the foregoing developments in the biological sciences will prevail generally in Asian countries will determine to a large extent the inputs that should go into science education assuming the political will is for the schools to serve the same ends as those of the nation.

The Physical Sciences and Education. In the near future we will see a more rational and systematic understanding of the origin and distribution of chemical elements as a result of studies on nuclear reactions that occur naturally or are induced by accelerators. Because of the explorations in space, there will be a better understanding of the extraterrestrial conditions which led to creation of our universe and the elements that comprise it. Many new elements and isotopes will be synthesized. Another area that will likely be advanced is how elements differ and how they can be identified in the presence of each other—analyses may extend to the detection and scaling of single atoms! The future promises to fill in the blanks than exist in our understanding to the origin and reactions of molecules and atoms. Accordingly, it is expected that many conventional positions in chemistry will be revised.

Appraisal studies suggest that in the near future (ten years hence) the main feedstock for petrochemicals and sources of energy will still be oil and natural gas. A breakthrough in the technological development of the major non-petroleum sources of energy may eventuate. These include coal, shale oil, tar sands, solar energy in the form of biomass; direct heating, photovoltaic technology or hydrogen generation. Nuclear energy is technologically developed, but its use will depend on political decisions and acceptance by the public. The chemical industry will continue to supply the essential needs of food, housing, clothing, transportation, drugs, health, recreation and so on—and become part of many aspects of modern life. The computer will play an important part in analysis of experimental data and technical calculations associated with many aspects of the chemical industry. It will become a major research tool and run complex chemical processes and produce better products with fewer problems. Environmental concerns will continue to be the focus of the public in relation to the operation of chemical industries.

Chemistry, physics and biology will overlap and intertwine increasingly. Biochemists will continue the probe into the chemistry of life. Space explorations may clarify and deepen the understanding of space and physical laws.

The rate of change in chemical education is slow. This may not be a bad thing. If education were to reflect all the changes immediately we may end up with an erratic curriculum which shows no direction. However, there is a need for restructuring curricula because pre-professional students are not receiving optional education to prepare them for work in the existing field. An examination of books in chemistry shows a preponderance of materials far removed from what the chemists are now doing in research and development.

Science, Society and Culture. In his article on the cultural impediments to scientific thinking (in Southeast Asia) S.H. Alatas (1978) identifies a type of mentality which he calls bebalisma which has the following characteristics: authoritarian, non-reflective, non-experimental, no power of anticipation, non-rational, unenquiring, no love for order in thinking, no capacity for sustained contextual appraisal, credulous beyond limit, lack of refinement, non-cumulative in the succession of thought and no maintenance mentality. These characterize an attitude of mind that obstructs the development of the scientific and technological spirit necessary to motivate industrialization and effective agricultural planning. Since the third world is suffering from a lack of science and technology and it is the will of most countries to move towards a more scientific society, there is then a need to develop scientific mentality in order to improve the situation.

Another view, point stresses that industrialization is itself a cultural concept. 'Technology produces goals and demands as well as provides the ways and means (far beyond the 'technical' ones) to attend to them, and prescribes the modes of approach and conduct' (Vente, 1978).

Some of the changes in values and behaviour patterns that are brought about by industrialization are: (1) work attitudes and relationships—industrialization implies segregation of economic activities from the traditional family community setting; (2) changing patterns of community life—urbanization is accelerated which in turn affects the life-styles of the population and their human interaction patterns; (3) family systems and family relations, e.g. the widening generation gap between parents and children; and (4) counter values and popular culture-industrial technology and innovations usually bring external values, fashions, life-styles (Chen, 1978).

Loss of culture does not necessarily follow from the introduction of industrialization. Changes undergone in Asian countries as a result of the impact of industrialization may fall into four categories according to Alatas: (1) eliminative changes; (2) additive changes; (3) supportive changes; and (4) synthetic changes. It is only the first category of changes that results in loss of culture. The rest enrich the indigenous culture.

For countries with many languages, the importance of language as a medium of instruction is a problem that keeps being raised. Because no books are available in the local language which are of the same quality as internationally accepted textbooks on the same subject, science subjects are taught in English in universities. (See for example Bhattacharya, 1978 and P.K. Bose, 1978). In the Philippines this is also true at the secondary and elementary levels.

The response of educators to government thrusts for national development has been in the main, in terms of science education projects that address the problems of rural development and disadvantaged areas of the country. Rural development is interpreted as a strategy designed to improve the economic and social life of the masses. Types of learning units prepared by the Science Education Center, University of the Philippines, in response to national development goals include those which are occupation oriented, those that improve on indigenous technology, those that relate to conservation and recycling, those on health, nutrition and sanitation. Even industrialized countries have concerned themselves with making science education more relevant to the real life situation of the students, and more practical. This was the theme of a seminar held in 1980 in Malvern, United Kingdom on the theme, 'Science, education and society'.

The students. A very important element of educational enterprise are the students in Asian schools. In the Philippines we have 8.2 million elementary school pupils, 2.7 million secondary school students About 79 per cent of elementary pupils finish grade IV; 66 per cent finish grade VI; 54 per cent reach first year high school and 34 per cent complete secondary level of education (fourth year high school). At tertiary level, 17 per cent enter first year college and 13 per cent complete four years of college education. India has about 60 million primary school children and about 50 per cent either drop out or do not proceed beyond the first level of education (Wanchoo, 1980). The problems related to school enrolment may vary in degree, but more or less most Asian countries would have the problem of accommodating (physically and in terms of the curriculum) larger numbers of students for two reasons: the large number of school children already born (population growth rates have decreased but not sufficiently to make a difference in actual school needs), and democratization of admissions at all levels of education.

Broadening the base of admissions (including entry of more women in the three levels of education) will change the nature of the school population. A lessening of the demarcation lines between formal and non-formal education (e.g., the use of equivalency tests to enable students who have dropped out of school to re-enter the formal system at the grade level he qualifies) will further contribute to the heterogeneity of educational needs.

Some of the studies on students have focused on cognitive development, particularly at the first level of education. Similar studies have been conducted on students at the other two levels of education, and even with teachers. (See for example, de Guzman, 1981). Most of the studies at the primary stage of education tend to confirm the findings of Piaget with respect to the sequence but not in terms of the time or age at which a given stage is manifested. Results of studies on the secondary and college levels in the Philippines show that students are mostly concrete thinkers. This has serious implications for the curriculum and instructional methods.

The age structure of the school population may not change much but there will be more school children from the disadvantaged areas and deprived families. Instructional materials and methodologies more appropriate to this group have to be utilized at least during the early years of schooling of this expanded school population. The characteristics of the student population would tend to change depending on the rate of change in the environment, physical, social and psychological.

Future Perspectives

Some ideas about science education in the future are dealt with in this section in the context of Southeast Asia, more specifically of the Philippines. As stated earlier these are not predictions but issues and possible developments about which decisions should be made in the future. Science education will not develop by itself; people in decision making positions will have to decide on questions such as those raised in the following paragraphs.

Curriculum development. How much stress should be placed on society's development needs, and the concerns of society in the science curriculum? The first is already a trend at least in some Asian countries. Science topics of the 'Science and Society'* type have appeared in modular form. It is not unlikely that new books will incorporate some of such topics.

Science taught with humanistic dimensions might be one way of meeting the interests of the large group of non-science

---

* John Lewis of Malvern College, England is Project Director of 'Science and Society.

oriented students. The teaching of values or a system of beliefs which permeate the entire curriculum (including science) may be a policy decision. Already some countries have incorporated moral education in their school curricula. The question arises, how much or to what extent can science education contribute to this aspect of the curriculum?

Should the science curriculum be developed locally or nationally? Should it be centralized or decentralized? In a small way decentralized curriculum development has been done in one or two regions of the Philippines via preparation of some modules specific to regional needs and interests. This type of grass-roots curriculum development enables the teacher to introduce local or community concerns into science education. The community becomes a learning situation or laboratory; learning hopefully becomes more interesting because of the reality of the learning experiences. A national text-book/syllabus is still used however; the community topics are introduced at relevant points. This is just one way of attending to this issue; several others may be developed and tried out.

Should the science curriculum attend to the development of both cognitive and affective dimensions? Much discussion and some research on teaching the logical core and the affective dimensions of concepts have been done, (see for example G. Schaefer, 1980) but science curricula have not yet reflected these in the formal curriculum itself. This issue is concomitant with the preceding one. Including community oriented topics and local problems would increase the perceptual awareness about things around us and correspondingly, the 'public' or scientific meanings of concepts as well as their 'private' or idiosyncratic meanings will enter into the learning situation.

Should school science education closely reflect what the discipline is all about and what scientists are doing? To teach science according to the structure of the discipline was an important objective of curriculum projects of the 1960s. It may still be considered as an objective but not as a primary objective particularly for students who will not go on to science as a career.

Should science education at the school level be integrated? To what degree should integration be introduced? Will such integration include the social sciences humanities, or other subjects, and which ones? In Philippine schools for example, apart from the elementary school science curricula, integrated science is taught at only one level; first year high school.

What does scientific literacy mean? Could this be defined in terms of competencies for each level of education? If this is done the curriculum could be examined to determine whether or not it provides at each grade level experiences for development of scientific literacy.

Is the curriculum future-oriented? Does it provide for the development of decision making skills, consideration of alternatives for the future course of human affairs and the diversified needs of students?

Does the curriculum reflect what is known about how learning takes place? Is there a match between the cognitive demands of the curriculum and the cognitive levels of the students? (See for example, Shayer and Adey, 1981).

Does the curriculum meet the requirements of the college-bound students as well as the non-science or terminal student?

Does the curriculum include some work on computers? They will be much used in various if not all fields of science. It is important that students become familiar with computers, if not all students at least special groups of students e.g., those in science high schools should be offered computer courses.

What do we know about factors which contribute attitudes adopted by students in helping them learn science, in helping them cross the secondary/tertiary interface, in helping the teachers create and environment for better learning? Results of research on this aspect of learning should feed directly to curriculum developers, teacher educators and classroom teachers so they can be used to improve learning situations.

Teacher education. The stress on humanism and values will demand the use of techniques of teaching which have not been conventionally used in science teaching. For example, in helping students think about the future some techniques have been used successfully but are as yet not commonly known among science teachers—the Delphi technique which involves an intuitive method of organizing and shaping expert forecasts about the future; use of the cross-impact matrix in which students assess the impact of several factors on each other; decision-making techniques like the decision tree which involved the student in analysing alternatives from a sequence of decisions; and so on (See for example R. Charlton, 1979; D. F. Hernandez, 1980).

More use of educational technology may become necessary in teacher education. In most teacher education programmes although hardware like video tape-recorders are known or heard about very few teacher training institutions actually use them. Their use may become necessary as more children enter the schools but at the same time less students opt to go into teaching careers. Other ways of using VTR than for microteaching need to be tried. (See for example Waring, 1980).

Teacher education programmes need more innovation to keep them abreast of the requirements of science programmes the teachers are expected to implement. Take as an example inquiry teaching:

> . . . it (inquiry) cannot be acquired by osmosis. It must be taught and practised by the instructor. It must be practised by the learner. And, it must be taught by the learner in the role of an instructor. Inquiry instruction cannot be accomplished in a one or two semester course. Instructions in inquiry must start early in the pre-service education of elementary teachers. . . (De Vito, 1980).

Improving the quality of teacher preparation by various means has been suggested many times in different international settings. Some of those suggested by Cheong, S.Y. (1980) include: more inquiry oriented learning; more interaction between trainees and tutors, trainees and materials and among trainees themselves; use of training methods that utilize small group instruction and to a lesser extent, individualized instruction, e.g., microteaching, mini courses, audio tutorials. Small group discussions, seminars and direct observation are used to complement laboratory based activities. Several types of teacher education materials have also been produced; but most of these are for the formal system. Software for learning informally and on their own has yet to make an impact on teacher education. However, in Asia, projects for distance learning (via radio and TV) are now ongoing or being initiated.

A review of teacher education developments would be incomplete without mention of one of the best known projects in this field—the Science Teacher Education Project (STEP). In this programme teaching practice becomes a time for inquiring into the job at the same time as it is a time for practising. STEP draws away from a programmed blueprint type of teacher education and relies mainly on a bank of good ideas offering the teacher what is possible at a given time. In doing so, it mirrors the real situation in which teachers teach for it is claimed they rarely manage the ideal planned programme but work on the opportunities they have (Holford and Sutton, 1980).

In teacher education as in pre-university education there is a cry for a 'return to the basics'. In this case the basics mean content. There are three positions regarding teaching of content. Some would stress professional education and methodology almost to complete exclusion of content. Others call for content courses and the doing away with educational philosophy, psychology, sociology. Still others argue for integration of subject and professional training.

The education of teachers needs to incorporate several experiences which are demanded of teachers once they are in the field. And, their training should be such that they can more easily adapt to changing needs in the field, make decisions about what is suitable for their own situation and accordingly undertake the necessary planning and implementation. There are however some experiences that are too significant to be left out of teacher training programmes altogether. For example, for some years now, science educators have been concerned with rural life and environment. Most of our teachers end up teaching in rural schools. Are they being educated for such environments? Most teacher training institutions are in urban areas; just providing practice teaching in rural schools would hardly meet this need. How could science teachers for example, use the rural environment more in everyday teaching? Another experience teachers need is the integration of various areas of knowledge.

This ability is expected of the practising teacher. How much (or how little) of the prospective teacher's courses are integrated so that the teacher really gets a feel of what an integrated course is?

In science and mathematics education it seems particularly necessary that there be constant interaction between practising scientists and practising teachers; or between those in the forefront of knowledge and discoveries and those involved in disseminating knowledge. University collaboration is necessary in curriculum development as such a relationship help keeps much trivia out of the books and it assists in developing a sense of inquiry. It is felt that such programmes could best be fashioned and implemented by greater school-university co-operation, i.e., among the schools, Ministry/Department of Education and the university in a given province or region. Teacher education must also be concerned with strategies for acquiring new knowledge, the aim should be not the production of polished practitioners but preparation of beginning professionals who have the capabilities and attitudes for lifelong learning (Sharp, 1975).

Science education and the public. Great progress in science and technology and the great strides made in electronics, computers, astronomy, communication and other areas, make it imperative to devise better ways of bridging the gap between science and the market-place. Too much misinformation and lack of understanding of these advances make decisions a risky process at both the everyday life level and the policy making level.

Projects like England's 'Science and Society' which is developed in readable short modules, intended for the formal school system could well be used by adults and youth who are out of school. A more common way of reaching the public is via mass media—newspapers and television. In some Asian countries the latter is already being used for this purpose. But science programmes as in the Philippines are imported and of rather a high level for the masses of the people. It will be necessary to prepare materials for national broadcast choosing topics and a level of delivery more appropriate to the present level of the masses of our people. This does not imply that the imported programmes should be stopped—they have an audience which could grow over the years as the people become more familiar with advances in science.

Whose is the responsibility for educating the public in science and mathematics? In some countries like the Philippines there is a government agency given charge of non-formal education. Extension programmes of industries, government and non-government agencies and institutions of higher learning, also contribute to this goal of educating the public. Science education teaching centres and science museums, have several advantages which can be put to good use for serving the public. Many of the science modules they prepare can be used for public education purposes. Most have facilities for producing multi-media materials which can be aimed at reaching the masses of the people. Our public education efforts however, have not undergone systematic evaluation apart from subjective statements from participants attesting to the usefulness and enjoyment derived from the programmes.

The ministry charged with public information may eventually have to assume the task of educating the public on scientific issues which affect everyday life and have implications for society. Issues on land management, fishery rights, displacement of people and entire communities due to building of roads, dams, bridges and atomic energy plants need to be publicly aired, the necessary scientific information needs to be presented, so people can form their own opinions based on accurate information.

In brief, every institution engaged in science education shares to some extent the responsibility for public education through their extension or service programmes or *ad hoc* activities offered for public consumption. But there seems to be a need for a more systematic way of educating the public particularly on issues that affect everyday life and the society as a whole.

Concluding Remarks

What was attempted in this paper was to present a review of current development in science education, some related issues and questions, and some alternatives. The shape of science education in the year 2000 may arise from many of the current developments and issues. No attempt was made at comprehensiveness; all that was intended at the outset was to present a paper which could stimulate a discussion that could produce more contributions about what the shape and future of science education will be like two decades from now.

REFERENCES

Alatas, Syed Hussein, "Cultural Impediments to Scientific Thinking" in Vente, Rolf E. and Chen, Peter S.J., eds. *Culture and industrialization*. Bonn, West Germany, German Foundation for International Development, 1978, p. 3-20.

Bhattacharya, S.C. "Status of Science Education", *Science and culture*. 44(12): 521-524, December 1978.

Bose, Purnenda Kumar, "Language Problem", *Science and culture*. 44(9): 385-387, September 1978.

Charlton, Ronald E. "Futuristics in Biuology: Some Techniques", *American biology teacher*. 41(3): 136-139, March 1979.

Chen, Peter S.J. "The Cultural Implications of Industrialization and Modernization" in Vente R.B. and Chen, P.S.J., eds. *Culture and industrialization*. *Op cit*., p. 115-134.

De Vito, Alfred, "The Improvement of Undergraduate Pre-Service and In-Service Teacher Education", in McFadden, C.P., ed. *World trends in science education*. *Op cit*.

de Guzman, Fe S. "The Status of Cognitive Development Research in the Philippines". Monograph No. 18. Quezon City, Science Education Center, University of the Philippines, August 1981.

Holford, Derek and Sutton, Clive, "Science Teacher Education: The Art of the Possible" in McFadden, C.P., ed. *World trends in science education*. *Op cit*.

Hurd, Paul Dehart. "The Teaching of Biology: A Possible Future", *Biological sciences curriculum study* 1(4): 20-21, 24 November 1978.

Schaefer, Gerhard, "Concept Formation in Schools Between Scientific and Community Demands" in *Biological education for community development*. Ed. by P. Kelly and G. Schaefer for CBE-IUBS and IPN. London, Taylor and Francis Ltd., 1980.

Sharp, William L. "The Regionalization of Teacher Education: The Next Step in Professional Development". *Science teacher education, 1974:*

issues and positions. Fred W. Fox, ed. Columbus, Ohio, Eric-Smeac, 1974, p. 16-25.

Shayer, Michael and Adey, Philip. *Towards a science of science teaching: cognitive development and curriculum demand*. London, Heinemann Educational Books, 1981.

Vente, Rolfe E. "Industrialization as Culture" in Vente, R. E. and Chen, P.S.J., eds. *Culture and industrialization. Op. cit.*

Wanchoo, V.N. "Nutrition, Environmental Sanitation, and Health Education in Primary Schools in India (a Pilot Project)" in McFadden, C.P., ed. *World trends in science education. Op. cit.* p. 150-154.

27

A Second Chance for School Systems and New Vision for Population Outside of School

PETER J. FENSHAM
Monash University, Australia

Introduction

'Science for all' is a contemporary slogan and challenge for science educators around the world in the 1980s. After a period of substantial depression in school science education in the United States, new funds have been announced in 1983 for another attempt to improve and extend the effectiveness of science education in that nation's schools.

Despite a general recession and cutbacks in educational funding in Britain and New Zealand, each of these countries has major projects underway in the field of school science education. In Britain an extensive five-year project, the Secondary Science Curriculum Review, began in 1982. In New Zealand, the Learning in Science project spent the years 1979-81 working on the lower secondary years and has now been extended for a further period to work at the primary school level.

In March 1982, the Commonwealth Office of Education hosted a Workshop in Cyprus of science curriculum experts with the theme 'Science and the world of work'. In Malaysia a new primary curriculum is being developed and there is a major debate about the place that science should play in it.

This interest in a number of countries in 'Science for all' has both a familiar ring and a new note. The great surge of curriculum activity in science education in the 1960s and early 1970s is too recent and too well documented for its great hopes to be forgotten.

Although this activity was focused initially on more specialized education in the sciences (and this level commanded much of the resources), many projects were aimed at more general levels of education—primary and lower secondary. Learners at all levels of schooling were to gain new excitement, new skills and new knowledge from the new curriculum projects and new materials that large sums of money launched in many countries in all the continents. If the United States and the United Kingdom were the first countries into the act as the 1960s moved to the 1970s they were joined by many others at all sorts of levels of industrialization. Internationally, Unesco, ICSU and numerous other bodies lent their support to these movements and the activity and exchange of ideas about science education was quite unprecedented.

The focus of these earlier hopes was very much on the schooling system via its primary and secondary levels. School education is still very much the concern of these new endeavours of the 1980s. However, in a number of cases the current concern is also about other target groups in the population. Those persons who are not at school need also to be enabled to share in some way in what science has to offer humankind.

With respect to this new and exciting aspect of the science for all concept, there is little we can learn from the past. Indeed, as it will be argued later in this paper, we will need to resist the obvious extrapolation from science education for schools.

However, with respect to the issue of science for all at school, we will be foolish indeed if we ignore these still fresh memories of earlier attempts to do just the same sort of thing. Lest we go over the same ground again and make similar mistakes, this paper devotes quite a large section to an analysis of what was done in the 1960s and 1970s and of the assumptions that led to it being done as it was.

It is a lot easier to be confident about that was achieved in these earlier efforts than it is to be sure about what was attempted and why it happened as it did. Nevertheless, in the later sections of this paper an attempt is made to raise issues that relate to this more complex task.

There is now a growing consensus in a number of countries about two things concerning science education in schools.

1. We now have (and curriculum materials are available) a much better curriculum for providing in education in the sciences to those at school (about 20 per cent of an age group) from whom the future scientists and science related professionals will be drawn.
2. We have not achieved an effective science education in schools for the 80 per cent or so who most probably will not continue with any formal education in science after they leave school.

The very existence of the new projects cited at the beginning of this paper are evidence for the negative assessment in the second statement. It is not however, intended that these statements belittle what has been achieved.

There is the very considerable achievement of the first statement and there must be a great deal of useful experience from which we can learn if we reflect on those earlier efforts that were made to educate a wider school population (the 80 per cent) through science.

This paper points to a number of sources of the failure of these first attempts at a science for all at school. Some of these sources involve quite fundamental features of curriculum development for schools such as (a) a naivety about the role of school systems in society and of science education in particular; and (b) an optimism about scientific knowledge and about educational pedagogy.

The Role of School Systems and Science Education in Particular

The curriculum movement of the 1960s and 1970s has rightly been criticized for so often behaving as if schooling and science education takes place in a social and political vacuum.

When it did acknowledge in its rhetoric, social demands that education is called on to meet, it often failed to distinguish between them or to recognize that they may even be in conflict.

Social theorists have often stated, but we easily forget, that school systems are established in society to achieve a range of purposes that relate to societal needs and social demands. For example, they are expected to reproduce the knowledge, skills and expertise that is required to maintain whatever is the existing *status quo* of society. Again they are often expected to produce new sorts of persons with hitherto unavailable skills and knowledge that have become essential to the development of an economy or to the changing needs of the society. Thirdly, they are often required to contribute to 'law and order' by passing on a respect and appreciation of traditional knowledge, values and culture. These three examples of societal needs that school systems have to meet are sufficient to illustrate the very different roles of reproduction, development and conservation.

The existence of a school system furthermore means, at the level of individual families, that some will endeavour to use it for social mobility, some for re-inforcement of their existing advantages and some will find it contributes little or nothing to alleviate their disadvantages.

It is obviously not easy for all these sorts of demands and needs to be met equally well and very often one or several will win out at the expense of the others.

Since the late 1950s two very distinct societal demands have been placed on science education in many countries. The first is the demand for specialist manpower so that societies and economies can keep pace in a world where scientific knowledge and technology is being exploited in a rapidly increasing way. The second is the demand for a more scientifically literate citizenry. That is, science education should produce more members of the society who will be able to benefit from the personal and social applications of science and will be prepared to support the changes of a scientific and technological kind that are needed for a good balance between development and environmental concerns. It is this second demand that now has as its slogan, 'Science for all'. These two demands are examples of conflicting ones and not complementary ones as was almost universally assumed in the first wave of the science curriculum movement.

It is of interest to note that, in the United Kingdom and perhaps in the United States, the initial pressures for the reform of the science curriculum did have some elements of the second demand but these were engulfed (although hence gaining establishment) by the demands of the first sort—the Dainton and Swann Reports in the United Kingdom and the post Sputnik response and Rickover Report in the United States.

The advocates of science for all, accepted the opportunity provided by the more powerful demand for more scientific specialists. They hoped that their own interest would be met along with the meeting of the first demand or at least soon after. But the first reforms of the curricula were almost always aimed at improving the science education in the school system that already was the source of scientific and technical manpower, namely, the elite disciplinary courses for mathematics and the sciences in secondary schooling. In hindsight it is possible to recognize this emphasis as ominous for the 'Science for all' movement but at the time we did not see it in that way. If there was naivety about school systems meeting different demands in the 1960s, it is important that a similar naivety is not displayed in the 1980s about the new interpretations of science for all that are now beings generated.

The supply of technological and scientific manpower is most important to the maintenance and development of the social, economic and defence needs of all countries. The educational system must therefore meet this supply need and in many countries there has been a significant improvement in the supply over the last 20 years. In some countries in the region some forms of scientific specialization, e.g. biological sciences and even medical sciences are so well supplied that there is a surplus over what the national economy can employ. In other countries there is still a shortage of these specialists in many fields but the targets for them are still of the order of 1-10 per cent of any age cohort rather than 30-70 per cent.

It is important to assess some of the prices that educational systems have paid in giving priority to meeting his national need and to consider the associated gains.

The ultimate formal education of this scientific and technological elite is in the hands of universities, colleges or institutes or technology. These educational institutions are under considerable international pressure to conform to the production of graduates who share a common body of knowledge and associated practical skills or experiences.

Although the growth of scientific knowledge generally has been and remains very rapid, this has not led to a great diversity of content in science courses either at undergraduate level or in the school system. Rather, there has been a consolidation of certain specific conceptual content in each of the sciences as the knowledge worth learning. A basis for choosing this conceptual content for undergraduate science courses is, no doubt, that it is 'powerful' in the sense that these concepts are ones that scientists use repeatedly as they consider new phenomena and new fields of interest. Nevertheless, the learning of these concepts (and their precursors in school science as it prepares this elite for university study) can take so much time that the excitement of contemporary science and its many possibilities for social usefulness can be, and are, often overlooked and omitted.

Two basic questions face any national system of education that is giving a priority to the development of this type of elite. Firstly, there is the question: Who shall be permitted to enter the training group (up to about 20 per cent)? and secondly, What prior preparation will they be given? These tasks of selection and preparation are, in most countries, associated with the secondary level of the education system. In some cases they may even extend down into the primary level. In even fewer cases there is a degree of openness that enables alternative forms of direct entry into science and technological education at the tertiary level. These are, however, rare and as yet little explored or even sought after. The lack of interest in 'second chance' education in these fields is, no doubt, a consequence of the clear message the majority have received at school that there is only one route, through schooling, for these fields of employment and that they lack the potential and the abilities for them.

It is usual to associate the two tasks of selection and preparation. That is, the content of science education that is deemed to be a suitable preparation for the study of the science disciplines at the higher level also turns out to be a useful selective device since comparatively few pupils successfully learn it. It is certainly possible to envisage alternative preparations in science education that would not serve the selection task. For example, a course that focused on relevant, practical skills of science may well produce more successful learners than are required. After all, a very wide spectrum of the population of most countries do now acquire the skills of driving a motor car—a much more complex set of skills than many of science's practical techniques.

This association has, of course, some strange and disturbing consequences. For example, if a science education at school could be devised so that most children were able to learn with substantial success, it would not suit the selection task as we now understand it. Such a course may, however, have heightened the interest of many more of the age group to seriously consider the scientifically related technologies and professions as possible careers. While failing to do the selection task, it may have broadened the size and the quality of the base from which selection would then be made.

The solution to the dual questions of selection and preparation has been found in most, or perhaps every, country by the creation of a secondary school curriculum in mathematics and the sciences that:

1. Involves the rote recall of a large number of not obviously socially useful facts and concepts;
2. Involves too little familiarity with many of the concepts to enable their scientific usefulness to be experienced;
3. Involves concepts that have been defined for high levels of generality among scientists without their levels of abstraction being adequately acknowledged in the school context and hence their consequential limitations regarding real situations is not indicated;
4. Involves an essentially abstract system of scientific

knowledge with examples of objects and events to illustrate this system rather than those aspects of the science of factual phenomena that enables some use or control of them to occur;

5. Involves life experiences and social applications only as exemplary rather than as the essence of the science learning;
6. Associates the role of practical activity in its pedagogy with the belief that it enhances the conceptual learning rather than being a source for the learning of essential skills;
7. Gives a high priority even in biology to the quantitative content, and in chemistry this priority is probably greater than it is for many practising chemists; and
8. Leaves to the continued study of these disciplines at the tertiary level the balance, meaning and significance that is lacking in 1 to 7.

Such a school curriculum has its content determined for it very largely by selecting out those simple but abstract concepts and principles that provide a good base for the continued learning of this sort that occurs in the specialist courses of study in the institutions of tertiary education. In other words there is no real discontinuity between what is regarded as knowledge of worth in specialist science education and the content that is regarded as worth learning for school curricula even down to quite early years of secondary schooling. Furthermore, the chosen content because of its conceptual and abstract nature lends itself to a sequential type of development that inevitably provides the selection part of the dual task. The learning sequence for conceptual knowledge shown in Figure 27.1 illustrates that this arrangement of a curriculum demands for success that learners have persistent motivation regarding knowledge and ability to consistently sustain dependent learning. If a learner loses motivation or fails for whatever reason to learn one stage, then it is almost impossible to recover. The sequences stretch on, only terminating because the curriculum says so. The learner is, at all times, dependent on the teacher or the textbook for what is 'correct'.

Figure 27.1. Learning sequence for conceptual knowledge

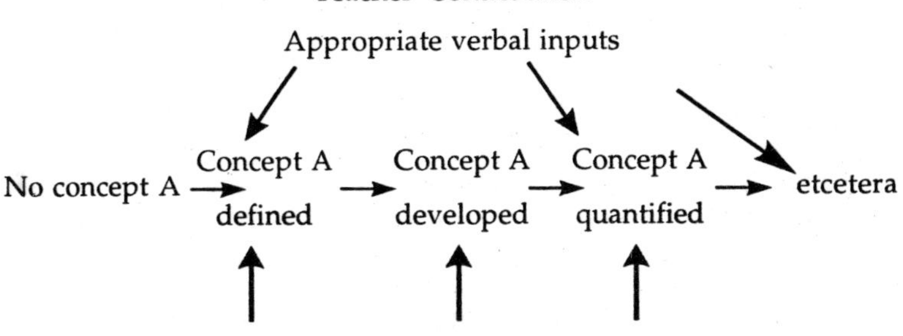

Optional associated experiences or applications

In many situations reasonable achievement in the learning of science subjects is not sufficient to allow a student to continue in a science stream (particularly for the physical sciences). A high level of learning in the even more sequentially arranged and abstract mathematics is also necessary.

There are many examples of the way in which the selection task operates in these curricula. In many countries quantitative aspects of chemistry (stoichiometry, etc.,) are introduced comparatively early although they are known to be very difficult to learn and although they are not essential to large sections of descriptive chemistry that follow them in the curriculum sequence.

There is probably little point in discussing whether these solutions to the selective and preparatory tasks are the only ones. They exist and are not likely to change in most countries. Furthermore, the provision of an adequate supply of trained specialists is being steadily achieved through them. Although not in any sense an example of education as positive social reconstruction, in a curious way, they have also allowed a significant degree of social mobility to occur. The very abstractness of this sort of knowledge content and its emphasis on the quantitative, lessens the advantage that certain socio-economic groups in societies always seem to have for the more culturally and language-based subjects in the total curriculum. It is often more common to find examples of human 'breakthrough' among the ranks of pure scientists than among the professions based on the humanities or those which are only partially science-related like medicine.

Accordingly, there is no likelihood of major changes in this manner whereby school systems (particularly secondary schools) meet this national need for scientific and technological manpower. As has been pointed out, this manner is not without its achievements—there has been an improving supply of manpower and at the same time a trickle of upward social mobility.

The major price of these solutions to the manpower demand is that the majority of the school population learn that they are unable to learn science as it has been defined. Furthermore, unless strenuous efforts are made to offer other forms of science for learning in school most students will identify science with what has been presented. Science to them becomes a subject that in some mysterious and not obvious way gives power eventually to an elite group of their peers who are rapidly distanced from them by the schooling process itself.

Several other prices have often also been mentioned. One is the degree to which the elite training group has to concentrate on science and mathematics education. Their opportunity to study the humanities and social sciences at the higher levels of the school so usually very limited. However, it is not such a problematic feature of elite science education that is our concern here. Rather, our concern is, How can we maintain the success of this type of science education and still optimize the chances that there can be an effective science for all? Some suggestions about these questions are made later on.

Optimism about Scientific Knowledge and Educational Pedagogy

Looking back at the last 20 years of curriculum endeavour in science education, it is now possible to see a number of rather curious aspects. At the time it was not possible to see them in this way, but that is what learning from history is about.

One of the most striking of these aspects is the optimism and enthusiasm shown by the curriculum developers of general science education. Given the chance of sharing their subject with primary children for the first time and with the rising mass of students everywhere who were moving into secondary schooling, they took up their tasks eagerly. Topics from the knowledge and content of science that they themselves had learnt in school or university were selected and reworked for presentation to these new generations of learners. If only the pedagogical approach was cleverly enough designed (guided discovery, stages of development, structured sequences, etc.), and the teachers followed it faithfully, the masses would learn and find the same satisfaction in it that the designers had done in their own education in science.

The evaluation and implementation findings now point to this optimism as either naivety or even arrogance. Only a relatively small percentage of a population historically have been fascinated by science knowledge for its own sake. Accordingly, it was expecting rather too much that the designers and teachers of the 1960s and 1970s could produce such a revolution of interest.

If the science of all of the 1980s and 1990s is not to make the same sorts of mistakes it will need to try to avoid imposing on the majority something that is and was important to a small minority. After all, some of the things that mark off many science teachers, all scientists and most science curriculum developers from the great majority of their peers is their interest in scientific knowledge as such and their willingness to persist in its learning.

It is neither surprising nor unnatural that persons educated extensively in science should look at the world and at schooling through eyes that are very conditioned by scientific knowledge. This, however, means that what they see as important, significant and worthy of learning is likely to be rather different from what persons uneducated in science see when they look to science as a phenomenon in their lives and in society.

For example, the person educated in science is likely to differentiate fairly clearly between science and technology. Many ordinary citizens draw no such distinction and when asked for examples of science give technologies they have experienced or heard about. Again, those educated in science give a priority to precise definition and explanations while the others are more interested in information and how to apply it.

Science educators, part of the educated in science, have tended to set out to create science education for schools that mirror their own (or science's) priorities. Hence the emphases on conceptual knowledge and on the intellectual processes that are used with, and in the generation of this sort of knowledge.

If we are to progress with science for all, it may well be necessary to reverse this process rather radically. If we are serious in our claims that science and our technological society affects, and can contribute to the lives of all citizens, then it is some of these points of contact and potential that we may need to identify.

This will involve a view of science from society rather than the other way round. It suggests that non-scientists may become rather essential members of the curriculum teams for science for all—a radical thought indeed. Science educators will still be needed to see how educational science can be drawn on and experiences can be made available so that these points of contact are illumined for the learners as they acquire knowledge and skills about them.

Some of the issues that will need to be faced if science for all is to succeed relate to the structural support, the possible content, the teacher support, and the population outside schools.

What is needed if science for all into succeed?

Systems of schooling and the organization of the curriculum. If the earlier analysis of the competing and conflicting interests of the education in the sciences for the elite training group and a science education for all is accepted, it will be important that this be acknowledged by the system and in the organization of any curriculum for science for all.

Some possible steps to deal with the competitive power of the education in the sciences of the elite training group are the following:

Step 1. Elite or traditional education in the sciences might be confined to (and not allowed to occur below) some agreed upper level of schooling—a containment policy.

Step 2. It might be identified for what it is—a limited and particular form of science education that is a precursor to specialized education in the sciences rather than 'science education' more generally.

Step 3. It might be retained as a possible course of study within the total curriculum, but only as one of the forms of science education that a school offers. If some of these alternative forms of science education are also mandatory for the elite training group the possibilities of these other forms of science education gaining acceptance, meaning and likelihood of success would be enhanced.

Each of these will now be considered in a little more detail.

Step 1. Containment Policy. A policy of containment means what it says. The education of the training elite in the sciences does not occur below the agreed level. Systems that operate a stream of education for this elite alongside a curriculum that attempts to provide a science education for the rest are not an example of containment. This is a policy of unfair competition with everything stacked against the science for the rest.

A few countries still see the primary/secondary transition as the appropriate level for containment since secondary education is only for an elite. However, a number of countries in this region are now in a position that does enable the level of containment to be raised if they so determine.

For example, Thailand has recently moved to a 6, 3, 3 structure with specific science curricula associated with each of the blocks of schooling levels. The separate groups of students who are still in schools for the last three years also, in this case, all study some form of science education. This organizational structure is shown in Figure 27.2 on the following page, and appears to provide very real possibilities for effective science for all that are lacking in many other countries' organization of schooling. The selective and preparatory type of science education is contained within the final three years of schooling.

In this organization of schooling, science is part of every level of schooling for all learners. There is a common science curriculum in the primary and lower secondary years. After these nine years of schooling, some pupils continue for more specialized academic or vocational education. In the academic schools there are so-called science and humanities streams. The former students study physics and chemistry and biology while the latter study another advanced but more generalized science curriculum. The students in the various vocational streams each have an associated science curriculum designed to support their vocational goals.

This organization clearly takes science very seriously as a part of the total curriculum of all school pupils. It also avoids some serious problems that exist in countries like the United Kingdom, Australia and the United States. Each of these have many students in the later years of secondary schooling studying no science at all and most of those who do not take the specialized sciences only take biology or the two physical sciences. This situation has the disastrous consequence that primary teachers (vital persons if there is to be effective science for all) tend to be drawn from these non-science secondary students or from the biology only group.

Figure 27.2. The structure of schooling in Thailand and its organization of science curricula

Level	Year			
Upper Secondary schooling	3 2 1	vocational Schools Specially designed science courses	Academic schools Science stream: Physics, Chemistry, biology	Humanities stream: Physical science
Lower Secondary schooling	3 2 1	General Science (all pupils)		
Primary schooling	6 5 4 3 2 1	Primary Science (all pupils)		

How will containment affect manpower supply?

At whatever level containment is to be established it is important to consider the possible or likely effect of this policy on the manpower supply process. The evidence from existing practice is not decisive. There are countries which begin the teaching of the above selective and preparatory type of science early in the secondary years. Others postpone the serious development of this type of science education until the third or even fourth year of secondary education, although they usually have a sequential form of mathematics so that achievement in that subject is still used as a lone selection device. There are examples of both developed and developing countries in each pattern. Established patterns thus do not provide an answer. Moreover, the content of the sciences that is learnt by the elite training group at the end of secondary schooling is surprisingly similar in most countries where there is six years of secondary education. This fairly common level of learning is achieved by the elite regardless of their number of years of formal science education. There is thus no inherent need to spend four, six or eight years of slow build up of this sort of scientific knowledge.

There is also the size of the training group to consider. There seems to be a particularly strong argument for the level of containment to be as high as feasible in countries where widespread retention in schooling is not yet established and the pool for the training group is still too small. The appearance at an early level of a difficult and excluding type of science education with its obvious cultural incongruities for the majority population would seem to be unhelpful to an expansion of the pool of learners from which the elite training group is to emerge.

The answer to the question cannot be given because there has not been sufficient experience of containment underpinned as this paper intends by an effective science education for all. If it is effective then there is little doubt that the pool for the training elite will be larger and of better quality. Two or three years of deliberate education in the sciences should then be adequate. If the science for all below the level of containment is ineffective the training pool could be weakened. It is, however, not usual to move forward on a project expecting it to be a failure.

Step 2. Identification as Academic Science. If a containment policy is established, the traditional and academic education in the sciences will begin *above* the level of containment and be available to all who wish to be considered for this preparation for the ultimate possibility of a science-based career.

Because it has to fulfil this preparatory (and selective) function the curricula for this form of science education is constrained to place a heavy emphasis on systematic factual knowledge that enables the basic and powerful concepts and principles of the science disciplines to be rapidly presented. In order that simple examples of these principles can be learnt and practised by these pupils, the real world becomes severely approximated with frictionless surfaces, ideal gases, biological classifications, and solutions in which concentrations can be used as if they were activities, etc. Many concepts will be introduced even though the empirical phenomena for which they exist cannot be shared with the pupils. The conceptual or theoretical aspects of the disciplines tend to be the controlling determinants of the content.

Judging by many examples of recent curricula at this level there is only limited room for the history of the subject, the study of its applications or its related technology, its societal and cultural impact, or its more exciting recent and contemporary frontiers.

In other words, the curricula of academic secondary science is an important but rather limited view of the rich-field we know as the sciences.

If an effective science for all can be established in schools below this level of containment, then some of these richer views of the sciences will have been shared with all pupils in the earlier years. The academic sciences will then be taken by some pupils for the proper reason that it exists in the curriculum and not for a mistaken sense that it is chemistry or physics or biology and that any other aspects of science are inferior.

Step 3. Parallel curricula for science education above the containment level. The existence of alternative curricula for science education above the level of containment would also be helpful in clarifying the purpose of academic science education. These of course exist already in a number of countries. Physical science in Thailand, is an example (see Figure 27.2) and is part of the total curriculum for the learners in the humanities streams of this level of schooling. As mentioned above, this is a major advance on the situation in Australia where biology has been pressed into the role of being the science subject taken by many non-science learners in senior secondary schooling and most states offer no alternatives to physics and chemistry. This damages academic biology in schooling and provides a very unbalanced education in science for most of its learners.

Some countries also do have alternative courses of science education in their vocational secondary schools or in the vocational streams of comprehensive schooling.

Despite the existence of these alternative courses for science education, it is possible to suggest that a number of them are not yet designed to serve the needs of most of their pupils within the intention of science for all. The problem again lies in the way science is defined in these alternative courses as learning of worth. When the content of these alternative science courses and the real priorities for their learning (as indicated by examinations) are mapped, it is usual for them to be not very different in emphasis and kind from the academic science subjects. Fewer concepts and phenomena are covered than in the academic curricula, and the quantitative aspects are reduced, but the expected learning is still largely characterized by conceptual and factual recall. The fact that conceptual coverage does not need to be so extensive has not been used nearly enough to allow a broader study of topics to be undertaken so that the interface between their science content and other fields becomes apparent to these senior students.

The content of a 'Science for all' in schools. Below the level of containment, wherever it is set, there will be a number of years of schooling in which all or most of the children of a society will be able to be offered science education. If it is to meet the concern behind this project, this science education must have in its content those aspects of human living that will be improved by studying in and from the sciences. In other words the content must be so compelling that everybody should have a chance to learn it.

Earlier in the paper a number of characteristics of schools' traditional education in the sciences were given. By using the converse of some of these and considering the concern and intention behind science for all, it is possible to list a number of characteristics that may be useful check-points for discussion as the science education below the level of containment is developed.

Some Possible Characteristics of a 'Science for all'

1. It should involve content that has immediate and obvious personal and social relevance to the learners. That is, it ought to begin as extension of what the learners already know from their experiences prior to schooling.

2. Its learning objectives (practical skills and knowledge) should have criteria of achievement that most learners can realize.

3. Its broad themes, topics or sections should constantly be visible to elucidate the component parts of the learning.

4. Its pedagogy should exploit the demonstration mode that is both inherent to much science and to the cultural learning that occurs pre- and outside of schooling.

5. The learning of practical and cognitive skills should flow naturally from the relevant and meaningful nature of the science topics rather than be a primary focus of the learning themselves.

6. Its assessment should recognize both the prior knowledge that the learners have of scientific phenomena and their subsequent achievements in all the various sorts of criteria of learning that make up the curriculum.

A next set of decisions will be those that begin to identify content that may meet these characteristics. As we so often find ourselves falling back on the past for our ideas, the list of sorts of content for learning in science education is longer than usual. Science is a really rich field of human endeavour and there are so many aspects of it that might become part of the curriculum and usually do not.

When the word 'content' is used in this paper it means the totality of the intended learning in science that makes up a course for study at some level of science education. The 'content' for science education can be made up of a number of different types of learning. Some of these are:

(a) knowledge—facts, concepts and principles used in science (thus knowledge content becomes a component of the total 'content');

(b) applications of knowledge—the direct and less direct use of concepts and principles of science to real or idealized situations;

(c) process skills—the intellectual skills like classifying control of variables, use of models, prediction from data, that are commonly used in science;

(d) practical skills—certain operations involving various sorts of equipment and instruments are common ways scientists investigate the natural world;

(e) problem solving—the combination of scientific knowledge and intellectual skills to solve theoretically presented problems. If practical skills are added, the solution may be actually carried out by the learner;

(f) science traits and attitudes—the pursuit and progress of science has often been associated with traits like honesty of observation and reporting, open-mindedness re-explanation and phenomena, sharing of results, and these combined are one sort of science attitude. Another set of attitudes are those that relate the learner to scientists and what science represents in the society locally, nationally and globally. There is also the attitude to science as a subject for study, for pursuit in leisure, and as a potential course of employment;

(g) applications of science and technology—an application of science or example of technology involves scientific knowledge that often comes from a number of science disciplines. The performance of a socially required task is the reason for the application of technology. In practice, there will also be a number of social implications of these performances that extend beyond the initiating task.

(h) personal and social needs—in all societies there is an existing set of personal and social operations that involve scientific knowledge and there is a great potential for sharing and harnessing this knowledge so that these needs are met better and more equitably;

(i) the evolution of scientific knowledge—science is a human invention which is expanding and changing. Some appreciation of the way this occurs can be obtained in a number of ways that could involve history of science, specially developed sets of experiences, and expository accounts; and

(j) boundaries and limitations of science—science and its applications can be helpful but sometimes it has been harmful. In critically appreciating science it is important to reiterate that popular knowledge and traditional views are also powerful and important. Science can only contribute in limited ways to many modern problems.

These possible components of the 'content' of science education apart from the first two familiar or traditional ones have been elaborated in some detail and with a more than usual degree of differentiation. The usual triad of *knowledge, skills and attitudes* has become too glib and too easily obscures the rich possibilities for science education in schools. This cryptic triad has also very often been interpreted as the same as the cognitive, psychomotor and affective domains of some learning classifiers, or as associable with the classroom, the laboratory and the overall experience of learning a science subject.

By and large with very few exceptions, the science curriculum projects of the 1960s and 1970s set out to extend science as it was known in the curriculum of elite secondary schooling to a much wider cross-section of school learners. In other words, the content and topics of these elite science curricula were taken as the knowledge of science that was worth learning and the projects spent their energies on devising new presentations and forms of pedagogy which it was hoped would achieve this goal of more and more learners acquiring some or all of this knowledge.

If science was to be taught earlier and to a much wider cross -section of pupils, there were obvious problems that its 'content' should not lead to overlap or endless repetition through schooling with what would in due course be taught to the elite training group.

Because of the heavy emphasis on knowledge content in the advanced science course for the elite group, one of the obvious ways to avoid this overlap was to emphasize another commonly recognized aspect of scientist's science, namely, the general umbrella often referred to as'scientific methods'. This also avoided the problem of deciding which knowledge content (factual and conceptual) was so important that it could be agreed to be appropriate for all these young learners.

So the most common and influential of the new approaches of the 1960s and 1970s were those that emphasized the cognitive processes that are used in the sciences for ordering observations, deriving measured records of material objects and events, developing generalizations about them, and then applying them to other like situations. This emphasis on the process skills of science (as well as, or as a means to traditional knowledge content) was also fairly readily linked to the more broadly based pedagogical approach that has been described as discovery, activity or experience-based learning. A pedagogical interpretation of Piaget's developmental studies of children's thinking, or the influence of other psychologists like Bruner was taken as a basis for this purposeful use of science's traditional laboratory. That is, practical work could be a source of science learning rather than merely be a demonstration or a confirmation of it.

These attempts to elevate the intellectual processes of science, to a status equal to or approaching science knowledge as learning of worth have failed in most cases. Most of the projects naively underestimated the power of the knowledge content of science as being learning of worth and as what teachers and learners alike perceive science largely to be.

As stated earlier, it is the degree of absorption of this sort of knowledge content (factual and theoretical) in an encyclopaedic fashion that marks off those learners who have traditionally succeeded in school science and even throughout the undergraduate years of most university science degrees. Few secondary school teachers go further than this level of science education themselves, and the worth of this knowledge content has been reinforced for them by the examinations they themselves passed year by year. Most primary school teachers, furthermore, are persons who also learnt by failing in these sorts of science tests that this was what science learning involved and that they themselves wee not very capable of it.

The popular presentation of scientists does involve some vague notion of experimenter but more strongly it again emphasizes scientific information—a name of this or an explanation of that, the basis of a new property or a novel and better product.

Research on school children has also suggested that they see the knowledge answers to questions as science and not the question itself in any equivalent manner. Likewise, the Learning in Science Project in New Zealand reported that science teachers themselves were very vague about the processes of science whereas they had no difficulty in listing the knowledge to be taught.

Some of the science curriculum projects like Nuffield Junior Science and the first Victorian (Australia) primary project so emphasized enquiry processes that particular content became almost irrelevant—a mere starting point for a trail of exploration. These two projects were largely rejected by primary teachers because of their lack of structure and specificity. Science—A process approach (in the United States and elsewhere) had plenty of structure and was more successful for that reason, but its gains were not reinforced by the content dominated secondary science that followed. Some of its adaptations as in Trinidad and Tobago tried to add sequential traditional knowledge to SAPA processes; but the knowledge content then tended to rapidly become what the course was about.

Elementary Science Study in the United States had the enquiry emphasis of Nuffield but this was not within a series of selected topic areas. The Science Curriculum Improvement Study had more traditional knowledge content added to an initial development of process skills. Brandwein's Concepts in Science (also the United States) had the least emphasis on process and the greatest amount of traditional knowledge content. Each of these had obvious knowledge content that could swamp the process learning which frightened the teachers, and each required a revision of later curriculum if overlap and repetition was avoided.

In the 1970s, Science 5-13 in the United Kingdom provided much clearer process skills to be learnt and tried to exploit knowledge content areas like wood, toys and other hobby areas that would not conflict with traditional science, and that were good contexts for the priority of process learning. In cases like this, there was, however, the danger that the process skills would lose the association with science (and hence their potential status for learning). A number of primary teachers did interpret the processes of these courses as ones they already taught more comfortably in social science contexts.

The intended priority for process learning in all these science courses raises other quite fundamental problems at the levels of basic schooling where classes tend to be large and teachers are generalists. This problem stems from the learning sequence for such process skills, its optimal human content (a small group), and the role required of the teacher (a clever and purposeful questioner acting as a steering chairperson of the group). Figure 27.3 attempts to set out this sequence.

While some teachers may be able to cope with it with one small group, it was not practicable or possible for most teachers in the large class setting. Others found the open ended nature of the learning threatening and many were very unaccustomed to such a subjugation of their role as knowledge transmitters.

This analysis of the problems of trying to make the learning of science process skills the priority content of science courses at the lower levels of schooling, where all learners are still present, seems to have led to a double bind or 'Catch 22' situation. If the processes are not associated with meaningful and acknowledged content, they will lose value. If they are associated with meaningful knowledge content of science, they will be lost in the face of this content of worth and in any case they are not necessary aspects of its learning.

Is there a way out of this dilemma?

There is, if quite fresh sorts of knowledge content from science are considered as the source of the 'content' of a science for all. Because this sort of 'content' emphasizes the application of worthwhile science knowledge it more naturally involves in its learning both the knowledge and the process skills (practical

Figure 27.3. The teaching/learning sequence for the acquisition of intellectual process skills used in science

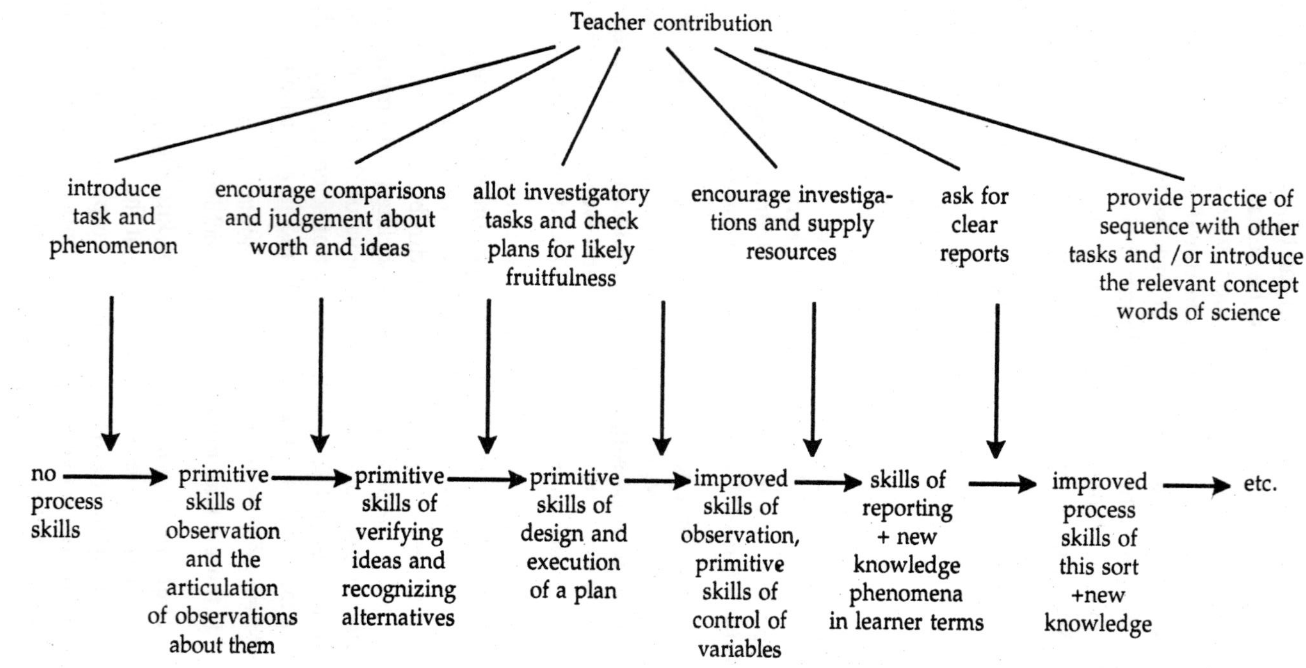

skills and a number of other components from the 'content' list at the beginning of this section are also involved).

Suggestions to establish such a fresh 'content' for the science education of all learners at school were made at the British Commonwealth Curriculum Workshop in Cyprus (March 1982). This meeting set out to spell out a minimum core of 'content' that *all* children should be given an opportunity to learn through the science education of schooling. This did not mean that this minimum core of science learning would be the only offering science education would make to the school population. Particularly for those who continue with the higher levels of secondary education there should be number of other forms (including the traditional ones) and opportunities for science learning.

The Workshop was asked to give a new priority to designing this minimum core and certainly not to be constrained by what has existed before or by trying to extrapolate downwards from the traditional science courses of selective secondary education.

The report of this Workshop indicates that the first step in determining the content of this sort of science education for all is to set up quite clear criteria against which available and new ideas for content can be checked.

The criteria that wee set up by this Workshop were:

1. The content (science knowledge and associated skills) should have social meaning and usefulness for the majority of learners; or

2. The content (science knowledge and its associated skills) should assist learners to share in the wonder and excitement that has made the development of science such a great human and cultural achievement.

By 'social meaning and usefulness', the first criterion meant that this learning would have the potential of directly enabling the learners to enhance and improve their life in their families and as citizens of the society in which they live. That is, this criterion is strongly pragmatic and any content chosen within it would be readily recognized as useful by the learners teachers, parents and community authorities.

The second criterion again requires a careful choice of natural phenomena (easily available to the learners and their teachers) that will make learning with the elements of wonder and excitement (when taught well) possible in these basic levels of schooling. In other words, this criterion rules out those many wonderful aspects of science which are reduced to prose descriptions or formulae in school science textbooks and that can only be learnt by reception of passed on verbal knowledge from the teaches to their pupils.

It was not intended that the criterion of social usefulness could be met if the essential 'use' of the content knowledge to be learnt is that it would be a basis for further science learning in the latter years of schooling. This sequential aspect of much science learning is, of course, important in the science those exploring a career in science may take later in their schooling. The first criterion is meant to be concerned, however, with justifications that are more externally relevant and in the comparatively short-term. Sequential usefulness is a bonus but not a justification in itself.

These two criteria enabled the Workshop to list 12 broad topic fields within each of which it could be readily seen that there were a number of examples of mini-curricula that would meet the criteria. These broad topics are listed in Table 27.1 and the associated broad justification in the report for two of them is shown under the list of topics.

It may seem that this approach is heavily knowledge-centred and that it has discarded process and skills altogether. This is by no means the case. Practice and encouragement of the acquisition of both intellectual processes (like careful observation, classifying, control of variables, prediction, etc.) and practical skills (like measurements, testing, construction, planting, etc.) were very much seen to be regular aspects of the basic science learning in school. They are, however, in this approach always associated with, or embedded in the learning of meaningful knowledge content. The knowledge content is chosen to have ready justification and acceptance by both the scientific and public communities. This in turn, it is argued, will lend more credence and status to the processes and skills that are also very much part of the intended learning.

Table 27.1. Umbrella topics for a basic minimum case of science education in schools (Cyprus Workshop)

1. The senses and measurement as extension of the senses
2. Our universe
3. The human body
4. Health, nutrition and sanitation
5. Food
6. Ecology
7. Resources (natural and man-made)
8. Population
9. Pollution
10. Energy use
11. Technology.
12. Quality of life

Examples of justification

Topic 1. Human beings explore the world around them through their senses. The use of these senses and technology related to them enables man to make a record of the world around him.

Measurement is a way human beings compare and communicate about objects, phenomena, space and time. There are many measuring instruments in existence that form part of our civilization. Measurement both extends our senses and overcomes limitations of them.

Topic 10. Efficient use of energy resources is a pressing personal and social need everywhere. All countries need to lower their dependence on imported energy resources and to reduce wastage. Understanding of efficiency in energy use can lead to an enhanced quality of personal and family life.

The outcome of the Workshop thus does not argue for abandoning science processes and skills as a lost cause in basic science education. Rather it suggests that such learning goals are a lost cause unless they are associated with knowledge content that has a strong claim in its own right as scientific knowledge of public with.

At this basic level of science education the treatment of topics will need to match the levels of ability and the interests of the learners. With the socially useful focus for the learning outcomes, the knowledge to be learnt will be more informed by (or based on) scientific knowledge than it will be the scientific knowledge itself. More recent approaches to the teaching of nutrition are of this type.

Rather than aim at knowledge of carbohydrates, proteins, vitamins, fats and minerals (common and appropriate in more advanced science education) as what is to be learnt under nutrition or foods, the knowledge to be acquired now under nutrition is that nutritious diets are more likely if each day's meals draw from each of the four groups, meat and fish, cereals and bread, fruit and vegetables, milk and milk products. Provided the process and practical skills of using this classification are also learnt, learners with this applied scientific knowledge are in a better position to improve nutrition than many more advanced students have been who acquired some knowledge of the chemistry of foods but often did not reach the point of making it operational as a nutritious diet. This leaves the food topic (No. 5) to deal with the important aspects of sources, production, preservation and distribution of various basic and relevant foods.

Support for Teachers

What help will teachers need? The experiences in every country have confirmed the generalization that the successful implementation of curricular innovations depends very greatly on the support that is given to the teachers in the classrooms. There will be no doubt that any developments of science for all will mean that teachers on whom we must rely for their implementation will need to be assisted with resources, and with in-service education.

These measures of personal support for teachers will not get far unless there is clear structural, organizational and administrative support. Some aspects of this type of support were elaborated earlier in this paper. The role of school principles is so important that they should be prime audiences for in-service education as without their understanding and co-operation it would be a waste for many teachers to try to equip them with appropriate skills and knowledge.

Whatever role examinations and tests play in a particular system, it will be most important that these powerful social instruments change in step with what is to be implemented in school. In the last 20 years so many good ideas in science curricula have foundered because they have not been confirmed and reinforced by the examinations that carry so much weight and influence. If a feature is worth learning it ought to be a regular feature of any tests of learning. It may be that paper and pencil testing is very inappropriate for some features of the 'content' for learning. If so, we should not leave them out but rather find new modes for the assessment of these features.

Undoubtedly new materials to support these sorts of curricula will need to be developed, and as hinted above, some rather novel persons may need to be part of this development team. Practising teachers will need to be very involved with the development since this will keep the project's feet firmly on the ground and because any involvement in the developmental stages is easily the best form of in-service education.

It will be interesting to see the reactions of teachers at the basic levels of schooling. Some of the topics of 'Science for all' are likely to be familiar to them and in other guises may have had a place in the total curriculum. Probably the topics in general may be less threatening because they are not so scientific (in the esoteric or trivial senses) as a number of the earlier basic science courses were seen by teachers to be. Topics that are more meaningful to the pupils should also be more appropriate to the teachers, and this may assist the new learning about them that many teachers will have to undertake through in-service education, or as they draw on the curriculum resource materials for their teaching of these new topics and courses.

We cannot expect rapid changes in the ways teachers interact with their pupils but these changes will occur faster if encouraged and supported in the ways suggested above.

Earlier in the paper two teaching/learning sequences have been mentioned. The one for conceptual knowledge (Figure 27.1) is relatively easy for teachers who have confidence in their own grasp of this type of knowledge. However, it has inbuilt features which make it a learning sequence that will have a higher failure rate for learners. The second one for learning process skills (Figure 27.2) seems to have reasonably higher learning rates but is very difficult for teachers to sustain in classroom settings and particularly with the class sizes that are common in this region. There are several other teaching/learning sequences with potential when some of the likely content of science for all is considered. The first is shown in Figure 27.4 and is the sequence for practical skill acquisition.

Figure 27.4. The teaching/learning sequence for the acquisition of a practical skill

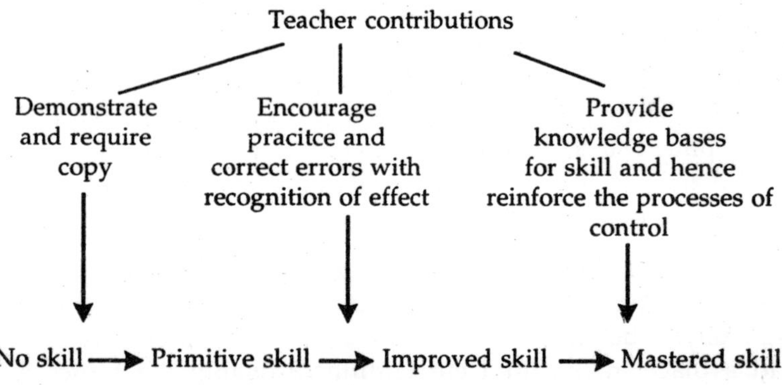

This is a learning sequence with high learning possibilities at least to the penultimage stage. It is not easy to teach to all pupils in large classes as it often consumes materials, needs space and a degree of skill expertise in teachers that they may well need encouragement to acquire.

A final pedagogy to mention is the teaching/learning of a scientific social issue, an application of science, or an example of technology. This is shown in Figure. 27.5.

Here there is no preferred or logical sequence apart from some personal experience (direct or simulated). After that the teacher and learners can approach the focus to be learnt from any of the directions that link them to it, each one of which adds more learning to the always obvious object of study. It is not necessary to complete all the approaches. This model of learning is rather different from the others and would seem to have great possibilities as it may be easier for teachers in class settings. Its obvious motivational focus and diverse possible approaches also offer something for many different sorts of learners.

Along several of these approaches each of the three previous teaching/learning sequences has potential and teachers can pick and choose between them as their confidence and experience allows.

Figure 27.5. Learning model for the acquisition of knowledge about issue, application or technology

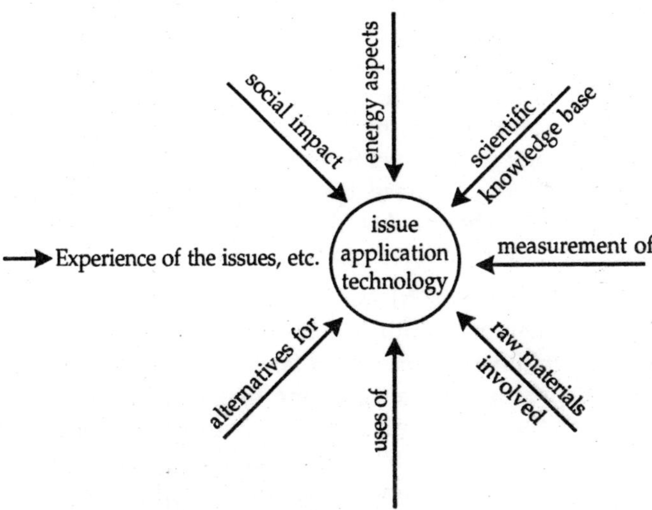

The Out-of-School Populations

What about the science for those beyond the schools? As the writer's own experience has been so largely confined to the formal system of education (including schools, colleges and universities), this paper has been inevitably biased to that part of science for all that occurs in schools. This bias is likely to be present in many meetings on this topic as those responsible for the vast and diverse population outside schools are much less organized, articulate, or even identified when compared with the representatives of school education.

It is, therefore, very important that we note that there may be many quite different educational issues in the science for those 'all' who are outside schools. The time this population has available for learning will vary considerably as persons out-of-school are very heterogeneous. Some types of workers may be encouraged by employers to attend short educational sessions. Others may only have precious leisure time. In any case, the process of teaching/learning will need to be more compressed than in school. As museum educators are learning, and the mass media have always know, adult learning is a more staccato affair. Motivation, for sections of the adult population will have to be quickened, precise knowledge presented, and consequential behaviour indicated in each segment of learning. For other adult groups motivation will be high and their need for learning will be clear. The dependence on the written word, for most adults as for pre-school children, has to be much reduced. There are many adult pedagogies available. Schools and school educators are not very practised in these types of education. Hence, 'science for the out-of-school all' is likely to only get a little way if it is planned by extrapolation from 'science for the school all'.

In 1982 the Unesco ROEAP published a report on Out-of-school science in member countries. This report indicated the variety and the patchiness of efforts so far in these areas. It also devoted (not surprisingly because of the bias of its writers) a large amount of its text to efforts that extend the science education of the school population (or probably the elite within that population) by using time and resources beyond the schools' time-tables and walls. If the out-of-school population is to be reached, quite radical initiatives will probably need to be used and less conventional sources (i.e. outside Ministries of Education) placed in charge.

One useful model for identifying the type of science education that may be useful for particular groups in the out-of-school population is shown in Table 27.2.

Table 27.2. Science education for all—
examples for groups of the out-of-school population

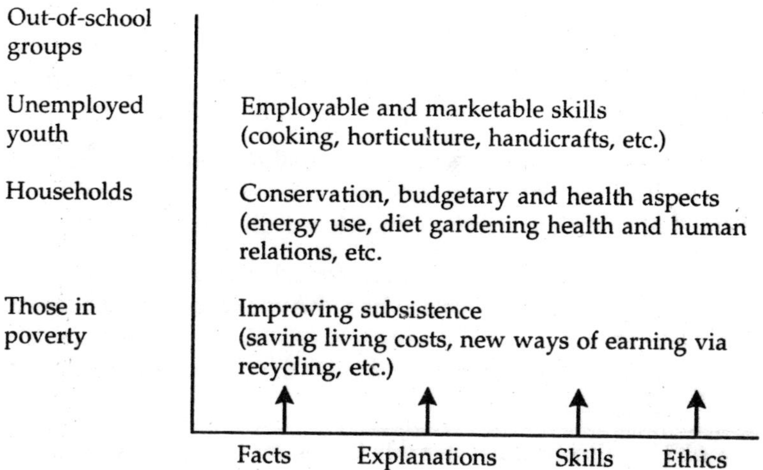

For each group on the vertical axis of the model, a number of needs are identified which could change the quality of their lives. Where science education has a contribution to make to these needs its component aspects of *facts, explanations, skills* and *ethics* are then identified as the content for learning. Appropriate pedagogies will then need to be devised. Educators will have contributions to make at some of these points.

The types of organizations that will best service and provide these educational opportunities for the out-of-school population will be quite diverse and will vary from country to country. Its target population certainly include all school-age children but go far beyond them to the adult and other out-of-school groups.

Unlike schooling systems which exist to service certain well—defined school populations with well-established procedures and organizations, there are many other types of organization both formal (under political ministries other than education) and informal, that have access to the wider target populations of science for all.

It may well be that the interests of these different sources of educational provision will need to be considered very separately. A focus on the interests of one source, e.g. the school system, will not necessarily flow on to the others. Only when these different sorts of providers recognize each others' roles are there likely to be fruitful interactions and positive outcomes.

Summary

1. There is a new recognition that science has much to contribute to the lives of all members of a society.
2. One substantial way the availability and evenness of this contribution can be improved is to make an appropriate science education available.
3. Such a 'Science education for all' will need to occur in school at the levels when the maximum numbers of pupils are present, and out-of-school in ways which affect many different groups in the post-school and adult populations.
4. In all countries, there is in the system of schooling an education in the sciences which serves the needs of an elite group from whom the future scientists and science-related professionals will be drawn.
5. It is argued that this important education in the sciences has been an inappropriate model for a science for all. Much of the failure of earlier attempts (1960s and 1970s) to extend science education to all pupils in school can be related to the conflict between the needs of these two forms of science education.
6. A science for all must have a content for learning that is recognized as worthwhile by the learners, their parents, employers, community leaders, It also must draw from the best understandings of science that are relevant to its various purposes.
7. Earlier science curricula for the general levels of schooling over-emphasized the processes of science and did not solve the problem of meaningful knowledge content.
8. Some new insights about meaningful content are now available.

9. Teachers, as with any innovation, will need assistance. This will not succeed if it stops at the usual forms of curriculum materials and personal in-service education. It will be most important that administrative, organizational and structural supports are provided that match the intended learning of science for all.

10. The education of the out-of-school populations in a science for all programme will be very different in kind from what happens in schools. Accordingly, it should not be planned by extrapolating from what is planned for, or is taking place in schools. It needs its own priorities and its own planners.

28

'Science For All'—The Strategies Involved and Problems Encountered in Reaching the Mass—The Indian Experience

D.C. GOSWAMI

Regional Research Laboratory, Jorhat, India

India really is a land of contrast. Here, the high science and technology of space and electronics go hand in hand with the bullock cart; atomic energy goes side by side with cowdung burning; highly sanitary conditions and nutritious food in big hotels go along with the stinky slums where penniless, jobless dwellers live in a primitive state. But the fruits of science and technology have percolated not only to the sophisticated urban life but to the simple life of the remote village which outwardly looks undisturbed by the change. The man in the remote village also occasionally listens to the radio, uses a contraceptive device, swallows a tablet, sprays insecticides, takes a bath with a cake of soap, rides a bicycle and a bus and receives a telegram. He may even be luckier and be able to see an instructional telecast, or a movie shown by a social welfare body that encourages him to get his children inoculated and vaccinated, to sow a high-yielding, disease-resistant variety of seed in his fields or to get his wife tubecotomized.

The course of science and technology has also touched the life of almost every Indian (like his counterpart in any other part of the world). The shock of rapid change and the unmanageable emotional adjustments; the ill effects of land, water and air population; the tilted balance of the ecosystem—all have echoed and re-echoed in his life either in an urban or rural environment.

Why Teach Science?

Thinkers opine that the practical value of every social invention or material discovery depends upon its being adequately interpreted to the masses. History also affords abundant evidence that civilization advances in direct ratio to the efficiency with which the thoughts of the thinkers are translated into the language of the masses. Hence the utmost need to improve public understanding of science. Scientific enterprise is expensive. India spends nearly US $900 million every year for research and development in science and technology, and India's sixth five-year socio-economic plan (1980-85) which recognizes science and technology as an important sector, envisages an outlay of $4,250 million in this sector. This huge financial support—fantastic as it is for a developing country like India—requires knowledgeable overseeing by the public.

Moreover, science yields practical consequences that require public decision-making: to fluoridate or not to fluoridate the public drinking water supply; to finance dialysis centres or not to finance them; to launch satellities and fund research and development agencies or to invest that huge fund for supplying the barest necessities to the public; are amongst a host of issues of a similar nature demanding public decision. Above all, science has been mankind's greatest intellectual adventure, as much a part of man's culture as music or art or literature. It is therefore imperative that every entity of the society participates in the decisions on and the activities of science.

For science education to be self-sustaining and self-generating, the general fabric of society will have to be rewoven with the weft strengthened by scientific methods and outlook. Any effort at science education which does not take the whole society as the target and which concentrates on a small advantageous group, will be heavily dempened. India has seen tremendous emphasis being placed on the delivery of science education to a small target group, viz. the children in school, during the last two decades. The mushrooming of schools and colleges throughout the country during the last few years is ample evidence of this. Enormous expansion has taken place in the science education delivery system also. But the number of school drop-outs had been frightening. Sixty-four per cent of the school-going children drop out before they reach grade V (about ten years of age) rising to 77 per cent before reaching grade VIII (about 13 years of age). Apart from this huge out-of-school population generated by the school drop-outs, a large percentage of the children of school-going age do not go to school at all—thus contributing to the vastness of the group.

Then there are the illiterate millions who cultivate their fields with the age-old traditional skills and equipment, work in factories in the same routine manner in unhygienic conditions, and who believe in the power of charms and talismen rather than in modern diagnostic and therapeutic methods when afflicted by disease. They are governed by superstitious beliefs in all aspects of life including health and habits, food and sex. They are poor people with their thoughts centred round their means of livelihood.

The group of literate, educated people living mainly in the urban centres also has its roots in the broader Indian society and is no different in its outlook and habits than any other group of people.

Moreover, India is a land of diversity—it has a large number of tribes, clans and races who speak different tongues, follow different goods and rituals and live in a variety of environments distinguishable from one another historically, culturally and geographically.

Therefore for any attempt at science education to be successful it will have to have a broader perspective and will have to keep the needs of the entire society in focus. An integrated approach with a local tinge will be the best prescription of any science education programme.

The Approach

To deliver science education effectively it is convenient to categorize the society into four target groups. These are: (a) the first ten grades of the formal school population, including those who will proceed further with science and technology education; (b) the out-of-school children and youth, including those who should have been in school under the universalizaton of education process; (c) the work force including the vast number of illiterates; and (d) the educated section of the populace.

Two clear questions arise. What science should be taught to each group? What is the most effective way to teach each group?

Certain general comments can be made before dealing with the individual target groups. One important observation is that by enabling only some to obtain a higher familiarity with and competency in science does not make science significantly beneficial to all. For science to benefit the individual it must become a part of everyday life. Therefore, any science education programme will have to identify teaching foci which can take advantage of the natural and social environment of the target groups and clearly establish the utility of science at the personal level. Science must be introduced as a way of investigating and solving problems and as an influence on a set of personal values which can enhance decision-making. While the utility of science and technology at the personal, community and national level must be clearly established, the learner must be informed of the limitations of science and technology also, without, of course, distracting him from the acceptance of its usefulness.

Formal school population. Realizing the importance of science as an integral part of life, India has placed tremendous importance on school science education programmes. Although education is a State subject, most states have accepted the guidelines and curriculum developed by the apex central council, the National Council of Educational Research and Training (NCERT). There is a concerted and integrated effort in curriculum development, teaching aid development and teacher training. The curriculum in science at the first level teaches science through environmental studies. In the first two classes it begins as a composite course including both that natural and social environment, but, in later years it is divided into environmental studies based on natural science, and environmental studies based on social science. The object is not to emphasize any particular content or syllabi but to sharpen the students' senses and train them to observe the environment to enrich their experience.

At the second level, although separate disciplines of physics, chemistry and biology are introduced, the broad perspectives of environmental education are kept so that science is interesting and meaningful to the students.

In spite of all these sincere efforts, the bias towards terminal examination with the old values in mind is the single reason why the expected results have not been achieved so far.

The science content, so far as this target group is concerned, is reasonably decided. How it should be taught remains open, although man trials and experiments have already been carried out. Some suggestions for further improvements could be:

1. Reduce the bias towards the terminal examination as it exists today;
2. Devise an examination system which can really assess the child's ability to use the methods of science;
3. Gradually withdraw textbooks that follow an inflexible syllabus and have an urban bias;
4. Introduce a comprehensive teacher training programme with an emphasis on using the whole environment as a learning experience;
5. Increase the out-of-school science activities for school children;
6. Produce out-of-school reading material in an attractive form and make it available to every school child to open up new vistas of knowledge; and
7. Make more effective use of radio, television, newspapers, posters and wall magazines, for science education, but without bias towards a syllabus.

It must be realized that teaching pupils disconnected scientific facts and meaningless formulas unrelated to the situations in their lives will only generate a negative attitude towards science.

Out-of-school children and youth. In spite of the various efforts and importance given to the programmes for the universalization of elementary education, a large percentage of the children and youth of school-going age remains out of school even today. What science do they need if they need science at all? A strict curriculum and scheduled routine cannot surely be the answer.

This out-of-school portion of the population will form a large percentage of the adult population in future. It requires to know basic health rules and hygiene, and how to prevent accidents. These might include such basic information as the treatment of cuts to prevent tetanus, the importance of sterilizing the baby's feeding-bottle and the possible consequences of not washing hands before eating. People also need to know something of the inexorable laws of physics, so that they do not step in front of a speeding bus, expecting it to stop; and the basis of sound nutrition so that all the body's needs for health are met.

The science education for this group must have a personal touch, and will have to be through a medium which can bring it down to the required level.

The illiterate population. What science should we teach the vast number of illiterate adults in society? Why must we improve the scientific literacy of these adults? A huge number of tragic examples of the superstitions and ignorance of this group can be cited that have led to illness or death. There are people who swallow their own blood from cuts in the hope that it will return to the blood-stream; others will deprive a child with acute diarrhoea from drinking water in the fear that it may enhance loose motions—thus causing fatal dehydration; or they feed their babies on tinned milk instead of breast milk in the belief that it will provide better nourishment.

More important than this is the alienation from science and attachment of some sort of magical and superhuman aura to science and technology by the general public and particularly the illiterate millions. Because of this, the general mass cannot participate in the decision-making, which leads to their exploitation and makes them subject to social manipulation.

A programme already exists, which is being taken up in a very isolated and half-hearted fashion to provide information on certain areas such as the prevention of epidemics, methods of family planning, and methods of use of fertilizers and pesticides. This is actually dissemination of science-related knowledge and not science, because these are bits of information and do not conform to the scientific method which is a logical, regenerative process and which prepares the learner for situations other than the context in which the knowledge has been given.

Science education for this section of the masses therefore has to be of direct relevance, centred round the individual in the society. The farmer, the factory worker or the skilled man will be concerned about his health, his family, his farm output, his productivity in the traditional skills, and his direct environment. His science must begin with these.

The educated section. Although otherwise educated, a large percentage of population in his group also continue to live in a state of scientific illiteracy and with an abhorrence for science. Included in this group is the scientist himself who is also influenced by superstitions and old beliefs and views things in his own life unscientifically once he goes out of the laboratory. While some of the old beliefs and rituals may have some scientific basis and require understanding in the right perspective, others are only blatant superstitions and are social retardants.

The needs of this group in the area of science literacy are not very different from those of the out-of-school and illiterate groups. All three groups require development of perspective and outlook, temperament and inclination.

The literate individual is a more informed consumer and because of his general level of intelligence could potentially use scientific knowledge for his own convenience and may distort information or wrongly interpret it. If he is against development or industrialization of a particular area or establishment of a particular industry, he may take recourse to out-of-proportion propaganda on pollution. Because of his access to media, credibility and megalomania he may distort the impact of a soiar eclipse to create panic to shut people indoors. He needs a better science education.

The Problem and the Strategies

The preceding paragraphs are indicative of science education in India. The variety of languages and dialects, religions and clans, castes and creeds; the disparity in economic conditions; the imbalances created by geographic and environmental conditions; the diversity of culture and tradition in so vast a country as India create myriads of problems for any activity as enormous as science education. The problem of creating a science climate, formidable though it may be, can be solved by sincere efforts. The government, the voluntary science bodies and the community science centres can make immense contribution to this effort.

There are a good number of voluntary science societies and community science centres which aim at popularizing science and creating a scientific literacy amongst the masses. That a voluntary science society can really start what may be called a 'peoples' science movement' can be exemplified by one particular achievement of the Kerala Shastra Sahitya Parishad (KSSP) of Calicut in Kerala. A rayon mill set up by a big business house near the bank of the river Chaliar near Walcad village started polluting the land, water and air. This resulted in respiratory and dermal diseases in man, and tremendous ill effects on plants and other animals. The villagers and assigned these to their fate and accepted everything with only a grumble. KSSP sent a team of medical students to study of the cause and effect of this pollution. When their report clearly indicated the rayon mill as the source of the pollution, a team of experts consisting of doctors, professors and engineers was sent to the village. The experts identified the cause-effect relationship and suggested remedial measures for arresting the pollution. KSSP than started conduction evening classes for the villagers to educate them with facts and figures, based on a scientific study, to build their perspective. The villagers started to agitate and had the rayon mill closed until a sufficient effluent treatment measures was carried out by the firm. KSSP also endeavours to reach even the remotest villagers through a network of volunteers and *jeepjatha* (jeep expedition) and *padajatha* (expedition on foot).

The Assam Science Society at Gauhati (India), apart from bringing out a very popular journal in the local language, runs a students' hobby centre and has started developing a big science complex which includes a modern-type science museum, an open air students' science activity centre, a planetarium, an aquarium and an exhibition ground. Through its many branches in various nooks and corners of the State, the Society carried out lecture demonstration programmes for village schools with the help of local lectures, professors, medical men and engineers. The Society's annual conferences and exhibitions at various towns and villages draw thousands of people from all walks of life.

In its efforts to promote scientific literacy in the country, the Ahmedabad-based, Vikram Sarabhai Community Science Centre has created a unique atmosphere for informal learning. This has helped fulfil, in some measure, the belief of the founder of the Centre that the development of a nation is linked with the understanding and application of science and technology by its people.

The Kishore Bharati Group of Hoshangabad in Madhya Pradesh also carried out various activities for the creation of a science climate in rural Madhya Pradesh and has been successful in generating awareness and scientific literacy amongst the rural masses.

These are only by way of examples. There are many other science societies in the country which are engaged in various science popularization activities such as organizing popular science lectures and demonstrations, running hobby centres and science museums, publishing popular science books and journals, displaying wall papers, organizing exhibitions, holding science talent search tests, running rocket clubs, holding evening classes for neo-literate villagers and, staging dramas based on science themes.

These science clubs have been doing a marvellous job, but the activities are very much localized; there is no central control and guidance mechanism and no interaction amongst these voluntary bodies, so one club cannot take advantage of the experiences of another.

What can the Government do?

The first thing the government can do is to establish a nodal agency which can guide, co-ordinate, plan, monitor and evaluate the activities of science education.

The government may set up a science news service which can effectively disseminate science news along with its perspective instead of allowing the mass media to carry such news in isolated fashion. Incentives can also be offered to the newspapers and magazines to carry science features regularly. These incentives could be in terms of tax relief and supply of newsprint at subsidized prices. More importantly, the government may encourage the voluntary science clubs and societies to co-ordinate their activities with the help of the nodal agency and work with a concerted effort to infuse scientific temper into the masses. The following are some of the important tasks for which the nodal agency can decide and assign priorities.

The Printed Word

(a) Popular science magazines should be brought out in various languages used in the country so that they can reach the various strata of society. Writers and editors will have to be trained to write in a way that conveys meaning and understanding of science to the reader. Scientists must be encouraged to write popular science;

(b) Profusely illustrated popular science books should be brought out in various languages;

(c) Popular literary magazines should be encouraged to carry features and supplements on science and technology;

(d) Science societies should take up the preparation of wall papers and start explaining newspaper reports on science and technology, thus putting them in a better perspective.

Exhibitions, museums and hobby centres. The science societies should be encouraged to hold frequent exhibitions in various localities and set up hobby centres and museums. These should not be static, but should be of a 'do ityourself' type. More and more children should be encouraged to act as demonstrators in these exhibitions, so that they feel a sense of participation.

Lectures, demonstrations and evening classes. Science societies should organize lecture-demonstration expeditions to villages and the local resource persons (like the local development officer, field publicity officer, medical man, or engineer) should be associated with these activities. Advantage of the local situations and problems should always be taken so that the target audience does not take a passive role.

Audio-visuals

(a) Radio and television should devote more time to broadcasts and telecasts on science and technology themes. For better planning of these programmes, directorates may be set up centrally with cells in all regions, separately for radio and television. Workshops should be organized to develop good science and technology communicators;

(b) Popular science films, filmstrips and slides should be produced with the help of experts in science and technology communication and experts in film production. The science societies can be relied upon to take these to the remotest of villages;

(c) Satellite instrúctional programmes similar to the Satellite Instructional Television Experiment (SITE) project, 1975, should be carried out because of its obvious advantages. Community television viewing should be encouraged in the remote areas where television with special antennae can be used;

(d) Traditional theatres, puppet shows, dance and drama programmes can be imaginatively used for transmitting the message of science.

It is now well recognized that the continuation of a medieval outlook and value system and social norms have been a hindrance to the development and integration of Indian society. The sixth five-year socio-economic plan (1980-85) recognizes this and emphasizes:

The task of creating a scientific temper is a vital necessity for the growth of science and its utilization in the development process. There is need to create a scientific climate and involve the people in discussions on various issues of science and technology which affect their life. There has to be dissemination of knowledge about natural phenomena and technological innovations through popular science journals and other media. There is also need for promoting public debate on major issues on science and technology. The full potential of science has to be utilized for eradication of irrational attitudes, which tend to hold back the nation from the path of progress.

29

Practical Work in Science Education

Practical work is a part of science curriculum. Practical work as well as practical examinations in science are far from satisfactory. There is over emphasis on measurement of product of performance while the processes of performance are quite often relegated to the background. The validity and reliability of the practical work and examinations are being affected by disproportionate weightages to different types of practical skills, inadequate number of laboratory exercises, lack of uniform instructions to the experts and examiners, inappropriate marking schemes, etc. The following details on practical work and examinations are the outcome of the Seminars on Practical Examinations and Workshop on Practical Examinations organised by National Council of Educational Research and Training (NCERT), India.

I. OBJECTIVES OF PRACTICAL WORK

It is needless to say that the purpose of science teaching is not only to acquaint the students with the knowledge of scientific facts, concepts and principles, but also to develop practical skills and scientific attitudes in the students, pertaining to these subjects. Science theory contributes a lot to the substantive structure of the subject, more emphasis is given to the development of scientific concepts while the syntactical structure of the subject is relegated to the background. It is only through various mode of inquiry that all scientific concepts and generalizations are arrived at. It is this aspect of science which refers to the development of practical skills. Development of practical skills in science subjects not only leads to learning of scientific concepts but also is instrumental in developing scientific attitudes among the students besides reinforcement of learning. It is, therefore, necessary that while formulating instructional objectives, care may be taken that proper weightage is given to the psycho-motor skills as also to objective in the affective domain which relate to appreciations, interests and attitudes. Psycho-motor skills include manipulative skills, dissectional skills, observational skills, drawing skills reporting skills, etc. All these skills must be taken care of while teaching the science subjects. There is need to define each of these skills into their component skills so that the nature and scope of practical work is properly delineated.

For the realization of the stated objectives various types of activities are to be selected and organized. The factors would select them according to the objectives of the discipline. Practical work, in any case, will play a major role in this respect. It will be based on the knowledge already gained and as such it will reinforce it. Doing with one's own hand leads to better understanding about the processes of science and will enable pupils to apply them to familiar as well as unfamiliar situations. A well organised programme for practical work will develop interest among students and appreciation of environments. Unlike objective in the cognitive domain psycho-motor skills can be developed only by doing practical work. Therefore, development of skills is the most predominant objective of practical work in sciences.

There are various types of skills like those of drawing skills, observational skills, manipulative skills, dissectional skills, collecting, mounting and preserving skills. But in each of these skills we can identify and delimit two aspects of performance. These are:

(a) Process of performance/performance in progress

(b) Product of performance/resultant outcomes

Both these aspects are equally important in teaching and

testing. It will be very desirable to specify them in terms of specific tasks envisaged under each aspect. This specification will help both the teachers and testers. Each branches of science will have slightly different specifications and will have to be separately defined to make them useful to teachers and evaluators.

As an illustration, the specifications of Process of Performance and Product of Performance in Physics are defined as under:

A. Process of Performance

Specifications

The pupil:

1. selects appropriate apparatus, tools, instruments, etc.
2. checks equipment, apparatus, tools regarding their working.
3. detects errors and limitations in the fitting up of apparatus.
4. rectifies errors. If possible, under laboratory situations.
5. sets up apparatus, tools, etc., for an experiment.
6. prepares a systematic and sequential plan for taking observations.
7. records observations in accordance with the design of the experiment.
8. states the principles, formulae and the symbols needs to report results in an experiment.
9. handles apparatus, tools and instruments with care while performing the experiments.
10. measures quantities and reads instruments, apparatus, etc. accurately.
11. takes necessary precautions in handing instruments, chemicals, and materials.
12. makes accurate observations of part, processes, etc.
13. draws graphs relevant to the experimental data whenever necessary.

14. calculates accurately the relationships to draw inferences or conclusions.
15. performs experiments with reasonable speed.
16. performs experiments with reasonable accuracy and precision.
17. performs experiments with neatness and in an orderly manner.
18. adapts himself with somewhat new and different apparatus in setting novel experiments.
19. explains orally the sketches of a given arrangements of apparatus or experimental set-up.
20. dismantles and cleans the apparatus, wherever necessary.
21. arranges the apparatus, substances, etc. at their appropriate places at the end of the work.

B. Product of Performance

Specifications

The pupil:

1. records the observed data in terms of objectives of the experiment in verbal, graphical or numerical form.
2. interprets the data or recorded observations to finalize the results.
3. draws conclusions from the recorded data or observations.
4. identifies the given specimen, apparatus, materials, substances, etc.
5. summarizes the findings to reject or accept a hypothesis.
6. reports the results in a systematic manner using technical terminology, graphs, sketches, etc.

The above list of specification is by a no means exhaustive but only suggestive. Each science subject has it own skills and can be defined separately in terms of processes and products of performance. Specification of drawing, observational, manipulative, dissectional skills, etc., and indicated in skill objectives given under instructional objectives of each subject.

Major purpose of such operational definitions is to enable the teacher to appreciate the hierarchy in development of skills and the sequence needed in development of these skills. It is through continuous evaluation at the various stages of skill development, like imitation, patterning, mastering, applying and improvising, that can help in diagnosing the inadequacies and proficiency in performance on the basis of which remedial programme can be taken up. Moreover, it is this specification of skills in terms of performance in progress or product of performance that provides the basis for instruction and evaluation of skills. It is on the basis of adequate coverage of these skills that a framework or design is worked out for setting question paper on practical examinations in science subjects.

II. IMPLICATIONS FOR TEACHING AND TESTING

Improved pattern of practical examinations discussed in the last few pages will be practicable only if only procedures are properly followed not only in the external examinations but also in school evaluation. Whereas the theoretical work in science is expected to promote pupils' growth mainly in cognitive domain, the practical work does not only promote pupils' growth in the psycho-motor domain but also helps to develop wholesome interests in the subject and scientific attitudes. Thus practical work in science is of great significance in all-around development of the pupils. However, for effective conduct of practical work and improvement of practical examinations the co-operation of different agencies and their special efforts would be required. The improved pattern of practical examinations envisages a number of implications for taking necessary steps by different agencies concerned with the improvement programme. The important agencies are schools, teachers, paper scatters, examiners, departments of education, unless certain conditions are fulfilled it will not be possible to implement the improved pattern of practical examinations. The implications relevant to each to these agencies are listed below:

A. Schools

1. School laboratories will have to be properly maintained

by providing adequate number of sets of the apparatus to provide opportunity to every student to undertake practical work.

2. Schools will have to reduce the rigidity of the time table thus enabling the science teacher and pupils to work with freedom in the organization of various activities such as demonstrations, laboratory work etc.

3. More initiative on the individual teacher and pupils will be needed in conducting such activities related to practical work. Teachers may be encouraged to undertake some projects to study different aspects of these improved procedures.

4. The practical examinations in the school will have to be carried out on the same pattern as recommended for Board Examinations.

5. The results of practical examinations will have to be used for improvement of instructional strategies to develop practical skills among students.

B. Teachers

1. The science teachers will have to change to present outlook towards practical work as merely an activity for verifying or just repeating what is done in the past. The tendency of mechanical repetition of some standard experiments will have to be discouraged. They will realise that this work is meant to develop experimental skills in a systematic manner. They will, therefore, organize the practical work in such a manner so as to realize the above objective of developing various psychomotor skills among students. They may equip themselves by receiving training in this field. For this they may take advantage of the various training courses and workshops and the literature produced in this field.

2. They should encourage the pupils to take initiative in undertaking small projects of practical nature, involving all the types of skills designated in the courses of study or the design provided by the examining agency.

3. They will have to organise the exercise in such a manner that the students get maximum opportunities in acquiring simple skills leading to more complex skills which can be attained as get more and more training and experience in undertaking practical work.
4. The practical exercises should be repeated in order to reinforce the desire skills. It is implied that these exercises will be in conformity with the objectives laid down for practical work.
5. It should always be kept in mind that the practical and theoretical work go hand in hand for effective teaching and learning, and to get better results in terms of proficiency in skills.
6. The teachers will prepare in advance the practical assignments on each expertise for students to make necessary preparation on the basis of which pupils can be allowed to undertake practical work. This is to be followed by practical work in the Laboratory with necessary briefing by the teacher.
7. Special emphasis to inculcate the habit of cleanliness and orderliness during practical work in the laboratory will have to be laid by the teachers.

C. Paper Setters

1. Paper setters of practical examinations will take cognizance of the objectives of practical work. They will set practical exercises to ensure adeqûate coverage of objectives and content as far as possible by giving short as well as long exercises. They will give weightage to different aspects as stipulated by the design supplied by the examining agency.
2. Whenever alternative experiments are to be given the paper setters should ensure that these are comparable in respect of skill tested, difficult level and time requirements.
3. The paper should frame the exercise in a manner that the tasks are clear to the examinees in terms of expected performance.

4. The paper setters will review their papers by preparing an exercise-wise analysis to check whether the requirements of the given design are fulfilled.

5. They will develop a detailed marking scheme as per requirements of the design. The marks will be distributed over various aspects of skill covering all the intended process of performance and product of performance. This detailed marking scheme will be sent to each examiner so that they could follow in during the conduct of practical examination.

6. They will issue necessary instructions which help in proper conduct of practicals and help to minimize the subjectivity in assessment of students and scoring of scripts.

7. They will use the proforma provided by the board for reporting significant details about the performance of pupils or develop one if not provided. Necessary entries regarding pupils' performance, laboratory conditions, services, record etc. are made. Consolidated reports of various examiners can reflect on practical work and suggestions for improvement can be made. This report will act as very useful evidence for schools as a feedback device for improvement of practical work in the institutions.

D. Examiners

1. Examiners will be very watchful throughout the time students are performing their experiments in order to observe the performance in progress and product of performance of the candidates and record them systematically in the scoring sheet provided by the paper setter or the board.

2. They will follow the instructions received by them regarding conduct of examination and scoring of scripts or evaluation of students.

3. If they find a candidate to proceed for want of specific information they should help them by supplying the necessary information. While scoring the performance

of such candidates the marks reserved for related understanding only, may be deducted and credit for showing proficiency in desired skills may be given.

4. If an alternative exercise is to given instead of original exercise for want of equipment the examiners will see that such an exercise is comparable in respect of the specific skills being tested, time requirement and difficulty level of the exercise.

5. They will prepare a very detailed report of their observations and findings about the performance of candidates and sent it to the examining agency in the prescribed reporting proforma. The examining agency will analyse these reports school-wise and send the same to respective institutions for necessary improvement in school practices. These reports will also be useful for the examining agencies for improving the testing procedures related to practical examinations.

E. Examination Agencies and Education Departments

1. School laboratories will have to be better equipped so that they may provide for all the experiments prescribed.

2. Practical syllabi, may be reviewed in terms of objectives of practical work and provision be made to include larger variety of experiments to provide for development of all needed skills.

3. Flexible time-table will have to be permitted so that the students may perform experiments in their spare periods and teachers concerned could organise practical work accordingly.

4. Better inspection and guidance programme will have to be ensured for proper instruction and evaluation of practical work.

5. Only qualified paper setters and examiners with training in paper setting and evaluation will have to be selected for practical examinations.

6. Examinations' reports will have to scrutinized and findings reported to schools for necessary action

regarding improvement of instructional strategies to develop experimental skills among the students.

III. RECOMMENDATIONS

In order to implement the improved pattern of practical examinations following suggestions are made:

A. Syllabus

1. Instructional objectives as stated in the syllabi of science subjects at present are not clearly defined in terms of pupils' behaviour and this creates difficulty in planning appropriate learning experiences for attaining the desired objectives. It is, therefore, absolutely essential that the syllabi in the subjects may be clearly stated and specified for providing proper guidelines for instruction and evaluation.
2. Present syllabi contain only the lists of the experiments to be performed but they do not indicate as to the various processes and products of performance to be emphasized. It is, therefore, felt that unless the various experiments as listed in the prescribed syllabi indicate the various types of skills to be developed as a result of practical work, it would be difficult to develop and assess the practical skills in a proper manner. For this some more practical experiments emphasizing different processes and more should be introduced for adequate coverage of skills, keeping in view the physical facilities available in the schools.
3. Demonstrations by teachers are prerequisite for guiding theory and practical work. To help the teacher in planning and execution of demonstrations it is felt that the syllabi should contain a list of demonstrations to be shown to the pupils before the pupils themselves perform the experiments in the laboratory.
4. In the recent past through scientific talent search and other agencies our educationists have encouraged independent projects by pupils. A list of projects could be incorporated in the syllabi with hints for planning and execution of the same for guidance of the teachers.

5. In order to develop spirit of inquiry among the pupils a suggested list of open ended experiments may be included in the list of experiments. Such as list could be prepared with the help of experienced teachers and lecturers.
6. For healthy competition among the students and proper record of pupils' practical work together the grading of their performance by the teacher on each experiment, a progress chart/performa may be devised by the board and circulated to the schools for use of teachers conducting practical work.
7. As improved practical examinations viz-a-viz instruction pre-supposes adequate laboratory equipment and material, it is recommended that the concerned departments should supply the necessary apparatus and materials well in time.
8. In order to prepare the students for practical examination at the higher secondary stage in may be quite useful to introduce practical examination in science subjects at the end of secondary school stage also. Unless sufficient practice is given in developing fundamental skills it may be difficult to expect good performance from the pupils.

B. Laboratory

1. It is also recommended that one qualified laboratory assistant in each of the science subject should be appointed.
2. Provision should also be made for training of the laboratory personnel in up-keep of laboratory and in assisting the teaching staff for conduct of practical work.
3. For proper conduct of practical work, essential services in the form of electricity, gas water, fume-cupboards, exhaust fans etc. should be provided in the laboratory.
4. Equipment, furniture, fittings, fixtures storage cabinets etc. should be so designed and arranged that it facilities the use of laboratory chemicals, apparatus and materials besides ensuring safety measures.

C. Mechanics of Examination

1. Analysis of question papers in practical examination revealed that there is no set pattern of emphasizing different skills or the coverage of content. It is, therefore, essential that a design of question papers for practical examinations may be got prepared with the help of subject experts and supply the same to the paper setters as well as to the schools. This would help sampling of skills for evaluation purpose besides proportionate coverage of various subjects areas.
2. Minimum pass mark in practical examinations should be 40%. This would help to emphasize practical work more in the instruction of science subjects.
3. As the improvement pattern of practical examinations entails a lot of work and time in evaluation students' performance, it is desirable that the examiner-examinee ratio should be at the maximum 1 to 15.
4. On the lines of the sample proforma worked out by the group for reporting pupils' performance in practical examinations the examining agency should get the reporting proforma prepared for science subjects and supply them to the examiners. Such as proforma would be very useful for consolidation and use of pupils' performance besides providing useful information for feedback to the schools. This would go long way in improving the instructional programme in science subjects.
5. In order to emphasize the importance of practical work and its place in teaching of science subject it is necessary that passing in practical examinations should be made obligatory.
6. Present number of exercises specially in the subjects of Physics and Chemistry appears to be inadequate and it is not possible to have good coverage of skills and different content areas. Therefore, it is felt that the number of exercises may be increased by replacing one or more major exercises by short exercises requiring less

time and testing different skills. This would ensure better validity of the practical examinations.

7. In Biology it is felt that viva-voce may be dropped as it is mostly based on theory that can tested better through written examinations. Moreover, it takes away a lot of time which can be used more profitably for observing students' performance. However if it has to be continued it should test only functional understanding related to the practical work in hand during the process of performance.

8. The paper setters should be selected only from among those who have received training in practical examination through seminars or workshops conducted examining agencies.

9. The paper setters should prepare a scoring sheet for use of the examiners giving all the necessary details of the allocation of marks and the criteria for evaluation. Such a sheet should be prepared in a manner that it facilitates scoring and minimize the time for recording.

D. Paper Setting

1. Design of question paper must be supplied by the board of school education.

2. Looking to the total volume of the work of paper setting in the new pattern it is considered desirable that there should be a panel of paper setters consisting of not less than two members. Out of these, one should be from the university/college and the other from experienced school teachers.

3. The panel should prepare the question paper/papers according to the requirements laid down in the design supplied by the Board.

4. It will be necessary for the paper setters to prepare instructions for the examiners along with the detailed marking scheme for each exercise. This will ensure uniformity in assessment which is highly necessary in public examinations.

5. It is suggested that there should be an internal examiner along with external and he should be suitable remunerated. In Biology, out of the two examiners one may be of Botany and the other of Zoology.

6. The load of work of paper setters and examiners will be much increased than what it is today. Therefore, it is suggested that their remuneration be suitably enhanced.

E. Production of Literature

1. In order to orient the teachers and the students about the new pattern of practical examinations, there is a great need for developing suitable literature. It is, therefore, recommended that a brochure explaining the framework of the new pattern of practical examination and giving some sample materials illustration the pattern should be produced by each board and supplied to all the schools.

2. It will also be desirable to produce laboratory manuals and teachers' guides in addition to the above-mentioned brochure.

3. Since different sets of question papers are needed every year for setting question papers, the need for variety of exercise cannot be over-emphasized. It is, therefore, suggested that examining agencies may develop pool of practical exercises in each of the Science subjects. Such a pool can be used by external and internal examiners for developing and evaluating students for practical skills.

F. Orientation of Personnel

1. For effective implementation of the new pattern of practical examinations it is desirable that the paper setters and examiners be oriented to this approach. It is, therefore, suggested that the examining agencies should organise such orientation programmes for their present and prospective paper setters and examiners.

2. In order to make this programme a success the teachers should also be made conversant with this new pattern of teaching and testing in practical work, so that they could prepare their students more efficiently for improved pattern of practical examinations. It is, therefore, desirable that in addition to the supply of suitable literature to the teachers, tailor-made training programmes should also be organised for teachers of science.

REFERENCE

Singh, Pritam (1983). *A Monograph on Improving Practical Examinations in Science.* New Delhi: National Council of Educational Research and Training.

30

Professional Science Teacher

MARLOW EDIGER
Truman State University, Kirksville, USA

The teaching science needs to be viewed as trained, educated beings within a profession. A teacher is a decision maker. Teachers make judgements pertaining to objectives, learning activities, evaluation procedures, as well as quality of the classroom environment. To be a teacher means to be a decision maker. Within an open-ended arena, problems arise and solutions need to be found.

Shepherd and Ragan[1] wrote:

> The present age is one of spectacular changes brought about by humans through science and technology. The past twenty years have witnessed more scientific and technological discoveries than had been witnessed in all previous recorded time. The achievement of many of our national goals, at home and abroad, depends upon a strong and growing science and technology. New insights into the processes of investigation, new knowledge in the various areas of science, a new information concerning what pupils at given levels of development can learn, all require a rethinking of the objectives of science in the elementary school. Science is included in the elementary school curriculum for the contributions it can make to the intellectual, social, and emotional development of children, and for the contributions it can make to the achievement of our national goals. It can interest some pupils in the excitement and satisfaction of a career in science; it can help all children to comprehend the kind of world in which

they live, and to participate effectively in an increasing number of local and national decisions which require an understanding of science.

Professionalization of Teaching Science

Classroom teachers need ample opportunities to grow, develop, mature, and change. Staying in the classroom continuously, experience the routine each day, feeling lack of challenge, having few opportunities to interact with other professionals, attending few or no professional meetings at home or away, and lacking motivation does not encourage meaning and interest in teaching. How then might the teaching of science truly become a profession?

1. Engage in doing research

Classroom teachers of science should actively be involved in conducting research. In conducting research, the teacher with the guidance of a research specialist, needs to identify an experimental group as well as a control group. Each group ideally should be selected at random. Instrumentation used in the study should have the necessary criteria pertaining to validity and reliability. The halo effect must be greatly minimized. If randomization was not utilized, analysis of co-variance should be used to equate the experimental and control groups, based on pretest results. Other variables that need to be taken into consideration are maturation, reactive measures, regression towards the mean, and history of study. Practical research should be emphasized generally by the teacher. However selected teachers may be interested in theoretical studies. With theoretical studies, the researcher attempts to attain a theory which explains or predicts what might happen under selected conditions. The theory is not a fact nor is it a generalization. Theory is hypothesis to be tested in a practical situation. B.F. Skinner, Jerome Burner, and David Ausubel, among others, developed valuable theories.

2. Do Professional Reading in Science

Each pupil school should have a professional library for teachers. The library needs to house teacher education textbooks, educational journals, audio-visual aids, pamphlets, and other materials on the teaching of science. These should be available to assist teachers to improve the curriculum. Teachers should be given special time during the school day to read and reflect upon what has been read. Ample opportunities need to be given to teachers to discuss content read.

3. Attend Professional Meetings

The National Science Teachers' Association (NSTA) and state affiliates have quality conventions and meetings for teachers to attend. Money and time off from teaching are needed to attend. The local school district should provide the necessary financing as well as substitute teachers. Here the school district is investing in in-service education. An end result should be improved teaching performance in science. Teachers should have ample time to discuss ideas acquired with other professionals.

4. Participate in Faculty Meetings

Administrators and supervisors must schedule an adequate number of faculty meetings during a school year. Each faculty meeting needs to pin-point selected problems identified by teachers. Solving the problems would guide teachers to do a better job to teaching. These problems could deal with such items as discipline in the classroom, providing for individual differences in science, individualised programmes of instruction, individually guided instruction, affective goals in the science curriculum, and peer mediated instruction among others. An agenda should be in the hands of participants of the faculty meeting two days before it is held. Faculty members should have much input in developing the agenda. Leadership for conducting each faculty meeting should come from administrators, supervisors, and teachers themselves.

5. Take University Courses

Teachers must be encouraged to continue professional education beyond the baccalaureate degree. Opportunities to continue professional education need to be available to all science teachers. Incentives and motivation should be inherent to encourage teachers to pursue a master's degree or higher. The graduate degree programme should place heavy emphasis upon content, subject matter, and methods of teaching science. Additional stress in the graduate degree programme needs to emphasize the philosophy of education, the psychology of learning, field experiences in the public school setting, methods of conducting educational research, the sociological foundations of education, and current issues in teaching science. The graduate degree programme should be challenging and meaningful to improve the quality of teaching science in the public schools.

6. Departmental Meetings

Teachers need to participate in scheduled meetings for their own grade levels taught in the elementary school or academic areas taught in a departmentalized plan of instruction. The sessions should emphasize problems experienced by teachers in teaching science. Related solutions need to be sought. Each meeting needs to be planned in terms of objectives, approaches to attain each objective, as well as means to appraise progress in goal attainment. Teachers should feel free to suggest items to discuss for each departmental meeting. Salient problems in teaching science need identification and discussion.

7. Plan an in-service education programme

Each teacher should plan a programme of growth and development. The ultimate objective for in-service education should emphasize curriculum improvement in the teaching of science. Plans for in-service education need to stress means of assisting students to achieve more optimally. The following are given as examples to indicate what a teacher might plan with supervisory guidance:

(a) how to motivate student achievement in science.

(b) how to achieve self-discipline among learners.

(c) how to guide students to increase problem solving skills in science.

(d) how to assist learners to stay on task.

The teacher needs to do research to secure information pertaining to the above named topics. The in-service project could have a due date and signed by both the teacher and supervisor. The in-service project could count as credit in moving to a higher level on the salary schedule. Results from the in-service project should be shared with others in the school setting.

8. Workshop Involvement

Teachers need to be involved an professional growth endeavours. Participating in work shops might well be an opportunity to develop well professionally. A workshop must have a theme. The theme should emphasize purpose and meaning for teacher participants. The first level of participation in the workshop is the general session. Here teachers and supervisors identify and choose problems to solve. Each problem needs careful consideration. Instructional problems should receive primary attention. The suggestions of each participants in the workshop must be respected.

The second level of the workshop emphasizes committee work. Teachers and supervisors need to select a committee which has an identified problem possessing perceived purpose. Thus the selected problem to be solved within the committee is worthwhile in terms of effort and time put forth.

A third level of the workshop is individualized study. Each science teacher and supervisor may well have relevant topics to pursue. The topic is vital to the participant and provides for in-service growth. A better prepared teacher or supervisor to improve the curriculum for students needs to be an end result. Gathering information on the topic should assist in implementing a quality science curriculum for students.

Problem solving in computer use might well be a suggested theme for a workshop. Flake, McClintock, and Turner[2] wrote:

> Problem solving is probably the major factor in successful computer use; therefore, teaching problem solving is a major goal of computer education. Writing an original programme is problem solving; the planning that leads to a programme is problem solving. In fact, from one point of view, the problem must be solved before the programme is written. Creative uses of computers require problem-solving processes.
>
> In general, problem solving is likely to become more central to education as society becomes more complex. Advanced technology requires sophisticated problem solving; at the same time, it provides the tools for sophisticated problem solving. The rapid alterations in today's world suggested that the form and the goals of education are changing. Some skills that used to be drilled for considerable periods are now replaced by the skills

of an inexpensive calculator. Rather than being memorized, some facts can be called from a computer's database. In modern society, knowing only facts, formulas, and specific solutions is not enough, because those can quickly become obsolete. Knowledge of how to approach and solve new problems, on the other hand, always will be applicable. Learning how to learn may become the focus of educational programmes designed for changing societal needs. Problem solving as a way of learning is not likely to become obsolete.

9. School Newsletter

Teachers and supervisors should keep arrest of current trends in teaching science by sharing teaching suggestions with each other by way of a newsletter. Each educator in the school setting should share ideas with other professionals on ways to improve learning opportunities in science for students.

The newsletter should be available to teachers and supervisors weekly. The purpose of the newsletter should stimulate thought and energy to develop the best objectives, learning activities, as well as appraisal techniques for students. Teachers should report back to other professionals how well each teaching suggestion worked in the classroom that came from the newsletter.

10. Self-evaluation

Each teacher should have ample opportunities to cassette record, or better yet video tap his/her own teaching. Peer evaluation, using quality criteria, should be utilized to appraise teaching. Lessons may be rightist following evaluation. The ultimate goal here is to improve the science curriculum.

To secure feedback from pupil achievement in science, Ediger[3] wrote:

> The teacher of elementary school science must use a variety of appraisal techniques to evaluate pupil progress. Thus, assessment procedure such as the following may be utilized to evaluate learner achievement:

1. observation by the teacher of pupil progress.
2. pupil participation in discussion.
3. written work of learners.

4. pupil's art products.
5. information conferences conducted with pupils.
6. pupils evaluating their own achievement.
7. teacher-developed tests.
8. use of standardized tests.

No appraisal technique is a perfect device to assess achievement. Thus several techniques should be utilized collectively to evaluate total growth of learners in—

1. intellectual growth.
2. social development.
3. emotional growth.
4. physical development.
5. moral achievement.

In Closing

Ten approaches were presented to assist science teachers in in-service education. These were the following:

1. engaging in research.
2. doing professional reading.
3. attending professional meetings.
4. conducting faculty meetings.
5. taking university courses.
6. being involved in departmental meetings.
7. planning an in-service educational programmeme.
8. participating in workshops.
9. developing a school newsletter.
10. doing self-evaluation to improve the quality of instruction in science.

Gega[4] wrote:

> Three compelling influences shape elementary science teaching: science as a discipline, society's needs, and the characteristics of

children. Understanding these imperatives enables us to judge what is basic, useful, and learnable.

Science is an organised search for patterns or regularities. Scientists construct generalizations to explain the patterns they observe and, when possible, to predict and control objects and event within the patterns. Non-scientists do this also but usually with far less precision and reliability. Evidence in science is acceptable only when it is collected and processed under objective rules generally agreed to be the scientific community. To conduct scientific investigations requires an integrated knowledge of process and content in the topic of study.

REFERENCES

1. Shepherd, Gene D., and William B. Ragan. *Modern Elementary Curriculum,* Sixth edition. New York: CBS Collage Publishing. 1982, p. 327.
2. Flake, Janice L., McClintock, C. Edwin, and Sandra Turner. *Fundamentals of Computer Education,* Second edition,. Belmont, CA: Wadsworth Publishing Company, 1990, p. 111.
3. Ediger, Marlow. *The Elementary Curriculum.* Second edition. Kirksville. MO: Simpson Printing and Publishing Co., 1988, p. 185.
4. Gega, Peter C. *Science in Elementary Education,* Sixth edition. New York: Macmillan Publishing Company, 1990, p. 18.

31

A Theoretical Framework for the Use of Scientific Method in Educational Research

A. SATYAVATI
S. P. M. University, Tirupati, India

I. The Systematic Character of Scientific Knowledge

The activities that go by the name of research involve mainly a research, i.e., activities undertaken to repeat a search. In a general way research is defined as a careful critical inquiry or examination in seeking facts or principles deligent investigation in order to ascertain something. Improving upon the above definition, research refers to a critical and exhaustive investigation or experimentation having as its aim, the revision of accepted conclusions in the light of newly discovered facts.

The Encyclopaedia of social sciences define research as the manipulation of things, concepts or symbols for the purpose of generalizing to extend, correct or verify knowledge, whether that knowledge aids in construction of theory or in the practice of an art. Research may be defined as the systematic and objective analysis and recording of controlled observations that may lead to the development of generalizations, principles or theories, resulting in prediction and possibly ultimate control of events (John W. Best & James V.Kahn).

The scientist controls things, concepts or symbols purposefully, in order to know their responses under specific conditions. Those responses are the generalizations or conclusions. Even in many repeated circumstances, the same responses must appear for the scientist or for others who control things, concepts or symbols under the same specific conditions. Those generalizations may extend the bounds of knowledge existing at a point in time or they may modify the existing defective knowledge on that particular point or they may confirm the correctness of the existing knowledge. Further, thus earned knowledge can be put into two possible uses—(1) theoretical, and (2) practical.

In its theoretical aspect, knowledge may be organised into propositions which in turn can be arranged into a meaningful abstract conceptual system affording estimations about a phenomenon under specified sets of conditions. Here knowledge is for the sake of knowledge only. In its practical aspect, knowledge can be used as a means to some practical or utilitarian goal.

Research is the systematic method of discovering the new facts or verifying the old facts, their sequences, inter-relationship, causal explanations and the natural laws which govern them.

Scientific research is systematic, controlled, empirical and critical investigation of hypothetical propositions about the presumed relations among natural phenomena. Two points require emphasis. Scientific investigation is so ordered that investigators can have critical confidence in research outcomes. It is empirical, subjective brief must be checked against objective reality.

II. A Systematic Character of Scientific Knowledge and Research

The characteristics of science have been analysed in terms of varying frames of reference. One description of science contains both substantive theory and methodology which are explained in such terms as empirical, proportional, logical, operational communicable, problem solving, abstract, tending towards a system and ongoing. Other interpretations of the term Science are in relation to the fields of subject-matter, universal laws, systematic procedures, technical methodology and pseudo-scientific schemes like, astrology, palmistry, phrenology, etc.

Definition of Science. Science is popularly defined as an accumulation of systematic knowledge. This definition ignores the fundamental character of science. Science is a method of approach to the entire empirical world. It is merely a mode of analysis that permits the scientist to state propositions in the form of "if-then". Thus whatever systematic anybody of knowledge may be, it is not science, if it merely begins with axioms, or self-evident propositions, and end with deductions from those axioms.

In the scientific world itself there are two broad views of science. (1) the static view where science is an activity that contributes systematized knowledge to the world. The scientist's job is to discover new facts and to add them to the already existing body of information. Science in this view is a body of facts and can explain observed phenomena. (2) The dynamic view of science regards it as an 'activity' what scientists do. The present state of knowledge is a base for further scientific theory and research. This has been called a heuristic view. The word heuristic means serving to discover or reveal. A heuristic method of teaching emphasizes student's discovering things for himself. It emphasizes theory and interconnected conceptual schemata that are fruitful for further research. A heuristic emphasis is a discover emphasis.

The Conflict Over Science. Early in the present century the definition of science and research was strictly in terms of mathematical precision and accuracy, objectivity, verifiability, impartiality and expertness. The behavioural sciences can not be reported in strict mathematical precision but can be explained only in verbal terms. In many areas of social sciences, the criteria of objectivity and verifiability can be only partially satisfied. Therefore, the natural scientists disagreed to consider the social sciences on the following points:

(a) Human behaviour changes from one time to the other rapidly, as such, the scientific and exact predictions are not possible.

(b) Human behaviour is too elusive, subtle and complex to

yield to the rigid categorizations and artificial instruments of science.

(c) Human behaviour can be studied only by other human observers and these always distort fundamentally, the facts being observed, so that there can be no objective procedures for achieving the truth.

(d) Human beings are the subject of such predictions and have the ability deliberately to upset any predictions we make.

It is clear that, if there are true, then social sciences have weak scientific foundations. It would then become the study of infinitely variable, unique and non-measurable situations, rather than the investigation of repetitive, simplifiable and observable behaviour. The most valuable outcome of the conflict was that the modern social scientists realized that it is not the models of physics but the underlying thought-ways of science that are significant. Further, this conflict brought the social scientists to re-examine their concepts, premises and procedures which in turn led to find out refined techniques for precise measurements for increasing theoretical and conceptual clarity. Although man has used procedures other than scientific methods, research sources and objectivity through the centuries for arriving at solutions to problems, it has been well-said that the greatest invention of the nineteenth century was the invention of the method of invention. One element in the method is just the discovery of how to set about bridging the gap between the scientific ideas and the ultimate product. The general utilization and acceptance of the method of invention or scientific method produced a stereo-type pattern of research over the years. This pattern includes crucial experiments growing out of previous findings and performed with great precision, results subject to the closest scrutiny and alternative interpretations accepted or rejected in accordance with canons of scientific rigour and finally confirmed discovery inserted in a systematized lattice of already available knowledge. This type of investigation requires the aid of intellectual equipment that includes logic, theory, scholarly knowledge, technical proficiency in statistics and a background of the history and philosophy of science.

It is mentioned that a theory, a statement of fact, a law, a concept and a model are all different things.

Theory: Its Meaning. The basic aim of science is to explain natural phenomena. Such explanations are called theories. Example can be cited that the investigator seeks general explanations of all kinds of problem solving, instead of children's method of solving arithmetic problems. Such a general explanation is called a theory of problem solving. Other aims of science are explanation, understanding, prediction and control. A theory is a set of interrelated constructs (concepts) definitions and propositions that present a systematic view of phenomena by specifying relations among variables, with the purpose of explaining and predicting the phenomena (Kerlinger).

The above definition says three things: (1) A theory is a set of propositions consisting of defined and interrelated constructs, (2) A theory sets out the inter-relations among a set of variables (constructs) and in so doing, presents a systematic view of the phenomena described by the variables, (3) A theory explains phenomena. It does so specifying what variables are related to what variables and how they are related. Thus enabling the investigator to predict from certain variables to certain other variables.

A theory is a deductively connected set or a system of related conceptions in agreement with known properties or behaviours and stated so as to guide in the search for properties or behaviours hitherto unknown. Examples: Gestalt Theory of learning, theory of relativity, identical elements theory, etc.

The Role of Theory. Theory is a tool of Science.

(a) *Theory as orientation*: It defines the major orientation of a science by defining the kinds of data which are to be abstracted. It narrows the range of facts to be studied to a specific angle. Any phenomenon or object may be studied in many different ways. Any science and each specialization within a broader field abstracts from reality, keeping its attention upon a few aspects of given phenomena rather than upon all aspects, only thus can the work of science be reduced to manageability.

(b) *Theory as conceptualization and classification*: It offers a conceptual scheme by which the relevant phenomena are systematized, classified and inter-related. Every science is organised by a structure of concepts. It is the relationships between these concepts are known as the facts of science. To explain these concepts, the scientist uses specialized vocabulary. They change as the science develops, for different phenomena come to be of major importance. If knowledge is to be organised, there must be some system imposed upon the facts which are observable. As a consequence, a major task in any science is the development of systems of classification, a structure of concepts and an increasingly precise set of definitions for these terms.

(c) *Summarizing*: It summarizes facts into (a) empirical generalizations, and (b) systems of generalizations. Empirical generalizations are the simple addition of data. These facts are useful and are summarized in simple or complex theoretical relationships. The social psychologist may gather data on the differences in the child rearing practices of various classes. Summarizing at this level is not even considered as theory.

Systems of propositions are those through which our common statements are interpreted. Facts are seen within a framework rather than in an isolated fashion. Example, a social group is not just the sum of its members. It is clear behind this statement, a complex series of observations, a set of assumptions about the effect of social factors upon behaviour.

(d) *Predicts facts*: Theory summarizes facts and expresses a general statement beyond the immediate observations which is called prediction. This prediction has several facets. The most important is the extrapolation from the known to unknown. For example, the use of A.V. aids gives better understanding of a geography lesson about oceans in VII Class A Section, we can predict that the same advantage we can achieve in Section-B by the use of A.V. aids.

(e) *Theory points to gaps in our knowledge.* Theory must also point to areas which have not yet been explored. If a theory states a general relationships, such as, in a class-room learning, the children of higher income groups show better performance than the lower income groups. To find out further facts, we have to break the higher income groups into their sources of income like jobs, cultivation, business and so on. It also can further divided into urban and rural children etc. If these gaps are being filled, changes in the conceptual scheme usually occur.

The Meaning of Fact. A fact is regarded as an empirically verifiable observation. They are thought to be definite, certain, without question and their meanings are self-evident.

The Role of Fact

(a) *Fact initiates theory*: There are certain important theories constructed basing on the accidental observation of facts. For example, the finding of pencillin, Newton's Law of gravity, etc. This kind of observation is called the unanticipated, anomalous and strategic datum (Merton).

(b) *Facts lead to the rejection and reformulation of existing theory*: Since research is a continuing activity, the facts must be fitted into the structure of a theory. If those facts cannot be fitted into its structure rejection and reformulation are likely to be going on simultaneously in the theory.

(c) *Facts redefine and clarify theory*: New facts that fit the theory will always redefine the theory. They state in detail. They clarify the theory, for they throw new light upon its concepts. They may actually present new theoretical problems. The new definition may be far more specific than the theory.

The relationship between theory and fact. Popular opinion generally conceives of theory and fact as direct opposites because, theory is thought of a speculation, while facts are definite, certain, without question and their meaning is self-evident.

For the scientist, theory and fact are quite different. A fact for him is an empirically verifiable observation while theory is an ordering of those facts in some meaningful pattern. Thus facts are theory are not opposing each other but they are intertwined. Facts must be systematically ordered (theory) without which science cannot predict. Without prediction, there would be no control over the material world. Thus theory is not a speculation. The development of science is a constant interplay between theory and fact.

Values in Science. Value neutrality is an important principle of science. It does not consider the goodness or rightness of a theory. The work of science is not persuasion or conversion but it is demonstration. It demonstrates that in a certain condition, certain events inevitably follow. Thus it establishes relationships between different facts. Science discriminates between problems, judging one as more important than another and thus more desirable of solution. Moral involvement in social sciences, generally tempt the investigator to bias his results in favour of his own values.

Values in Educational Research. Educational research owes a prominent place to certain concepts that are common in our culture. They are purpose, motive, teleology, values, feelings and emotions. The values are basic to human living. Earlier times, the over emphasis was on statistical and measurement techniques in education and psychology. If scientific out look emphasizes on value-neutrality, those basic human values drive man to humanitarian outlook and the spiritual ends of life and faith. Without such a philosophy of values, science is blind and lacking direction. Science may be good or bad in the degree it contributes to the basic needs and goals of human life but scientific knowledge may serve as one of the great instruments if higher ends.

The pure scientist traditionally prided himself on his concern for facts and his indifference to values. But values are inseparably present in educational research. Therefore, it is recommended that value orientations be brought in the open, dealt with as objectively as possible and made known to all, who are personally affected by value aspects of professional behaviour.

The difficulties of evaluation in the area of values, we must face the fact that instruments for measurement of moral values have weaknesses which limit their utility for psychology and educational research.

(a) *The difficulties of evaluation in area of values*:

(i) Questionable assumptions about the relationship of moral behaviour in realistic contexts.

(ii) A focus on moral abstractions rather than moral behaviour in realistic contexts.

(iii) Reliance on subjective and interentional scoring procedures that stress correct moral values.

(iv) Inadequate standardization.

(b) *Values involved in the following areas in Education*:

In the area of evaluation of instruction and learning, typically by the method of controlled experimentation, judgement of necessity plays an important part in each step. It is because objective data may be either unavailable or untrustworthy.

Judgement and the investigators system of values are involved in the following decisions, situations and steps.

(i) The decision to make an evaluative study.

(ii) Determination of the grade level at which to make evaluation.

(iii) Selection of appropriate subjects for investigation.

(iv) Decision concerning the length of the period of time to be included.

(v) Analysis of the content and of the objectives in rival programmes, for the purpose of selecting only what is common to them or of determining what is to be done about unlike content and objectives.

(vi) Decision regarding the kinds of data to be collected. For example, correct answers on tests or levels of thought process.

(vii) Choice of available tests or other instruments, or the making of original tests.

(viii) Determination of measures to assure equal quality of teaching or of means to allow for differences.

(ix) Selection of the statistical methods best suited for the treatment of data.

(x) Final interpretation of the findings.

III. Educational Research

The field of education is a mixture of science and art. Many teachers do not know about educational research. There is no direct impact of educational research on educational practice, even though educational research is to develop new knowledge about teaching and learning and administration.

Major purposes of Educational Research:

(a) to provide answers to operational questions;

(b) to assess educational programmes, practices and materials;

(c) to build up a body of information about educational enterprises;

(d) to provide the outlook, stimulation, and guidance for educational innovation;

(e) to develop more adequate theory about educational processes.

Steps in Educational Research: Educational research is the application of scientific method to the study of educational problems. When using the scientific method, man engages himself in a thinking process called reflective thinking.

(a) *The Research Problem*: Man comes across some obstacle, experience, or problem that puzzles him or he may select a problem from the area of his own interest. He has to observe and gather facts so as to define his problem more precisely. It must be presented in a form that makes absolutely clear what data or evidence must be obtained in order to solve the problem.

(b) *Formulation of Hypothesis*: Educational research should make use of carefully formulated hypotheses. They may be formally stated or implied. They are tentative generalizations, calling attention to fundamental relationships or possible solutions. So that the investigator should give much thought to it.

(c) *The Method to be used*: The selection of research method to be used is of utmost importance in the research process. It refers to the general strategy followed in collecting and analysing the data necessary for solving the problem. The research methods are generally classified in three categories: (i) Historical, (ii) Descriptive, and (iii) Experimental. The method used in the study is dictated by the nature of the problem and the type of data required for answering the questions relating to the problem.

(d) *Data Collection*: This step is concerned with the procedures and techniques to be adopted for data collection. It refers to the nature of the sample to be chosen for study and selection and development of data gathering devices such as tests, questionnaires, rating scales interviews, observations, checklists, etc.

(e) *Analysis and interpretation of data*: Good research is characterised by the care taken in the analysis and interpretation of data. It includes the selection of appropriate statistical and other techniques to be used for processing the data collected for the study.

(f) *Reporting the results*: This is the last and important step of the research process. It is characterized by carefully formulated inferences, conclusions or generalizations. The researcher must be able to report his procedures, findings and conclusions in an intelligent form to others who may be interested in his study and its results.

This is not to be considered as the only scientific method. There are many ways of applying logic and observation to problem solving. Inspite of the application of scientific method and refinement of research techniques, tools and designs, education is no exception to face limitations as other social sciences in strict mathematical accuracy of physical sciences.

IV. The Position of Educational Research in India

Educational research in India is still in its infancy. After Independence, a systematic effort to develop educational researches in curriculum and text-book development and evaluation procedures, along with the development of elementary and secondary education and vocational education and guidance—Extension Service Departments in Training Colleges. These organisations financed for certain research projects. Even though the quantity of research work is increased, significantly its quality is poor. The NCERT and the UGC played an important role in the development of researches in Education. Some journals were also started to spread educational researches.

Third survey of Research in Education (Buch M.B. 1987) and Educational Research and Innovations Committee of the NCERT, New Delhi have suggested some priority areas in educational research, keeping in view of the National Policy of Education 1986: Programme of Action (1986) and Role of Education in the Total Programme of National Development.

REFERENCES

1. Foundations of Behavioural Research by Fred, N. Kerlinger (1973).
2. Research in Education by John W. Best & James V. Kahn (Sixth Edition) (1989).
3. Methods in Social Research by William J. Goode & Paul K. Hatt (1952).
4. Methodology of Educational Research, by Lokesh Koul (1989).
5. Educational Research—An Introduction by Walter R. Borg & Meredith D. Gall (Fourth Edition) (1984).
6. Encyclopaedia of Social Sciences.
7. Webster International English Dictionary.
8. Theory and Practice in Social Research by Hans Raj.
9. Methodology and Techniques of Social Research by Wilkinson & Bhandarkar.
10. Scientific Social Surveys and Research by Pauline V. Young.

32

Evaluation of Pupil Achievement in Science

MARLOW EDIGER
Truman State University, USA

There needs to be a variety of approaches used to evaluate pupil achievement in science. Since no approach is perfect, it behooves teachers and supervisors to use diverse methods to determine learner progress in science. Then too, there are numerous facets of a learner's achievement that need to be evaluated making it necessary to use different procedures. These facets include knowledge, skills, and attitudes, among others. I would like to start with discussing teacher observation to appraise pupil achievement.

Teacher Observation of Pupil Progress in Science

Observation by the teacher of each pupil in the classroom during time devoted to teaching science can be rather continuous and ongoing. Perhaps, it is the most common way to evaluate achievement in science teaching and learning. The teacher needs to use quality criteria in appraising pupils in ongoing lessons and units in science. These criteria should include the following:

1. Pupils being on task and not digressing from paying attention to ongoing learning activities.
2. Pupils being actively involved in identifying and solving problems.

3. Pupils developing and testing vital hypotheses in problem solving situations.
4. Pupils working harmoniously with others in committee settings and with the class as a whole.
5. Pupils making application of what has been learned previously.
6. Pupils putting forth optimal effort in individual endeavours.
7. Pupils reading science materials with comprehension.
8. Pupils writing content clearly and meaningfully in science.
9. Pupils evaluating their own achievement in science in a conscientious manner.
10. Pupils observing carefully during time devoted to science experiments and demonstrations.
11. Pupils speaking accurately and precisely so that quality communication in science takes place.

What has been observed by the teacher may be recorded periodically so that retention of learner achievement is as optimal as possible. One approach in recording pupil achievement is to use anecdotal records. Shepherd and Ragan (1982) wrote the following:

> Teachers have many opportunities to observe pupils in the classroom, on the playground, in the cafeteria, and in the auditorium. Observations over a period of time in these situations may provide information not revealed in an artificial test situation. For example, pupils may answer yes to a test item, "Do you prefer to work with others rather than by yourself?" When careful observation of their behaviour may reveal that they seldom participate in the activities of a group. Observation also provides an opportunity to report actual behaviour. The pupils who are asked to report on their own behaviours in a formal test situation are likely to give what they perceive to be the expected answer. The report of direct observations is likely, in this instance, to be more reliable than test results. The teacher may also learn a great deal about the personal-social development of children by observing their creative activities. Do the pupils enjoy the

activity for its own sake, or do they primarily work for good marks? Do they express their own feelings in their drawings and paintings, or do they prefer to copy the ideas of others?

Anecdotal Records

With anecdotal records, the teacher recor[illegible]rn progress individually at selected intervals. Photocopies may be made to make it convenient in using anecdotal records to record each pupil's achievement. The following form has been used very successfully by teachers whom I have supervised to record information about a pupil through teacher observation:

Name of Pupil Date Observation Made

What might be written, for example, pertaining to pupil's achievement in the classroom, according to teacher observation? The following is provided as an example:

Alex Smyth September 10—Alex worked well with others in the committee to develop a mural on volcanic eruptions. He needed to do more reading and looking at a video so that the opening to the volcano looked more real. Alex seems to enjoy working on the mural with others. He read additional materials on lava and magma, beyond what was discussed in class. Alex enjoys discussing current events items pertaining to volcanic eruptions.

From the above anecdotal record, it appears that Alex tends to do well in science at this point. If a pupil is deficient in an area, the science teacher may then assist the learner in overcoming a difficulty. By looking at the anecdotal record, the teacher may quickly notice what a pupil needs more help in. The teacher may write anecdotal statements on two or three pupils per day so it does not become an overwhelming activity. There must be a purpose in writing anecdotal records and that purpose being to assist pupils to achieve more optimally.

There are other procedures whereby a teacher may observe learner progress and file the results also, in addition to anecdotal records. Journal writing is another procedure for the teacher to use in recording observations made of pupil progress.

Writing Journal Entries

As is true of anecdotal records, journal writing stresses

contextual situations of evaluating pupil progress. "Contextual" means pupils are being evaluated within specific learning activities in terms of observations made by the science teacher to notice what the strengths and weaknesses are of a pupil's progress. Journal entries are written in narrative form, not as precise statements as was true of anecdotal records. The science teacher may focus upon one or two pupils per school day when writing journal entries. It is good to have records of pupil achievement in science. The date for writing in the journal is important. Companies might then be made of later with earlier journal entries. A good science teacher is a good evaluator in that he/she knows where each pupil is in achievement and can guide pupils to make continuous progress.

When field studies are being made, pupils need to record comprehensively what was achieved and accomplished. Pertaining to pupils doing field studies in connection with Prince George's Community College, in Largo, Maryland on ospreys and whooping cranes. Cunniff and McMillen (1996) wrote the following:

> At the end of the research week, students rank the four research areas in order of preference so that project directors can establish teams to do the data analysis, research presentation, and poster for each area. As expected, working with each species, the ospreys and cranes, is the first choice of many students. However the project directors are able to place students in their first or second ranked research area. Letting students work in their area of interest promotes a sense of ownership and motivation.
>
> For each research area, the student teams make numerous null and alternative hypotheses. Statistical analysis, done both by hand and computer, is then used to test these hypotheses.
>
> This final week is intense. Each of the four groups analyse the field data along with data from existing databases. Students are graphing software packages to analyze and graph data, test hypotheses, and help reach conclusions. Students develop posters to summarize the research methodology, data analysis, and conclusions. Each team develops a 12 minute presentation, and every student is required to speak. Research presentations are given the Thursday evening of the fourth week to more than 100 persons—parents, teachers and friends. This activity gives

students an opportunity to strengthen communication skills, learn how to give a scientific presentation, use overheads and slides, and work together as a team to deliver a final project, all under a very tight deadline.

There are numerous skills being acquired by pupils in the above named science project; these include doing research, using statistics, reporting orally, and writing observations made.

Using Portfolios to Appraise Pupil Performance

Pupils individually or in committees with teacher guidance need to develop a portfolio to indicate the quality of school work that has been accomplished. Isele (1995) raises questions and provides answers pertaining to portfolio development:

What are student portfolios? A purposeful collection of work that illustrates the student's efforts, progress, and achievement in given areas.

What is the purpose of a student's portfolio? Portfolios provide an ongoing and authentic record of student performance that enable:

Students to reflect upon and articulate their progress.

Teachers to tailor their instruction to the student's strengths and needs and to use the student's work as a basis for instructional planning.

Parents to gain greater insight into their child's learning.

Administrators/policymakers to base decisions about student achievement on authentic and meaningful information.

What are benefits of portfolios? Portfolios.

- Portray students' processes as well as products.
- Involve students in reflecting upon their learning, and thereby, provide individual responsibility, self-sufficiency, and active involvement.
- Increase time spent on learning and the quality of teaching.
- Provide a tangible and meaningful basis for discussions among students, teachers, and parents.

- Link curriculum, instruction, and assessment.
- Inform instruction.

Portfolios have a rather recent history in their use to appraise pupil achievement. I have observed portfolios to be wisely used by student teachers and cooperating teachers whom I have supervised in the public schools. What should go into a portfolio containing products of pupil achievement in science?

1. Snapshots and videos and pupils working on science experiments.
2. Cassette recordings of pupils working on committees in collaborative endeavours.
3. Art products and written work of the pupil in ongoing lessons and units of study in science.
4. Diary entries kept by the learner on a daily basis and dated pertaining to what was learned in science. Written products may come from word processor use.
5. Log entries which summarize the diary entries.
6. Pupil summaries of major concepts and generalizations acquired in science units of study.
7. Descriptions of pupil/ teacher conferences covering a science unit of study.
8. Self evaluation by the pupil on strengths acquired during the entire unit of study. The pupil may wish to list what areas he/she needs more assistance in.
9. Results from teacher written, standardized tests, as well as norm referenced tests.
10. A listing of computer packages completed. Internet may well be used to obtain information in problem solving experiences. A table of contents should be developed for the portfolio.

Collins and Dana (1993) suggest that four kinds of data or evidence be in portfolio; these are the following:

1. Artifacts are documents normally created or used in schools such as tests, book reports, work sheets, projects, etc.

2. Reproductions are items that typify events of activities in which students normally engage but often are not captured. For example, audio/visual taped discussions, presentations or photographs of projects or other work.
3. Attestations often take the form of a letter prepared by someone other than the student verifying his/her work or contributions.
4. Productions take two forms, both of which are especially created for the portfolio. The first is a reflective entry which articulates what was learned from the project or activity. The second is a caption affixed to each portfolio entry describing what it is and why it is included.

Pupils with teacher guidance need to have definite categories in mind when having the former develop a portfolio. These identified categories assist the learner in thinking about how to organize the portfolio and its contents. A wide variety of processes and products should be in evidence in a portfolio. Interested, responsible persons, especially parents, may then see what the learner has accomplished and what needs to be worked on to further the progress of the pupil.

After appraising diverse procedures used to evaluate pupil achievement, Ediger (1995) wrote:

> Approaches used to appraise pupil progress depend upon the philosophy of education involved. Each specific philosophy has uniqueness attached in determining that which learners have acquired.
>
> The testing and measurement movement stresses the utilization of predetermined objectives written in measurable terms. The objectives are written prior to instruction of learners. With appropriate learning opportunities, either a pupil does or does not achieve one or more precise objectives. Measuring pupil progress against the stated objectives emphasizes the concept of criterion referenced testing (CRT).
>
> The testing and measurement movement also advocates using norm referenced tests (NRT). Pupils are spread out on a continuum from highest to lowest based on test scores. Predetermined objectives tend not to exist when utilizing norm

referenced tests to measure pupil achievement. Norm referenced tests spread pupils' results in terms of test scores much more so than criterion referenced testing. Pupils attempt to attain predetermined objectives with CRT's. The measurably stated objectives represent absolute standards. A high number of pupils might well achieve the measurably stated objectives, as the teacher usually intends.

Self evaluation by the pupil is an opposite approach to appraisal of learner progress as contrasted with the testing and measurement movement. With self evaluation, the responsibility rests upon the learner himself/herself to acknowledge strengths, weaknesses, and modifications to attain at a higher level. Learners when evaluating the self need to perceive the processes and products completed from the frame of reference of personal improvement. Truth, in results from the evaluation, may well reside within the pupil. Subjectivity in results is to be expected, since open-ended criteria are utilized to appraise progress. With self evaluation, the pupil might well perceive increased purpose in assessing the self. The teacher is a stimulator and initiator when guiding the self evaluation process.

Testing to Determine Pupils Achievement

Using tests as a sole determiner to ascertain pupil achievement has lost its popularity and luster than what it once had. However, test results can still provide the teacher with feedback pertaining to a pupil's achievement. Testing occurs in a noncontextual situation and thus does not have the utilitarian features that a contextual situation has. For example, if a pupil writes a "thank you notice" to a person or place where the classroom took an excursion, the situation is practical and the letter will be mailed to the proper destination. The involved letter of appreciation was written in context in a lifelike situation. Tests taken by pupils are outside the framework of a utilitarian situation. People in society then do not take tests to show how well they are doing their work. Rather they are appraised in terms of how well they perform at the work place. An automobile mechanic might then be appraised in terms of how few complaints are received from customers as to faulty work having been done on their cars and trucks. The carpenter on the job does not take a paper/pencil test to show how well he/she did in building a home or other structure. Instead, the carpenter reveals proficiency by his/her skills and abilities to build a cabinet in the house, shingle the roof of the dwelling, and lay tiles for the basement floor, among other needed tasks.

To use the same analogy, the pupil in school has purposes for writing such as writing a "get well notice" to a friend who is ill, inviting friends to a birthday party, sending a thank you notice for a gift or favour received, and/or corresponding with pen pals. Here, the pupil is not evaluated in letter writing through a paper pencil test using multiple choice test items. In context, the pupil should be appraised in how well he/she writes, not how well a test can be taken. The term 'constructivism' is also given to appraising pupil achievement in writing within a contextual situation. The contextual situation stresses practical and utilitarian situations. Knowledge and skills are put to use. Application is then made of knowledge and skills possessed by the learner.

Now getting back to testing of pupils in the curriculum. Should testing be avoided? I think not. Why? Testing is one method of appraising pupil achievement. The teacher when writing these test items needs to use quality standards. Subject matter contained should be valid for the test. In other words, the teacher in teaching and learning situations has covered the content written as test items, generally multiple choice in nature. The teacher needs to be certain that the test items are clearly written; ambiguity has been omitted. The stem of the multiple choice item is grammatically correct with each of the four distracters. The following is given as an example:

Reptiles have all but one of the following characteristics:

(a) Temperature readings are comparable to that of the environment.

(b) Their live are born from eggs that have hatched.

(c) Babies are very dependent upon adults for at least a month.

(d) In their phylum are animals such as turtles, snakes and alligators.

The responses should be quite similar in length when writing multiple choice items so that clues are not available to the pupil as to which the correct answer would be. It is much easier to write multiple choice items measuring factual responses as compared to higher levels of cognition.

Many teachers write true-false items to measure pupil achievement. If a test item here is false, pupils should correct what is incorrect so that a minimal amount of guessing is involved. In the following true-false item, the pupil needs to correct what is false:

Fish start their lives breathing through the use of gills and later develop lungs.

There are teachers who write matching test items to measure pupil achievement in science. What is matched is usually factual in nature. There are important facts for pupils to understand in science. To match column A with column B, there needs to be more items in one column as compared to the next so that the process of elimination may not be used excessively. There should not be more than ten items in one column for intermediate grade levels. One column in the matching test should have single words of phrases; it is difficult to match column A with column B if both have lengthy sentences.

Teacher written test items should possess reliability. Thus if a test is taken a second time by the same set of learners, the results would be similar from one testing time to the next for individual learners. Should these test results vary much for one child from one testing to the next using the same items, the test would lack reliability. It would not be too useful to notice where a pupil is, on the same test, if on the first testing, John has 90 per cent right and for the second testing 30 per cent correct. The question would then arise as to where is John in achievement since the scores vary much on the same test from one testing to the next. There are basically three kinds of reliability statistically. These are test-retest, split half, and alternative forms.

Teacher written tests are one kind to be taken by pupils. Generally teachers align their tests with what has been taught. Thus, there are degrees of validity there.

There appear to be weaknesses no matter which procedure is used in testing. Thus, in standardized testing, teachers have no objectives to go by to know which subject matter will be covered in the test. The manual section will say how the items were selected to be on the standardized test. But, it leaves the science teacher in a precarious situation in terms of having some guidance as to what pupils should learn in ongoing science units of study in order to do well on the standardized instrument. Quality standardized tests will contain in the manual section the validity and reliability figures from schools having used these tests. Reliability figures given are high since it is relatively easy to develop quality reliability figures when spending a considerable amount of money to secure needed test-retest, alternative forms, and/or split-half reliability. It is much more difficult to obtain quality "validity" for the standardized test. The science teacher should have statements of clearly stated objectives so that he/she may teach in a manner which will assist pupils to achieve desired objectives. The learning activities in science would then be valid for the stated objectives. Otherwise, the teacher would be uncertain in knowing what to teach so that pupils do well on the test.

A publishing company of standardized tests has specific rules to follow, indicted in the manual, as to how to administer the test. Each pupil taking the test follows the same rules and has the same time limits. Thus there are standard procedure in test taking. To score the tests, the same key is used for all pupils and with machine scoring, no errors should be made in checking each pupil's paper. Test results, if checked again, should be the same for each pupil no matter who or what scores the tests.

From pupil results, there should be quite a range from high to low in pupils' test scores in any one grade level. The standardized tests are constructed in ways which make it possible to have this wide spread of scores.

Criterion referenced tests have taken some of the weaknesses out of standardized testing. Here, teachers have statements of objectives to use in teaching science. The teacher needs to choose learning opportunities in order that learners may attain the objectives. Thus the learning opportunities harmonize with the stated objectives and provide for validity. The testing device also aligns with the stated objectives, thus making for validity in testing. Ideally, there should be a small range in pupils' test scores from a criterion referenced test. Why? The science teacher teaches so that so many pupils as possible achieve the stated objectives. Thus, it can be expected that the range of scores from high to low on criterion referenced tests will be much more marginal as compared to standardized tests.

There are numerous states that mandate criterion referenced tests for pupils to take on selected grade levels. Accountability of teachers may be tied in with criterion referenced testing. Thus, teachers are held accountable for pupils achieving the precise objectives whose subject matter is being measured on the criterion referenced test.

There is considerable debate presently as to how much should test results count as compared to portfolio content in appraising pupil achievement. Tests possess much subjectivity when subject matter is selected for inclusion. There certainly would not be agreement on which science content should go into a test. Objectivity occurs here when the results from pupil testing is being evaluated. If the results are scored accurately, there should be no subjectivity involved providing all scorers use the same scoring key. With portfolios, subjectivity is involved when two or three raters appraise any one portfolio. It will be difficult for these raters to come up with the same results when evaluating each person's progress. Kane and Khaturi (1995) wrote the following:

> Some questions related to performance assessment remain to be answered by future research. They have to do with basic and secondary issues in educational reform . . . What knowledge and skills are pupils to demonstrate after a certain period of schooling? What other systemic reforms must be undertaken in order for assessment reforms to be effective? What assessment formats are most useful for which specific purposes? The greatest challenge ahead lies in designing systems of reform that synergistically support the core educational functions of teaching and learning for which teachers are the most powerful "engine".

Conferences with Pupils

The conference method can be an excellent way of assisting

the teacher to determine what pupils have learned in science. Ediger (1996) wrote:

The teacher may conduct conferences with pupils individually or in a group setting. If a pupil, for example, has completed reading a library book directly related to the ongoing unit of study, the teacher may conduct an informal conference to determine attitudes and comprehension of the involved learner. The teacher might also conduct a conference with a small group of pupils who have read the same or related library books. Thus, learners may read library books on the following topics relating to the present unit being studied in science:

1. The Seasons, Plants, and Animals.
2. Plants and Animals of Prehistoric Times.
3. The Uses of Nuclear Energy.
4. Uses of Magnets and Electricity.
5. Constellations and the Universe.

Pupils may reveal learnings such as the following in a conference setting pertaining to content gained from reading selected library books:

1. Obtaining skills in reading critically and creatively.
2. Acquiring selected facts, main ideas, and generalizations.
3. Selecting ideas which come in a certain sequence.
4. Reading to solve problems.
5. Wishing to engage in reading for recreational purposes.

Conference methods of evaluating pupil achievement may be used along with other appraisal procedures. A conference may take a very short period of teacher time. Others may take longer depending upon the agenda of the science teacher. I believe conferences are a marvellous way of getting to know pupils better as individuals as well as guiding learners to achieve more optimally. In conferences with pupils as well as with any facet of the science curriculum, I believe teachers need to think about four questions pertaining to science lessons and units of study that Ralph Tyler (1949) raised:

1. What objectives should pupils achieve?
2. Which learning activities should be chosen to assist pupils to achieve the stated objectives?
3. How should these learning activities be organized?
4. How should we evaluate to know if the objectives have been achieved?

These four questions might well provide for a framework for planning and implementing a quality science curriculum.

Discussions and Pupil Achievement

Pupils with teacher leadership should have ample opportunities to discuss content acquired in science. Learners need to understand and attach meaning to what has been learned. Rote learning and memorization of subject matter is not adequate. Pupils also need to comprehend and use what has been learned. Discussions can be lively and engaging. They certainly do not need to be dull. I have observed teachers lead discussions in classrooms whereby each pupil was truly involved wholeheartedly. If discussions seem to be boring and lead nowhere, pupils with teacher assistance need to determine causes for these occurrences. Science is a fascinating curriculum area in which pupils may truly ponder over questions and problems as well as being actively involved in each learning opportunity. Pertaining to discussions, Ediger (1977) wrote the following:

In discussion settings, feedback from learners is obtained in terms of relevant concepts and generalizations gained in a specific unit of study. Thus, learners may reveal the following understandings in a discussion:

1. What causes earthquakes, cyclones, and hurricanes.
2. What causes diverse kinds of weather on the earth's surface.
3. How gasoline and electrical engines operate in terms of involved scientific principles.

Using discussions as a technique to appraise learner progress, pupils also indicate.

1. If they can stay on the topic being pursued.
2. If they can communicate ideas orally in an effective manner.
3. If they respect the thinking of others.

By listening of oral reports given by pupils, the teacher may notice learner growth in the following ways:

1. Has the report been carefully planned and prepared?
2. Is there appropriate sequence of content being presented?
3. Does the reporter really understand the content being presented to listeners? Thus if a pupil is reporting on cirrus clouds, does he/she understand how these clouds are formed as well as have accurate perceptions on their physical appearances?
4. Does the learner speak clearly enough so listeners can clearly understand the contents being presented?

There should be ample time given after the oral report for listeners to ask questions and make comments in an atmosphere of respect. It is very important for pupils to learn to accept and respect each other. In an atmosphere of acceptance and belonging, pupils probably will learn more subject matter content than would otherwise be the case.

In Conclusion

The development and use of portfolios should be a way for pupils to reflect upon their strengths and weaknesses in working toward higher achievement levels. Bimes-Michalak (1995) believes that a major reason for developing portfolios is for pupils and teachers to reflect upon what has been taught and learned. There is a motivating ingredient in portfolio development and that is active involvement by learners in compiling a truly excellent device to inform others of personal progress in science. The pupil is involved in a hands on approach in determining what should go into a portfolio and why. Gilman and Rafferty (no date given) list the following advantages of using portfolios to appraise pupil achievement:

1. They evaluate both process and product.
2. They allow an integration of learning and assessment.
3. Evaluation is not limited to a single score.
4. Provide more information about a student's progress.
5. They encourage students to take charge of their own learning.
6. Students feel they are a part of the assessment process.
7. They help develop the skills for lifelong learning.
8. They may actually reduce the daily burden of grading papers.
9. The information gained from portfolios is meaningful and substantial.
10. They provide a continuous example of a child's work in a context that is relevant and understandable.
11. They assess global understanding and thinking skills.
12. It is a form of evaluation that is bound to have parental approval.

Wolf (1996) suggests teachers also develop their own portfolios. He wrote the following:

> Why this interest in portfolios? Although portfolios can be time consuming to construct and cumbersome to review, they also capture the complexities of professional practices in ways that no other approach can. Not only are they an effective way to assess teaching quality, but they also provide teachers opportunities for self reflection and collegial interactions based on documented episodes of their own teaching.
>
> Essentially, a teaching portfolio is a collection of information such as lesson plans, student assignments, teacher's written descriptions and videotapes of their instruction, and formal evaluations by supervisors . . . .

Teachers and administrators need to look for better means of evaluation of pupil progress than what was used previously. Changes need to be made when moving from *what is* to *what should be*. What should be is based on the best thinking possible in education. Using test scores largely to reveal learner progress and achievement was weighed and found wanting. Norm and criterion referenced tests provided some data on pupil achievement, but the scope was very narrow in showing what a pupil knows and can do. Test results show numerical data scores, such as norm referenced results indicating how well a pupil compares with others in taking the same test. Percentile ranks, standard deviations, grade equivalents, and quartile deviations are given to show how well a pupil is doing in the curriculum. Or in the case of criterion referenced tests, information is given if a pupil has or has not achieved predetermined objectives. Numerical test results do not indicate how well a person communicates orally or in writing in a contextual situation. The tests also are taken outside the framework of the ongoing lesson or unit of study being presented. Pupils then lack ownership of indicating how well they are doing in the curriculum area of science.

REFERENCES

1. Bimes-Michalak, Beverly (1995), "The Portfolio Zone," *Education Digest*, 60: 53-57.

2. Collins, A., and T.M. Dana (1993), "Using Portfolios with Middle Grade Students," *Middle School Journal*, 25: 14-19.

3. Cuniff, Patricia A., and Janet L. McMillen (1996), "Field Studies," *The Science Teacher*, 63: 51.

4. Ediger, Marlow (1995). *Philosophy in Curriculum Development*. Kirksville, Missouri: Simpson Publishing Company, pp. 114-115.

5. Ediger, Marlow (1996). *Elementary Education (A Collection of Essays)*. Kirksville, Missouri: Simpson Publishing Company, p. 149.

6. Ediger, Marlow (1977). *The Elementary Curriculum: A Handbook*, Kirksville, Missouri: Simpson Publishing Company, pp. 215-216.

7. Gilman, David Alan, and Cathleen D. Rafferty. (no date given). "Portfolios: They're Just Not Work Folders Anymore," School of Education, Indiana State University, Terre Haute: Curriculum and Research Center.

8. Isele, Frederick (1995), "Performance Based Portfolios". Paper presented at the National Council Social Studies Convention, Chicago.

9. Kane, Michael, and Nidh Khatri (1995), "Assessment Reform," *Phi Delta Kappan*, 77:32.

10. Shepherd, Gene D., and William B. Ragan. *Modern Elementary Curriculum,* New York: Holt, Rinehart and Winston, pp. 109-110.

11. Tyler, Ralph (1949). *Basic Principles of Curriculum and Instruction,* Chicago: University of Chicago Press.

12. Wolf, Kenneth (1996), "Developing an Effective Teaching Portfolio," *Educational Leadership*, 53:34.

33

Futurism in the Science Curriculum

MARLOW EDIGER
Truman State University, Kirksville, USA

Science educators need to study the objectives, learning opportunities, and appraisal procedures in the present science curriculum. The science curriculum is then being evaluated and described in terms of what exists presently in ongoing lessons and units of study. Science educators should not stop with describing what is in the present curriculum. Rather problems need identification and solutions sought in terms of what should be in teaching/learning situations in science. Predictions of the future science curriculum is a necessity. Science instruction needs to move away from the present to a better future. Futurism and its studies are necessary in order to develop excellence in the science curriculum.

The Science Curriculum of the Future

The teacher will have more adequate opportunities to determine where a student is in science achievement presently. To start where a learner is achieving and work for optimal continuous student progress is an ideal for the science teacher to follow. A futuristic science programme will emphasize determining a student's entry level of achievement with ordered opportunities for optimal achievement.

Second, better approaches in sequencing student learning will be in evidence, be it a psychological or logical science curriculum. Students then will experience increased success in sequential lessons and units. The lack of ordered learnings will be minimized while appropriate sequence in achievement will be optimalized.

Third, learners will perceive increased purpose in learning. Thus, students will accept inherent reasons for acquiring facts, concepts, and generalizations. Science teachers will have definite knowledge and skills pertaining to assisting learners to perceive purpose in learning.

Fourth, materials and methods of teaching will assist science teachers to secure student interests more effectively. With increased interest in science lessons and units, the student will put forth increased effort to learn. Increased interest in science will make for more effort to attain relevant goals of instruction. Interest and effort will be one and not separate entities.

Fifth, harmonious balance among diverse categories of objectives will be in evidence. Knowledge objectives stressing students acquiring vital subject matter will become increasingly salient. Skills ends are equally significant for student attainment. With skills objectives implemented, learners apply content acquired within the framework of knowledge objectives. The last of the three categories of objectives—attitudinal—are the most significant. With quality attitudes, students are positive in their wanting to achieve knowledge and skills ends. Science teachers in the future will become increasingly professional in guiding optimal student progress in knowledge, skills, and attitudes. Improved philosophies, psychologies, and research results will assist teachers to increase learner progress in science.

Sixth, new materials and procedures of teaching science will assist teachers to individual instruction more thoroughly. With more knowledge available to teachers in providing for diverse achievement levels, each student regardless of past levels of progress will be guided increasingly to attain as much as possible. Developing, growing, learning and achieving in science lessons will become more optimal for each student.

Seventh, science achievement of essentials will be a life-long process. Growth in science learning will have no end beyond itself. Achievement is continuous and cumulative. Development in knowledge, skills and attitudes has no ends in the science curriculum. Knowledge for its own sake as well as for utilitarian purposes will become a goal in science for each person. School and society will both emphasize vitality in its diverse manifestations of life-long learning in science.

Eighth, school and society will increasingly integrate its goals in science instruction. What transpires and occurs in science in the societal arena will provide content in the school curriculum. The realness and reality of scientific phenomena will provide objectives for instruction, learning opportunities to attain objectives, as well as appraisal procedures.

Ninth, more appropriate means to ascertain student attainment in science will be in the offing. These appraisal procedures will appraise not only cognitive learnings, but also skills and attitudes. Skills to be appraised include critical and creative thinking, as well as problem solving. Appraising student progress in the attitudinal dimension will include determining the quality of feelings, beliefs, and appreciations of contributions of science.

Tenth, quality in-service means of updating science instruction will be in the offing. In-service education programmes will be varied, purposeful, and provide for individual needs of science teachers. The major objective of in-service education will be to provide the best possible objectives, learning opportunities, and appraisal procedures in actual classroom teaching situations.

In-service Education and the Science Teacher

Each science teacher should provide for individual differences in the classroom to provide the best science curriculum possible for students. In-service education in its diverse manifestations many well assist each science teacher to do the best possible in teaching-learning situations.

First, a quality professional library needs to be in evidence for science teachers in the school setting: Teacher education text-books, professional journals for teachers, as well as audio-visual materials need to be available to teachers to benefit from. Science teachers should have time to read and view these materials to update the profession of teaching science.

Second, teachers should attend state and national education conventions devoted to the teaching of science. Each teacher needs to attend meetings in conventions which assist to provide quality ends, means, and appraisal procedures for students. Attendance at these meetings for science teachers should be fully funded.

Third, science teachers should be involved in a local school district or in a regional meeting involving a planned series of meetings to improve the curriculum. With interaction among participants, quality science lessons and units should be in the offing. Each science teacher has opportunities to share with others means of improving teaching-learning situations.

Fourth, workshops should be conducted to provide science teachers with opportunities to identify and solve problems in teaching students. A general session with all participating should emphasize teachers selecting problems areas. The general session should be followed by committee endeavours. Here, each participant works on his/her chosen problem(s) to solve in the committee setting. Ample opportunities should be provided for teachers to work on individual tasks, projects, and endeavours. Feedback from committee and individual endeavours should be shared with the general session. Practical situations should be emphasized in the workshop whereby each secures valuable suggestions to improve the teaching of science.

Fifth, faculty meeting conducted within a school should assist in identifying and solving problems related to the general areas of curriculum and instruction. These problems could involve discipline, inductive teaching, inquiry learning, as well as utilizing a variety of materials in on-going lessons and units. The general areas of curriculum development in terms of problem areas identified should also relate to teaching science in the school setting. Hopefully, solutions decided upon will improve the teaching of science.

Sixth, departmental meetings might be an excellent means in improving the science curriculum. Stimulating discussions on new methods in teaching science should aid in curriculum improvement. Content taught in science also needs appraisal to determine if key generalizations, concepts, and structural ideas are being emphasized in on-going lessons and units.

Seventh, team teaching is a way of learning from others in the teaching of science. With team teaching, member splan cooperatively objectives, learning opportunities, and appraisal procedures. In large group instruction, each team member may appraise and provide feedback to the teacher teaching students. Quality criteria need to be utilized in the feedback. Small group work as well as individual projects and activities for students provide teaching team members ample opportunities to work with learners in committees as well as in individual endeavours.

Eighth, models in teaching science may come from selected audio-visual materials such as video-tapes, films, filmstrips, and slides. Teachers need to analyze and appraise each method, prior to its implementation in the classroom.

Ninth, student teachers, when assigned, are a source of new ideas, methodology, and content for the regular science teacher. The student teacher and the regular teacher need to plan ends, means, and appraisal procedures cooperatively. Each new approach having quality criteria needs to be tried out in actual teaching situations. Feed-back from students provides information as to the effectiveness of new approaches utilized.

Tenth, science teachers need to have paid leaves of absence to secure advanced degrees in their area of expertise on a college/university campus. The advanced degree, be it a Specialist in Education or a Doctorate, should assist the science teacher to become increasingly professional and competent in teaching. Achievement, growth and development are key concepts to emphasize when a science teacher works on and secures an advanced degree.

In Closing

A forward looking science programme will emphasize:

1. Determining specifically where a student in presently achieving.
2. Sequencing learning opportunities for optimal student progress.
3. Feelings of purpose on the part of the student for learning.
4. Securing the interests of students in on-going lessons and units.

5. Emphasizing balance among diverse categories of objectives in teaching-learning situations. Thus, each category of objectives—knowledge, skills, and attitudes—will receive appropriate emphasis.
6. Providing for individual differences in order that each student may achieve as much possible.
7. Learning as being life-long and continuous.
8. Integrating school and society.
9. Appraising student progress for diagnostic purposes as well as to determine progress of learners.
10. Increasing opportunities for in-service education for teachers.

Inservice education opportunities for science teachers will emphasize:

1. Quality libraries in the school setting. Content will be readily available for teachers to use to improve the science curriculum.
2. Attendance at state or national professional teacher education conventions to improve science teaching.
3. Regional meetings convened to develop quality objectives, learning opportunities, and appraisal procedures.
4. Workshops emphasizing large group and small group sessions as well as individualized study for participants to solve problems in the teaching of science.
5. Faculty meetings scheduled to plan a quality science curriculum.
6. Departmental meetings to view present trends in teaching with effort put forth to upgrade the curriculum.
7. Teach teaching as a means of learning from each other in developing the science curriculum.
8. Observation of audio-visual materials to update content and methodology.
9. Cooperative planning with an assigned student teacher.

10. Work toward an advanced degree in science teaching on a college/university campus.

REFERENCES

Beane, James A. et al. *Curriculum Planning and Development*. Boston: Allyn and Bacon, Inc., 1986, pp. 241-42.

Cruickshank, Donald R. *Teaching is Tough*. Englewood Cliffs, New Jersey: Prentice-Hall, Inc., 1980.

Ebel, Robert and David A. Frisbie. *Essentials of Educational Measurement*. Fourth edition. Englewood Cliffs, New Jersey: Prentice-Hall, 1986.

Esler, William K. *Teaching Elementary Science*, Belmont, California: Wadsworth Publishing Company, Inc., 1973.

Friedl, Alfred E. *Teaching Science to Children: The Inquiry Approach Applied*. New York: Random House, Inc., 1972.

Gronlund, Norman E. *Measurement and Evaluation in Teaching*. New York: Macmillan, 1985.

Henson, Kenneth T. *Secondary Teaching Methods*. Lexington, Massachusetts: D.C. Heath and Company, 1981.

Herman, Jerry J. *Developing an Effective Elementary Science Curriculum*. West Nyack, New York: Parker Publishing Company, 1969.

Joyce, Bruce and Marsha Weil. *Models of Teaching*. Third edition. Englewood Cliffs, New Jersey: Prentice-Halls, Inc., 1986.

Joyce, Bruce et al. *The Structure of School Improvement*. New York: Longmans, 1983.

Kuslan, Louis I. and A. Harris Stone. *Teaching Children Science: An Inquiry Approach*. Belmont, California: 1972.

Lewis, June E. and Irene C. Potter. *The Teaching of Science in the Elementary School*. Englewood Cliffs, New Jersey: Prentice-Hall, Inc., 1970.

Mehrens, William A. and Irvin J. Lehmann. *Measurement and Evaluation in Education and Psychology*. Third edition. New York: Holt, Rinehart and Winston, 1984, pp. 14-15.

National Society for the Study of Education. *Staff Development*, Part II. Chicago, Illinois: The Society, 1983.

National Society for the Study of Education. *The Humanities in Precollegiate Education*, Part II. Chicago, Illinois: The Society, 1984.

34

Project 2000+

Declaration

We, participants in the Project 2000+ Forum, meeting at UNESCO, Paris, France, from 5 to 10 July, 1993:

1. ***Recalling*** the World Declaration on Education for All, in particular its recognition that 'sound basic education is fundamental to the strengthening of higher levels of education and of scientific and technological literacy and capacity and thus to self-reliant development' and, further recalling recent worldwide expressions of concern for the environment and for the quality of human life, especially those contained in Agenda 21, the output of the United Nations Conference on Environment and Development, Rio de Janeiro, 3-14 June 1992,

2. ***Believing*** that scientific literacy and technological literacy are essential for achieving responsible and sustainable development,

3. ***Declare*** our full commitment to the promotion of science and technology education for all in keeping with the World Declaration on Education for All, and our readiness to contribute through Project 2000+ to the concerted action set out in the Framework for Action to Meet Basic Learning Needs;

4. *Call* on governments, industry, public and private sector interests, and education and other authorities in all countries to:

(a) Review critically existing provisions for science and technology education at all levels and in all settings with the aim of giving appropriate attention to development and maintenance of learning programmes responsive to the needs of individuals and communities;

(b) Assign priority to the development and introduction of programmes leading to scientific literacy and technological literacy for all with the aim of achieving responsible and sustainable development;

(c) Take such steps as may be necessary to ensure equity of access for everybody to science and technology education, notably for women and girls, young children and other under-represented groups;

(d) Develop appropriate in-school and out-of-school opportunities, programmes, curricula and assessment procedures for science and technology education responding to the human needs of a scientific and technological society;

(e) Ensure and support appropriate pre-service and continuing in-service provisions for those responsible for all forms of science and technology education;

(f) encourage and support evaluation, research and development in science and technology education in both formal and non-formal sectors;

and to this end:

(g) Establish and support task forces involving partnership with public and private educational bodies and councils; these might include universities and other institutions of higher and further education, research institutions, libraries, interactive science centres, environmental areas and nature reserves as well as public and private bodies active in the fields of agriculture, natural resources, environment, health, industry, commerce and the media, and also organizations and individuals specially concerned with science and technology education;

(h) Recognize the central role of teachers in achieving scientific literacy and technological literacy for everybody, and enhance the status of careers in science and technology education at all levels;

(i) Recognize the capital role of institutions of non-formal education, such as museums and scientific centres, of the media (radio, television and the press) and of all other out-of-school channels for communicating knowledge of science and technology, in fostering scientific and technological literacy for all; and develop activities designed to set science and its applications in a wider social and cultural environment;

(j) Ensure and adequate resources are available to achieve these aims;

5. *Urge* United Nations Agencies and other inter-governmental organizations to work together to initiate and support programmes which will advance the ability of counties and of populations to shape their own future in a scientific and technological society and which will increase the capacity of countries for designing, planning and implementing scientific literacy and technological literacy programmes;

6. *Urge* non-governmental organizations active in fields of science and technology education, as well as the social sciences, and professional associations of teachers and educators and educational organizations at all levels to:

Enter into partnership with, and make their knowledge and experience available to, United Nations and other inter-governmental bodies as well as establish innovative programmes in a common effort to achieve the goal of scientific literacy and technological literacy for all; and

Participate in national, regional and international programmes for the enhancement of scientific literacy and technological literacy for the improvement of the quality of life in all societies and for the achievement of sustainable development;

7. ***Recommend*** that UNESCO makes provision, within its Medium Term Plan (1996-2001) in the field of education, and in the context of Project 2000+, for an international programme to develop co-operation among all countries in the field of science and technology education, with particular reference to the promotion of scientific literacy and technological literacy for all:

   This programme, conducted in partnership with the relevant and competent governmental and non-governmental organizations and agencies, should focus on regional and subregional co-operation and on strengthening networks for exchange of ideas, information, human and material resources for science and technology education, and actively seek to promote world-wide:

   (a) Understanding of the nature of, and the need for, scientific literacy and technological literacy in relation to local culture and values and to the social and economic needs and aspirations of each country and its peoples, and also in accord both with the general aims of education for the all-round development of human personality and with human rights and basic freedoms;

   (b) Identification of those issues concerning the applications of science and technology which are of special importance for personal, local and national development and their embodiment in educational programmes;

   (c) Establishment of teaching and learning environments as well as supporting structures conducive to the achievement of scientific literacy and technological literacy for all;

   (d) Formulation of guidelines for the preparation and continuous professional development of science and technology educators and leadership coupled with assistance to countries in giving effect to them;

(e) Development of effective communication, both verbal and visual, assessment strategies and evaluation programmes designed to enhance general levels of scientific literacy and technological literacy;

(f) Support for the non-formal and informal sector in its own right and support for development strategies which will help to stimulate and maintain lifelong scientific literacy and technological literacy;

8. ***Recommend*** that by the year 2001 there should be in place appropriate structures and activities to foster scientific literacy and technological literacy for all, in all countries.

THE WAY FORWARD

1. The nature of Project 2000+

The target has been set:

> appropriate structures and activities to foster scientific literacy and technological literacy for all, in all countries, should be in place by the year 2001.

There is, therefore, urgent need not only for action but also for reflection on current practices in formal, informal and non-formal education at all levels as well as on the meaning to be attached to scientific and technological literacy in different national settings.

To this end Project 2000+ is working to:

- Identify ways of promoting the development of scientific and technological literacy for all;
- Put forward educational programmes (formal and non-formal) which will empower all to satisfy their basic needs and be productive in an increasingly technological society;
- Provide guidelines for continuous development of science and technology educators and leaders;
- Encourage the formation of broadly based national task forces to initiate programmes for greater scientific and technological literacy;

- Support the development of a wide range of projects designed to promote solidarity and co-operation in achieving scientific and technological literacy for all;
- Support the evaluation of existing and projected programmes in this vital area.

Project 2000+ involves a long-term co-operative effort to move forward on a broad front developing and strengthening interlocking links between the United Nations and other intergovernmental agencies, governmental bodies, bilateral donors and non-governmental organizations.

Time is now short.

2. What does the Declaration mean in each national context?

To implement the Declaration and promote action, it is proposed that national task forces be set up to work closely with existing Education for All task forces or to form an integral part of them. Although the structure of Project 2000+ task forces may vary from one country to another, all should involve partnership between public and private educational bodies, governmental and non-governmental organizations concerned with science and technology education and institutions of both formal and non-formal education. They should also have links with those sectors of the economy underpinned by science and technology, including notably, agriculture, natural resources, environment, population and health, commerce and the media.

The first function of a national task force would be to analyse the Declaration in terms of the country's national and local needs and to identify priorities for action. These priorities should take into account both qualitative and quantitative factors.

Qualitative issues to be considered might include the following:

- Science and technology education which does not lead to *understanding* cannot lead to scientific and technological literacy. Is the science and technology education now being given in the schools leading to such understanding and if not why not?
- Scientific and technological literacy implies that science and its applications should be set in the wider context

of the *social and cultural environment*. Are activities being undertaken to achieve this?

- The role of *teachers* is central to the achievement scientific literacy and technological literacy for everyone. Is their training adequate? Is their career status appropriate?

In quantitative terms, scientific and technological literacy for *all* calls for an outreach through *non-formal education* of many kinds. Institutions providing non-formal education have a capital role to play in this regard. They include: museums, science centres, the media (radio, television and the press) and other out-of-school channels for communicating knowledge and understanding of science and technology and of their applications.

- How can the impact of such institutions and bodies be enhanced?

It also implies outreach to groups which are often under-represented in both formal and non-formal science and—technology education - women and girls, ethnic minorities, the disabled, the poor, refugees and those who live in remote rural areas.

- What can be done to engage such groups more effectively?

The second function of the task force would be to draw up an overall strategy for establishing the structures that are deemed necessary to prepare projects for action. It may, for example, be necessary to:

- Create centres or facilities (or reinforce, adapt, equip, or restructure those already existing) for supporting the improvement of science and technology education throughout the country;
- Provide support for the establishment or reinforcement of science and technology teachers' professional associations which will make important contributions to achieving both the qualitative and the quantitative goals of Project 2000+;
- Provide support for groups or institutions working or willing to engage in the popularization of science and

technology (museums, exhibitions, the media, etc.) particularly for helping them to focus on people's needs and to establish good links with the educational system.

Relevant projects may include:

- Revising school science and technology curricula and assessment procedures to make more relevant to national needs, problems and priorities;
- Revising pre-service and in-service teacher-training programmes, paying special attention to re-shaping the institutional culture so as better to prepare teachers to deal with current scientific and technological issues and face the challenge of those which may arise in the future;
- Developing teaching and learning materials suited to local needs, both for use in schools and in the training of teachers;
- Integrating knowledge about relevant science and technology into literacy, post literacy and adult education programmes;
- Promoting and supporting activities designed to improve the participation of women in scientific and technological occupations and professions and to open up to them the benefits that they can derive for themselves, their families and society at large from better access to a basic understanding of science and technology.

3. Finance

To accomplish this task, it will be necessary to mobilize financial resources from both public and private sources. Although the pattern of financing eduction is specific to each country, channels exist in all countries for requesting international and bilateral funding. If high priority is accorded to scientific and technological literacy in national plans, United Nations agencies, such as UNESCO and the United Nations Environment Programme (UNEP), are willing to support well-prepared projects in co-operation with United Nations Development Programme (UNDP) or under funds-in-trust arrangements. UNESCO's own Regular and Participation Programmes are also able to provide seed money for the support of task forces, while programmes developed with World Bank loans may also have a scientific and technological literacy component.

4. Secretariat

Communications should be addressed to:

Project 2000+ Secretariat
Science and Technology Education Section
UNESCO Place de Fontenoy, 75352 Paris 07-SP
FRANCE

Contact may also be made with UNESCO regional and sub-regional offices (Addresses may be obtained from UNESCO National Commissions) or with any of the other members of the Steering Committee.

PROJECT 2000+

STEERING COMMITTEE

United Nations Educational, Scientific and Cultural Organization (UNESCO)

The World Bank

United Nations Children's Fund (UNICEF)

United Nations Development Programme (UNDP)

United Nations Environment Programme (UNEP

Commonweath Secretariat

International Council of Scientific Unions (ICSU)

International Council of Associations for Science Education (ICASE)

International Organization for Science and Technology Education (IOSTE)

Gender and Science and Technology (GASAT)

World Council of Associations for Technology Education (WOCATE)

Organizations represented on the Steering Committee, March 1994.

The International Forum on Scientific and Technological Literacy for All brought together participants from the following countries and territories

Algeria
Angola
Argentina
Australia
Austria
Barbados
Belarus
Belgium
Benin
Bolivia
Botswana
Brazil
Bulgaria
Canada
China
Colombia
Cote d'Ivoire
Czech Republic
Denmark
Ecuador
Egypt
Finland
France
Germany
Ghana
Greece
Hong Kong
Hungary
Iceland
India
Indonesia
Iran (Islamic Republic of)
Ireland
Israel
Italy
Japan
Jordan
Kenya
Korea (Republic of)
Kuwait
Lebanon
Lesotho
Luxembourg
Malawi
Malaysia
Mexico
Morocco
Netherlands
New Zealand
Niger
Nigeria
Norway
Palestine
Panama
Papua New Guinea
Philippines
Poland
Portugal
Romania
Russian Federation
Rwanda
Sierra Leone
Slovakia
South Africa
Spain
Sudan
Sri Lanka
Swaziland
Sweden
Switzerland
Syrian Arab Republic
Thailand
Trinidad and Tobago
Tunisia
Turkey
United Arab Emirates
United Kingdom
United Republic of Tanzania
United States of America
Venezuela
Zimbabwe